ROCK ODYSSEY

A Musician's Chronicle of the Sixties

IAN WHITCOMB

Dolphin Books
Doubleday & Company, Inc.
Garden City, New York
1983

FOR MY FATHER,
WHO IS WITH ME ALWAYS

Library of Congress Cataloging in Publication Data
Whitcomb, Ian, 1941–
    Rock odyssey.

    Includes index.
    1. Rock music—History and criticism.   I. Title.
ML3534.W53   1983   784.5′4′009046
                         ISBN: 0-385-15705-3
Library of Congress Catalog Card Number 80-2992

ROCK ODYSSEY

ACKNOWLEDGMENTS

Like most of my other books, this effort took three years to assemble. To put it mildly, the going was rough and included some moments in hell. But I hope you find the result a pleasant journey through the key years of the pop sixties and the arcane alleys of my imagination. Of course, much of the factual material came from my reading of books, magazines, and newspapers.

But a number of friends and colleagues have been tremendously helpful and patient and encouraging—and I want to thank them in print. The germ of these chronicles was a series of chats with my London literary agent, Leslie Gardner of London Management. She spread the word to Elaine Markson, my New York agent. Elaine fixed me up with Barry Lippmann of Doubleday and the result was that I set about writing a proposal which eventually was accepted. We were on our way. Unfortunately, I took such an unconscionable time completing the book that, by the time I finished, Barry had left Doubleday, my next editor—Kathy Tiddens—had moved to the fiction department, and Gerry Helferich was left holding the baby. All three were always willing to take my calls (collect, too!) and to hear my cries and give me advice and encouragement. Then Gerry left and Shaye Areheart became the final editor—and a first-class job she has done. Nor must I forget Mark Hurst's careful copy-editing-cum-research.

In California, I spent hours and hours with Barry Hansen (the famous Dr. Demento of KMET) as he talked me gently through Dylan, the Doors, acid rock, and a few obscure items that I wasn't familiar with; and as he talked he taped me dozens of examples of sixties' rock. At Bomp Records, I was lent records, magazines, and books galore by Greg Shaw, another pop expert. He also listened to my theories and stories when the book was still in its embryonic stages. Many of the characters in the chronicles—George Sherlock, Bud Fraser, Jerry Dennon, Hal Shaper—have remained dear friends of mine and, while writing about them, I begged them to bear with me. I hope they're happy with the result. During the writing about the San Francisco scene, I was able to call upon the great knowledge of Charles Perry, an associate editor of *Rolling Stone* and a historian of the Haight-Ashbury period. Andy Wickham, a vice-president of Warner Bros. Records, was an active member of the music scene in the sixties and also an extremely witty observer. As a friend, he has regaled me (at countless dinners where he frequently picked up the tab) with story after story about the absurdities of this music game. I owe him a great debt for his insights; much of my outlook springs from our dinner exchanges. Our mutual friend Robert Mundy, the screenwriter and bon vivant, read my almost-completed book very carefully and presented me with pages of well-reasoned comments. He also said that he laughed heartily and learned a little. Now he's spreading the word about what a good read *Rock Odyssey* is and, as a result, I'm getting on the "A" lists of Hollywood parties again. In order to make sure I hadn't made any factual errors, I had the manuscript checked by Ken Barnes, an authority on the sixties, an author himself, and currently a staff member of *Radio & Records* magazine.

Finally, I thank once again my mother—for letting me type on her dining room table, for understanding the need for my remaining in America in order to get this weighty conceit off my chest and onto paper, and for her continual support of and love for the family eccentric. Like America, she has always seemed amused and charmed by the carryings-on of this generally happy child.

Ian Whitcomb,
Altadena, California,
1983

CONTENTS

"To receive a new kind of music is to be guarded against as endangering the whole of the constitution. Forms and rhythms in music are never altered without producing changes in the entire fabric of society and its most important political forms. It is here that we must be so careful, since these new forms creep in imperceptibly in the form of a seemingly harmless diversion.

"But little by little, this mischief becomes more and more familiar and spreads into our manners and pursuits. Then with gathering force it invades men's dealings with one another and goes on to attack the laws and the constitution with reckless impudence until it ends by overthrowing the whole structure of public and private life."

Plato, *The Republic,* circa 375 B.C.

"Wooly Bully!"
Sam the Sham, 1965

Prologue:

1949: "THE CALL OF THE WILD"

It was a typically gray day in the summer of 1949 and I was sitting on the lavatory. We were on our holidays in the South Coast resort of Felpham and I was eight years old. ("But he acts like he's five," my aunt liked to say.)

Lunch in the boardinghouse was over and the afternoon's activities had not yet begun. A delicious pause in the race of life. So I sat on the lavatory with my books and comics and I became whomever I liked and went wherever I wanted to go. . . .

If I cast my fate to the tide and just lay back in a war-surplus rubber dinghy, I might well be swept away from Unjolly Old England and, many moons later, might break through swirling sea mist to suddenly chance upon the Blue Lagoon in the flesh! Then it would be off with the sticky flannel trousers and into the luscious jungle to run free with my dingle-dangle squashed between my fat thighs.

But in reality the rubber dinghy was punctured, the sea was green and ended in France, and I was feeling poorly. My stomach was gurgling, due perhaps to the rhubarb tart and custard served up at lunch. Why couldn't they serve treacle tart? Lack of treacle and sweet things in general, I supposed. Britain still at attention, in a state-of-war economy. Before the war, they most likely had treacle tarts falling out of their ears.

I closed *The Blue Lagoon* and picked up a comic book annual, *The Knockout Fun Book*. Slap-bang on the cover was Billy Bunter, the fat owl schoolboy of Greyfriars, gorging himself on custard pies, macaroons, and indeterminate yellow cakes with snow-white icing and red cherries. Thumbing through the dog-eared pages, we find Our Ernie, silly little plum pudding from the dreary North of England, capturing crooks by rolling them into a snowball. He's rewarded, in the final frame, with a slap-up supper of mashed potato mountain stuck with plump pork sausages.

Why didn't they write songs about food these days, when food—especially sweet food—was what the country wanted? I remembered the chocolate bars the GIs used to give us during the war. They'd drop them into my baby carriage. The GIs were big, lusty brutes with chiseled faces and precision-drawn builds—like the heroes in the comic books. American comic books were so much more . . . filling. British ones were OK for a laugh, but why was everything over here just OK for a laugh?

I put down *The Knockout Fun Book* and picked up *The Rio Kid*, an American comic. Then I heard my aunt calling me through the lavatory keyhole to remind me about the revue we were going to see that night: "Follow the Fun" at the end of Felpham Pier. But the Rio Kid! He's been outlawed for a crime he ain't done—which is a very tingly sensation. To be abused and cursed and then found innocent and to have everyone tell you how sorry they are! Stupendously exciting!

After an hour or so, I felt I'd gotten enough satisfaction in the lavatory. It was time to get going down to the seaside. Today, unbeknown to my uncle and aunt, I was going to attempt to escape from this postwar concentration camp called Britain.

Let us examine this "prison" more closely. The second half of the century was almost rolling and should have been motored by new drive, new energy, and *progressiveness*. And yet!—World War II was still lowering about, drizzling and dripping and leaving rust marks all over the Isles. Rust, for example, on Felpham Pleasure Pier (built 1886): splotches, stains, and streaks on the chunky pig-iron slot machines that had cranked out chocolate bars before the days of Hitler & Company; rust on the mechanical Al Jolson puppet who, for a consideration, would blubber out a scratchy "Mammy"; rust on the Mutoscope peep show featuring torn and creased silent cowboys and keyholing Edwardian butlers; rust on the wheels and hinges of disused bathing machines beneath the pier, those closed chariots in which stout ladies had been rushed pell-mell toward the ocean by excited donkeys before the war. *Before the war!* When, as the grown-ups kept telling us, things were better, brighter, and more typically English. *Before the war,* the British may very well have looked like those strapping lads and lassies with healthy legs a-working as they hiked happily down the Ovaltine Highway toward a radiant horizon—as depicted on the mural on the crumbling wall of Felpham's Moo-Cow Milk Bar, closed indefinitely.

No—on the eve of the New Elizabethan Era, the Britishers looked poorly. They were tired and badly fed and their clothes knew nothing of Technicolor. They were worlds away from the all-American glamour folk decorating the pinball machines down at the amusement arcade near the pier. Here were incendiary blondes, milk-fed and honey-smooth, squired by rough guys (not mere blokes) wearing gangster suits and T-shirts shaped by their muscle bulges. Both guys and gals displayed gleaming rows of even teeth. Exactly even, not like British teeth, which were raggedly serrated and rotten, too. "I've said it all my life and I'll say it again," opined my Uncle Jeremy. "Teeth are at the root of life's problems—have 'em removed and get false ones." He was careful to refer to "false teeth" and not "dentures"; Uncle Jeremy was a stickler for correct King's English because the family was keenly aware of being *upper-middle-class.*

Uncle Jeremy and Auntie Iris were hosting me on this seaside holiday. They would have preferred to stay at the Old Ship Hotel in Brighton (four stars), but their money these days wouldn't stretch to it. *Before the war*—that was a different story: that was when the family had Rolls-Royces and chauffeurs and silver tea sets and a hunting lodge in Scotland. But now in the Age of Austerity and in the wake of a rather stiff family business setback, they were living in reduced circumstances. In short, they were distressed gentlefolk—and there is no minority in this world with greater bile and venom and unadulterated fury than distressed gentlefolk. It's shocking to find yourself sliding backward when the whole world and its politicians and news editors talk constantly about marching forward. But Uncle Jeremy and his people clung to their old ways, attaching enormous importance to the details of life. "Once our lingo goes, we're done for—*poof!*" Uncle Jeremy liked to say as he stirred his cup of hot water in the darkest days of the war, when even tea was beyond his means. Still, in those days, one was doing it for the sake of Great Britain and the War. Nowadays, the war was between the classes and Uncle Jeremy wasn't going to let his little details go: the family still had values and good manners, never saying "toilet" or "pardon" and always giving up their seats to women on crowded trains or buses.

The class war continued at Mrs. Moore's SeaView Family Hotel (read "boardinghouse"), where Uncle J. had selected a table in the southwest corner, as far away as possible from the common herd. From here he could comment on the other guests, how they held their knives and forks like pens, how they ate their peas off knives smeared with honey—and how the devil did they manage to afford honey anyway, not to mention that spotted bow-tie man with his endless supply of thick, nonstreaky bacon and real butter? The man was probably in scrap metal or war surplus or American nylons. Never trust a prematurely bald man, by the way, especially when he wears tartan socks, corresponding two-tone shoes, and nonmatching tweeds. "You see," said Uncle J. to Auntie Iris and me, "no matter how much money they spend on their clothes, even if they dress up to the nines, you can always tell the lower breeds by the shape of the nose, the setting of the eyes, and the overall blotchiness of the complexion."

But at lunch on this particular day, Uncle J.'s bile had settled down. He'd actually nodded and smiled to the melancholy little man in the gray cardigan who, like Uncle J., sat apart from the rest of Mrs. Moore's holidaymakers. The little man always ate alone, slowly and thoughtfully, often gazing through the other guests and often interrupting his meal to write in a notebook. "That's a fellow called Charlie Danvers. Common but nice. Amusing," said Uncle J. as he spread a dab of margarine on a corner of his bread, being careful not to coat the whole slice in the vulgar manner. "Danvers asked me for a round of golf today, so of course I asked him what school he'd attended, and when I found out it was the 'School of Life,' I offered him nine holes."

On the golf links that morning, Uncle J. had discovered that Danvers was, of all things, a theatrical—a comedian. Odd, because he seemed so sober and civilized. "Yes, but you ought to see me in my music-hall gear," said Danvers. "Why, my checked jacket shrieks so loudly I had to force the salesman to sell it me." A buxom woman sporting twin tremblers had passed them on the fourth tee: "I'd like to climb her north face," said Danvers matter-of-factly, adding, "Course, I'm a free man, being a bachelor. Know what a bachelor is? He's a man who has no children—to speak of." His timing was impeccable, which was why it had taken him and Uncle J. a long time to play their nine holes. Uncle J. had regretted that he hadn't invited Danvers to play eighteen. The fellow was damned amusing. At the eighth green, Danvers had told him about a tart he'd met up in London who'd said she was doing so well she only wished she had another pair of legs so she could open a branch in Manchester.

Uncle J. roared so loudly at the table that some of the other lunchers looked around in shock. "The *idea!*" said one woman. Then Danvers had wandered over from his far corner and, removing his napkin from under his chin, had invited Uncle J. and family to see him that night in the pier revue, "Follow the Fun." With a wink he'd added, "Try and show some respect for my jokes—they're older than any of the audience." He'd fished a porkpie hat from his pocket, plunked it on his head, and said, "Well, toodle-oo! All right behind?" "All right behind!" replied Uncle J., entering into the straight-man spirit. "Then off we jolly well go, TTFN [Ta-ta for now] and Abyssinia, and I leave you with this riddle: if a fly going east passes a flea going west, what time is it in Hong Kong?" "Give up!" shouted Uncle J., as Auntie Iris looked deep into her custard. "Fly past flea!"—and Danvers had exited swiftly, stage left. "The *idea!*" had said the fat woman again. "Telling jokes at dinnertime." Uncle J. had faced her and said proudly, "*Lunch*time, madam. For us—*lunch*time!"

It was now two-thirty and, having finished my ablutions, I was ready to set off on my date with destiny. Charlie Danvers, with his sudden show of dining room cheek, had spurred me on. I was determined to have a go, if only because success might remove me from the prison of middle-class life. I mean, *upper*-middle-class life. An entertainer, like Bob Hope, Bing Crosby, Al Jolson—or Charlie Danvers! I might join the ranks of the roving vagabonds!

As I opened the front door of the SeaView, I was assaulted by a delicious, enticing smell that even whisked from my nostrils the boardinghouse smell of overboiled vegetables. This new smell was the smell of oil: *oil* from eating shops where cooks suffering from batterer's elbow and fryer's eye stirred deep-sea vats crammed with rock salmon, plaice, cod, sausages, and chips; *oil* from the great clanging, hissing, chugging fun machinery that worked the Dodg.'em cars, ghost trains, switchback roller coasters, and all the other marvelous mechanical entertainments of the modern seaside.

Stomach now rumbling, I huffed and puffed down the steep street that our boardinghouse topped, down, down, down to the excitement zone—to the Shangri-La Amusement Park and its annex, the Super-American Fun Palace. As fast as my flat feet would allow, I passed the grim terraces of the sturdy red houses, all individually named ("Mon Repos," "Bill-Beth," "Dun-Rovin") and yet all identical. I ignored the glares of beet-faced retired officers and the moony looks of exshopkeepers and the moving curtains operated by ancient spinsters who now dreamed of long-dead matinee idols and Rupert Brooke. Around the corner at the bottom of the hill and soon I was rushing along the seafront, past rows of once-grand hotels now tear-streaked by the revolting weather and a changing world—expensive five-star hotels that had seen better days before that last long, lazy afternoon in August 1914 when bees droned on the idle slopes of the South Downs just behind, while in front, on the sands, the hot and shiny pierrots beat their way through ragtime songs about grizzly bears and Alexander. By 1918, most of the pierrots had been smashed to smithereens by Boche shells while entertaining the troops in Flanders fields.

At last, I came to a halt in the Modern Age: 1949. *Boing, boing, clung!* went the fleet of pinball machines in the Super-American Fun Palace. Then TILT, TILT! And *boing, boing!* I passed the newsstand where they were doing a brisk trade in real American *Action Comics*—thick and glossy and smelling of wood pulp. The ink came off in your hands. "68 Big Pages—Don't Take Less!" Then more *oil*—this time from a vast metal vat where floated real American doughnut rings, not to be confused with those stodgy suet balls the British called doughnuts. Should be "donut"—that's the way it's spelled in the comics.

And as I stopped for a donut, I drank in the wonders of the nearby Dodg.'em car rink. Beneath a firmament of electric sparks, laughing, giggling, screaming girls (in headscarves mostly) were being poked and banged and mauled by local Burt Lancasters in bumper cars. And all the while, grimy kid employees hopped from car to car collecting fares, chewing gum, and combing their hair, all so nonchalantly and gracefully. Greasy gazelles. From a Tannoy system high above—four big bullhorns—crashed a barrage of inspirational pop music: "Chattanoogie Choo Choo," "On a Slow Boat to China," "Enjoy Yourself, It's Later Than You Think."

I knew all the words to all these songs and lots more besides. I could take you to the land of "Cuanto le Gusta" or any Deep South state. But today, at 3 P.M., I was going to sing of domestic life. I had entered the Merrymakers Concert Party Amateur Talent Contest—to be held on Felpham sands (weather permitting)—and I was going to offer the judges my version of the Phil Harris recording of "Never Trust a Woman."

As I left the snug and oily amusement area and headed for the yellow sands, I grew stronger and I grew wings and pretty soon I was soaring high above the gray sky, even over the British Isles, the World, the Universe. . . .

Only a wooden stage on the rippled sand. Only a small audience of holidaymakers, chilled but friendly. Only a bunch of kids conducted by an uncle type in a red blazer and straw hat. He introduces a pimply girl who taps badly, then a boy who gets his conjuring tricks wrong and exits—presto—and a weedy youth who dries up in the middle of his Kipling recitation and blubs loudly.

Only a free show, a kiddie amateur hour—but the stage is now a world for me. Legs strutting, arms flaying, voice piercing like a demented magpie, I bash and biff the song home without any accompaniment.

I was truly transported. The audience was transported. The straw-hatted uncle type awarded me first prize: a record of "Twelfth Street Rag" by Pee Wee Hunt and his band. JWIW! (Just what I wanted!) But in the mad dash to tell everyone about my success, about how I hadn't stumbled over one word, about the shouts and cheers—I tore too hard at the ribbon around the record and I busted that 78. (They busted so easily.) Hot tears followed. From a terrace house, a curtain moved ever so gently. Blast it! Now I hadn't any proof of my seaside victory over shyness, fatness, and a mild stutter.

But the gods were looking down at Felpham—and they nodded. I was to be given another chance. At Charlie Danvers' "Follow the Fun" revue.

That night, the curtains opened to a line of high-kicking chorus girls singing "We're in Favour of Friendship." Uncle J. leaned forward keenly, Auntie Iris said something to the effect that this was "romance," but I was fascinated by the backdrop painting. For Felpham sands—that gray and dismal stretch—had been transformed. Certainly the scene was of Felpham, but this was another Felpham, an ethereal watering spot of blue skies, silver sands, gleaming pier, and dreaming tall hotels. A happy ship snaked off toward the horizon. A moment of bliss captured for all time. Life as it ought to be. . . .

But now a disembodied voice, amplified and tinny, was announcing: "Make welcome your host for the evening, that cheery chap himself—O. *Stoppit!*" And onto the stage strode Charlie Danvers! He was transformed, too. I turned to my aunt. "It's romance, dear, romance." Danvers was wearing a screaming plaid jacket that drooped to below his knees, plus a homburg hat that reached for the stars.

"You like the outfit? Got it for free. Came home the other night and found it draped over the wife's side of the bed—and I've been wearing it ever since." Hoots of laughter and Charlie/Stoppit stepped right to the front of the stage, put one foot forward onto the apron, craned his neck out into the audience, and, after glancing into both wings, rattled on in a loud and lecherous whisper:

"Course, my wife does take pains to look attractive—she puts so much cream on her that when I gave her a squeeze the other night she shot out the ruddy window. So she went to the doctor and he asks, 'Have you had a checkup lately?' And she replies, 'No, but I had a couple of Hungarians.'" Uproarious laughter. Auntie Iris fiddled with her bag. Uncle J. said, "Vulgar but good," and the stream of comic postcard humor flowed on like a beggar's opera, reaching a climax with:

"Nice spot, this town—I was sunning meself on the seafront just before the show. I was next to a vicar fellow and we got talking. Turned out he was here on his honeymoon. I said, 'Pleasant little spot, isn't it?' He replied, 'Yes—and how *cunningly concealed.*' I've been asked to do a request, but the mike's the wrong shape, so I'll give you a British number—Brighton 2386. No, seriously, here's an old song called 'You Made Me Love You—You Woke Me Up to Do It.' What a job for a grown man, eh? If my mother knew what I was doing, she'd be ashamed—she thinks I'm in prison. No no, but seriously—and settle down now—I'd like to leave you with this poem. . . ." And with a nod to the band, O. Stoppit went into a lovely song, whose lyrics seemed to sum up the very essence of the show-business life and whose pop tune seemed to echo every haunting phrase hewn by pop songwriters since the business had begun at the end of the last century. Then Stoppit bowed and went off to thunderous applause. Just as he was about to vanish into the wings, he found a coat hanger in his jacket and he waved it to one and all.

I was in a transport of delight. I didn't pay any attention to the following act and I was startled when Uncle J. nudged me in the ribs and ordered, "Go on up—they want volunteers from the audience. Go on and show 'em, but remember the old school." Aunt Iris didn't really approve, I could tell. But I didn't need much encouragement now to get onstage and in a flash I was next to the trampoline act and the acrobat was still saying, "Come one, come all, and have a bash on the old tramp. Enjoy yourself—it's later than you think!" Maybe they thought I'd make a fool of myself, but I don't think I did. I felt that elation again, like on the sands. And soon I was bouncing, high and funny, and the audience was roaring *with* me, not *at* me. It was ecstasy. Next thing I knew, I was telling jokes as I bounced and then I caught a glimpse of O. Stoppit winking at me from the wings and giving me the thumbs-up. So I bounced higher and higher and finally I launched into a current song, "I've Got a Lovely Bunch of Cocoanuts."

Suddenly, I was aware of the acrobat near me, very near. He was hissing harshly: "You'll have a loverly bunch of coconuts soon, my lad, if you don't get off my stage!" *Your* stage indeed! *My* stage now! I could feel the warm waves of one-sided, irresponsible love splashing all over me and I drenched myself in this perfumed water where Jolson, Crosby, Garland, Hope, Frankie Howerd, Tommy Trinder, Vera Lynn,

Frank Randle, and O. Stoppit had all bathed. I had found my calling and I was only eight years old.

So into the fifties I stepped, secure in my world of pop. Soon I was making my own music at prep school. Amusing the boys, keeping bullies at bay. The prize record had been busted, but there would be others. And anyway, I'd make up my own songs and jokes, based on the dream of America and its call of the wild.

And when the outside world—that dull and flat and sensible thing—got rough or went wrong, I'd lull myself into a better one with O. Stoppit's song, that hymn he'd ended his show with those years ago on the pier:

> "Goodnight to you and see you soon again,
> I hope that you will miss me now and then.
> I know the glow of your applause will burn,
> But I hope that you got something in return.
> Goodnight to you—God bless you, one and all,
> You make my life worthwhile.
> And when the shadows turn to endless night,
> I'll live forever after in your laughter and smiles.

1

1955–62:
"AMERICA,
I LOVE YOU"

Just before he died, Bill Haley, the great square-dance caller of "Rock Around the Clock," anthem of classic rock 'n' roll, told me this:

"I'm the first to admit that I didn't invent that rocking train that just keeps a-rollin'—but I can lay claim to being its first conductor. I got on board at the start and I had a darned good ride. Thank the Lord I got off safely!"

I well remember when I first became aware of that good-news train clickety-clacking across the weeping gray skies of Austerity England, belching beat and dropping molten rock 'n' roll on the history-laden, good-taste-riddled islanders. It was after lights-out in my dorm at a private boarding school deep in the heart of Thomas Hardy's Dorset. Huge with valves and hissing and stuttering, Smythe-Crotchford's shortwave radio, secreted under his blankets, had lit upon "Radio Luxembourg" and they were playing "Rock Around the Clock." I responded at once to this "Marseillaise" and to hell with *Tess of the D'Urbervilles* and *Alfred the Great!* There was to be no stopping this train—certainly not by the headmaster and the other arbiters of taste. Haley was now Chief Scout of the great brotherhood of rockers and his train carried no grim history of Afro-America—no suffering jazzmen, bluesmen, ghettos, shacks, or lynchings—no complications. His was a clean and sparkling train bringing the good news that rock 'n' roll was here to stay.

So that midnight, March 16, 1955, I wrote the magic words in fresh snow on the school's front lawn: ROCK 'N' ROLL IS HERE TO BLOODY WELL STAY. Next day, there were severe repercussions.

It was just about time for a fresh bundle of beat from America. The old stuff was getting extremely stale and dry: dreary dance bands still dreaming of past jitterbuggery, drippy crooners from Balham whose only action was in their Adam's apples, elevated shop girls who wailed of unrequited love till Mr. Right came along to whisk them into wedlock. All performing in slavish imitation of American models. Miniature Americans.

Since the arrival of ragtime, just prior to World War I, Britain had been in the thrall of the double eagle. How we loved these friendly invaders! Oh boy, OK buster, hey baby, stick 'em up, you're darn tootin'! Bunny-hugging, Charlestoning, jitterbugging, boogie-woogieing, we'd gladly followed the U.S. pop culture trends as they were dropped on our island. These Yanks seemed to know how to sing and sway and emote. Where was our Welsh jazz, Highland swing, or London lope? Was "The Lambeth Walk" the best we could offer?

Over the years, custodians of culture had spoken out against the American invaders. Expatriate American T. S. Eliot had written in his British-based *The Waste Land:* "'Is there nothing in your head?' But O O O O that Shakespeherian Rag." Rudyard Kipling had objected to the new syncopation, complaining of being "hummed at nasally by an alien." John Buchan, the thriller writer who later became Governor-General of Canada, founded a society for the prevention of cruelty to the English language (by American vulgarisms). And in the 1950s, Gilbert Harding, pundit of the BBC's "What's My Line?", had thundered against the spectacle of "half-naked Yankee sailors yattering coarsely and incomprehensively as they sprawl across the stage of *South Pacific.*"

British comedians did their best to poke fun at the vocal and physical contortions of the American entertainers. Sterling work was offered by Frank Randle with his slapstick jitterbug; by Frankie Howerd with his travesty of the swing nonsense song "Three Little Fishies"; and by Tony Hancock with his drape-suited Johnnie Ray-style crooner bound like Prometheus to his microphone.

But it was all to no avail. We couldn't come up with anything better than the American beat—and the people seemed to love it.

I certainly did—together with American donuts and comic books and movies and jeans. It was all part and parcel of the image of a land where one could be free to cast off the restrictions of heavy serge and gray flannel shorts. A land where the possibilities were endless. The beaty, beefy punch-first-and-ask-questions-afterward Americans were saviors whose pop culture snatched us momentarily from England's green and boring land. When, in the early 1950s, before the R&R train descended, Tennessee Ernie Ford was released on wax with his stupendous country-and-western chugalugs "Shotgun Boogie" and "Kiss Me Big," I was thrilled and amazed. Such dynamism coming from a thick, safe 78 r.p.m. record manufactured in England and bought at the High Street record shop, next door to the friendly sweet shop! "Kiss Me Big" infuriated the staff at my prep school. This, of course, is an important function of art.

But Tennessee Ernie was only the John the Baptist of R&R. In 1955, as we have seen, Bill Haley—the Rocker Chief himself—descended with his rock-a-beatin' boogies, razzle-dazzles, rocking around the clock, and his axioms like "See You Later, Alligator" (zingy as tabasco sauce). And he was followed by the legendary disciples of rock 'n' roll: Elvis Presley, Gene Vincent, Eddie Cochran, Jerry Lee Lewis, Little Richard, Fats Domino. These gods of wax, springing at us seemingly complete and fully armed, were the culmination of the years of peaceful penetration by the friendly invaders from the land of syncopation.

The new heroes were wild and natural men stepping into the shoes of those lost heroes of the immediate past—leaders of strong and certain morality like Winston Churchill and Douglas MacArthur and Field Marshal Montgomery and Mountbatten of Burma. We had been reared in the atmosphere of World War II—the only "just" war—and that feeling lingered. Only the circumstances had vanished, together with our supremacy.

For three years, the wild rocker men ruled, supported by Miss Connie Francis, Siren Queen of Sufferers with a voice that was a real bleacher-reacher. And acting as camp counselor, a waffle-syrup crooner with a smidgeon of beat, was Pat Boone. He told us to think positive and tackle those exams and be mindful of God because Elvis certainly was—and El was a good friend of his.

It was delicious to experience the rocker records blazing out of tinny Tannoy speakers as we rolled round in Dodg.'em cars. It was even more satisfying to lie on the bedspread in my room with the rain pitter-pattering outside, and with pop newspapers like the *New Musical Express* and the *Record Mirror* spread around me, and Danny and the Juniors testifying on the hi-fi that "Rock and Roll Is Here to Stay." They affirmed what I'd written in the school snow and now I was lapping up the entire scene—jeans, checked shirts, haircuts, and all. I was even interested in the star's fave foods. And Elvis's gold suit and gold Cadillac were so right for the world of endless summers, ten-mile-long cars, swaying palm trees, and rivers of root beer and mountains of hot fudge sundaes served by top-heavy, pneumatic blondes on roller skates.

This then was the wonder world conjured up by classic rock 'n' roll, particularly by one who, though he didn't have heroic looks, wrote and recorded songs that epitomized the U.S. teen heaven described above— Chuck Berry, of course.

But the heroes had not, in their native land, been created by a munificent god as I had dreamed. They had actually sprung from the maverick branch of the all-American music biz, which had spawned hillbilly and rhythm and blues in a netherworld of hole-in-the-wall record outfits that paid their artists in jugs of wine—or bullets, if they didn't behave. This was the other American music, hitherto spurned by New York's Tin Pan Alley and Broadway. The moon-in-Juners and the sophisticated songsmiths (with rhyming dictionaries and a knowledge of French romanticism) were shocked to see the craft and culture they had so carefully nursed up from the gutter days back at the turn of the century (when there was little but Irish-American tearjerker ballads and ragtime songs) dragged back even beyond ragtime to barbaric shouts and screams and tom-toming evocative of dark continents.

The music establishment, supported by ASCAP, even got a congressional investigation to determine whether rock 'n' roll was part of a plot dreamed up by radio and record interests to brainwash the Youth of America. They didn't prove their case, but next year started the infamous payola investigations that resulted in the downfall of deejay supreme Alan (Mr. Rock 'n' Roll) Freed, the man who had taken the magic sex-play phrase from blacks and first applied it to teen music. Freed and Haley were good buddies in those early embattled years when the new music was being attacked by the old fogies of "good music": the Alley and Broadway. They were also pals with Dick Clark, a deejay-cum-rock-entrepreneur. Clark, more than either Haley or Freed, knew how to play the game—and that game was to establish rock 'n' roll as a legitimate, well-organized, squeaky-clean, nonaggressive show-biz world. A kiddie version of the big Broadway example, a continuation of the great American sales pitch started by P. T. Barnum back in the nineteenth century, a game that needed two teams: the flimflam men and the suckers. And remember—nobody is forced to buy the product, whether it be a glimpse of circus freaks (including the "Egress") or a record of Fabian singing "I'm a Tiger."

And so it was that by 1960, when our story starts, Dick Clark— together with a new breed of teen beat music and fan mag publishers, TV producers and leisure clothing manufacturers—established Teendom, where even moms and pops could enjoy themselves, learning the new steps like the Madison and, later, the Twist. God-fearing, taxpaying folks could relax in peace with the knowledge that their kids were in safe hands. See them harmlessly enjoy themselves on "American Bandstand," dancing away their rites of passage before they enter the real adult world of work and marriage. Pat Boone published a book of moral-conduct tips, *'Twixt Twelve and Twenty*; Connie Francis wrote for the fan mags about losing baby fat and gaining confidence by thinking positive. Before his demise, Haley himself had vowed in print to "clean up rock 'n' roll" by taking it out of the world of switchblades and delinquency. Land sakes! It was only music—and fun music at that. *Recreational.* The new team ran a clean ship on the surface—and surface was what counted in America, the land of the everlasting personal deodorant.

New pop publishers set up offices in and around the old Brill Building, flagship of Tin Pan Alley, and they sported shiny desks and business suits and intercom buzzers and sliding-glass doors and, if you thought *that* was smart, you ought to have seen their apartments! Ira had *oak paneling* in his bathroom! So even though his business was teen music full of nonsensical *sha-la-la*s and *shooby-doo*s, the man had money and taste and earned his fortune in the Good Old American Way. And just as in the past, there were cubicles in the new publishing offices, where toiling songsmiths like Neil Sedaka, Carole King, Mann and Weil, Goffin and King, and Leiber and Stoller all turned out perfectly workmanlike songs that could be understood in print, complete with the correct dotted quarter notes and rests. "Itsy Bitsy Teenie Weenie Yellow Polka Dot Bikini" was written by decent craftsmen plying their teen trade. The danger period of rock 'n' roll was over. The girl fans were soon calling the tune and there were even violins behind Ray Charles and the late Buddy Holly. There was noble ambition in the air too. Frankie Avalon, Bobby Rydell, and Fabian had aspired to be all-around entertainers and, having paid their dues in teen music, would learn to tap dance, to give song segue patter (with perhaps a joke or two), to bow, even to act—so that eventually, God willing, they would graduate into household names like Lawrence Welk and Frank Sinatra.

Already there were signs that "good music" was returning: Gene Vincent, notorious rock wild man of "Be-Bop-A-Lula" fame, had covered "Over the Rainbow" and the soul-shouting Isley Brothers had revived the Irving Berlin standard "How Deep Is the Ocean?", while the popular black novelty group the Coasters had a bash at "Besame Mucho." And can you believe that streetcorner doo-wop hero Dion (with his Belmonts) had released "When You Wish Upon a Star"?

To celebrate a new decade and to set a fine example Elvis the Pelvis Presley himself updating a *classical* song. Fresh from military service in Germany, neat and dapper and polite, Elvis & Company found that the old chugging, shuffling rock numbers weren't enough for a man who was now a film star and an all-around entertainer. "Stuck on You" and "Mess of Blues" had done well, but "It's Now or Never" shot to number one in no time at all—and that was pretty terrific for a rocked-up version of "O Sole Mio," the old Neapolitan classic originally published by the esteemed Ricordi Company. The new 1960 Elvis Presley was no longer a word-mangler—and gone were the hiccups. Why, this man could develop into a fine tenor!

Back in Britain, I could still be found sprawled across my bed, scanning the pop papers for any news of the Heroes, even as the 1960s arrived and the steam of these wild men evaporated. As in America, there were plenty of old-line pop pundits—believers in musical literacy and vocal standards—who were glad to see the end of a period when pop had gone off the rails and strayed into a jungle of *yahoos*.

For example, the *Record Mirror* summed up the fifties as a decade distinguished by "a disc boom, by television as the New Religion, and by the Big Beat Blitz," and the publication waved a relieved good-bye to "the most appallingly infantile and talentless decade in living memory." The real talent, maintained the *Mirror,* lay in the backroom boys —those skilled arrangers and conductors like Nelson Riddle, Hugo Winterhalter, Ray Conniff, Gordon Jenkins, and Britain's own Geoff Love. Pop establishment journalists eagerly published Frank Sinatra's reference to the rockers as "goons" and his order to Mo Ostin, head of Sinatra's Reprise label, to release no rock 'n' roll records since neither Sinatra nor Reprise would have anything to do with such "junk."

A reader of *Disc,* a more liberal weekly, wrote in 1961 of "Hopes for a Rock 'n' Roll Comeback" and bemoaned the unfortunate demise or emasculation of most of the Heroes: Elvis had returned from the Army as a model American and a balladeer; Buddy Holly and Eddie Cochran were both dead; Gene Vincent had gone "Over the Rainbow"; and Jerry Lee Lewis was licking his wounds after being hounded out of

Britain by a puritan press campaign against his marriage to a thirteen-year-old second cousin. Little Richard had gone the other way by re-nouncing R&R as devil's music, throwing all his rings away, and be-coming a lay preacher. The pop papers reported that he'd last been seen spreading the Lord's Word in L.A.'s Pershing Square on behalf of the Seventh-Day Adventists and getting quietly moved along by the police.

The *Disc* reader ended by expressing hope that the spirit of R&R might be found in recent records by Barrett Strong ("Money, That's What I Want") and Jesse Hill ("Ooh Poo Pah Doo"). These records were, of course, examples of rhythm and blues (R&B), a parent of R&R that was being increasingly discovered by Britishers turned off by the shlocky-wet state of the pop scene. "Money" summed up succinctly one of the two basic needs of society and "Ooh Poo Pah Doo" expressed that shout of abandon that Little Richard had done so well on records like "Tutti Frutti." There was no language barrier in such exultant shouts, which were the essence of R&R—a sound of high energy con-ceived in an absence of restraint.

For the moment, though, our pop charts were free of the strong vi-brations of R&B. We would have to look for these rare records in im-port shops or get them from pals who'd been to Darkest America. Turn-ing the page of *Disc*, we would read that Brian Hyland was following up his hit "Itsy Bitsy Teenie Weenie Yellow Polka Dot Bikini" with "Lopsided Overloaded and It Wiggled When We Rode It."

But even worse than this drippy nonsense—as opposed to the righ-teous rock nonsense of *a-wop-bop-a-lu-bop*—was the adulteration of R&R by the incursion of Ideas: Adam Faith, once just Terry Nelhams and a simple skiffler, was now a big pop star with such hits as "What Do You Want?" and was rapidly becoming the Thinking Man's pop star. He was interviewed by an intellectual, John Freeman, on BBC-TV's very serious "Face to Face," and later he even pontificated with the Archbishop of York on the BBC's Sunday religious show, chal-lenging the Archbishop's contention that Faith's songs claimed that sex was all that life was about.

Pop was going egghead, pop was steering into the middle of the road again, pop was even going jazzy. Led by Chris Barber's "Petite Fleur," a number of trad-jazz bands had broken into the charts, bringing a healthy, optimistic, and slightly tipsy brass-band flavor. Barber was a dedicated jazzman with a well-rooted historical perspective and his fifties band had included Lonnie Donegan, a banjoist who had gone on to start the skiffle craze via an EP made with members of the Barber band. ("Rock Island Line" had hit even in America and Donegan had

gone on to become a pop idol with a leaning toward Woody Guthrie
songs and comedy-novelty material, such as "Does Your Chewing Gum
Lose Its Flavor on the Bedpost Overnight?" A host of kids took up the
guitar, thanks to Donegan and his skiffle, a real do-it-yourself music.)
Barber was also a fan of authentic rhythm and blues, an enthusiasm
which caused no little fuss within the doctrinaire ranks of the traditional and revivalist jazzmen. To these die-hard fans, R&B was a bas-
tardized, appreciated form of the true rural black blues from the Deep
South. But Barber appreciated the electric urban blues of, say, Louis
Jordan and Muddy Waters.

Meanwhile, other bands were springing up that took less care of the
traditional forms. Kenny Ball's Jazzmen swung standard melodies, such
as Cole Porter's "Samantha," the old Russian folk song "Midnight in
Moscow," and Rodgers and Hammerstein's "March of the Siamese
Children." Acker Bilk's boys from Somerset wore bowler hats and fancy
waistcoats and boasted "good scrumpy music" (cider music) for "trudging over muddy fields in big boots." Rollicking through "The White
Cliffs of Dover" and the pseudo-Italian "Buona Sera," they caused a
near-riot at a jazz festival when their raving fans—identified by their
fondness for long hair and beards; shaggy, baggy sweaters; and top hats
and bowlers—got overenthusiastic and prevented several important
black bluesmen from appearing. True jazz fans and R&R lovers joined
together to condemn the archaic crassness of these traddies—Hooray
Henrys with their Henriettas, obviously from the layabout upper-middle classes. Their private school accents gave them away.

The most British and perhaps most worthy of the ersatz jazz bands
were the Temperance Seven. They made no pretense at being serious
jazzmen; they were in it for fun and perhaps money. They wore their
British eccentricity on their sleeves: their wardrobe—a satirical reminder of the past glories of the British Empire—consisted of pith helmets, officers' tropical kits, full-dress Victorian, and lots of junk gathered from antique shops. The Temps had started as an art school jape
(most of the band held day jobs—one was a sculpture teacher, another
a graphic designer) and this good humor was retained on their more
commercial records when they went on to be produced at EMI by
George Martin, a staffer who specialized in odd-job, offbeat productions. Peter Sellers, the Luton Girls' Choir, brass bands, Scottish reels—
Martin had done it all, except real down-to-earth gutsy rock 'n' roll.

As we have seen, the good old safe Establishment pop industry had
spayed the wild men of rock—and it was business as usual on both continents. Even comedian Benny Hill had no trouble getting high on the
British charts, with his "Gather In the Mushrooms" (February 1961).
Asked about the pop/rock scene, he told Disc: "Pop is amusing. A few

years ago, it was just three chords—now it's graduated to four and I only know one! But I'll tell you something: we're definitely in the age of knobs. It's marvelous what these engineer chappies can do!"

However, in this same *Disc* was a voice crying in the wilderness, exhorting the beatmen to put some fire under themselves and get cracking again, shouting in headlines that the current 1960s pop scene had NO NEW IDEAS! and was SO BORING! Jack Good, Britain's (and the world's) visionary TV pop music show producer, had gotten himself a weekly column in which to sound off about the dreadful state of affairs. He did so brilliantly, lashing out at the industry like a headmaster at recalcitrant schoolboys. One week, he actually published an end-of-term report in which he reprimanded Head Boy Elvis. "Too much responsibility has taken the edge off his originality." In general, Good felt, the rock school had lost its raucous energy: "Singers have learned to hop about a bit and not to offend grandmothers. Elvis is now an all-around entertainer, being nice to babies and friendly to foreigners." He begged Elvis to drop insipid ballads like "Are You Lonesome Tonight?" and to please record more of the old "real, low-down, raunchy, scraunchy rhythm and blues that'll knock the guts and beat the hide." Jack, too, saw R&B as the fountain of youthful vigor for an ailing rock scene.

Jack Good had been an extremely important figure in British beat. He had put our rock dreams into pictures on the TV screen. He had realized the pure melodrama inherent in the rock 'n' roll record. Without him, there would have been sound and fury—but no *style*. Television and the movies, in that order, were the media that made the rock stars. The point is very important: without "The Ed Sullivan Show," Elvis would not have made such across-the-board impact; and, looking ahead, we shall see that the Beatles accomplished the same thing when they managed to get early exposure on this same show. Jack Good, in fact, was to produce their first TV spectacular, "Around the Beatles."

In the late fifties, Jack became TV's Rock Svengali. An Oxford graduate, with a grounding in Greek drama and Shakespeare, he scoured the coffee bars and skiffle cellars for potential stars. In one of these hangouts, he scooped up Adam Faith. Other stars-to-be were brought to him at the studios. Cliff Richard (born Harry Webb) was a shy boy with sideburns and a skiffle group; Good made him learn the quintessential Elvis movements and eventually transformed him into a sizzling, sexy property. Marty Wilde, Joe Brown, Vince Eager, and a host of other ordinary boys had their burning inner fantasy selves brought out by Jack Good. He dressed them carefully, he shot them cunningly, he rushed up and down behind the cameras, endlessly exhorting them into histrionic actions by hooraying and bravoing and jiggling and flaying his own limbs. From "Six-Five Special" (BBC) to "Oh Boy!" and "Boy

Meets Girl" (both ITV), he invested British TV screens with his fiery vision of high-speed America—which he in turn had absorbed from American movies, records, comic books, and magazines. This was America as it ought to be, filtered through its own pop culture, but now made more intense, larger than life, more vital and stripped-down. This was America seen at 200 m.p.h. through smoke and dust-bleared motor-cycle goggles.

Of course, the real McCoy was better. Slowly but surely, the American rockers were arriving in Britain—Jerry Lee, Eddie Cochran, Buddy Holly. Elvis kept promising he'd come someday. Although hot on disc, some of the U.S. rockers were rather a letdown in person. Bill Haley's record sales slipped dramatically after his 1957 tour of Britain. Too avuncular, not threatening enough. Gene Vincent presented a challenge: a nicely spoken, charming Southern gent in a red-felt ice-hockey jacket. Good soon got to work, making use of the singer's wan El Greco face and his stoop (caused by a gammy leg encased in an iron affair). For his first TV appearance, Good dressed Vincent from head to toe in black leather and instructed him to limp around the set as he moaned his hit "Be-Bop-A-Lula." Thus was born the Richard III of Rock. The effect was sensational, as Good himself discovered when he attended a Gene Vincent show at a London music hall: lots of the audience were similarly dressed in black leather.

The line show was presented by Larry Parnes, the theater version of Jack Good. In America, the late fifties had seen the arrival of pretty-boy stars like Frankie Avalon and Fabian, together with their idol-maker Bob Marcucci, a manager who could work wonders on teenage boys once he had found a suitable face to sculpt into an idol. Parnes was achieving similar successes in Britain with his stable of likely lads. Parnes dreamed up glamorous stage names to hide their humdrum origins and to perhaps suggest a key sexual characteristic: Nelson Keene, Vince Eager, Dickie Pride, Johnny Goode, Johnny Gentle, Duffy Power, Marty Wilde, Billy Fury, and Georgie Fame. He carefully groomed his boys to walk, talk, and dress like silky satin stars. Otherworldliness was the goal, the sort of mystery that Marlene Dietrich had. This charm school for rockers had, of course, an obvious absurdity and was ripe for satire. George Martin produced a hilarious sketch on record featuring Peter Sellers as Major Ralph Ralph, an ex-horse owner who has moved into the newly lucrative teen idol scene. The major's interview is interrupted by one of his rock stable. The intruding lad is ordered to remain with the other rockers and to remember that he must always stop where the carpet begins.

Jack Good never had much time for the pop industry; he was only interested in pop as a state of spontaneous combustion. But he did use

some of Parnes's raunchier rock boys on his TV shows, so long as they
didn't go soppy on him and start balladeering. Jack never cared for serious love songs. For him, pop had nothing to do with serious music. If
he wanted moonlight and roses, he could get them from Chopin and
Beethoven. Nothing less.

The split-personality syndrome was elevated to utter grotesqueness in
this period (the last great period of American cultural domination) in
the case of Billy Fury. One of the most fiery runners in the Parnes stable (and favored by Good), Fury had formerly been plain Ronald
Wycherley, a shy Liverpool lad with a taste for drainpipe jeans and
ornithology. Off-stage he was jittery and tongue-tied, but once released
into the spotlight he seemed possessed by a demonic power. Roaring
and raging and hopping frenziedly, he symbolized the bursting of a
dam of pent-up emotion. For too long, we British had been holding
back our passion, even proud of this repression (immortalizing it into
stiff-upper-lip art in the film *Brief Encounter*). Now R&R was providing a vehicle for us to release rivers of sweat and waves of body odor.
However, the vehicle was Made in America. We were still a distant
outpost, a dumping ground for American pop products, and we could
do little more than tribal Africans who imitated their white colonizers
by dressing up in epaulettes and cocked hats. We were still Little
Americans. And we were building up in our own little Tin Pan Alley
a pop/rock industry on American lines.

In March of 1962, Jack Good, in his *Disc* column, described the
local scene as a "mess." The excitement had gone and there was "no
unity of purpose." Recording techniques, he said, were getting so sophisticated, what with multitracking and so on, that pop had gone too
"cerebral." The purpose of a rock record was to "catch a fleeting moment, not to bottle, pickle, and then cube it all up later." Wise words,
but unheeded because too much money was being made by the denizens of the newly tamed industry. Good wanted not dissection but
"overall noise." The industry wanted professionalism and teamwork.
Executives wanted to prove that they were of more use than ashtrays
on motorcycles. And the kids were going along with this plan. "The
kids don't want to rock anymore," said Jack. "They want to retire. The
adults have taken up rock 'n' roll and are twisting. Ugh!"

Pop was becoming eclectic again; string sections sawed, banjos
plunked. Yodeling was not far off (in the shape of Frank Ifield). Arrangers were calling the tune again. EMI's Norrie Paramour, an arranger and producer (like Parlophone's George Martin), claimed that
1961 had been pop's "finest year for a long time. We're beginning to
think for ourselves in arrangements. It's been a year when quality has
counted. Singers are getting more professional and we are developing

excellent session players to back them up." Many of these new musicians had started as skifflers but had now achieved mastery of the
pop/rock idiom. From another direction came actors like John Leyton,
Oliver Reed, and Bernard Cribbins, who took up pop recording and
managed, through skillful engineering and canny producers, to make
the charts. Joe Meek, a wizard engineer, made Space Age music via his
group the Tornadoes and got them to the top of the U.S. charts with
"Telstar." Acker Bilk, the onetime earthy cider drinker with the clomp-
ing trad-jazz sound, went ethereal with soaring strings and breathy clarinet on the ballad "Stranger on the Shore" and in April he shot to
number one, not only in Britain but also in America. High hopes and
prayers were put on Cliff Richard, our own answer to Presley, that he
might soon conquer America in his new, carefully earned role as all-
around entertainer.

All this "progress" was anathema to Jack Good. He felt he had done
his bit and yet Britain was going under with the crooners and violins.
In July 1962, he left for America and a new life. He wanted to keep
his status as an excited and engaged amateur, a gentleman of R&R.
America was Abroad, a potential whirl of excitement, a pool of pulse.
"I am fascinated by America as a *way of life,* not as a place," he said.

So our spokesman, headmaster, and idol-maker deserted us for foreign parts just when we needed him most.

And yet, I have to admit that Man cannot live by Beat alone. He
does need the softer ballad from time to time and I adored both Connie
Francis's cries of suffering and Brenda Lee's perky pouts about being
"Fool Number One." I thought Frank Ifield's yodeling was pretty nifty,
but then I'd always been a pantomime fan and panto is a catchall for
all kinds of things. However, even for the beat purist, there were bea-
cons in this early-sixties darkness, singers and sounds on the charts that
had individuality and originality, plus a healthy sense of the great traditions of show business. These exceptions successfully mixed art with
commerce—not an easy thing to accomplish.

I must also admit that I was introduced to these originals by girls.
Alison, Diane, and others carried around little boxes of 45s and handy
portable record players to augment our petting sessions on beach,
bench, and boat. At first, I frowned on such background music, but
soon I found it to be ideal accompaniment—and sometimes a positive
lubricant! In this way, I was exposed to such standouts as Roy Orbison,
Del Shannon, Neil Sedaka, Dion Di Mucci, and Frankie Valli and the
Four Seasons. And as always there were a host of one-hit wonders like
Bruce ("Hey! Baby") Channel to provide a few minutes' joy and then
vanish in the best R&R manner. These one-hitters are absolutely crucial
to healthy pop—gorgeous butterflies who flutter by and die quietly out

of sight after giving us a moment's bliss before we return to the everyday business of life. This is the true purpose of pop: to be a leisure arm
of real life. And sometimes it nagged me that I was spending too much
time absorbed in this lightweight leisure music when I ought to be
tackling weightier subjects, like the works of Joseph Conrad or Boris
Pasternak. But I got by, reading the *Classics Illustrated* version of *Lord
Jim* and seeing the movie of *Dr. Zhivago*. Conscience was cleared and
I could hold my own at intellectual gatherings.

And after our discussions of literature, the Bomb, and the relative
talents of Truffaut and Chabrol, it was refreshing to go out under the
moon and stars and romance to the music of Roy Orbison, whose
minimelodrama operas told achingly of the battle to win the girl in a
ten-speed voice shot full of anguish. He was the loser's troubadour—
only, sometimes, through sheer musical power, he managed to win her.
"Running Scared," for example, rat-tat-tatted along in dramatic Morse
code, finishing in another key and another realm. A natural high pla-
teau. The struggle continued through "Crying," "Falling," and "It's
Over"—and it was made more dramatic by the contrast between Roy's
melo-operatic voice and his appearance. Behind the all-black image—the
hair, the garish costume with its cape, and the shades—was a slight
squint and a pudgy face. Yet dashing around inside him was an arch-
romantic with wonderful lungs. His self-written epics rose like steeples
as he built them and often they teetered on the edge of that delicious
valley of self-pity.

Del Shannon, on the other hand, was plainly of the earth. He looked
like a working stiff, stocky and bullish, with a lantern jaw. He sang,
roaring out his own compositions about runaway girls, accompanied by
a marvelously cheap, rocking fairground sound characterized by a
cheesy organ that splattered out sliding toy notes. It was no surprise to
learn that he had written "Runaway" while working as a carpet salesman in Michigan shortly after serving as a GI in Germany.

In Britain, we had a brief flash of righteous R&R from native Johnny
Kidd. His creation "Shakin' All Over" was an eerie, slow raver full of
wobbling guitar. The wobble, made by bending a lever on the side of
the guitar, was to become rather overused by groups like the Shadows,
Ventures, and Tornadoes, but Kidd's song and voice packed terrific
power and danger and the record has become a classic. However, Kidd
expressed a desire to become an "artist," recorded things like "If You
Were the Only Girl in the World," and generally adulterated his raving righteous brand of rock. He vanished. But at least he was an original, for a while, even if he did have that midatlantic twang. The
rest of the British boy and girl chart-makers were the usual run of Little Americans, together with too many guitar-wobble groups copying

the Shadows (Cliff Richard's old backing group). Indeed, George Martin of Parlophone was quoted as saying that this "overabundance of beat groups presents a problem. They *must* achieve a distinctive sound." And for my tastes, the only distinctive sounds were being made by those still carrying on the British music-hall comedy tradition—Bernard Cribbins ("Hole in the Ground," and "Right, Said Fred"), Mike Sarne ("Come Outside"), and, of course, Benny Hill and Peter Sellers. Why was it that we seemed incapable of making effective beat records? Were we still a race of motheaten, dull-colored clerks and louts and middle-class excrement living on increment, ruled by the Old School Tie Establishment? Did Lady Chatterley's comment about the Midlands in the 1920s hold true for Britain in the early sixties: "The utter negation of natural beauty, the utter negation of the gladness of life, the utter absence of the instinct for shapely beauty which every bird and beast has, the utter death of the human intuitive faculty"?

From America, home of Greek gods like Elvis, Jack Good reported back to *Disc*. En route to a Hollywood *Nirvana*, with a head full of ideas to showcase R&R talent on U.S. TV and to bring new life to that medium, he stopped off in New York, where he noted that British singers were having a tough time making any kind of impact. Acker Bilk and the Tornadoes had had freak fluke hits, but an English sound had not been established. Jack had supposed that Lonnie Donegan, who had had U.S. chart success, would have done well there, but he found the chief skiffler with his back to the wall at a steamy folk club in New York's Greenwich Village, an area Jack described as very "artsy-craftsy." Poor Donegan had spent his first show battling for attention from folk fans who were not tuned into his spikey music-hall jollity, nor impressed by his stage gear of dinner suit and gold-buckled patent leather boots. "Have a Drink on Me" was lost on them; herbal teas and the occasional weed were more to their taste. Across Broadway, our Cliff Richard was part of a laundry list of acts on a rock show, billed as "An Added British Attraction." Jack noted that his off-stage accent had gone completely American. Britishers were still Britishers and interesting only as curiosities from the land of the derby hat. For us, the impossible dream was to make it big in America.

Speedily, Jack Good turned his method on American talent, seeking to spotlight all that was bright and airy in the New World. He devised a wham-bam show on the lines of his British "Oh Boy!" (which had been billed as "the fastest show on television"). "Young America Swings the World" was born of Jack's sweeping view of beat music as a mobile force for good. His view was clean, clear, and single-minded. The world would be changed for the better by music boiling from the American melting pot. Give them back the old verities, the primeval pulse and scream, in the new shape of R&R served up by bright young things!

He put his vision in a letter to Robert F. Kennedy, asking for government funding for this noble cultural mission. "Young America," he suggested, would be distributed free around the world as a goodwill gesture by an altruistic nation. He got a letter back from President John F. Kennedy to the effect that rock 'n' roll was not the sort of thing that American dollars should be spent on at the moment. A hootenanny might have been more to the point.

Jack went ahead and made a pilot show, featuring P. J. Proby, Jackie De Shannon, Leon Russell, the Blossoms (with Darlene Love, who had sung on many of the Phil Spector "Wall of Sound" epics), and Johnny Cash (at that time in a state of commercial eclipse). ABC liked the pilot, but brought the vision more down to earth, cutting away the religious fervor. "Shindig" was the result, the first (and, possibly, *only*) American TV series to capture visually the speed and excitement of beat music. The very first show of fall 1964 mixed the Everly Brothers with Sam Cooke in a typical and marvelous Good theatrical framework. The house bands were under the direction of Ray Pohlman, a young bass player who had won his spurs playing on Spector records, and Pohlman rounded up some of the best rockers in the world, most of whom could, at this point, be found playing sessions in Los Angeles. Rock playing had been perfected, after years of stewing, by James Burton, Jerry Cole, and Glen Campbell on guitar; Jim Horn on sax; Larry Knechtel and Delaney Bramlett on bass; Leon Russell on piano; and Mickey Conway and Earl Palmer on drums.

Black segued with white, as people sang and danced together and shouted the hosannas of beat music to millions of homes in a still-divided country via network TV. But ultra-close-ups of a sweating Little Richard proved to be too much for many of the affiliate stations and soon Jack was getting calls from New York telling him to lay off the black close-ups. He asked to see this directive in writing and on official ABC stationery. No reply. Later, when confronted by a slur about leering tinted TV faces, Jack knocked the speaker, an ABC veep, clean through a plate-glass window.

In Britain, some of us had been going Jack's route and discovering for ourselves the freshness of modern, urban rhythm and blues. We were digging "parent rock," as a satisfying alternative to pop pap. And in so doing, we were carrying on a traditional passion for Afro-American musical research that dated back in Britain to at least the end of World War I, when the Original Dixieland Jazz Band had visited us and started a love affair that lasted till Beatle time.

In Britain, we had always taken our American pop (from rag to rock) far more seriously and studiously than most Americans. For them, jazz and swing and boogie and blues were passing moments in a land of crazes, food for the American need for constant change. But we collected our syncopation records carefully, filed and cross-indexed them, and some of us so treasured our early Gennett 78s that we never actually played them, just stared at them and memorized the matrix numbers. From World War II on, some of us began to get quite popular playing revived forms of early jazz.

When I say "we," I'm referring to my own class—the educated middle class. I'm also referring, of course, to a minority. For most people, pop collecting was on a par with stamp collecting. In an American context, class may seem irrelevant, but in Britain it's the key to an understanding of every aspect of life in the Isles. We are riddled with it. We can fine-grade an islander's social position after hearing a few seconds of his speech: *accent*.

We—a large number of us being university liberal arts undergraduates, art students, design students—have tended to be more taken by older pop cultures than brand-new ones. The higher the social scale, the more likely the fan will go for really ancient jazz, possibly even ragtime. Humphrey Lyttelton led one of the best fifties' trad bands and he was an "honorable," an aristocrat. The Queen's cousin had a pretty sizable collection of early hot jazz and used to lecture us at school on the subject. In the early fifties, my prep school teacher delighted in playing me his Louis Armstrong records and next minute he was telling me to turn off that bloody racket on the radio—which happened to be a brand-new boogie by Tennessee Ernie Ford, "Kiss Me Big." Just too modern and threatening and vulgar for him.

Although I instinctively adored Elvis when he first burst out of my radio on "Radio Luxembourg," I eventually gave in to peer pressure, denouncing him and all R&R around 1958. I was told to mature and either appreciate the gray-matter music of the Modern Jazz Quartet or Dave Brubeck (using a slide rule to work out the rhythms) or start seriously researching Ye Olde Blues from the Golden Age: Bessie Smith was the prime example, but if I really insisted on living people then Big Bill Broonzy or Josh White. The reason for this love of the past and distaste for the present was this: the past could be invested with the romance of the carefree or suffering Negro; R&R was made by aggressive urban blacks or hopelessly conservative hillbillies, smelling too strongly of modern working-class life. The archaeologists, dubbed "moldy figs" by modern jazzers, preferred a pastoral setting for their blues: a dear old Rastus on the ole front porch, twangin' the plangent blues as de evenin' sun go down. R&R by contrast, was not played for personal expression and aesthetic pleasure but for *money*. Big white show biz was deeply involved. This was anathema to middle-class, liberal-minded Afro-American aficionados. "Ban the Bomb" marches were generally pepped up by the toots of a New Orleans-style jazz band in duffle coats and suitably rakish headgear.

It was one such traditional jazz band leader who started the British rhythm and blues movement. Chris Barber, you will remember, had formed a group within his band to play skiffle, the good-time jug band rent party music that was the flip side of the introverted blues-'roun'-my-bed solo style. His singer, Lonnie Donegan, went on to score lots of skiffle hits and to break away and up from traditional jazz circles. And the skiffle craze in its overground pop form inspired lots of kids to form guitar groups which later became R&R outfits, especially in Liverpool and the North. However, Barber continued to stick to the straight and reasonably narrow path of jazz-related music. Skiffle had been a fifties version of black twenties and thirties music, but next Barber strode forward into the forties and early fifties to discover urban electric blues. He started importing urban bluesmen and providing accompaniment with a special R&B group within his jazz band. Cyril Davies played a splendid moaning mouth harp and Alexis Korner strummed a mean electric blues guitar. Korner, the son of an Austrian cavalry officer, went on to form, with Davies, Britain's first electric R&B band—Blues Incorporated—in 1961. Ian Armit, a jazzman, was on piano (later replaced by another jazzman, Johnny Parker), Jack Bruce played string bass, and Charlie Watts was the drummer (later replaced by Ginger Baker).

Blues Incorporated left the old jazz ways behind and entered the Age of Electricity without the crassness of silk band uniforms, gold cars, and Uriah Heep-like managers. Thus, their big-city blues (with lots of songs by Willie Dixon and Muddy Waters) was still rural-rooted and never took in the more hip, taut, contemporary "soul" of such black favorites as Ray Charles, Sam Cooke, or Solomon Burke. Motown music, just beginning to make a mark on the American charts, was far too commercial for Blues Incorporated and its followers. Too slick and shiny and arranged.

But Korner and Davies were our instructors in British R&B and, despite their slightly academic bent and unglamorous appearance, they set the local R&B movement rolling. Over the years, Blues Incorporated alumni would join pop supergroups like the Rolling Stones, the Animals, Manfred Mann, the Cream, and Led Zeppelin. The group's first regular gig was at the Marquee Club in London's West End in 1961. Jack Good was still around and looking for something meaty to get his teeth into. He came, saw, and raved. He persuaded Decca to let him produce a live album at the Marquee and the result was sturdy and boisterous and included the Muddy Waters' favorites "I'm Your Hoochie Coochie Man" and "Got My Mojo Working." These two were to become R&B standards and staples for any fledgling R&B band.

Jack wrote up the R&B movement in his *Disc* column and he did his best to get the stuff onto the charts. He produced a dynamite version of Buster Brown's "Sugar Baby," using Jimmy Powell, a local lad, but the record failed to click. I read Jack and I bought the record and I was very impressed and excited by the potential of R&B. I started buying reissues of 1940s "race" records—boogie-shuffle things by Big Maceo and Jazz Gillum—and I read and digested the learned liner notes by Alexis Korner. Then an art student friend told me that Dick Heckstall-Smith, who'd been connected with our old school, was tooting sax with Blues Incorporated down near the Ealing tube station. Would I like to come? Blues Incorporated by this time, spring of 1962, had left the Marquee and opened the Rhythm and Blues Club in Ealing, a dreary South London suburb.

At Ealing, I found most people dressed in the usual sloppy casual gear, a sort of planned thoughtlessness. It was the music that was important, not the clothes. I was wearing baggy Daks and a dull, vomit-colored sports jacket, *de rigueur* for G.B. R&B, but I was yearning to get slim enough to be able to wear tight jeans and a form-fitting T-shirt. Instinctively, I knew that sexiness was at the essence of pop music in its most popular form. And who doesn't want to be popular? To hell with ethnic authenticity when popularity's the name of the game! Anyway, at the Ealing club, the bandsmen looked like the audience—there was none of that show-biz gap between performer and fan. All that was to come later when the bonds were burst by other kids who felt, like me, irked by the straitjacket of blues.

So—no glamour and no show. But so authentic was Blues Incorporated's powerhouse of pulsing modern electricity mixed with good ole down-home earthy picking and hollering, that when I closed my eyes during "I Got My Brand on You" (or it might have been "I'm Gonna Put a Tiger in Your Tank") I could imagine being in a real funky Chicago blues bar. We'd never seen a full American blues band in action, but had been visited only by the odd solo blues entertainers like Champion Jack Dupree or Speckled Red. Fine old varmints, true, and full of colorful tall tales and folksy music performed by head, hands, and feet ingrained with a pain learned in the "Varsity of Life" ("School of Hard Knocks"). But nevertheless, these charming black men always remained several degrees removed from our own experience. Not accessible. They could never be role models.

Blues Incorporated was showing us that even we white chaps could make reasonable R&B—with no wasteful and pointless overheads like band uniforms, choreographers, or publicists.

Mick Jagger, Brian Jones, Keith Richards—all jammed with Blues Incorporated from time to time at the Ealing club. Later, they borrowed drummer Charlie Watts, roped in bassist Bill Wyman and boogie piano wizard Ian Stewart, and took their name from a Muddy Waters number, "Rolling Stone Blues." Not far from Ealing, in the comfy dormitory town of Richmond-on-Thames, they were soon established as the hot resident band at the Crawdaddy Club in the Station Hotel. Being younger and prettier and more antsy and less academic than Korner & Company, there was very little ethnic authenticity to block the flow of pure hedonistic rave-up. They played a lot of Chuck Berry, as well as the more dignified Muddy Waters. They shook around and showed off their flaming youth. In Mick Jagger, the tousle-haired gamin schoolboy with the sensuous rubber lips and girlish hips, they had a potential pop figure reeking of sex for all tastes. There was a crowd collecting to see and hear R&B, not purely for the Afro-American blues sound but also for a highly charged mixture of sex and violence and blues, plus some cheap thrills when Jagger pouted in that cute surly manner, naughty but nice. R&B was starting to roll in the motion of the sixties and was becoming relevant to the feelings of white middle-class youth.

Mick Jagger and the Stones were only one manifestation of the new British flesh-and-blood R&B. All over London, but especially the South, R&B clubs were mushrooming: on Eel Pie Island, at Klooks Kleek in Hampstead (where John Mayall's Blues Breakers were to reign later), at the Scene and Studio 51 in London's West End. Within the term R&B lay a variety of styles. Some favored the rural, down-home sound of Cyril Davies; others mixed more youth-oriented influences like Chuck Berry and Bo Diddley. At the Flamingo Club in the West End, the slicker and more modern "soul" sound was favored. Georgie Fame and the Blue Flames and Zoot Money's Big Roll Band were to be the favorites here, playing a fat and sassy, sometimes even Scotch-velvetlike music with sax sections and throaty organs. This, of course, was no more native British music than that of Billy Fury and the other local apers of American R&R. But one noticed that the Flamingo fans wore suits and ties and neatly clipped hair. Not exactly Savile Row tailoring or Trumper's haircutting, but certainly evidence of more sartorial awareness than the average Ealing R&B fan and far removed from the shapeless and scruffy clothes of the trad-jazz crowd.

Then into the Flamingo sauntered one Rod (the Mod) Stewart and he was a sight for eyes used to the monochrome drabness of male fashions of the fifties. Men were in color again for the first time since

Queen Victoria! The peacock struts, the hair back-combed and teased into a look of electric shock, the leer from a fully painted but hollow-cheeked and slightly skeletal face, the sway from a tight-panted satin ass made visible by the shortness of the bum-freezer box jacket—and all in a riot of many hues! Carmen Miranda had strong competition—and your regular bricklayer or truck driver would have pronounced Rod and his ilk (for he was one of a growing cult) "queers." But Rod was not gay; his style was just the start of an androgynous strain in pop which was to be puzzling to outsiders. There was no sexual substance to the outward appearance. Inside, beneath the powder and paint, lay a boy who fancied women just as much as his mates. Second to soccer, of course. When he gave out with that Scotch-whisky voice, he hit those girls at bull's-eye and he sounded very soulful in the best modern American manner. *Modern*—that was important. None of this old fuddy-duddy cottonfield stuff. Rod and the Mods were up-to-date, were Modern, and music was only a part of their sixties life-style.

Like British R&B, the Mod movement had started in London and remained centered there. First cropping up as the fifties died, its origins are mysterious, but there's little doubt that it was spontaneous and not generated by entertainment industry types, who were busy congratulating themselves on the success of their exploitation dance craze, the Twist. The Mods were a new generation because, like the fifties rockers, they were reaping some of the benefits of "The Affluent Society." Prime Minister Macmillan was boasting that "You've never had it so good," meaning that there were more jobs, more leisure time, more spending money for the young, and no threat of National Service call-up. The New Youth could look forward to material wealth coming to them in this Great Age of Progress. The Mods, in particular, were reacting against the grimy grimness of the fifties. They expressed a loathing for that era's coarseness and brutishness as shown in its Teddy Boy music and clothes and general coating of grease. By the 1960s, Teddy Boys and rockers were to be found only up in the unspeakable North and in the rural wilds of the West Country. The Southern working class was to express its newfound sense of social mobility through the life-style called Mod. Display (or "flash") has always been a useful form of instant expression in working-class culture: you're doing well, you feel good, and you show it with gold teeth, gold Cadillacs, huge diamond tie pins, and fur coats galore.

The English upper classes had always spent a good deal of money on clothes, but the object had been to look as unostentatious as possible. Discreetness in costume as in life. Only the tailor knew the price and then it was only in guineas. The Mods, however, were reviving a narcissistic flamboyance not seen in Britain since the days of Beau

Brummel and the Regency dandies. The early Mods had a hard time assembling their wardrobe because as yet there was nobody in the rag trade to cater expressly to their needs, so they had to search in all manner of places. For their tight trousers and bright sweaters, they went to casual wear shops around Carnaby Street, which normally catered to the homosexual trade. For the short box jackets, winkle-picker shoes, and trousers with no cuffs, they went to the snappier West End shops that specialized in the Italian look. And for their hipster trousers with flares and their matelot shirts, they went to the few stores that stocked the St. Tropez style. Even sports shops were invaded for their Fred Perry tennis shirts.

Let us, for the moment, leave our prince of Mod on the eve of his major breakthrough into overground pop and, of course, exploitation by Big Business. He is to be a new Prince Valiant, together with his Northern countrymen, in a massive Invasion of America. The tables will be turned.

Our average young Mod is racing along the pavement in short, stabby steps, with shoulders swaying and feet turned slightly outward. He's clicking his fingers and talking rapidly—to no apparent music or being. He now wheels around the corner of this Shepherd's Bush street and enters a place called the Goldhawk Club. Inside, he joins others of his kind, finger-clicking, fast-talking—and pill-popping (which causes the fast actions). Soon he is on display at the bar, careful not to be touched in any way, standing elegantly with the top button of his jacket undone and his trunk angled so that the line of the jacket isn't spoiled, and his legs slightly crossed, but not so much that they will stretch the razor-sharp trouser crease. A cigarette is held in a certain prescribed manner, a Scotch and Coke sits nearby. He could have a vodka and lime or, possibly, a vodka and orange juice. He has spent many evenings at home at the ironing board, getting ready for such a night. He walked to the club rather than coming by bus or tube, not taking the chance of wrecking his trouser crease by sitting down or getting jostled. He is a dedicated follower of a certain fashion. He is a Face.

At the moment, his ears are prickling nicely to the satin sounds of specially imported American soul records. He knows he is part of a new, cocky, confident elite. He is talking rapidly to any Face that comes near because he is bursting with boss feelings. And he's waiting with high expectancy to hear the resident group sing out their praise to Dr. Feelgood. The Who will be onstage very shortly.

2

1963: "SURFIN' HOOTENANNY"

Others prefer the sign of the cross, but I used to say "*Elvis Presley!*" to ward off evil spirits and to help me keep a stiff upper lip in times of trouble. Whether I was en route to boarding school, in haunted houses, or in nightmares, this incantation used to exercise a mental magic: "*Elvis Presley!*" and—*poof!*—the evil vanished. One spin of his music and I could escape to Wonderland, U.S.A., where, amid palms and pines, the King ruled with a glowering lopsided grin as he watched his court of comic book heroes taking swims in malted milk and root beer, helping themselves to mountains of squishy nursery food such as hamburgers and hot fudge sundaes. Strumming beside the King was the court bard, Chuck Berry, and every now and then he'd come up with a choice song of praise about the wonders of the Promised Land. Some

ditty about a ponytailed, blue-jeaned, petal-lipped teen queen or a tail-
finned, chrome-clad, elongated supercar. Girl and car—interchangeable
objects of worship in the worldly other world summoned up by *"Elvis
Presley!"*

But, unfortunately, most of the time I just got on with the job, as
most of us have to. "Living and partly living," as T. S. Eliot wrote in
his play *Murder in the Cathedral*. (This was required reading for the
English Lit. course I took during my last year at boarding school. I felt
it was a cheat because the play's thriller promise never materializes, but
Murder in the Cathedral was art and rather awesome.) I had finally responded to peer pressure and put away childish things like Haley,
Presley, and Jerry Lee. At least publicly. But my heart was still in
Wonderland, U.S.A., and I determined to get there someday, just as
any child would love to visit the icy fun factory where Santa Claus
loads up.

Meanwhile, I found it acceptable to pursue the historical. I began to
find that I enjoyed marching backward, musically. It was as cozy as
Wonderland, and had nothing to do with Today. Fortunately for me,
the early sixties was, as we have seen, a time when my class was examining out-of-date R&B. I had shot back much farther—to the twenties and even before. I'd been dabbling around with revivalist kitsch
bands, wearing a wing collar and long-tailed coat, playing debutante
parties where swan-necked girls liked to swing their pearls to "Yes, We
Have No Bananas." But now, inspired by the intellectual respectability
of Alexis Korner and the animal magnetism of Mick Jagger, I buried
myself in R&B. I pored over liner notes. I combed specialty record
stores. I consulted an Old Etonian who had a very decent collection of
R&B imports. He helped me choose numbers that suited my style, bearing in mind my respect for the great tradition of the British music hall.
We came up with stuff like "Built for Comfort" (Willie Dixon) and
"Who Drink My Beer When I Wuz in Der Rear?" (Dave Bartholemew). Nothing too deep or taxing. I didn't have the right to sing
"Every Day I Have the Blues" because I hadn't experienced hundreds
of years of slavery and oppression and, anyway, most days I felt pretty
happy.

But I did like the sound of the music.

In the fall of 1961, I took this new interest over to Ireland, where I
was enrolled as a junior freshman at Trinity College, Dublin, the ancient Protestant bastion in a Catholic republic. In those days, the campus was a haven for oddities: obscure Scottish peers, eccentric offspring
of ancient British families, an Egyptian count, a Mauritanian Teddy
Boy, and a couple of African tribal chiefs. The Africans fascinated me
because I was now reading anything I could find on the subject of

blacks and black music. To my great joy, I discovered that there were several blacks in my history class. I was absolutely dying to be black myself, as it seemed to be the answer to all my musical desires. My misconceptions were soon corrected through experience—as I narrated in my book *After the Ball* (Penguin, 1973):

"In our class was Mr. Anangoola, who had tribal scars on his face and applauded everything, especially lectures. I persuaded him to come out to my digs one evening to hear jazz records. He turned out to be a disappointment, enjoying the tea and iced cake but not really responding to the jazz. I thought it might trigger him off so that I could then quiz and study him but it didn't and that night I learned a truth: not all black men have innate beat."

Mr. Anangoola returned to his history course and I returned to my search for the source of the Big Beat. I last heard of Mr. Anangoola through the Trinity Old Boys' magazine. As a brigadier-general, he'd been killed leading his men into action during a recent African war; the magazine thanked him for willing his Gilbert and Sullivan record collection to the college. I was to learn further that most young blacks I met had no interest in black music unless it was of the Here and Now. But most young whites ate it up, especially the girls. And if you played it on an instrument, you were assured of being shown a good time.

So from then on, I determined to combine scholarship with sex in a blend that was to be my very own R&B, which was to become the hit of Trinity and then of Dublin. Next stop—America!

Changing my name temporarily to Warren Whitcomb, I gathered an assortment of disgruntled college jazz musicians to form an ad hoc blues band. We were soon in demand for nuclear disarmament demonstrations and "Ban South African Fruit" marches, as well as the odd rugby game. I even inserted a few protest blues of the "nobody-knows-the-trouble-I-seen" variety because in Dublin there were scenes to feel blue about, what with the street beggars, roaming lunatics, and crashing drunks. And there was a very practical reason for setting up a pounding rhythm: it was so damned cold wherever you went.

After a few terms, our fame spread outside Trinity's walls and we got offers to play ballrooms, monasteries, and castles. With money and vision, I expanded the band to include young Dublin electric guitarists with real amplifiers and mikes and knowledge of how these gadgets worked. As a result, we lost the clarinet player and the banjoist (thank God). Inspired by Blues Incorporated, I concocted our new name—Bluesville Manufacturing. But the locals insisted on calling us "The Bluesvilles," slotting us into the long line of Irish showbands. These showbands were pretty dreary affairs of enervating ballads and schottisches and wet-rock, accompanied by demure high-kicking and the swinging of instruments from right to left in strict unison. So when Bluesville Manufacturing came along, a feast of shambolics, Young Ireland was roused to a frenzy not seen since the Troubles. Our noise was not unfamiliar: we were transforming the whoops and hollers of the black shouters into the grunts and bellows of a post-rugby game crowd in full cry.

Lectures were skipped, trysts were made, many pints of stout were downed—and Bluesville flourished. Even my political science lecturer grew intrigued, discerning a contemporary vehicle for the dissemination of neoanarchist didactics. "One hears a certain universal cry of the common man's *angst*," he told me over a Guinness. "One hears echoes from the nineteenth-century street barricades, from the clarion call of Bakunin, and—dare I say?—from the ghosts of a thousand Republican Freedom Fighters lost in the mists of the Celtic Twilight!"

You can see that it was an innocent time, but you must remember that President Kennedy was in office. We still believed in the theory of the Great Man, Pop Art was safely in its separate slot from genuine art, and I hadn't the faintest idea what my political science professor was ranting about. Terms whisked by in a whirl of ale and stout and hunting and, of course, rocking and rolling to rhythm and blues. I still yearned to find the source of my solace and inspiration. In the summer of 1963, I did. I took a student charter flight to America. Would Wonderland materialize? The child was still lurking in the student.

While the other students visited traditional tourist attractions—places like the Grand Canyon, Disneyland, and breathtaking San Francisco—I perversely set out alone by Greyhound. I soon discovered that I was in a very foreign country when the mysterious "rest room" or "comfort station" touted by the Greyhound people turned out to be a garden-variety lavatory. I had been expecting a recreation parlor with at least a bar and billiard table and possibly a piano (on which I could show off some British blues). This was my first disappointment (the burgers and malts had really been up to par). My next letdown was the general absence of American ethnic music in the hills, valleys, and swamps of offbeat America. Everyone appeared very clean and pressed and clearly intended to Sta-prest. Frequently, I was given little gifts of personal deodorant spray cans.

Still, for the time being, I plugged on, finding little ragtime or jazz without the accessories of sleeve garters, straw hats, and pizza. (The pizza was scrumptious, though.) I was shattered to find, after trekking up and down the Blue Ridge Mountains of Virginia on the trail of the lonesome pine and finally hearing some bluegrass picking, that the bearded mandolin player was a musicologist studying for a Ph.D. in folklore. He didn't like me much, either.

Where had all the folk gone? Of course, I hadn't realized that real American folk music was now urban. It was in the cities that I should have looked. By chance, I found myself stranded at the Nashville Greyhound station and, in an enterprising moment, decided to waltz into the nearest radio station, WLAC, and announce myself as British. They immediately put me on as a news flash, as few Britishers had been seen around these parts in a coon's age. On the news, I was quizzed intently about the Profumo scandal and in particular about the call girl Christine Keeler. Americans were fascinated to hear that sex could stir the britches of members of the British Establishment. Hitherto, they had visualized Britain as a tight little island of ruins, castles, and MGM cottages. Frequently, I had been greeted by Americans with the cry of "What ho! Tea and crumpets, ho ho ho!"

WLAC was a country station which also played quite a bit of rockabilly. It was here I sat in on a down-home cracker-barrel show hosted by an avuncular character who began his six-hour shift by ringing a cowbell and who introduced me to a remarkable country record by Dave Dudley. "Six Days on the Road" was the most masculine song I'd ever heard, a trucker/cowboy telling us in a rich and lusty voice about his "rig" with its ten-four gears and Georgia overdrive and about how he could have had lots of girls but he wasn't like some other fellows, while the backing lolloped and chugged, whooshing every now and then like air brakes. The covered wagon had become the truck and these machismo drivers were the new (and bulky) knights of the road.

With this Tarmac vision in mind, I was taken by the WLAC people (I'd quickly been adopted by the station owner's son) to the famous Grand Ole Opry and it was there that I found busloads of the urban folk clapping on cue to spangled cowboys who sang of sex, sin, and salvation in suburban settings. Then, later that night, as a special treat I was taken to my first recording session. It was at the RCA studio, as big as an aircraft hangar, and I marveled at the lines of backup singers, violin players from the local symphony, and the rhythm players specially imported from Hollywood. The drummer had just flown in from a movie session with Elvis himself. The arranger was from New York and he was awesome, even though he was dressed in a Hawaiian shirt. It had something to do with the way he shifted his cigar. The artist was a performer named Jerry Wallace and he sat at the back on a stool downing endless soft drinks. The production was everything and, without so much as a bead of sweat showing, these professionals got the song in three takes. Then they knocked off a B side.

This was "country" music in 1963.

I wanted to meet Roy Orbison, but I was told he was in Germany seeking out more acquisitions for his collection of World War II Ger-

man mementoes. But I did see his house as part of the Music City bus
tour. We also saw the site where Hank Williams was found dead in
the back of his car and, as a finale, we were welcomed by Webb Pierce
to his guitar-shaped pool and were invited to buy samples of the water
and copies of his latest album.

By this time, I was feeling homesick, so I took time out to see
Lawrence of Arabia. The epic made me burst with British pride (after
all, we had united the Arabs, a "silly and barbaric race," to quote Peter
O'Toole in the picture) and, during the intermission, I made a point of
talking very loudly in my best clipped accent to no one in particular. I
wanted to be noticed as a representative of good manners and breeding.
I felt like Lawrence himself—an eccentric Englishman in a desolate
place. Anything to avoid being a tourist.

Continuing my travels, I set off for the Promised Land, the Eldorado
of California. On the way, I thought I'd better stop off at the blessed
Grand Canyon, just so I could say I'd seen the thing. I wasn't that
impressed. True, it was certainly a long drop. But my view down was
constantly being blocked by herds of Americans on mules. I'd never
seen so many fat bottoms and bulging thighs in my life. The women
had a penchant for hair rollers, while their menfolk were crew-cut to a
man. And even though they'd just risen from the bowels of the canyon,
their shoes winked with shine.

At last, grimy and flushed, I arrived in Eldorado, which was the
downtown Los Angeles bus station. It looked rather like the seedier
parts of New York City. But my sense of anticlimax was alleviated by a
wash of music I heard coming from a nearby record shop: to the
chugalug boogie beat of a Chuck Berry tune ("Sweet Little Sixteen"),
came a fantasy that all Americans, even those Kansas-bound, should
have their very own ocean, so that soon the whole republic would be
"Surfin' U.S.A." I liked the word "ocean." I'd been brought up on
"sea," because that's all we'd known in England; a day by the sea
where you paddled and built sand castles and huddled in bathing huts
when it rained (or escaped into the comforting darkness of the cinema). The seaside was where I'd had my first intimation of a career in
show business. But the *ocean!* That was quite another matter, akin to
the universe or outer space. The ocean suggested limitless opportunities
and therefore was daunting. The word sounded grand *and* pretentious.
(Although there was a hint that it might turn out to be like a "comfort
station"—in other words, just another sea.)

As I was standing on this hot downtown street, another song filled
the air. "Surf City" was the center of "Surfin' U.S.A." You rode a '34
wagon (called a "woodie") to get there. You wore a wetsuit, not a dinner jacket, to join a community where there was a promise of two birds

for every chap. To land one of these sea nymphs, all you did was wink and the beauties were easy to find because they were either surfing or partying. No time wasted studying Marx, Bakunin, and political science. This was indeed the millennium that the nineteenth-century prophets had predicted! As for the lads, they'd probably let you have as many sea nymphs as you could handle because they had their work cut out waxing down their boards, checking out the surf, and flexing their muscles at undesirable gremmies and ho-dads.

My mind was bursting with visions evoked by record after record that poured from this store. I thought it curious that this wild world summoned up by the records and accompanied by an exciting eight-to-the-bar boogie beat was sung poker-voiced and slightly pampered. The singers were certainly well versed in harmony and intonation—far superior to most teen rock singers—but their expressionless nasality and emotional carelessness suggested that they felt smug to be in the center of the universe. One almost felt honored to be allowed to share this surfing world. After all, they were doing us a favor to tell us so explicitly about this phenomenon and, having sung us so many details, they would flop down on golden sands to take a siesta while pneumatic blondes oiled up their physiques.

Whereas Chuck Berry's song characters had lusted maniacally after cars and girls, even making long-distance telephone calls in hopeless quests for "Sweet Little Sixteens," these surf guys had it made, sitting plum in the middle of Lotusland-by-the-sea. Could this be a part of my Wonderland, U.S.A.? Where exactly was this "Surf City"?

I rang my hosts, an expatriate British family now living on the Palos Verdes Peninsula, hard by the sea, I mean, ocean. Perhaps I would now be able to examine this surfing at close quarters and pick up a few surfer girls too. While waiting for my ride, I strolled into a record store to discover the names of these surf singers who sounded so satisfied and who said their *rrr*s like Peter Sellers or Spike Milligan doing a parody of an American. Don't get me wrong—like most Europeans at that time, I was both attracted and repelled by flagrant Americanism. Envy is another word for it. And a touch of culture shock. But I also told myself I was a social scientist.

Of course, the "Surfin' U.S.A." singers were the Beach Boys and the "Surf City" barkers were Jan and Dean, all of whom were riding high on the charts at the time. Jan and Dean, bleached and blond and well knit, did look like outdoors types, but one or two of the Beach Boys didn't look so athletic. Too many burgers and fries perhaps. They wore woodsman checked shirts and had stripped-down ancient cars in their album pictures. There were many more surf albums in the store, but most of the covers were of huge waves curling with wiry Greek god types riding in on boards. I wasn't too certain of the exact nature of surfing, but the record industry was able to supply a detailed description of this new activity. It seemed as though singers and executives were keen to fill in the world on every aspect of surfing. Very thoughtful, really: "A water sport in which the participant stands on a floating slab of wood resembling an ironing board and attempts to remain perpendicular while being hurtled toward the shore at a rather frightening rate of speed on the crest of a huge wave."

By this time, the record store owner—a beefy fellow swarthy of face and beady of eye—was demanding whether he could do anything for me, so I put my notebook down and bought a banjo, which was a step backward in terms of pop progressiveness, but I had to do something. Thankfully, before I bought anything else, my British host arrived and we set off in his car down to the Palos Verdes Peninsula.

By an extraordinary coincidence, my host and hostess had firsthand knowledge of the Beach Boys. And, after the obligatory game of paddle tennis and tour of the area (which included Marineland; several new luxury housing developments; a couple of beach clubs where you had to wear jacket, tie, and shoes; and the site of the last earthquake), we sat down on their terrace, mai-tais in hand, and a $250,000 ocean view in front of us, while Mr. Barry Haven, my host, told me about their old friends, the Wilsons—parents of the Beach Boys.

"Course, I don't know much about this pop song racket," he started, betraying a lower-middle-class origin in his nasal vowel pronunciation (he was only a passing oil acquaintance of my uncle's), "but when the wife and I first came out here, we did a little business with Murry Wilson, who was in the heavy machinery trade. We were their guests at their Hawthorne house while we looked around for suitable diggings (haven't done too badly have I, since '61?). Well, they kindly arranged to take us to Mexico on a three-day trip—pretty dodgy country and some awful smelly people—and they left several hundred dollars for their three boys—Carl, Dennis, and Brian—to live on. When we got back, they greeted us with some songs they'd written and played on instruments they'd bought with the food money. Guitars, bass, drums, you name it. They gave us a miniconcert and it wasn't bad. The wife and me almost got up and did some twisting to it. She's a pretty good hand-jiver when the spirit moves her, by the way. Anyway, Murry was furious when he first saw what his boys had bought with the food money and he wasn't a man to spare the rod and spoil the child. But his attitude changed pretty fast after he heard the songs. Oh, they had the teen beat and all that, but also some pretty melodies and chords that really made you feel like relaxayvooing. So immediately he went into a huddle with his boys about getting these songs published and recorded. He was quite a nifty songwriter himself, the sort of moon-over-Waikiki variety. I remember going back to see them a few months later—I had to see Murry about some machinery or other—and I arrived to find him administering a real old pep talk to his lads, just like one of those ruddy football coaches they have here. They're quite a Germanic race in some ways, these Yanks. But it gets results. He got them into the studio and onto a record and now, with him managing them, they're so rich that we never see them. C'est la vie and all that."

Next day, I went out and bought a whole bunch of surf records. I really wanted to dive deep into this California cult, a cult which seemed to be spreading to the size of a national phenomenon. I learned about shooting the curl, surfing the wedge (a "shaped peak formed when incoming swell meets outgoing backwash"), hot doggin', and getting wiped out after being stuck in a pipeline. "Wipe Out" and "Pipeline" were instrumental hits and I noticed that lots of the surfing records had no lyrics. Sometimes the downward chromatic guitar runs simulated wave crashes, but at other times the music sounded very similar to the space music of groups like the Spotniks and the Tornadoes and there were honking sax numbers with surf titles that were very similar to the earlier hits of Johnny and the Hurricanes. But "Balboa Blue" by the Marketts was such an enticing title and all the beach names looked wonderful when you saw them on the map, on the West Coast, on the edge of civilization with only the deep-printed blue beyond: La Jolla, Huntington Beach, Santa Monica, Redondo, Zuma. Far more exotic and full of foreign promise than names like Clacton, Weston-Super-Mare, and the Isle of Wight. I was itchy to explore these zones of athletic hedonism, but I was stranded—the Haven boys had commandeered the family autos to drive to school, while poor Barry himself was reduced to busing it to work. But Mrs. H. kept me amused with stories about her difficulties in purchasing Old Country products like Branston Pickle and Jacob's Cream Crackers. "As for a pork pie, that item's quite out of the question!" she insisted, slapping a copy of the Illustrated London News to emphasize her point. "It's a bit of a desert out here, let's face it." "Yes," I replied, "but we British are noted for our ability to cope in desolate places—and we rather enjoy it too." I was thinking of Lawrence of Arabia. "You're a deep one and no mistake," chortled Mrs. H., nodding down at my everpresent notebook in which I was scribbling.

She seemed to rise to the occasion, waxing eloquently about life along the Southern California coast. But she was especially enlightening on the immediate hinterland. Suburbs like Hawthorne, Gardena, Lawndale, Bellflower, Compton all looked samey-samey, she explained —endless boulevards, identical tract homes and supermarkets, lines of tired palm trees—but she had learned to differentiate the neighborhoods by careful study of the palm tree bark. A clever woman—and one who was learning to cope with the impersonality of modern American life.

Her coffee table talk was lively and she had retained the native lilt of her downtown Nottingham accent. A pleasing singsong. The same could not be said of her eldest son, Frankie (after Laine—a name he hated and which may well have spurred him onto a taste for the tougher aspects of surf punkery). Frankie had returned from school to interrupt our conversation with the slow drip of his one-note voice. The note spelled "I want," but with little feeling and no music. At that moment, he wanted "eats," pointing to his mouth and muttering about fast foods. While I was trying to talk surf lore to him (and bum a ride to a nearby beach to see if the real surfers matched the songs), he made several raids on the cathedral-like fridge, leaving his mother's authentically prepared toad-in-the-hole uneaten. Years of snacking had taken their toll on the Haven boys. Like so many of the American youths I had encountered on my travels, these expatriates had developed bulldog jowls and flab grips on their sides. Southern rockabillies and Eastern ghetto doo-woppers sang with hunger pangs, but Southern California was a cornucopia and highly visible fat was not the only result: as I have said, their voices reflected the plenty—bored, plain, uninvolved.

This was California Cool, the art of the laid back, the art of not being fazed by anything, whether it be nuclear disarmament or an impending earthquake, the art of not showing emotion but just existing at the precise moment—for example, the peanut butter sandwich hits the lips and one does not register the fact that it's jolly good. The Sound of Cool from the Land of Pamper had been captured beautifully in the records of the Beach Boys and Jan and Dean—and now I was experiencing the life those records reflected.

I didn't mention this lack of *hooray* enthusiasm, but waited patiently while Mrs. H. operated the dishwasher and her son costumed himself for his beach recreation—"baggies," tennis shoes with no laces, and a Scotch-plaid shirt with the tail sticking out. Everything had to be just so, including the brand of chewing gum. For a fat boy, he was extremely narcissistic.

After what seemed like an age (and I had read *Surf Monthly* from cover to cover, noting the odd sexlessness of the lithe surfers), the Haven boy was ready to be seen by his peers and grudgingly agreed to drop me off at a beach en route. According to Mrs. H., neither of her boys actually surfed, yet I couldn't help noticing that Frankie was carrying a small surfboard under his arm. It was all very complicated and yet, as I was to learn as time went by, all very Californian. The surface is fake and the fake is reality.

At the beach, I did at last encounter specimens of Golden Youth. Admittedly, they were in a special roped-off section called "Muscle Beach Surfer Party," but nevertheless I was seeing in reality what my dreams, *Classics Illustrated,* and the surfing vocal records had suggested. A slight fog obliterated the far blue yonder, thus limiting the quantum-leap possibilities of the vista, but I could certainly make out a circle of sea nymphs in bursting bikinis and Greek god youths in modest shorts sporting and playing in sea, surf, and sand. There was an Aryan splendor to gladden the heart of any neo-Hitlerian—and I was glad to be apolitical.

So transfixed was I by this vision—I couldn't hear their talk; I didn't want to hear their talk—that I was unaware of the lifeguard with the bullhorn. He had been blaring at me for some time apparently and finally he confronted me with a stomach rippling like a washboard: "Please remove your person and rubber raft from the affixed surfing area, sir." I was prepared for his tone, having already come across this kind of regimentation and compartmentalism even in small motel swimming pools in the East. Part of a lingering World War II mentality. I didn't mind; I enjoyed being called "sir" and, with a sigh, I moved along the beach to join the other gremmies.

We must now leave these personal recollections in order to take a more objective look at surf music (and its partner, hot-rod music) for it was, unwittingly, the last truly all-American pop phenomenon and it marks the end of the Age of Innocence in pop music themes. And in this craze were signs of the mayhem to come—when the inmates took over the asylum in the latter sixties. But I must restrain myself. . . .

In the fifties, the pioneering days, surfing had been a specialized sport for adults—and for big bruisers at that. You had to be really strong to manage those giant wooden ironing boards. Oddly enough, though, this surfing fraternity had something in common with the sport-shunning Beats. (We'll be dealing in more detail with their movement in a later chapter.)

Both party-pooped on the Eisenhower family-style regime, refusing to bring home the bacon to the little wife/cook who'd wash the button-down shirt (and mind) in return. Both had no visible, or acceptable, means of support; both used psychedelic drugs to aid them toward a state of oneness with the universe. A wishy-washy mysticism of the Oriental variety kept both surfer and Beat away from real Dale Carnegie style.

But the Beats were inner-city people, lovers of the neon light and the cracked coffee cup, patrons of the greasy spoon, neglecters of physical health. The original surfers were nature boys, scanning the oceanic horizon for signs of the Big Kahoona, that legendary monstrous wave of ineffable beauty. And even if that wave *had* been describable, the old surfers couldn't have done it. Words weren't important to them, as they were to the Beats. The old surfers wandered the beaches, digging the sun and sea, riding only the tastiest azure scrolls, grinning and nodding to each fraternity brother from beef-jerky faces. And as the years rolled by and their skin turned to parchment, they prayed that someday they'd actually meet the Big Kahoona and mount in mystical sexuality that great wave which had been set in motion by the Prime Mover way back when.

However, by 1960, such guff was strictly for the birds. The new breed of surfer kid had no time for these burned-out Ancient Mariners with their panhandling and tall tales. And as for that dribbling and tuneless modern jazz they liked, well, that was no big deal compared with the real stuff spat out like Spanish spitballs by Dick Dale, King of the Surf Guitar. Tough tunes, bitchin' stomp music, a sound wash to fit the mood of a wave.

Fender Stratocaster through Fender Showman amps—ace technology and mucho energy! Spacey ocean music for surfer punkos! How could the little devils carry the big boards? Easy! Technology had been *their* Prime Mover and He'd brought them the Fiberglas surfboard. Lightweight, convenient, no sweat, no nothing.

By 1960, the Cal kids were spilling out everywhere, but especially in the postwar tract home 'n' supermarket bedroom communities along and behind the beaches. They were bouncy and healthy, these products of the war and postwar baby boom, and they saw nothing ticky-tacky about their packing-crate homes nestling near a spaghetti of freeways. They had no memories of orange groves, cow pastures, tumbledown missions where aged dons had once strummed small guitars. They had no time for the past and its vanished glories and outdated moralities. The new white mañana kids took the conveniences of man's inventiveness for granted and used them without misgiving. From Fiberglas to Telecaster guitars to dental floss, the kids reveled in the new conveniences, settling in easily as the beneficiaries of the Southern California success story. Man's triumph over a nothingness of rock and sand. By the sixties, California was a bursting cornucopia, containing all your salad makings, your aerospace technology, your latest automotive trendsetters, your most intricate electronic developments.

Leo Fender, electronic boffin, worked not far from the beaches and had been as steadfast as a surfer in his application to his guitar work. How the kids responded to the thudding deep notes and spacey trip notes and twists and twirls that shot from Leo's Stratocasters and Telecasters! How they cheered and stomped for the neat guys in the instrumental surf bands that pumped out such wondrous music!—not knowing that this square old-timer had played a highly creative part in that super surf sound.

Hundreds of electric-guitar surf bands—like the Challengers, the Rumblers, the Defenders, the Chantays, the Surfaris, the Pyramids—were splashing away in the three great surf craze years from 1961 to 1964, local heroes every one—and some even bona fide surfers. But the Boss Man was Dick Dale and he not only looked like a real surfer with his piratical face and single gold earring, but he was also a helluva surfer. He'd started out picking country songs in local beach clubs and throwing in a few wild instrumentals. He had misgivings about his lack of slick technique as a lead guitarist, so he'd developed a heavy stacatto style, a *daga-daga-daga* on the low strings, plus fast chromatic flurries on the high ones. Leo Fender's reverb units were a real friend here. The reverb echo strung out notes so that they emulated the shape, color, and even texture of the wave. They also sounded pretty neat to the kids in the club who called for more, more, more instrumentals and can the hillbilly stuff! Dale had been born in Beirut and he remembered an old Arabic melody called "Miserlou." One night, he served that eerie thing to the kids and they ate it up. In later years, he liked to talk about that night:

"It was weird, man! Like I changed the tempo on that old folk tune and just started cranking on that mother. Eeriesville! The people started rising up off the floor and they were chanting and stomping. That was the start of the surfer stomp. I knew I'd tapped into some sort of power and that power came to be labeled surf music."

He dusted off some more of these old numbers, like "Hava Nagila" and some Latin-tinged stuff and blues-based riffs for good measure, and soon he and his group, the Deltones, were the rage of the beach, attracting four thousand to his gigs at the Rendezvous Ballroom at Balboa Beach. Of course, a good part of these fans had been drawn from inland communities and weren't surfers at all but just dug the music they'd heard on their local good-guy radio station. San Bernardino, eighty miles inland, was a hotbed of surf nuts eager to wet their imaginations. And the bands were eager to play for them, especially when a San Berdoo jock invited them to play at his local hop. The pay was sometimes just free Cokes, but you never said no to a boss jock—because if you did, *bang* went your airplay.

Radio and records—the bridge to the Big Time. You didn't need big bucks to cut a single and there were a few local labels to help spread the sound. Dick Dale was quick off the mark here. Early on, he'd been signed to a local label and soon his records were hitting the local top tens. In '62, "Miserlou" was number one in L.A. and then there was "Let's Go Tripping" and "Surfer Stomp." At one time, he had the top three records in Southern California and he was the pride and joy of KFWB, "Color Radio" and the surfer's choice. Sure-voiced jocks stayed loyal to the ocean, even as they sweltered in stucco above the asphalt of Hollywood Boulevard.

And around the corner on Vine, in the Capitol Tower,* the executives of this lonesome West Coast major label were also responding to the call of the ocean. They grabbed up Dick Dale and the Deltones and did their damnedest to spread him around the country. No dice, unfortunately. Dot records had jackpotted with the Chantays' "Pipeline" and the Surfaris' "Wipe Out," which were bought straight out from little local labels who couldn't handle the national distribution of a regional breakout monster.

So they blew a few hundred thousand bucks on Dale. They could absorb that because they'd clicked on the surf craze with the Beach Boys, thanks to one of their in-house A&R kids, Nick Venet, as sharp a cat as you'll ever find, part of the new breed of L.A. record-biz whiz kids who were rapidly challenging the New York vets.

But to go really big, the surf sound craze needed some captions to go with the wave pictures. This was accomplished by Brian Wilson and his disciples.

Brian's vehicle was the Beach Boys, mainly a family affair—he and his brothers Carl and Dennis, their cousin Mike Love, and their good friend Al Jardine. (Another kid, David Marks, had subbed for Al for a time, but the kid was too beachy for the organization, not reliable enough.) The Wilsons hailed from Hawthorne, one of those look-alike instant suburbs, about three miles from the beach. It was so instant, in fact, that when the Wilson boys were growing up there weren't even any sidewalks to roll up at eight in the evening.

The Wilsons were a musical family, coached by their excitable father, and their family sing-songs were pretty impressive. Father didn't spare the rod. This rough treatment may have turned Brian into a bit of an introvert, who knows? Maybe he was always that way. Certainly, in high school he seemed a gung-ho regular and even made some sports teams. But he was different in that he liked to spend a lot of time in his room with his one good ear cocked close to the record player. And the music he dug wasn't exactly to the taste of your average nerd: his earliest favorite had been *Rhapsody in Blue;* he also loved the thick, almost gooey harmonies of the Four Freshmen. He'd rush home from

---

* This famous Hollywood landmark was erected in the early fifties, sending aesthetic shocks through EMI Records, whose British organization had recently bought Capitol Records. The circular building was designed to resemble a stack of 78 r.p.m. records. Working inside could be a dizzying experience.

school, lock himself in his room, and practice their high parts. He fired his voice astronomically till it was ready to burst through his hair, but eventually he'd gotten his range up so high he could hit that falsetto with no sweat at all. He was no slouch at keyboards either and when his neighbor Gary Usher, who was also into music, dropped around one day Brian impressed the baggies off him by running through a slew of nifty modern chord progressions.

Brother Carl was more in tune with current R&R and knew how to play all the Chuck Berry guitar licks. Dennis had an excess of energy and therefore gravitated to drums when the brothers formed their first group. He was blond and outgoing and he knew how to handle a board and all the surfing lingo. One day, he came home from school and said that surfing looked like it was going to be the next big craze and that instead of writing songs about Barbie Dolls and rah-rah stuff for school assemblies, they should write about this surf world.

Their father encouraged them and got them into a studio to record. He told them to do this and do that and to tighten up here. He gave them discipline and sometimes the boys got fed up with him. But they were signed by a local independent label, Candix, and their first record, "Surfin'," got on the local chart in 1962. Then Murry stormed Capitol Records, the local big-time company, and parlayed them into taking a Beach Boy record. Nick Venet thought that their "409" song (which Brian had written with Gary Usher) was the hit side. It was real cool the way Mike Love eased out the line about a four-speed dual quad positraction 409. However, it was the surf side, not the hot rod, that became the hit—"Surfin' Safari." Capitol execs saw the act as merely a bunch of silly children and the next release was a version of the playground nursery rhyme "Ten Little Indians." No go. But then Brian put new words to the old Chuck Berry number "Sweet Little Sixteen" and made the surf world one that everybody was welcome to and wished that everybody could do it, even if they were plowing fields in flat old Kansas. Sprinkle some sand on the floor of your room and make believe. Hell, Brian himself avoided the water but liked to have a little sandbox to rest his feet on as he tickled some surf songs out of the piano. "Surfin' U.S.A." went Top Ten while the boys were still in high school. It was all so fast, but Murry was now their manager and he ran a tight ship. He scolded Brian for singing the high part on Jan and Dean's smash hit "Surf City." Even if he had co-written the number, he should remember that Jan and Dean were on a rival label. But they were all buddies in this surf and car thing. There were Jan and Dean and Bruce and Terry and Gary Usher—and they had the scene sewn up. When a new fad came along, they'd be the first to ride it. They sang on each other's records, they wrote together. They under-

stood this world—and they didn't need auto manuals and surfer magazines to enlighten them.

Roger Christian was one of the boys. His main job was exercising his
honey voice as a deejay on KFWB, but after hours he was a deft hand
at car lyrics like "Little Deuce Coupe." One time, he was pulled over
for drag racing down Hollywood Boulevard, but the cop let him off
when Roger explained he was doing research for a hot-rod record.
Maybe the cops understood how important show biz was to the local
economy. Anyway, Brian would meet Roger after he got off his radio
shift at midnight and then they'd huddle over hot fudge sundaes at
C. C. Brown's down near Chinatown and scribble out songs until—hot
dog!—they'd written fifteen or so! Brian didn't care for Capitol's studios
—too big and antiseptic. He wanted the kind of fat and funky echo that
Phil Spector got on his little epics. Brian idolized Phil Spector, but that
teen tycoon was a hard guy to get to know. Murry went along with
Brian's desire to experiment in other studios and he told the Capitol executives to get lost. Who was paying their bills? Who paid for Stan
Kenton?

More and more, Brian was becoming a perfectionist, taking this craze
into the realm of fine music and nifty record production. Music was his
life, even if he was seemingly singing about trivial things like being true
to your school and having fun on the beach. With "Surfer Girl," he
showed he could write a pretty ballad and make it a thudding flowerpot
of a hit. "In My Room" (co-written with Gary Usher) showed the
reclusive Brian in his own private world, but even so a lot of teenagers,
especially acne-sufferers and butterballs, could identify with this song.
Brian was in touch with millions all over the world. They'd be surfing
in London, even if they didn't have an ocean. Besides, he was spreading the good news about the California life-style. This thing went
beyond surfing to include hot rods and woodies and baggies and
Twinkies. Even special South Cal rules of petting.

But the old hands at Capitol couldn't see it that way. Hell, they had
standards to maintain—Johnny Mercer, wordsmith jeweler who'd
crafted such gems as "Jeepers Creepers," was one of the company's
founders. No, this surf 'n' car group was a passing teen fad and they'd
exploit it as much as possible and then dump it the way you dump your
old car. "The Lonely Surfer," "The Rocking Surfer," "Surfer Moon"!
Could you really ask them to take this junk seriously as music? Anyway, there was plenty more Beach Boys-type stuff around; they weren't
unique. Look at Jan and Dean. And in the boondocks there were gag-
gles of these guys who seemed to be able to make the kind of surf noise
the kids liked: the Astronauts from Colorado, the Trashmen from Minnesota, the Rivieras from Michigan and Indiana. The record company

execs knew that those Dick Dale licks came right out of black blues-men like Freddie King. As for this so-called special aural evocation of the ocean, you only had to go back to 1960 and the Ventures' "Walk— Don't Run" to find out where that cool reverb guitar sound came from: up in the great piney woods and lakes of the Pacific Northwest, where there was no goddamn surf!

So Capitol packaged their goodies together on *Surfing's Greatest Hits:* Dick Dale, the Beach Boys, and a bunch of session men ho-dads. Shelly Manne, the great jazz drummer, had a lot of laughs with his contribution, "The Monster Surfer."

Just a job, man. The Marketts were another bunch of L.A. session men capable of evoking the blue yonder at the call of a record pro-ducer. Ray Pohlman played bass with them, but he'd also played bass on a lot of Phil Spector extravaganzas. If required, Ray could strum rhythm guitar, whistle in tune, even bark so well it had Lassie fooled. Of course, it was all "just a job"—but these days pop/rock session play-ing, engineering work, and supervision (now called "production," as in the movies!) required plenty of know-how. The guys were pretty mel-low about their skills and they didn't brag. They could play R&R in their sleep because they were all still callow and they grew up on Presley. Many of them were from the redneck Deep South, where the brimstone black backbeat is part of their white heritage. Take Al Casey —a real casual guy: he played guitar on the Duane Eddy twang hits; and remember that lapel-grabbing hook lick on Sanford Clark's "The Fool"? That was Al. Like so many of the Southern pickers and honkers, he drifted up to L.A., where he was playing the teen pop game and making good bread. There were a slew of little independent local labels scattered around the L.A. sprawl and, as stakes are small and the dice might roll right if you catch a willing deejay, guys like Al Casey could even rope a hit. Al cut a clever novelty called "Surfin' Hootenanny" that climbed to number forty-eight nationally. He combined two trends. He could lay back and strum away with ease because it was all basic blues root music, with a touch of tabasco.

BUT—*attention!* Eyes *right!* When Phil Spector, the diminutive gen-eralissimo of pop, hit town for another epic onslaught on the ears of the world, there'd be no standing at ease. The players had to sit up and strum, pick, blow, bang, rattle, shake the tambourine, click the castanet, ting the triangle—sometimes till the blood flowed. The Spector super-production day would almost certainly turn into a long night because the maestro King of the Cavernous Sound, ruler of the Kingdom of High Kitsch, architect of the Wall of Sound, was a perfectionist in the intricate, tiny art of making hit singles for tinny radios and record players.

"I'm making Little Symphonies for the kids," he liked to tell the press. "I'm bringing a Wagnerian concept to rock 'n' roll." Was R&R ready for this? "From a simple start, my records build and build into a thunderstorm of *Götterdämmerung*, ending with a climax of Force, Meaning, and Purpose!" Hadn't Roy Orbison's records (produced by Fred Foster) been building and building from simple starts (for example, "Dream Baby") for years? And what was this high Purpose? To make art—or money? Never before had such grandiloquence been applied to the little circle of plastic fun which never dared spin its dream over more than three minutes!

But such claims were not unexpected from this weird, wacky figure, whose appearance was quite unlike the usual L.A. record gang. For a start, his hair was too long, making him look like an unemployed page boy. Few knew the color and message of his eyes because he always wore dark glasses—and certainly not because he was under the sun a lot. Spector, like Brian Wilson, was no sun-worshiper. One glancing blow from a surfboard and this itsy-bitsy man would be a goner. Actually, he'd've been spurned by the beach beauties as a trifle on the creepy-crawly side. Nor was he a joiner, one of the guys for locker room talk. Funny, because he made records about he-man antiheroes of the James Dean type, naughty but nice.

So here he was in town again, hot off the jet from New York, ready to tape-sculpt another teen drama at his favorite studio, Gold Star. Old-time A&R men might shake their gray locks and call Gold Star a hole-in-the-wall tacky little substandard shack good only for demos. But it was here that Spector had developed his apocalyptic *sound* in which the individual was submerged by the clang of the universe. At Gold Star, he had found an ideal echo chamber, a low-ceilinged room good for elementary drum-thudding, and a very co-operative engineer. Bring in the army of accommodating session folk, point the magic baton, and welcome to the world of Phil Spector! How could he wear all those clothes, though, in sunny Southern California? Brocaded vest, frilly shirt, velvet suit, pointed shoes, and *spats!* When he walked, he often took one step back for every step forward like some baggy-pants vaudevillian; when he talked, it was likely to be littered with grunts and *aaarghs*; and when theorizing about his art, he could get eggheady. Of course, beneath the wacko exterior was a shy guy. He was a loner like Brian Wilson and Brian had idolized Spector ever since "Uptown." Which all-girl group had sung that one? Was it the Crystals or the Ronettes? Doesn't matter, they were each just another brick in the Spector Wall. Like a Hitchcock movie, a Spector record had the master's handwriting all over it.

The summer of '63 was a golden year for Spector. Everything

seemed to be coming up roses, pushing through the concrete of urban hustle. Here was a kid of twenty-two showing that he could wield corporate power—a tycoon, heading his very own record company, Philles, and marshaling his session army like a Rock Prospero, creating a wonder world of sound and fury (signifying nothing?), and street-surfing millions of kids into the blue yonder, propelled by his very own sonic boom. The pride and envy of the Music Business.

Let the track record for 1963 speak: "Zip-a-Dee-Doo-Dah" (Bob B. Soxx and the Blue Jeans)—number eight on the national charts.

"Da Doo Ron Ron (When He Walked Me Home)" (the Crystals)—number three.

"Then He Kissed Me" (the Crystals)—number six.

"Wait 'Til My Bobby Gets Home" (Darlene Love)—number twenty-six.

"Puddin' 'N' Train" (the Alley Cats)—number forty-three.

"Be My Baby" (the Ronettes)—number two.

Next stop, *number one!*

And just to thank his public for being so kind to him, Phil Spector was now spending much time and energy, regardless of cost, recording a Yuletide album featuring all of the singers from the Philles label and entitled *A Christmas Gift for You.* Quite a present from a fellow born to the Jewish faith! Shows his determination to be accepted into the Great American Family. Mind you, he made his employees work their fannies off on this gift. Every track was treated as if it were a single. No fillers, the kind of junk that most A&R men stuck on an album along with the one hit single. This time he had a *concept,* something new in this game. After six grueling weeks slaving over a hot console, Larry Levine, the engineer, spoke for everyone concerned when he said, "I never wanted to work with Phil again. My nerves were shattered and everyone was exhausted."

At the end, Spector himself delivered a Christmas message to his subjects. In the dark studio, surrounded by the metallic heat of L.A., over a backing track of the orchestra and choir doing "Silent Night," he chirped with a delightfully childish lisp:

"Hello, this is Phil Spector. It is so difficult at this time to say words that would express my feelings about the album to which you have just listened—an album that has been in the planning for many, many months. First, let me thank all the people who have worked so hard with me in the production of this album, and in my endeavor and desire to bring something new and different to the music of Christmas, and to the record industry which is so much a part of my life."

Behind the soft words and the shades was an aged child who had single-mindedly fought his way up the charts. He loved the record business, which had finally allowed him to carve his own monuments in plastic. Like Mae West, Noel Coward, and Elvis Presley, he was his own contribution to twentieth-century culture. Nothing, it would seem, had come before him. That was the self-created myth.

Behind the myth were several years of apprenticeship to other masters of pop. These masters—Leiber and Stoller, Lee Hazelwood—had been encouraged in turn by patron Lester Sill, an ex-promotion man who had given them the push to start experimenting with colors and brushwork that were later to become essential to a Spector aural painting. Perhaps all that these masters lacked was the Spector vision—or, shall we say, *chutzpah?*

The record producer as *superstar* was something new. But since the early 1920s, there had been record producers. Uncle Art Satherly (Columbia) and Ralph Peer (Victor) had journeyed "into the field" to dig up obscure hillbilly singers, to set them on wax, and disseminate that wax into worldwide acceptance. (The resulting stars weren't very grateful; they would have been discovered sometime, they reckoned.) In the 1930s, John Hammond, a jazz buff of independent means, had organized sessions with Bessie Smith and Benny Goodman; in the early 1960s, he was to A&R the first Bob Dylan sessions.

But these producers were supervisors rather than creators. They weren't interested in writing their signature all over the finished product. They simply got the machines switched on and let the artist perform. Capturing a live performance. Trapper producers.

The first person to actually *interfere* with the music was Mitch Miller of Columbia Records. He was the first truly active A&R man. His cheerful arrangements surrounded such crooners as Frankie Laine, Guy Mitchell, and Rosemary Clooney with ear-catching effects—whip cracks, french horns, harpsichords. Often the songs were sappy or trifling, but the Miller sauce made a piquant platter and very often sold in the millions. Trouble was, Miller developed an antipathy toward rock 'n' roll. He didn't mind dressing up a rude hillbilly number in satin and lace, but he drew the line at presenting the new raunchy sound in its own blue jeans and heavy grease.

The first flush of rock 'n' rollers were left wild and unchecked. The wild men—Elvis, Jerry Lee Lewis, Gene Vincent, and Little Richard, notably—were left to the trapper producers. Switch on the recorder and let 'em rock. The record industry was amazed and much of it was aghast. Where were the songs, where the arrangements and production values, let alone taste? But a whole lotta shakin' to the tune of an evangelical roar and scream and pant could be effective for only so long: continued success needed strong songs. The song was the key. Always and forever. So from *a-wop-bop-a-lu-bop* there was a search for new material for the rockers to tackle—and their advisers turned to oldies-but-sturdies. In the forties, there had been a practice of jazzing the classics; in the fifties, it was to be rocking the oldies. Pat Boone revived "Love Letters in the Sand"; Fats Domino revived a load of old songs, including "Blueberry Hill" and "My Blue Heaven"; Elvis Presley went back as far as the Civil War for "Love Me Tender" and later searched the 1920s for "Are You Lonesome Tonight?" Connie Francis found the twenties and thirties a particularly rewarding era: "Who's Sorry Now?", "Happy Days and Lonely Nights," and "Together" were just a few of the standards revived in the fifties and early sixties. In all these cases, the songs were left unharmed; a light rock beat and vocal interpretation were all that was added.

But in 1957, when Billy Ward and the Dominoes produced their version of "Stardust," the result was something else. They had hit upon an exciting combination: black gospel voices complete with all the usual twists and turns; a heavy, pounding, Germanic drumbeat; and a lush symphonic background in which the strings, in particular, lifted the general earthiness of the rest made the whole effort take off and fly. Of course, the lyrics became a little lost in the grand process, but they'd never meant very much in the first place.

Phil Spector must have loved this epic.

But there were only so many standards suitable for rocking and pretty soon the search for fresh material was on again. Into the breach stepped a new breed of songwriter, youngsters who understood rock 'n' roll and yet also were grounded in the formalism of the written melody and the written word—the European tradition. They were to give this gutsy sound of the city a suitable frame. A gaudy one, maybe—but certainly more exciting than the Middle America singalong jingle of Mitch Miller. The new songwriters and producers grew up alongside other developers of teen music: disc jockeys, teen TV show entrepreneurs, record distributors, teen magazine publishers, shoestring record company owners who produced in their garages and distributed out of the trunks of their cars. Wildcats operating way outside of the major labels.

The West Coast was the last frontier and it was wide open for spunky independents with a few bucks and some chart visions. Two young songwriters, Jerry Leiber and Mike Stoller, got involved with one such little local label and, in 1953, they hit with their R&B production of "Hound Dog." The song, bluesy and full of funny imagery, was theirs and the singer, Big Mama Thornton, a feisty mountain of a woman, was just right. She left the lyrics intact and intelligible. Then Elvis discovered "Hound Dog," switched it around, and spread it around the world—in the process smothering the whole point but mak-

ing another point, the Presley one, with full use of the quivering phal-
lus at the heart of his voice. Soon Leiber and Stoller were writing special material for Presley—blues-rocker songs that showed a white
understanding of ghetto music coupled with a working knowledge of
old Tin Pan Alley verities.

But trailing in the shadow of a giant star wasn't satisfying from an
artistic viewpoint. Leiber and Stoller needed a vehicle to show off their
witty work—and they found it in the Coasters, a black vocal harmony
group, one of thousands in search of the right material. They were easily manageable and it was easy to replace lost members. One black face
was very much like another (as far as the public was concerned). The
Mills Brothers, Ink Spots, Platters—standouts in the long line of black
vocal groups. But lately there'd been a host of groups with similar-
sounding names and sound-alike voicings. Great fun but indistinguisha-
ble from one another. As one jaded old Alleyman said, "Once you got
your song, you're there. If you want a group, just go down to Harlem
and whistle!"

Using the Coasters as their putty, Leiber and Stoller produced a
series of classic comedy records, including "Yakety Yak," "Charlie
Brown," "Poison Ivy," and "Little Egypt." Lyrically and musically,
they raised the Coasters records above the general run of R&B vocal
group efforts. They didn't leave them in a slough of *sh-boom, dum-
dum-dum-be-oo-bee,* and *sha-na-na.* They chose other chord sequences
to go alongside the time-honored but wacked-out "Blue Moon" se-
quence (C/A minor/F/G seventh) so beloved of black groups.

And Phil Spector listened to and loved the Leiber and Stoller productions.

However, young Spector had a soft spot for the seemingly repetitive
vocal groups (later to be dubbed "doo-wop"). He knew black from
white—and there were plenty of white groups who reached a moment's
wax only after singing for years on Philadelphia street corners. Spector
loved the rigid rules of doo-wop; he even liked the wobbly harmonies
and downright mistakes. It meant honesty. He was proud to be able to
tell one bird-named group from another. And it depressed him to realize
that it would be ultra-hard to make a record as good as "Little Star" by
the Elegants. Who the hell were the Elegants? Five Americans with
Mafia-sounding names who got their name off a whiskey bottle and had
their fling in 1958. But Spector revered and remembered, even while
he was digging Wagner.

The more accomplished black groups—with their soaring vibratos and
curlicues and sudden breaking of the sound barrier as they shot into
falsetto—made you think you were at a hot gospel meeting and getting
ready to testify. Many of these better vocal groups had originally been

gospel groups or had sung in school choirs. For example, the Chantels had been in their Bronx school's choir and so had some of the girls in the Shirelles and the Chiffons. The latter two groups were inspired by the success of the Chantels and they too brought that rich and righteous gospel feel to their records: the Shirelles with "Will You Love Me Tomorrow?", a song shot through with Protestant-hymn harmonies and suspensions and with a lyric brimming with moral worries and postcoital guilt; the Chiffons with "He's So Fine," a secularized gospel roundsong (which was later resanctified by George Harrison into "My Sweet Lord").

So there was no lack of groups and singers. Leiber and Stoller could take their pick. They went to New York and, perhaps inspired by the Billy Ward "Stardust" sound, they added violins behind the black-voiced Drifters. And they started adding refinements to the basic drumbeat of R&R. They grew very fond of a lilting stop-start rhythm that had previously been characteristic of Latin-American music, a *boom-pause-bah-boom* repeated figure that was called the *Baion*. Hitherto, it had been confined, in North America, to certain New Orleans blues artists like Professor Longhair and, when this rhythm had previously surfaced in mainstream pop, it had been as an exotic novelty like the samba or the rhumba as played by Xavier Cugat or Perez Prado. A *novelty*—but in the hands of Leiber and Stoller's Drifters recordings, the *Baion* beat was to become, like syncopation itself, a basic pulse of R&R. New York studio instrument rental companies got used to assembling a special bag of exotic percussion instruments for Leiber and Stoller sessions. Many kinds of guïros and cabaças and different timbres of African and Caribbean drums were delivered, together with finger cymbals and triangles. The triangle was also to become an important item on Drifters sessions. A little tinkle to add delicacy to the hearty beat.

Phil Spector loved that hesitating *Baion* beat, a slow and sinuous rock 'n' roll tango.

Leiber and Stoller were not alone as songwriter-producers in this new teen form. They were simply the best. There were others, like George Goldner and Bumps Blackwell, but too many times their considerations were ones of commerce or ethnicity. Leiber and Stoller recognized the wit and the fun of teen life and didn't take it all too seriously (except regarding copyrights and royalties). And there were other songwriters, too: in and around New York's Brill Building, H.Q. of Tin Pan Alley, contemporary song factories were being established. In the tiny cubicles where once Alleymen had sweated and pounded piano keys and dreamed up new scenes from nature to describe lovemaking were now installed youngsters hip to the new beat. The newcomers didn't alto-

gether throw out the old harmonies and tunes and rhyming couplets—
but they utilized the new teen topics and they articulated the grunts
and groans and joy gibberish of this newly secularized gospel and blues
music.

Flagship of the new Alley pop was Aldon Music, started by Al
Nevins and Don Kirshner, and they ran a tight crew: trimmed,
squared, and institutionalized. Their team of Howard Greenfield and
Neil Sedaka scored first with special material for Connie Francis, siren-
voiced Queen of the Oldies. "Stupid Cupid" was perfect. There were
other notable teams: Barry Mann and Cynthia Weil, who were to become specialists in songs with a sociological touch; Gerry Goffin and
Carole King, who gave the Shirelles their hymnal "Will You Love Me
Tomorrow?"; Ellie Greenwich and Jeff Barry, who were experts at nursery-rhyme rock jingles. Soon Neil Diamond was to join the factory.
The hits came rolling in. The formula was working. Aldon Music had
successfully filled the gap between the old moon-in-June Alley pop and
the new teen demands. Aldon had proved that R&R wasn't simply an
anarchic mess produced by the switchblade set, as Congress and the
old-line music establishment claimed, but a well-organized business.
And isn't that what America was all about? Why, Aldon was doing so
well that they'd opened up an office on the West Coast, run by a real
sharp businessman named Lou Adler.

So all the elements of the new pop/rock industry were there. All that
was needed to make this business higher than humdrum was an eccentric, a maverick, may we say *genius*? Phil Spector forged his way in and
started spinning his web of teen dreams. . . . Like a flying shlemiel, he
was to give this whole seedy little world a grandiose sweep.

Spector had grown up in the Fairfax district, an unfashionable part
of L.A., where many poor Jews lived. In junior high, he was no sports
hero; not for him the sharing of jokes in the locker room. He was a Big
Man only in his mind. Surrounded by bronzed Alexanders and Dianas,
young Philip directed his thoughts to the record biz. And while still at
high school, he put together a vocal group called the Teddy Bears and
damned if he didn't land himself a number-one national hit with their
very first record, released on a putzy little local label called Dore. Of
course, he didn't reap much money from his hit, but that was par for
the course for kid groups in those days. Still, it was an education. The
song was one he wrote himself, "To Know Him Is to Love Him." The
title was the epitaph on his father's grave! A bit cheeky to throw private
family sentiments into the public eye, but nothing is sacred in the artistic struggle.

The record was sweet and innocent and lulling, like those by the

Fleetwoods. The bridge had some nifty hymnlike changes and there was a good hook in the repeated lyric lines.

Dore, being a hole-in-the-wall operation, couldn't keep up the steam on the Teddy Bears and the group was destined to be a one-hit wonder. But Spector had made a dent in the business and the buzz was out about him. After all, L.A. didn't produce that many smashes back then. It was shacksville compared with snazzy New York where the real pros were. Spector made himself visible and soon came to the notice of one Lester Sill, a promotion-man-cum-record-entrepreneur. Sill seems to have had a keen ear for future moneyspinners and was prepared to gamble dollar advances. Already he'd helped put Leiber and Stoller on the map and currently he was working with producer Lee Hazelwood.

Out in the unlikely desert city of Phoenix, Arizona, Hazelwood had been bringing in a batch of hits featuring the twangy guitar of Duane Eddy. Record people wondered how Hazelwood got that heavy *clank twang* with its boondock echo. Phoenix? You gotta be kidding! How cheap can you get? Lester Sill decided to serve as patron to the irrepressible Spector, who was begging, pleading to learn the biz. So he sent Spector out in the field, to Phoenix, to apprentice with Hazelwood and the Eddy sound. He gophered for coffee and so on and grabbed every chance to watch how the sound was created. He eagle-eyed Hazelwood fixing the right speed for tape echo reverb. What was the speed, what was the size? He marveled at the makeshift echo chamber they'd erected out in back of ramshackle Ramco Recorders: a huge grain storage tank through which Duane Eddy's twangy guitar reeled and rocked —and sometimes bothered by errant birds, delinquent kids, and thundering desert rain. He peered and inspected and pestered. The coffee got neglected. Spector was in the way.

Sill got the message and sent his protégé off to New York to study under Leiber and Stoller, the old masters. In L.A., he stayed at Lester Sill's apartment; in New York, he slept on a couch in the Leiber and Stoller office. People were very nice, very accommodating. Now he was allowed to do more than gopher—he strummed some rhythm guitar on one or two Leiber and Stoller productions; he was put in with some Alley pop writers to see what would happen—and nothing much did. But then one day, when Mike Stoller was out of town, he and Jerry Leiber went in and cut some numbers with Ben E. King, among them a number that Spector had written with Leiber. "Spanish Harlem" was full of precise "romance in the concrete" lyrics and Spector's folk Latin melody had a simple splendor and catchy syncopations (reminiscent of Irving Berlin in his ragtime phase). And the *Baion* beat was there in stark glory. The record smashed up the charts. Sometimes Spector liked to claim he'd produced it. Time to split.

Spector was always more of a romantic melodist than Leiber and Stoller. This was apparent in "Spanish Harlem," with its pretty thirds moving satisfyingly with just a touch of folk flavor. Now he was to get his chance to produce independently and experiment with the swirl of sounds rushing around his feverish brain. Singer Ray Peterson's people allowed him to try a version of the old folk song "Corrina Corrina." The result was a long way from blues shouter Big Joe Turner's lusty version. Spector paralleled a classical soprano with Peterson on the first line of every chorus. It was different and catchy and it went high in the charts. He punctuated Gene Pitney, another established singer, with chicken-nervy strings and, at the end, as the record faded, he set the strings on a dizzying spiral so that you sat up with a start and asked, "What was that?" then wanted to hear the whole thing through again. Little touches like that were to become typical of Spector productions.

Spector was then handed a pretty-boy Fabian type called Curtis Lee and with him he was able to indulge his love of East Coast doo-wop on "Pretty Little Angel Eyes." Again using Lee, he experimented with deep, thudding bass drums and became an expressionist on "Under the Moon of Love." Listening to "Under the Moon of Love" was like opening the "Green Door" and experiencing at full blast all the smell, sweat, and good times at a fantastic party, as if a single mike had trapped moments of pure pleasure. From "Under the Moon of Love," it was also clear that Spector had been influenced by the thudding party sound of Gary "U.S." Bonds records (produced in Norfolk, Virginia, by Frank Guida). Geniuses don't exist in vacuums and even Spector was no exception.

By this time, he was hopping from coast to coast, still under the kindly wing of Lester Sill. The boy was shaping up, even if he did sport strange clothes (like ascots and spats), wear his hair much too long, and utter odd *aaarghs* every so often. In L.A., Spector had found the studio of his dreams in Gold Star. Now, not many ace A&R men would have thought of using Gold Star for top-flight A sides. On the tacky side, it resembled a motel for quick tricking. But some funky R&R sides had emerged from the studio in recent years, notably Eddie Cochran stuff like "Summertime Blues," but generally you didn't use craft at Gold Star; you just got the machine switched on and hoped your act was in good form. However, what Spector coveted was the extraordinary echo chamber—deep as a dungeon or spacey as infinity. With such a chamber, he could navigate the world, conjuring up heaven and hell like Dr. Faustus.

His early Gold Star productions weren't exactly earth-shattering. Some of them had a lot of heavy breathing, like the Teddy Bears.

Close-miked and cute. He took the Paris Sisters, as cherry pie a white girlie group as you could imagine, and a Barry Mann song called "I Love How You Love Me" and added some very spare but tasty strings: the result was irresistibly sexy, if you're into telephone breathers. The record went to number five and Sill felt rewarded, even if his sleep had been often interrupted during the production, when Spector would summon him at unearthly hours to listen to his latest mix-down of the record. And Sill, in his pajamas, would stagger from his bedroom to his protégé's room to listen and nod and mumble some encouragement in true West Coast style. Spector was to remix those goddamn strings over thirty times.

But Sill went on letting his boy learn his craft, regardless of cost. Unlike most A&R men of that time (who cut corners, always trying to get the sessions finished as fast and as cheaply as possible), Spector spent as many hours as were necessary to satisfy his artistic sensibility. This was something radically new in the pop field: not just a guy doing a job, peddling popcorn music to silly little kids, but an *artist!* A man who was taking the music seriously! Was this a portent of things to come? No one said so, probably no one thought so. As long as the weirdo went on bringing in hits, who cared that his life-style and work methods were off-the-wall? And Lester Sill kept signing the checks.

In 1961, Sill and Spector cemented their partnership in a record label: Philles. Phil and Les. Spector's job was to concentrate on product, I mean, music. Not for him the scatter-gun technique of the major labels—fire out the buckshot and hope some will hit the chart. Every Philles release was carefully crafted and only one was released per month. The love and labor were all directed to the A side. The B side was usually a nondescript jam by the studio musicians and unlikely to get any airplay by the deejays. So three things were achieved: the deejays were forced to listen to just one side; the session men were able to blow out some of their jazz frustrations after hours of being told exactly what to play by General Spector, the Erich Von Stroheim of Pop; and the master would sign his name to the B-side copyright form, thus reaping as much money as the writer of the A side.

Spector was still making records in New York but, increasingly, he was jetting in to Gold Star. For here, in the funky shack in the rather seedy business area of Santa Monica Boulevard, he had an amenable workshop with workers who would carry out his plans without complaint. Malleable, obedient, laid back. Important qualities if you were working for Spector. Too many of the New York session musicians were unco-operative, muttering about playing crappy kid's stuff, feeling they'd sold out their jazz talents to the demands of the pimple market. But in L.A., there were, as we have seen, younger players who had actually grown up in R&R, who thus understood the feel, and who, fed by balmy sun and ocean breezes, were quite content to play anything so long as they got paid.

Among this accommodating band were some future rock "heavies": Leon Russell, Larry Knechtel, Glen Campbell, Sonny Bono. On the drum battery—and superimportant to the Spector Wall of Sound—was Hal Blaine (later replaced by Earl Palmer). Blaine played superb *crash-bang-wallop* drums in the fine tradition of Barnum and Bailey circus drumming. He was a show in himself, thrashing around the drum kit with true American extroversion, calling to mind not only the "Yankee Doodle Dandy" days but also Gene Krupa and the flashy, exhibitionist show drummers of Las Vegas. He was assisted by a kitchen crew of thumpers and rattlers and pingers, including Nino Tempo (who'd hit with April Stevens on "Deep Purple") and Sonny Bono, as well as other pals of Spector's who happened to be passing through.

On the more cerebral and "legitimate" side, Spector used a good string and horn arranger named Jack Nitzsche, who was soon sporting dark glasses by day and night, like his master. At the Gold Star console knobs was Larry Levine, a young engineer who appeared to be able to summon up just the right mix and echo to satisfy Spector. It was not an easy job interpreting the wishes of the wonder kid. But there was something inspiring about the little fellow when he got all worked up.

As for artists, it was simply the old "whistle down in Harlem" technique. There were plenty of black all-girl vocal groups around. As for songs, there were the hit factories in and around the Brill Building. Spector had finished his apprenticeship and was ready to amaze the *goyim!* In no time at all, he had bought out Lester Sill and had Philles all to himself. The hits were about to roll in and he was soon to be the Tycoon of Teen.

Let us look at the records from this golden period of Spectorsound (1961–63). "Uptown" by the Crystals was the first big hit for Philles. Hitherto, the cute-kid black girls had been used for demo discs, but Spector thought their cuddly, tight piping could be commercial. On the intro was some shivering flamenco-style guitar and then in came the girls with their semisociological story (by Barry Mann and Cynthia Weil of Aldon Music) about a little guy, a nobody, who works downtown in an angry jungle. By day just a face in the crowd, but when he comes home to his low-rent tenement uptown, she treats him like a king and he's everything to her! Supporting, almost smothering, the Crystals on all sides were castanets a-clicking, violins a-plucking, and an array of percussion; underneath was a solid foundation of nifty harmonies and cunning slides from minor to major. It was brainy and commercial. It zoomed into the Top Twenty. Brian Wilson, not yet famous, bought the record and went back to his Hawthorne room to quietly dissect this rich plum cake. "Uptown" was a very influential piece of plastic.

The follow-up was too clever by half. "He Hit Me (And It Felt Like a Kiss)" was a Goffin and King composition whose title grabbed like a headline in the *National Enquirer*. But when you got beyond that shock, the record turned out to be a new angle on the old love story and it had a queer, edgy melody, like something from a Berlin cabaret. Though *Billboard* hailed it as a "serious ballad with a telling message" and *Cash Box* called it a "fabulous beat-ballad romancer," the record met with a barrage of radio resistance. Program directors got the jitters when they realized that masochism was in the story. Freudian stuff on the air? Violence in Kiddieland? No way! Philles was forced to withdraw #105. The maestro licked his wounds and chalked up another one to experience. What Philistines! Still, you gotta play by the rules if you're gonna stay in the game.

Philles #106 was again by the Crystals, sounding as sexy and cuddly as ever. You could almost see their bubble buns swaying. "He's a Rebel," written by Gene Pitney, was full of perfect pop imagery. Soft outlawry—surefire sales and radio acceptance. "He's a Rebel," stated the girls, because society doesn't understand a greasy guy in leathers on a bike. But society ought to see him at home. He's a real pussycat on the hearth—and so kind.

Near the fade, there was a terribly addictive riff: the girls shot out "He's a Rebel" over and over and very fast. "He's a Rebel" rolled off their tongues and bounced merrily into the sunset of the fade.

The make-believe group idea was pursued further. Two of the Blossoms, plus a fellow called Bobby Sheen, were paid to come in to Gold Star and sing over an extraordinary backing track. Rumbling and clanking like an old ironclad wreck lying at the bottom of the Atlantic and being rocked slowly by a rhythmic earthquake, the track was unidentifiable as a song—until the sessions singers were laid on top. Then suddenly it became the dear old tune from *Song of the South*, a Walt Disney film of the forties: "Zip-a-Dee-Doo-Dah." An amazing transformation! The record went out as sung by Bob B. Soxx and the Blue Jeans. Spector spoke about them publicly as if they really existed. And they did exist in his child's garden of characters. The record sleeve showed a rustic lane in nursery colors winding away deep into cartoon country.

"Zip-a-Dee-Doo-Dah" went Top Ten.

Then, in 1963, came Spector's Big Three Smashes. The Wall of Sound perfected at last! The team and captain in perfect mesh, in tune with the radio and kiddies. A triumph of matter over mind. First came

"Da Doo Ron Ron," written by Spector, together with the Brill Building's Jeff Barry and Ellie Greenwich. How could any sane person *write* "Da Doo Ron Ron"? Wonderful nonsense, it had all the repetitive charm of a nursery rhyme or a child's street-game song. The rhythm fairly marched along at a brisk goose step, propelled by Hal Blaine and his drum kit. At regular points, he'd fire off a couple of cannons that sent their balls thumping into your gut, telling you to pay attention. A terrace of grand pianos banged out a mesh of chimes in strict tempo of very straight eighths and the real Crystals uttered their love syllables on top of the ever-rolling military band.

"Then He Kissed Me," their next release and another Top Ten'er, started with a good guitar hook line, followed up with castanets, then opened into a grand vista of symphonic strings and horns all playing long lines of harmony that moved like the seasons. Again Sergeant-Gunner Hal Blaine caught us with a regular *whoomph* in the stomach.

But the masterpiece arrived in August with the debut record of the Ronettes. Their voices, deeper and more experienced, were alleys away from the teasing Crystals. You felt that these Ronettes could really follow through on their promise. Lead singer Ronnie Ronette had a quivering serpent of a voice and, when she begged the world to "Be My Baby," the world had to obey.

Boom . . . bah-boom! Tish! The record began with the familiar tattoo of the old *Baion,* except that now it was to the strict precision of the Spector march. No lazy afternoon in Latin lands with a jug of wine and a friendly rhythm. After the rousing tattoo, in marched the massed basses and grand pianos and squads of guitars, all repeating their assigned notes squarely on the beat. Snare drum explosions from Blaine broke up the rigidity and later on the show drummer was allowed to let rip around his drum kit. "Be My Baby" was no nursery song, but was positively churchy, especially in its chord changes. The record evoked the feeling of a great cathedral (albeit with an army tramping around inside). Never had the Gold Star echo chamber sounded so good. Never had Spector's engineer, arranger, and players done so well and so precisely. Never had there seemed to be so huge a choir on a pop record. All of Spector's pals and colleagues and hangers-on appeared to be chiming in. Cher was there, it is alleged. Perhaps Kilroy was there, too. Passersby in the street heard the joyful chorus giving praise and wondered what new religion had just been invented.

"Be My Baby" was the climax of Spector's romance with Gold Star. It was possibly the climax of his career. He had finally built more than a Wall of Sound—he had built a pop cathedral. Quickly, the record shot to number one. Everybody had to buy it. Brian Wilson said it was the best record he'd ever heard.

Phil Spector was now Master of the Pop Record Game. He had discovered a formula and nothing was impossible. The keys to the kingdom were his. His arranger was fond of telling interested parties exactly what that formula consisted of. And it sounded most scientific.

The girl sitting next to me on the Greyhound bus was cute—if you went for even features that might have been bought in a mail-order kit. She had a lot of accessories, though: hair piled up in a beehive shape, eyes heavily painted with mascara, sexy halter, and tartan Bermuda shorts. Every so often, her dimpled knee would nudge my leg and I'd say, "Sorry!", but she didn't hear me. I could note all these details because she was totally absorbed in her portable radio. She was humming, swaying, and kicking my knee to "Be My Baby." And I had to admit I was getting a kick out of the record, too. It went so well with the chromey radio, with her hair, eyes, halter, and shorts. It was very manufactured, of course, but it was a glorious example of the Great American Confidence Game.

Pretty soon, it had ended and some commercials came blending in—beautifully. The record dovetailed so smoothly into the general radio sound. But the next records weren't of the same quality and I turned my attention to the terrain that was whizzing by me as we rolled up the marvelous coast road en route to the Great Northwest. My destination was the great city of Seattle, where I had a cousin, Anna, waiting for me. She was a student at Seattle University and had promised to get me a real university sweatshirt and, possibly, a letterman jacket. I had seen these in films and found them most attractive.

Once you've seen one spectacular, breathtaking view of the ocean (as opposed to the sea), you've seen them all. So after a while, the scenery became much of a muchness and I wanted to save my breath. Anyway, there were too many billboards obscuring the view and most of these billboards were telling me to do this or that. I hadn't yet learned to appreciate the Pop Art of advertisement reading. I was still too cultured, too English.

My conscience told me I should read something more substantial and educational. So I pulled out one of my college texts, a thick book on British constitutional history. In the autumn, we were to sit for our Trinity College finals (part one). But after only a few minutes of "Leges Henrici" and the place of "sake and soke" in the medieval system, my mind began to wander back to the recent days I had spent down at Palos Verdes and the beach communities as a guest of the Barry Havens. The expatriate British family had been most solicitous and the Haven boy had introduced me to the Southern California surf culture, for which I would be everlastingly grateful.

Sometimes my researches had led me down dangerous paths. One afternoon, we had been tearing down Pacific Coast Highway in the woodie with the rag top down and the radio blastin' out a bitchin' Jan and Dean number—while the surfers were hoping for some real hairballs (big waves) and even hydrocoffins (waves that enclose the surfer then break on him), possibly even a few tubes (perfect waves), rather than the mush dogs (waves that never break) they'd been getting at Zuma recently, and praying they wouldn't be zoo'd out (crowded) by wannabees (neophyte surfers)—when the Haven boy asked me if I'd ever done a "gas and run." I looked puzzled and he said that if I really wanted to complete my researches and also get properly initiated into surfing life, I should do it—and do it now. I was remarking that this was all part of the rich tapestry of American life, when suddenly the Haven boy tipped the wagon on two wheels and pulled into a gas station. No sooner had the old gas station attendant finished filling the car than the Haven boy roared off in a cloud of filthy smoke. "That's 'gas and run,'" he shouted at me. "Put that in your poetry book!" Next minute, he was doing a "Twinkie and run" and a "burger, fries, and run," but then I had had enough and excused myself at Malibu. I certainly didn't want my visa revoked.

I was to discover that the Haven boy knew a darker side of surfing life. Beer busts were one thing, but "gang bangs" and heavy drugs were not for me. This was not the "Surf City" I wanted to inhabit. But his twisted attitude did result in one amusing curiosity: he took me one evening to witness a veteran surfer's burial in San Clauso Bay. The ashes were paddled out a few hundred yards in an old Hawaiian outrigger; the brief service was followed by a ritual casting in of flowers, followed by a small beer can. The Haven boy had to spoil the solemnity of the occasion by dumping in a whole keg of beer, soaking all and sundry. Why is it that so many of the British lower classes, when abroad, have to let the side down by desecrating native customs?

Realizing I was in danger of becoming a parody British colonel type, due perhaps to my being alone and in a strange country, I was glad of the dinner break in Portland, Oregon—because I found a cafeteria that sold marvelous individual pecan pies, an extraordinary delight I'd first come across in a Greyhound station in El Paso, Texas. After dinner and with some time to kill, I wandered around and happened to see a decent ukulele for sale in a pawnshop window. A Martin and the very best make, if you like ukuleles, which I did. I bought it for a song. Unfortunately, as I was to find out in the years to come, America no longer takes the uke seriously and this purchase was to turn out to prove a fatal mistake for my career.

As we headed north up the coast, the country got greener and lusher and quite like the better parts of Scotland. There seemed to be an enormous amount of shooting brakes (station wagons) around, mostly driven by stout women in scarves or curlers, and the menfolk for the most part wore their hair very close-cropped on their bullet heads. Near Seattle it started to rain pretty hard and, as we pulled into the bus terminal, I realized that my "boomer" surf trunks and T-shirt were the wrong costume. Of course, while in Nashville I'd worn a blazer and cavalry twill trousers and sweated like a pig. I just couldn't get the rig right.

Anyway, my cousin Anna was there to meet me and immediately got me fixed up with the right clothes. She said she was working on the campus wear and would soon come up with a letterman jacket, but did I mind Idaho U.? Of course not—the "I" could be for "Ian"! We left her college apartment and headed downtown for a snack at a student hangout called 92 Yesler, a basement coffee house in the famous Skid Row area. There was a piano on the stage and nobody playing it, so in order to show I wasn't the complete idiot that I looked in the oilskin and galoshes my cousin had lent me, I dashed off a few snappy songs. The two student owners approached me. Would I like to perform here regularly during the next two weeks? Would I indeed? I had been planning to journey on to see more breathtaking sights, but to hell with Yellowstone National Park now! I was to get room and board in return for performing blues, ragtime, comedy, and rock 'n' roll. Talk about carrying coals to Newcastle! Still, after the initial shock of seeing a Britisher let his hair down, the audiences seemed to like it. I was told that the local rock 'n' roll station, KJR, was going to send a disc jockey down to see my act, but if the man ever showed up he didn't introduce himself. KJR was always intoned with great reverence. Get KJR to go on a record and you were made. You might get to be a "national breakout." It happened to local groups, like the Ventures with their "Walk—Don't Run." The Ventures? Weren't they the group who set up the sound that surf music used? I was quickly informed that the Ventures were from nearby Tacoma, but that if I thought their music was tough I ought to go hear the Counts, or the Sonics, or the Frantics because those guys would blast me out of my Bermudas. They played real "tough" stuff and were keeping the rock rolling and the Frankies and Fabians at bay. This was lumberjack country, or nearly, so watch out!

I determined to see some of these local groups play at my earliest opportunity. Trouble was, my student employers never gave me a night off. When I wasn't singing "MacNamara's Band" or "Nobody Knows You When You're Down and Out," I was busy putting pizzas together. After a while, I grew heartily sick of the coffee house—but mainly because of the other music acts they featured. These acts were forever celebrating what they called a "hootenanny" but it looked to me like an after-tea entertainment put on by the local vicar. Night after night, tidy, crew-cut college boys got up and sang folk songs breezily and scrubbed acoustic guitars, sometimes singly, sometimes in groups. They sang folk songs, but they certainly didn't look like the folk I'd seen stamping and cheering at Nashville's Grand Ole Opry. They sang of cotton fields, and three jolly coachmen, and particularly of Tom Dooley, a murderer who got hanged, and they always sang with a smile. The audience—old and young and women and quite small children—joined in by singing along, clapping their hands, or banging cheap tambourines rented out by the student management.

The whole business appeared to be like a Sanforized skiffle movement to me. And I was slightly annoyed to find that some of the purer folk singers objected to my singing "Chantilly Lace," the classic rock song by the late Big Bopper, because it was too "commercial." I was to brush against these killjoys again later, but for the moment I got on with making the pizzas and ignoring the endless campfire singalong onstage.

In England, I'd come across folk music lovers. One thing they hated was any kind of pop music. "Noxious weeds—the debased street music of the vulgar" was how Cecil Sharp, famous collector of folk songs, had described pop. For the most part, the folkies I'd known had been weak-kneed creatures who abstained from meat, slung herbs into everything they ate and drank, and had a fetish for sickly medieval mead. They were also fond of donning antlers to perform ancient Morris dances. Recently, there had been a fad among redbrick university people for songs about working down in the mines or in coal ships and steam engines. In the songs, the workers forever had steam popping out of their brows and they never ceased to heave and ho. This was the contemporary style of folk song and the heroes were invariably from up North. Of course, the real working people had no time at all for this coal mine music and they much preferred Frank Sinatra, Johnnie Ray, and Glenn Miller. Lately, their children had taken to Elvis Presley as a role model for escape from coal mining or any other such grubby, dispiriting, and soul-destroying "real" work.

I didn't like folk singers and their world—and I don't think they cared much for me, those few that had run across me, I should add.

But I was wrong to believe that the folk craze was simply a matter of singing and banging along to ballads like "Tom Dooley" and "Green

Grow the Rushes, O!" The singers and their audiences took their music seriously and, like surfing, a small culture and industry had grown up around the craze since it had first started spreading from campus to campus and coffee house to coffee house in late 1959. They had their own television network show, "Hootenanny." At least, it had them. I thought it fairly pleasant in the campfire scouting sense, but I was told that some of the more thoughtful and idealistic singers had been banned from appearing. Grand old master Pete Seeger had been black-listed because of his leftish leanings. However, I did read that the show's producer, Richard Levine, claimed he hadn't invited Seeger to sing because the man was a rank amateur and couldn't hold a tune. This I could understand: many of my fellow performers at the Seattle coffee house were stronger on energy than entertainment skills. Still, they excused themselves by telling me it was the words that counted. Thinking Man's pop, I suppose.

The folkies had their own magazines, too. The covers were bright and glossy, with lots of exclamation marks and smiling faces. These magazines looked not so very different from the movie and pop fan mags. But the words were different, very different. The "Be My Baby" and "Da Doo Ron Ron" sentiment was nowhere to be seen. To me, the language was a foreign one. Take *Hootenanny* mag. I'll admit it did give a definition of the "hootenanny": "a meeting of folk singers for public entertainment." But farther inside were the thoughts of one Bob Dylan and they sounded like the ramblings of an aged varmint drunk on Mark Twain and James Joyce. Dylan and a friend had been to a show in which two intoxicated blacks sang and danced like old Uncle Toms, clad in gold-striped red silk shirts and nylon pants that were "kinda tight." But what was worse, they'd told jokes about "Negroes an' bears, Negroes an' Tennessee Williams, Negroes an' Negroes." And after every joke, the audience would "howl an' laugh madly an' guzzle down more beer t' the tune a their satisfied hearts poundin' with a happy-go-lucky beat." Could this have been authentic ragtime, I wondered? Then I'd like to have been there. And who was this G-clipper to start complainin'? Dylan had cried, "I don't believe this!" Then his thoughts had winged to "civil rights marches an' Miles Davis, Paul Robeson, James Baldwin." He had his ramble regularly in the glossy *Hootenanny*. In a rambling column called "Blowin' in the Wind," he described some of the denizens of his new world. Some of the names I recognized and even admired. But what were they doing all lumped together? What did they have to do with pop music? What did they have to do with a magical other world?

And yet this folk music fad was apparently stirring up some authorities. It threatened the awful real world, unlike Spectorsound or surf music or even, now, dear old Elvis. I read that a certain Los Angeles civic organization—the Fire and Police Research Association—had described folk music in one of their newsletters as "an unidentified tool of Communist psychological or cybernetic warfare." Folk music was a part of the Communist arsenal of weapons. However, a bold politician named Senator Keating had taken the Fire and Police Research Association to task in a brilliantly witty speech in the Senate. He considered American folk music to be thoroughly American, though containing some un-American influences, like Elizabethan ballads, Protestant hymns, and Scottish reels. He realized that the folk song was grounded in movements of political, economic, and social unrest. He'd personally run across songs in praise of Jesse James, Pretty Boy Floyd, and Billy the Kid. "No one could possibly imagine the members of the board of directors of General Motors sitting around a conference table composing ditties in honor of defense contracts, while it is not surprising that coal miners have come up with a protest song, 'Sixteen Tons.'" I well remembered "Sixteen Tons" as a jolly rhythm number by Tennessee Ernie Ford in the fifties—I didn't know it was political. Times were a-changin' for me. Finally, the good senator considered the charge by the L.A. Fire and Police Research Association that the song "Down by the Riverside" used "subtleties and verbal subterfuges of applied Marxist dialectics." If this song was to be condemned, then one must also condemn "The Best Things in Life Are Free," with its socialist lines about the moon belonging to everyone. He ended with this resounding statement: "Thank God for the Constitution! To stop the amateur ferrets of the radical Right."

I found all this rhetoric quite enthralling, but also a bit too close to the work I was doing at Trinity College and had come to America to get away from. So it was with some relief that I journeyed out with a beer-bellied kid to a dance hall called the Spanish Castle to hear some of the instrumental groups who specialized in the Northwest sound. I was lucky enough that night to hear the Kingsmen play their current hit, "Louie Louie." They wore band jackets and looked fairly clean cut, but when they blasted out on this number the kids went wild and not a few beer bottles were smashed. Crew cuts glistened and eyes popped. The kids couldn't explain their music like the folkies could. They just got with it bodily like kids used to at the beginning of rock 'n' roll. I couldn't understand a word of "Louie Louie," but it was supposedly dirty in the collegiate "making out" sense (what we called "snogging," meaning heavy petting, in Britain).

From the Spanish Castle, we went to Parker's Ballroom and then finally the Lake Hills Roller Rink—where I met Lan Roberts, one of the top deejays from KJR, a man who could make you a star by a spin of a disc. He was polite but puzzled by my accent. He thought I must be Australian or, failing that, Dutch. He went on to tell me that this summer of '63 marked the "Louie Louie" battle. The song itself went back to 1958 and a record by a black singer named Richard Berry. Over the years, the song had become a local underground classic. It was ultra-simple, having only the three basic chords and a blunt, shunt melody and change. The song was very akin to the chants one heard at soccer matches. Any fool could sing and play the number, but it required that extra *oomph* to make it count. "Louie Louie" was fast becoming a folk song of the rock 'n' roll world. In 1961, the Wailers had a local number-one tune on the mighty KJR and now, in the summer of '63, Portland's Kingsmen were battling it out with Paul Revere and the Raiders. The Kingsmen were winning and pretty soon they were to bust out of the local scene and go national. Feelings were high right then and local pride was at stake. I was amazed that there were these local labels and it did occur to me that perhaps I too could someday get a contract and bust out big.

Meanwhile, I had to get back to my coffee house gig—singing and pizza-making. It was about this time that I met Billy Roberts, an itinerant guitarist and singer who lived far from fraternity row in a shack on the wrong side of the tracks. He ate steak tartare and drank pure apple juice. Yet he wasn't a wet folkie of the British kind. His clothes were baggy and he had a scraggly beard. But he sang wild and exciting songs at the coffee house and he had a passing interest in ragtime and British music hall. He showed me his song "Hey Joe," a weird circular song that ran through some startling changes. I didn't dare demonstrate any blues piano because I felt I needed to be black or at least poor white to impress Billy. Instead, I sang "Your Baby Has Gone Down the Plug-Hole" and he laughed fit to burst and pronounced me "crazy."

But there were others who trooped in to perform at the coffee house who weren't as pleasant as Billy, who didn't take life so expansively: testy, gaunt men who fired their guitars like guns and whined of dust in their lungs from too much hard travelin'; innocent-looking young girls who sang with eyes closed and hair streaming down and seemed to be roaming down roads thousands of miles from home. One night, one of the girls suddenly stopped in the middle of a long lament and announced that she was leaving the stage because people were talking. A dreadful void yawned and I quickly stepped in by banging out "Whole Lotta Shakin' Goin' On" in the style of Jerry Lee Lewis as my entertainer sense told me to do. The show must go on. The audience clapped and the talking stopped, but some of the gaunt folkies scorned me for playing such "capitalist crap, the opiate of the masses." But I noticed how the girls liked it and gave me knowing winks.

My historical sense urged me to find the roots of this whole damned hootenanny folk thing. My cousin Anna steered me in the right direction. One of the courses she'd been taking at Seattle University was "Great Irish-Americans" and the teacher, Professor Jack Feeny, was something of a folk music buff. Unfortunately, American universities being what they are, I had to sit through a lot of other Feeny classes before I could collar the man and get some chronological folk facts. Classes on "The Ten Books That Shook the World," "The Nose Music of the Plains Indians," and even one on "The Salmon Culture of the Great Northwest." Clearly, Feeny liked the sound of his own voice and it was a pretty resonant one. Very masculine. He reeked of after-shave. Meanwhile, I took the opportunity, during his interminable lecturing, to catch up on my college work—"Leges Henrici" and all that.

Eventually, he gave me the nod and we retired to his rooms, where he made a lot of fuss about making the coffee—striding around the floor, grinding the beans, shaking the grinder as if it were a cocktail, and all the while reeling off facts and figures through perfect teeth that clenched a meerschaum pipe. I got a few words in edgewise: I expressed bewilderment about the fact that, while the folkies sang of old-fashioned subjects like "Three Jolly Coachmen" and the "Sloop John B.," off-stage they forever banged on about such contemporary issues as rampant commercialism in the pop industry, H-bombs, etc.

"Hold it, Iron!" replied Professor Feeny in a firm and manly voice. "What you call 'banging on' is really a sense of 'involvement,' of 'commitment,' of a general concern for the perilous condition of mankind. What we're talking about here is no passing pop craze, no mere quest for the almighty dollar by fooling the public, but a folk *movement*. We must trace its origins back to those years just prior to World War I, when Tin Pan Alley, an American corporate triumph, had established a monopoly on popular music. The Alley sold bread and circuses, dreams and escapism, while the true music of the people was left a-moulderin'. But the working stiff found a hero in Joe Hill, the laborer who put meaningful words of protest to the pabulum of pop and thus lit the torch of folk. He put new words to current hits like Irving Berlin's 'Everybody's Doing It Now' and changed it into a real hunky-dory union propaganda song, 'Everybody's Joining It Now.'"

"Joining what?" I asked.

"Why, Iron . . . one big union. A dream we have yet to see realized —but then, you see, some people have to be forced to be free." I contributed a wink, which was not appreciated. "Anyway, Joe Hill wrote these songs to *fan the flames of discontent* for the *Little Red Songbook*, issued by the Industrial Workers of the World. The capitalist bosses didn't like these Wobblies or Joe Hill. They got old Joe executed on a trumped-up murder charge in 1915. But old Joe didn't die, no siree. You can't put out that kinda torch—it burned on and, in the thirties, it was taken up by Woody Guthrie, a genuine working Oklahoman with a zest for learning, a strong moral sense, a feeling for the little man, and a store of great songs."

"Would this be the same Guthrie who co-wrote many of the hit songs recorded by Lonnie Donegan in the skiffle era? Do you remember Donegan's 'Rock Island Line'? Or maybe 'Does Your Chewing Gum Lose Its Flavor on the Bedpost Overnight?'" I had a good memory for song titles. I was also trying to find a point of contact between my interests and Feeny's.

The professor waved his hand with slight impatience and continued his saga: "Woody had real dust in his lungs from the famous dust bowl storms in Oklahoma in the Depression and pretty soon he went hard travelin', picking fruit in California, garnering experience, *payin' his dues*. Note that.

"Eventually, Guthrie turned up in New York in 1938 at a time when there was a growing interest in American folk songs, stimulated by folklore projects set up by the Roosevelt administration. And at the Library of Congress archives, Alan Lomax and his assistant, Pete Seeger, son of a folklorist himself, had been publishing uncensored versions of the old songs, complete with all their blood and guts, sex, protest, and suffering. None of that Gene Autry hillbilly nonsense.

"When Woody was discovered by Lomax, it was like a research project in the flesh. Guthrie was to radicalize what had been a pursuit of intellectual antiquarianism. In person, he could be quite ornery—one time at a swank New York hotel reception, he got insecure and went around tearing down the drapes and running riot. He was an undependable performer, too—he might turn up at the show or he might not; he might or might not sing what you wanted to hear. But there was a consistency to his contrariness—he believed in people doing what they wanted as long as they didn't upset anybody. In a wider context, he believed in one big union, one big world, everybody together. He was a real patriot, you know. He said America was basically a good place, but a few things needed to be changed. He wrote 'This Land is My Land' and he meant it."

I told him I remembered singing that song in the school skiffle group back in the days of Lonnie Donegan and Bill Haley.

Feeny continued, "Alan Lomax introduced Woody to key people in the fast-growing New York folk scene, in particular, the denizens of Almanac House, a co-operative settlement down in Greenwich Village. Here Guthrie lived and worked with such luminaries as writer Millard

Lampell and folklorist Pete Seeger. As part of the quartet called the Almanac Singers, they went out to tour the 'subway circuit'—colleges, labor rallies, antifascist meetings—during the forties.

"All this was small potatoes. Their intention was to change the world, to make democratic music for the people of the republic, to wake them up politically through aesthetic joys. But the Almanacs were preaching to the converted. In the early 1950s, a new group called the Weavers, whose members included Pete Seeger, were spotted by arranger Gordon Jenkins while they were appearing at a coffee house called the Village Vanguard. Unlike the Almanacs, this new group actually rehearsed, had harmonies, and were getting to be very professional. Jenkins put his orchestra behind them on their version of what was thought to be a traditional Israeli folk song, 'Tzena, Tzena.' The Decca recording went on to sell a lot of records and make the best-seller lists. [Unfortunately, "Tzena, Tzena" turned out not to be an anonymous folk song but a relatively new number written in 1921 by a Palestinian, Issachar Miron. Legal action corrected the claims of Gordon Jenkins and Spencer Ross as writers and copyright holders.] That same year, 1950, the Weavers had a two-million-copy hit on their hands with "Goodnight, Irene,"† which they had excerpted from an Alan Lomax book, *Negro Folk Songs as Sung by Leadbelly*. Like Woody, Huddie Ledbetter (or Leadbelly) was another Alan Lomax discovery, a real find—a dyed-in-the-wool black man who was serving time for murder in Angola prison, Louisiana, when the roving folklorist chanced upon him. Lomax used to carry around a recording machine like you do. So there we had a genuine hillbilly—Guthrie—and a genuine singer-songwriter Negro. Both had paid their dues. And we folklorists had put them on the map and put their songs into the laps of the American people."

At this high point in the story, Feeny invited me to join him in a bottle of specially imported Power's Irish whiskey. When we resumed our conversation/lecture, Feeny warned that he had reached a dark era in the story of folk:

"The Weavers seemed to be on top of the world—at least, 'On Top of Old Smoky'—to quote the title of one of their hits. Others included 'Kisses Sweeter Than Wine,' 'Rock Island Line,' 'Sloop John B.,' and the South African song 'Wimoweh.' But already signs of repression were appearing: Decca, the Weavers' record company, didn't like the mention of dust storms on their version of 'So Long, It's Been Good to

---

† "Goodnight, Irene" was based on a number of nineteenth-century ballads whose origins have been lost to time. No one knows who owned the original copyright. This "borrowing" from the work of others has been a characteristic of folk music-makers until at least the early songs of Bob Dylan.

Know Yuh,' nor the criticism of organized religion. They got writer Guthrie to deliver a new set of lyrics.

"Remember that the Iron Curtain had crashed down and America was on a paramilitary alert against Communist attack. The fifties were a decade of fear and soon the fear turned from H-bomb attack to infiltration from within—Commies under the bed. Even liberals were seen as potential Reds. Folk radicals were branded as 'unfriendly' by the House Un-American Activities Committee and, in 1955, Pete Seeger was hauled up in front of them to answer questions—questions he called 'immoral and improper.' Six years later, they nailed him with a jail sentence that was reversed the following year, but the damage had been done and Pete found it hard to get bookings. He appeared at quite a few colleges, but even there he found disapproving administrators.

"However, though the folk flame was only just a-flickerin', there were some among this bleak and silent button-down student generation who were to carry on by spreading the message, albeit a rather watered-down one. I'm thinking of the Kingston Trio, a group of students who originally got started by playing at fraternity parties for free beer. Their leader, Nick Reynolds, admits that he and the boys had been admirers of both the Almanac Singers and the Weavers. They were singing up a hootenanny storm at the Purple Onion in San Francisco when they were discovered by Capitol Records. To everyone's amazement, their version of an old backwoods murder story, 'Tom Dooley,' was a million-seller. The show-business papers like *Variety* began to mention this novel sound: HILL SOUND UPSURGE—FOLKNIKS ON THE MARCH. Of course, the dedicated folk music fans fumed in their little magazines: I remember Dan Armstrong in *Broadside* complaining that the Kingston Trio were spurious folk, mere 'panty raiders on a weekend vacation in Dad's Rambler.' But you gotta remember that the Kingston Trio's easy-listening style turned on a lot of pop fans to the real folk music."

"What's new in folk music?" I asked, finally understanding how the movement fit into the grand scheme of pop.

"Today, in this hopeful young country, you'll find that the kids who are singing around campfires at barbecues—or in coffee houses or wherever—are also involved with current issues: they are anti-John Birch Society, antisegregation, and pro-Peace Corps, pro-civil rights. You'll find them freedom marching in Alabama, facing Bull Connor's dogs and whips, sitting-in at segregated diners; you'll find them marching for nuclear disarmament, protesting against militarism and fascism everywhere. And you'll find them full of hope for America—because, Iron, like our wonderful young President, they feel that the future will and must be *better*. So long, it's been good to know ya."

"That Feeny's full of bullshit," said folk singer and folk-liver Billy Roberts, as he and I tramped along a street in downtown Seattle, site of the original Skid Row. "The guy's just towing an Old Left line that's out-of-date. Folk music's bigger than his cant—I mean, man, we don't all do the community get-together singalong. And some of us—including me—dig rock 'n' roll. Hell, we grew up on it and Presley was our first hero. He made us sit up in front of the TV—instead of slumping—and made us think, 'Hey, maybe I can make it big, too!' "

I was glad to know of this connection between the folkies and Elvis and the Rockers.

"Hell, some of us are individuals!" He kicked hard at a beer bottle in his path, scattering a group of winos nearby. He took a sharp left and marched straight across the street, causing traffic to screech to a halt.

In his pad, Roberts indicated a pillow for me and proceeded to fill a long, decorated pipe. He wanted to turn me on to what he called "the twentieth-century minstrel boy, our very own weather cock." He handed me an album cover showing an angel-faced boy with curls sprouting from under a peaked cap. He was cute and fey, with a faint, wry smile playing on his lips. *Bob Dylan,* said the cover. I thought that there was an awful lot of G-clipping going on, but for the moment I held my peace.

At first, Bob Dylan's voice was abrasive and irritating to me, like a vile old Dublin tramp begging for a handout. But the historian in me said to give the boy a chance so I stopped analyzing: it was surprising, this disparity between the cute cover boy with the alabaster face and the rasping recorded voice of a decrepit varmint. A clearing of the throat was needed, a good gargle with salt, and possibly a set of better-fitting dentures.

The song "Freight Train Blues" was pretty standard folk fare—about being stuck yet again thousands of miles from home and having to tramp on down that dusty road. (Why not hop a Greyhound or hitch a lift? I thought.) As accompaniment, a single guitar scrubbed away rudimentarily—skiffle without the group and the campfire jamboree fun—and that whiny voice buzzed *around* but never actually *on* the note. Sometimes the voice got so excited it sounded like a fingernail dragging down a blackboard. A far cry from the painlessness of Feeny's hootenanny music. How I yearned for that soothing stuff!

Billy, noticing my reaction, hastened to assure me that this was Dylan's first album for Columbia Records and consisted of traditional folk material interpreted in his own unique style but before he had really learned his craft and revealed his true spirit. "Bobby's still playing the folk game; he's still one of the boys in the hard-travelin', forever-ramblin' way of Woody & Company," he told me.

As he pulled at his pipe (I stuck to cigars), he grew more expansive about his pal Bob Dylan. Turned out he'd known the troubadour quite well in the early days. That was when Dylan was Robert Zimmerman, a dropout from the University of Minnesota who used to hang out in the bohemian bars and folk clubs in the hip off-campus Dinkytown. Dylan and his crowd would keep warm in the snowy winters by strumming fast on their guitars and whipping up visions of better times in warmer climes. The Promised Land and a pot of gold might be just down the road apiece, but, as they were all students, it wasn't hip to pursue that goal via R&R—however, the folk route to fame and riches was OK.

Billy met Bobby one snowy day in Dinkytown. Billy was wandering the country, hitting bars and clubs, and he'd found recently that the best pickings were around university towns. The students seemed to be getting fed up with their regular courses and turning on to meaningful music. In a coffee house called the Scholar, he found Zimmerman struggling with the chords for the old song "House of the Rising Sun" and Billy obliged by showing him the changes. Next thing he knew, the boy was performing the song around Dinkytown as though he'd just written it or, to be more exact, as though he'd just hacked it from the rock of his personality. Billy didn't mind because the boy had a riveting personality—better known as "charisma." Whenever Bobby walked into a room, he got everyone's attention and he could do crazy things and get away with it because he wore that sweet, innocent, little-boy look. Girls went for him in a big way; they dug his Chaplinesque walk and his elfin-cute face, which counterbalanced the cutting musical style he was developing. Billy admired the way Bobby could spit out some venomous words and then soften the impact by burying his face in his harnessed harmonica and blowing away. Billy had to admit that Bobby's harmonica playing was dreadful and his guitar playing pretty rudimentary—but he got your attention and he kept it.

Bobby was very secretive about his family background, but Billy ferreted it out. After all, Billy had been around. For instance, he knew straight away that Bobby was from a middle-class Jewish family. You learn that sort of thing on the road. But he had to approach some fraternity members to find out that Bobby had actually been in a Jewish fraternity for a short while. From Bobby's ex-fraternity brothers, he learned that the Zimmermans were well-to-do business people in Hibbing, Minnesota—his father operated a hardware store and his uncle ran the local cinema. As a kid at school, Bobby had organized a perfectly terrible rock 'n' roll band, but this lack of success hadn't stopped him. He was determined to escape the suffocation of middle-class life in hicksville Minnesota, where most of the year was spent under snow

and the only things they had to boast about were the lakes, the occasional bumper crop, and the Minnesota Vikings football team. He
could have escaped into R&R like his fellow Minnesotan Bobby Vee,
but instead he chose a brainier route: folk music for the college audience. Zimmerman immediately set about creating his myth—he was really Bobby Vee, he was an Okie, he'd played piano in carnivals, he'd
rambled and gambled and paid his dues. Billy was amused by these dis-
guises, but he reminded Bobby that their mutual hero Elvis hadn't
needed to cover up his background. Bobby paid no heed. "Hey, man,"
said Billy one day when they'd drunk quite a bit of mulled wine and
toked up a mite too much. "Who are you? Vee . . . or Guthrie . . . or
Brando . . . or Chaplin . . . or Dean?"

"I'm Bob Dylan and I'm gonna be bigger than Presley!" he replied
with that curious smirk that made you wonder if he was putting you
on. Billy had no idea that his pal was hip to the Welsh wizard of poetry, Dylan Thomas, but he agreed to play along with the persona that
Bobby had chosen and with the whole atmosphere of mysterioso. Billy
could sympathize: after all, his dad was in the aerospace industry and
Roberts wasn't his real surname either; it was actually some unpro-
nounceable name by way of Serbo-Croatia.

Billy moved on to another college town where the pickings were better and he lost touch with his pal. Then, a few years later, he blew into
Greenwich Village and found everybody that mattered talking about
this musician who had set the scene in a whirl with his cutting songs.
"Listen, he's taken up the Guthrie torch and dragged folk screaming
into the twentieth century. No more folderol and cowboys and 'Lord
Randal, my son'!" explained one folkie. Billy went out and bought the
albums by his old pal and was pleased to see he'd made it to Columbia
Records, home of Mitch Miller and Rosemary Clooney. Same league as
RCA, Elvis's company. Bobby was making it—and how clever to take
the old tunes like "Lord Randal" and write new lyrics—"A Hard Rain's
A-Gonna Fall." He was really getting into the *angst* of the time; even
his salute to Woody Guthrie had an editorial about the sad state of the
world.

And then there was "Blowin' in the Wind," which was fast becoming the anthem of the civil rights movement, as popular and potent as
"We Shall Overcome." Very clever, this one, in the best metaphysical
tradition, posing a lot of questions and suggesting no clear answers, the
real stuff of art. Again we had the poet rambler walking down those old
highways, but we also had a white dove sailing seas and cannon balls
flying and mountains waiting to be washed to the sea. And the question
was, how much longer were they gonna have to wait for justice to be
done?

Anyway, you can't argue with success, at least not in America—and
success was what Dylan was getting. "Blowin' in the Wind" was recorded by the easy-listening folk group Peter, Paul, and Mary, as was
his excursion into love problems, "Don't Think Twice, It's All Right."
This showed that, although Dylan could satisfy the protest set in the
Village with such songs as "Masters of War" (in which he castigated
the bomb builders who put guns in kids' hands and then ran off and
hid behind desks), he could also write as decent a love ballad as any
Alley songsmith. In fact, his songs were being published by the old
firm of Witmark, who had a heap of moon-in-June and ragtime classics
among their copyrights. And Dylan had teamed up with Albert Gross-
man, as tough and astute a manager as Colonel Parker.

When Billy played me "Don't Think Twice, It's All Right," I commented that I found the ungrammatical phrases like "I never knowed"
and "If'n you . . ." a bit affected coming from a Minnesota U. student.
And I said that the bit in "Masters of War" about the authorities duck-
ing behind the lines and leaving the young men to fight had already
been better expressed in World War I songs like "If you want to know
where the colonel is—he's fifty miles behind the line."

"The trouble with you, pal," said Billy, "is that you know too much
goddamn history. *Today* is where it's at. Stop stifling art!"

I started arguing again—about the doggerel rhymes in, say, the sheet
music of a Dylan song that was lying on Billy's mattress: "The Times
They Are A-Changin'." I mean, why was it necessary to put in the redundant "they"? Why not just say "The Times Are Changing"? Why
G-clip, too—was it part of the belief that somehow the unschooled folk
had more wisdom than the educated? And this medieval troubadour
opening of "Come gather 'round people . . ." with mothers and fathers and senators and congressmen being invited to gather around and
listen to a rather biblical warning of an impending apocalypse: "And
the first one now will later be last." Wasn't this simplistic Sunday
school stuff? Hadn't the youth rebellion been better stated in Presley's
warning not to step on his "Blue Suede Shoes"? Or Danny and the Juniors' affirmation that "Rock and Roll Is Here to Stay"?

In short, wasn't Bob Dylan a bit of a throwback to God knows
when? Perhaps to periwigged rebels in the dreary days of the Boston
Tea Party and "hey-nonny-no"?

"You're really out of step. If you could only get into what Bobby's
saying, you'd see that he's talking about youth telling parents they're
beyond their command and they better lend a hand if they don't
wanna get run over. Same with the politicians—they better get hip or
we'll stampede 'em. Look, man, he's talking about Cuba and segrega-
tion and poverty and so on—and blah, blah, blah."

Then Billy got tired of talking and, taking another pull at his pipe, he relapsed into a brown study, smiling beatifically. After a while, he forgave me and said he knew where James Brown and the Famous Flames were playing that night and invited me to join him. He said Brown could whip up the same sort of spiritual fervor that Dylan was doing. He told me again to stop rationalizing—millions of thinking people, not just folkies, were digging Dylan and Dylan was far from being a closeted purveyor of ethnic antiques—he was gonna be the voice of his generation.

One consolation, I thought, at least these Dylan addicts aren't rock 'n' roll fans. They aren't going to foul up the fun that is pop (I still felt that R&R was best experienced over a tinny Tannoy speaker while roaring around in a fun-fair Dodg.'em car). They want no part of overground pop, of the glamour of exotic America with its spangled cowboys and long-oppressed blacks. This Dylan could certainly never be the next Presley.

Feeling buoyant and better informed, I went with Billy to a ramshackle high school gym on the outskirts of Seattle to join the black throng at the James Brown show. How thrilling to be wedged in this mass of humanity, white dots in a black ocean undulating to the hypnotic beat of talking drums which had sustained their message of perpetual hijinks despite decades of white oppression. Do it here, now, today, not tomorrow! Do it on the floor, in the street!—the drums proclaimed. And Brown himself was the High Priest, stomping and shouting his congregation into a state of euphoria.

Phew! I thought as we swayed. Precious few Britishers have experienced this sort of celebration. Stanley and Livingstone came to mind, rather than Prince Philip watching the independence celebrations of some far-flung African colony. What a country was America! Everything from the wholesome frankfurter steam of the Kingston Trio to the deep-fried pig's trotters of James Brown and his Famous Flames. That night, I had a perfect dream: a surfing Adonis coming in on a huge creamy Pacific roller to the beat of a monster tom-tom.

I was still in this frame of mind when I turned up at New York's Idlewild Airport for the return home (except that my spiritual home was now America). But my oafish student colleagues were unimpressed by the letterman jacket with a huge purple "I" (for "Idaho U."), nor had they much time for my Seattle University sweatshirt. Why go to such off-the-wall spots when there were the Grand Canyon, Disneyland, and the splendors of the National Parks?

But once in the air and fueled up by a glass of wine, I left such mundane plodders behind and I began to feel elated, expansive, and thoroughly historical. Suddenly, I saw the perspective in the great tap-

estry of popular music. Looking below at the vanishing American
landmass, I reflected on the enormous cultural impact of this New
World on the Old one, on how Britain had been host to these friendly
invaders ever since the arrival of the black minstrels, followed by the
ragtimers, and then jazz and swing. And how the island people had
made asses of themselves as they slavishly copied the bunny hugs,
Charlestons, and jive steps and inserted "ain't-chas" and "oh yeahs"
and "OKs" into their conversation. Yet at least this peaceful penetration had offered a colorful alternative to the otherwise dreary life in the
British Isles.

Yes indeed, American pop was a Santa Claus scattering gifts from
the faraway land of make-believe. Of course, we British were no good
at the syncopation game ourselves. We were good at being Jeeves and
silly-ass types like Jack Buchanan and we were good at being homely,
sincere ballad singers like Vera Lynn. I suppose the closest we got to
our own homegrown syncopation was in the high-speed ukulele-banjo
strumming of George Formby. I remembered a droll song that my
great-uncle, Stanley J. Damerell, had written for Formby (at a time
when he was the top box-office draw in British cinemas):

> "Baby dear, never fear, never mind your beer.
> Come and look at these lads,
> From the pitch-black coal mines down in Wiganland.
> And when they play on Wigan Pier so grand,
> All the people fill their ears with sand!"

3

1964: "ALL I WANT FOR CHRISTMAS IS A BEATLE"

That winter of 1963, a few days after arriving home from my American adventures, I got on a London bus. As it was bitterly cold, I felt quite justified in wearing an ensemble collated from the U.S. male apparel that I'd brought back: a beanie cap, an Alaskan parka, a genuine McGregor plaid shirt, and a military-gray sweater that stated quite categorically: SEATTLE UNIVERSITY.

"Wot's that, then?" demanded the cockney bus conductor, dragging a grimy finger across this perfectly obvious sweater insignia, "Beatle University, eh? Ha ha!" "No no," I replied quickly (for the passengers

had all sprung to attention at this "beetle" word). "This is the official
Seattle Uni—" But my words were left to trail off into window conden-
sation, the conductor having already moved off down the bus and the
passengers having grumpily returned to their newspapers, knitting, and
colds.

I had only gone up West to look around the shops and perhaps buy
some toilet requisites—but I soon became aware of a phenomenon: the
city was in the grip of this "beetle" word. Having left America roistering in healthy, happy hootenannies, I now found my own countrymen
in the thick of what became known as "Beatlemania." These were no
insects, but a beat group. I had thought that guitar bands like the Shadows and the Tornadoes were passé and I certainly felt that such punning (insect/rhythm) was the sort of silly pastime only inky schoolboys
indulged in.

But who was I to cast a shadow on the festivities? Everybody was entering into the Beatle spirit: mums and grannies were trying on Beatle
"moptop" wigs in the stores, adolescent girls were shouting "fab,"
"gear," and "stick it in your jam buttie" at each other; youths were trying on pointed boots with elastic-sided gussets and Cuban heels and
bum-freezer jackets with no collars. At other counters, I saw Beatle
wallpaper in assorted colors, Beatle talcum powder, Beatle chewing
gum, and the confectionary department displayed a fine line of Beatle
cakes—guitar-shaped and party-sized (or individual lozenge-sized). I
beat a retreat into the record department to see what blues records they
had in stock. The shop assistant asked, "Is it the Stones you require?"
Thundering out of a nearby speaker came a Christmas novelty, "All I
Want for Christmas Is a Beatle." This was sung by a serious actress,
Dora Bryan, who should have known better. I heard a woman in twin-
set and pearls, up from the country, no doubt, ask for a record of the
national anthem. "Are they a group?" was the reply. I heard a bearded
jazz buff ask for Louis Armstrong's Hot Five, only to be told: "All
groups are divided into cities." This was amazing but there the records
were, neatly sorted into Liverpool (Beatles, Searchers, Swinging Blue
Jeans, Billy J. Kramer and the Dakotas, Gerry and the Pacemakers,
Fourmost), Manchester (Freddie and the Dreamers, the Hollies, Wayne
Fontana and the Mindbenders), Birmingham (the Strangers, the
Rockin' Berries, the Kavern Four), and dear old London town (the
Dave Clark Five and Brian Poole and the Tremeloes). "You mark my
words," a friendly clerk told me. "The Tottenham sound of the Dave
Clark Five is going to topple these cheeky Beatles." Then he saw my
perplexed look and added, "It's all a bit of a lark, really. Don't be a
Scrooge—get into the Christmas mood!"

I went home and listened to the radio, watched the TV. Pretty soon,

I realized that the Beatles were a sort of British Marx Brothers. You didn't have to hear a note of their music to realize they were huge jokesters, up to a lark, not taking themselves too seriously. "Why do you wear so many rings on your fingers?" asked a reporter of Ringo. "Because I can't get them through my nose." A rather more avuncular interviewer said, "Well, lads, almost unknown in January and now going into the Royal Command Variety Performance in December. This is quite a rise even for your business, isn't it, Paul?" "We've been very lucky," said the cherub-faced Paul, the one who was most polite, most like the normal pop singer. "Obviously, this sort of thing can't go on," opined the interviewer, straining to make himself heard above the high-pitched shrieking of "Yeah! Yeah! Yeah!" "But," he continued, "do you think you can settle down to a life in show business?" "Not exactly a *life*," answered the gracious Paul in that thick Liverpool accent, "but at least a couple more years—if we do as well as Cliff Richard and the Shadows, we won't be moaning."

Gradually, some individual personalities emerged: Paul as diplomatic and cuddly; Ringo as dopey-simple but country-canny; George quiet and craggy, content to play guitar, it seemed; and John Lennon! Well, John emerged from my media watch as the one with the ragged edge, the burr in the show-biz saddle, the outspoken one. He was good at cracks all right: When the Beatles were on "Juke Box Jury," one of the records was by Paul Anka, a rather gooey crooner by this time. "I don't like people with a crack in their voice," judged Paul. John chipped in with, "It's in his head." Funny but tough. John could come out with quite acid comments about society, too: "People say we're loaded with money, but by comparison with those who are supposed to talk the Queen's English that's ridiculous. The more people you meet, the more you realize it's a class thing." Cliff Richard or even Elvis, the King himself, never made this sort of statement. Something novel in pop. At the Royal Command Variety Performance, he invited the audience to clap along—and the nobs to just rattle their jewelry. And they all laughed. The Queen Mother was very amused.

The press was having a field day. The Beatles were heaven-sent, great copy. You could get grunts and earthy stuff from the other Northern Invaders, but there was something very precious about the Beatles. They were already a race apart. What a relief to turn from the sordid details of the Profumo scandal to these hijinks, these champagne-and-ale bubbles of pure relief!

The *Daily Mirror:* "You have to be a real sour square not to love the nutty, noisy, happy, handsome Beatles. . . . They're young, new. They're high-spirited, cheerful. What a change from the self-pitying moaners, crooning their lovelorn tunes from the tortured shallows of lukewarm hearts."

Our local paper, the Putney *Herald,* took a nationalistic approach: "How refreshing to hear the cheerful music of our own British youngsters instead of the American-accented slop of the Bobbys and Frankies who hitherto have dominated our hit parade! America, watch out! Britons never, never, never again will be slaves to your popular culture!"

The writer had obviously never been exposed to the true Afro-American blues, nor to the Anglo-American country music that I had been privileged to absorb on my American trip. And just wait until the surf sound hits Britain! How could puny, stoop-shouldered Northern lads compete with the sunburned masters of the wild surf guitar? But then what could you expect from ignorant journalists who for decades had shown only a passing interest in pop music? To most people, to their readers, pop was merely a tune you hummed as you worked; or danced to while waiting for a wife; or it brought back a poignant memory of Able Seaman Harry going down with his mates in a destroyer in World War II, singing, as they drowned, "Roll Out the Barrel."

In the past, before this Beatlemania, press and public had left pop to its own closed world: an industry run from London by older men with cigars and bulging stomachs and presentation desk pen sets who lunched on the best brisket and salt beef, calling the name of the game, dispensing contracts to the right boys and girls—those who had been properly groomed, with teeth fixed and posture corrected and stage moves choreographed—who in interviews repeated what their managers told them to say, ending with their life's ambition, which was to perfect their craft in show biz so that they might become all-around entertainers. They might finally play the London Palladium with the big American stars.

Now this cozy, set world was being disrupted. "I'm certainly not going to learn to tap dance," said John Lennon. The Beatles' favorite group was Sophie Tucker and they wanted the Queen to star in their first film because "She sells."

After I'd finished my extensive research on the Beatles, I thought I'd pop over to Chelsea and get some brain food from Ffiona and Margaret, two bluestocking students at Trinity College who shared a London flat. I was in dire need of a good bout of dialectical materialism. But imagine my amazement when I arrived to find them both dancing around in Beatle wigs to the strains of "Merseybeat" by Somebody and the Somebodies. Plunking myself down on the sofa, I was further disgusted to find I'd gotten a jam sandwich stuck to the seat of my U.S. military fatigues. "I say," shouted Ffiona, "Mind out for me jam buttie!" I ignored her remark and picked up a copy of the *Times* from her coffee table. My eyes fell immediately on an article by their "serious" music critic, William Mann. Even he had fallen for the new fad and was writing thus:

"Since the decline of the music hall, England has taken her popular songs from the United States, either directly or by mimicry. . . . But the songs of Lennon and McCartney are distinctly indigenous in character, the most imaginative and inventive examples of a style that has been developing on Merseyside during the past few years." He went on to baffle me with references to "chains of pandiatonic clusters" in their song "This Boy" and in "Not a Second Time" he discovered "an Aeolian cadence," which he said was "the chord progression that ends Mahler's *Song of the Earth.*" Mahler! Never had the classical masters been compared to pop merchants. For relief, I picked up a copy of William Burroughs's novel *Naked Lunch.* Margaret, sweating, came over to me and said, "Paul says he'd rather read *Packed Lunch* by I. B. Greedy. What a tonic these boys are, eh?" I replied by asking whether anything was taken seriously in England today. Then I went on to criticize the music by saying that much of the Beatles stuff consisted of clumsy copycat versions of obscure American R&B records or tired reworkings of Chuck Berry or Little Richard classics. I said the beat was bottom heavy, much too gallumphing and unsubtle and that when the Beatles shouted they didn't do it musically like the black soul singers. Had they ever heard James Brown?

"Oh, do shut up," interrupted Ffiona. "Why are you such a killjoy, such an egghead? I can't see what this refreshing blast of fun from the North has to do with a bunch of Americans. Stop analyzing and enjoy. . . . Yeah! Yeah! Yeah!" I told her this was not a time for mindless enjoyment when a great American President had only recently been assassinated. "That's *exactly* why we're losing ourselves in the Beatles & Company," she replied. "We need their happy faces after all this tragedy." I gave up and returned to the literature on her coffee table. The girls had started dancing again, this time with each other. First the *Times* and now the *Observer*—one could understand the tabloids covering this phenomenon, but one didn't expect it of the quality papers. *However:* "You usually think of film stars, pop singers, and so forth as living in glamorous places—Hollywood and so on," a girl fan told a reporter from the *Observer.* "But the Beatles aren't like that. It's *Liverpool*—where 'Z Cars' comes from." ("Z Cars" was a popular BBC-TV series that I tried to avoid.)

Finally, I turned to *The Daily Worker,* a very serious Communist paper. Surely there would be some sense here?

"The Mersey sound is the voice of 80,000 crumbling houses and 30,000 people on the dole," it reported.

I am trying to be as honest as I can about my reactions to the Beatles and the other Northern Invaders. Clearly, I was baffled—the shock of the New. We in the comfortable South, in the Home Counties, had for years viewed all territory north of Birmingham as a foreign country. As for Scotland, it was beyond redemption, beyond the pale. Oliver Cromwell, they say, took one look over the Scottish border and decided it wasn't worth conquering. The North was cold and harsh and full of no-nonsense plain speakers who had no time for us posh, lazy exploiters in the South. We in turn saw Them as figures of comic relief. Comedians came from there: men like George Formby, Sr., with his catch phrase, "I'm coughing better tonight," and his famous son who played high-speed ukulele and sang about "Granddad's Flannelette Night-shirt." Or Frank Randle from Blackpool, a clown who used to open his act by chucking his false teeth into the orchestra stalls with, "Ee, ah don't need these!", then proceed to urinate into a potted plant (which promptly collapsed). There were frightening stories of Southern travelers stranded in woebegone, depressed cities and suffering under the rough natives. For example, a well-known Shakespearean actor, having missed the last train out of Crewe, knocked on the door of a hotel. A cadaverous figure opened it and gave the actor a harsh look. "Er, do you have special terms for actors?" the traveler asked. "Yes—and here's one: *Fuck off!*"

And if they weren't being aggressive, the Northerners were acting daft. One heard of a Lancashire lad down in London demanding another helping of dressed crab (in the shell): "Give us another of them pies—but don't make the crust quite so hard."

So that had been our picture of life north of London—a prejudiced mixture of fear and amusement. Much of this knowledge had come to me from comic strips like *Andy Capp* and from B movies which starred these comics and in which the ruling class always got their comeuppance in the last reel. But since the late fifties, a new North had been emerging on the screen: in films like *Room at the Top, Saturday Night and Sunday Morning*, and *The Loneliness of the Long-Distance Runner*, a new antihero emerged—pushy, insolent, self-confident, and with no time for the niceties of society. No longer would there be any attempt to ape our betters. Take us as we are, muck and all. If we spit, then we spit. We *sweat*, not perspire. Authors like Alan Sillitoe and John Braine and actors like Albert Finney and Tom Courtenay electrified the page and screen with this new Northern presence that was impatient for equality. Enjoy your freedom now, these films said, before the prison of dirty diapers and the dole and the football pools.

So far, though, this new and truculent antihero had been confined to book and screen. He had not been seen in the flesh, nor had he really touched the public with a special magic. Rock 'n' roll, more instant and earthy than either books or films, was to be the vehicle which would carry our lusty lads into the hearts and minds of millions. Guitar groups bashed away merrily but were presented thoughtfully by knowing entrepreneurs who came to exemplify this new breed of cheeky-chappie swashbucklers who refused to bow and scrape and stay oop North like their forefathers.

And the character came with a musical form, too: the British blues, the Merseybeat, the scouse swing. For the best of the Northern groups offered no mere slavish copy of American beat, but infused their performance with a peculiarly English raciness and charm. And, in so doing, they were carrying on the great British music-hall tradition which had been in decline since the incursion of ragtime just before World War I. The spirit of "Boiled Beef and Carrots" and "Knees Up, Mother Brown" was being revived in the cloak of rock 'n' roll. At last, Britain was to find its own authentic pop voice, vox/pop, and the storm center of the movement was a dirty old seaport, a relic of the Industrial Revolution, squatting on the edge of England.

"Liverpool is not, conventionally, a very beautiful city," wrote Beatle manager Brian Epstein in his autobiography. A characteristic understatement—for if the industrial North, with its belching factories, polluted canals, and satanic mills, was colloquially called the "Arsehole of England" (the rear end of smooth-faced London society), then by the 1950s, that is, on the eve of rock 'n' roll, Liverpool was a great carbuncle on that arse.

Built in solid brick on the parvenu money of nineteenth-century cotton merchants, shipowners, and slave traders, on the premise that "Where there's muck, there's brass," this once proud and splendid monument to Victorian enterprise had gone to seed. By the 1950s, after a series of unfortunate setbacks to the Empire—which included two world wars and, in between, a shocking General Strike and a Great Depression, with its ominous hunger marches and working-class restlessness—Liverpool had deteriorated into a dreary mass of soot-blackened buildings dominating endless terraces of redbrick houses and festering slums, where "Land of Hope and Glory" had become a bad joke played by ex-Northerner Gracie Fields (living in luxury on the sunny isle of Capri). Bomb sites abounded (Hitler's efforts at slum clearance) and on these played embryonic rockers whose only music was the dripping tones of the big band crooners beloved by their sisters. Away from the dirt, grime, and decay were green fields and trees—but who needed the gentle English countryside with its soft, refreshing rain? Certainly not anyone with any sense of get-up-and-go! The ruined fortress of once-proud Liverpool intoned like a killjoy priest: "Thou Shalt Not . . ." warning those with any spunk—any "nouse" or guts—that the game was up. Great Britain, as far as the North was concerned, was out of the race.

Liverpool was different from other Northern cities in one important respect: it was a *seaport* and seaports are both an entrance and an exit to the outside world, welcoming exotic products, from Persian rugs to R&B records, and releasing restless souls seeking excitement, change, maybe that pot of gold at the end of the rainbow. By comparison, Manchester, in the hinterland and the self-styled capital of the North, was a hick town. Liverpudlians burned with a fierce local patriotism, proud of their "scouse" accents and their stable of famous comedians. The maritime connection meant that the city was a melting pot of different races, a carnival of nations, and the Liverpudlians reveled in this glorious hubble-babble. In any case, a large majority had Celtic blood flowing in their veins and owed little allegiance to their Anglo-Saxon masters: Liverpool had long before been dubbed "the capital of Ireland," due to the enormous influx of Irish that had started after the Great Potato Famine of the 1840s.

In the Liverpool eight districts was a kind of minor Harlem, along with Beat poets and painters and folk musicians, all living the bohemian life of jam butties and hot, sweet tea. Jack Kerouac and William Burroughs were avidly read and the work of Beat poet Allen Ginsberg was much admired. Some of the local poets experimented in the American manner by setting their poems to a jazz accompaniment. The cosmopolitan atmosphere of Liverpool was reflected in the wide variety of music performed around the city. The art set, mentioned above, liked to frequent pubs and clubs where Old English folk ballads could be heard one night and avant-garde poetry 'n' jazz the next, while outside in dark alleys roistering sailors sang ribald songs about Maggie May, the legendary Liverpool prostitute, and looked for a "knee-trembler," a few cheap minutes of furtive sex up against a wall.

Then there were the clubs (like the Cavern, which opened in 1957) where traditional and modern jazz could be enjoyed. The more studious buffs had read up on the music and there was a fringe who'd memorized record matrix numbers. The latest jazz names from the London scene were much appreciated.

Unlike the Southern Counties, there was a large and well-organized following for country-and-western music and lore up in Liverpool. The top gathering place was the Philharmonic, a sort of Lancastrian Grand Ole Opry, where Slim Whitman, Ernest Tubb, and other riders of the vinyl range were celebrated and saluted by local look-alikes. Ten-gallon hats, high-heeled boots, and Western drawls were much in evidence, while on the bandstand Mersey cowboys twanged out the songs of hill and range on big, booming acoustic guitars. To most people, the guitar was associated solely with the Wild West.

The intensity of the jazz and country buffs was offset by Lancashire's continuing ability to turn out comedians, particularly drolls. Gracie Fields, George Formby, and Frank Randle all hailed from here and each had been a number-one cinema star in Britain during the thirties and early forties. Each was expert at playing knowledgeable simpletons: "I may look daft, but watch out!" They were country-canny, a wily combination and one likely to get hold of cash and keep it. More recently, the city of Liverpool had spawned radio comedians like Arthur Askey and Tommy Handley and in London there was always a demand for Northern funnymen. Southerners found their accents alone a source of much mirth.

But the best outlet for comedians—live theater—was on its last legs in Britain. The music hall had been on the decline since the end of World War I and the start of the American cultural invasion. The comedians had fought bravely against stupid Yankee jizzy-jazz, jitterbuggery, and crooning, but it was a losing battle. Yet, somehow in the 1950s, music halls still existed and still presented stand-up comedy. Liverpool boasted hundreds of halls and, in them, despite the barbarians of rock 'n' roll howling outside and soon to tread those very boards, could be heard songs on the sacred subjects of boiled beef and carrots and recalcitrant mothers-in-law.

Of late, however, blue material had been slithering in. Comics winked and leered at skimpily clad chorus girls; there were lots of jokes about wanting to climb the north face of one of Marilyn Monroe's twin peaks. Comedian O. Stoppit was hauled up before a judge for lewd language and gestures in a public hall on numerous occasions, but in 1957, O. Stoppit got off lightly. He used as his excuse that he had been doing an impression of Elvis Presley. The judge understood. These were not lewd gestures but a comment on an American crooner who was threatening the very fibers of civilization. Fair game for satire.

The youngsters were getting out of control, no question. Before this rock 'n' roll fad, youngsters had looked and acted like diminutive adults. They had worn suits and ties and caps and hats and they had listened to the music of the shop-girl adults and had done what they were told, in the hope that they'd soon meet Miss or Mr. Right, but now the youngsters had become "teenagers," a separate class of humanity. They were casting about for their own "identity," mainly by trying on new costumes and customs, to the accompaniment of American rock 'n' roll. And in their rejection of the glorious days of Empire, the teenagers had been encouraged by recent events. In 1956, Britain had finally lost its "Great" in the botched invasion of Egypt. From then on,

Britain was to be a second-rate power, later sliding to an even lower position in world politics.

Within Britain, it became the sport to poke fun at our institutions and class structure. John Osborne's petulant scream of a play, *Look Back in Anger,* was hailed cheerfully by disillusioned intellectuals and fit neatly into the demolition work of the Angry Young Men brigade. Teenagers had no interest in this, though. But they did warm to the anti-Establishment hijinks of BBC-Radio's "Goon Show." Using an aural surrealism (or childish nonsense, as some saw it), the Goons hacked away weekly at the idea of Empire. Peter Sellers (as Major Denis Bloodnok) seemed the epitome of bloody old fools. On record, he was produced by Parlophone's George Martin.

America provided our teenagers with the rebel image portrayed to its finest surl and stutter by James Dean and Marlon Brando. The motorcycle, hitherto associated with adult speedway sports and the working-class family "car" (by way of a sidecar attachment for the wife and/or kiddie), now became the weapon of the leather-boy gang. But on foot, Britain's teens came up with their own contribution in the Teddy Boy, whose costume was guaranteed to annoy old fogies because it was a parody of the Edwardian dandy. This fashion seems to have originated in London and its life-style consisted largely of lounging around street corners and coffee bars looking for action, usually of the milder kind: a scuffle here, a coiffure mussed up there, and maybe a slashing or two. Coffee cups were a popular item for throwing around, but these proved hard to destroy, as they were now made of plastic. The Teddy Boy gangs felt like rebels, even if they didn't effect a rebellion, and the *feel* was the important thing. A certain satisfaction in dissatisfaction.

Bill Haley's music and films had provided an excuse for mildly riotous behavior, though most of it was the invention of febrile press minds. In 1957 when he toured Britain, he turned out to be a rather benign and avuncular figure. As a rocking and roly-poly square-dance caller, he was easily eclipsed by the more menacing image and sound of Elvis Presley, who reeked of a sex appeal that found a home in the hearts of both boys *and* girls. He was also the perfect model for quasi-rebels everywhere—a singing Dean and Brando—and was, in fact, deeply influenced by both these stars. After Presley, the door was open for the wild men of early rock 'n' roll: Gene Vincent, Jerry Lee Lewis, Little Richard, Chuck Berry, Eddie Cochran, and so on. It was a wonderful time to be young because, for a short spell, while the music industry reeled in disbelief, wild, uncontrolled, real rock 'n' roll was allowed to run free. In Britain, the Teddy Boy gangs were ready to exchange their metal-studded belts and bicycle chains for guitars. Haley and Presley had introduced the idea of the guitar as a weapon. No longer was this instrument for cowboys and Spanish fandangos.

It wasn't long, of course, before Britain's Tin Pan Alley started manufacturing its own rock 'n' rollers—and a pathetic bunch they were. The best of them, like Tommy Steele, soon found their true calling as inheritors of the music-hall tradition, because comedy was their best bent. Meanwhile, the London pop bosses kept trying to find a British answer to Presley and agents like Larry Parnes served up countless young studs with sexy names to TV producer Jack Good, who did his best to dramatize this rather dim material. At least the theatrical potential of R&R came across. All over Britain, the kids began to realize that to be a rock star you had to join the ranks of show business by getting apprenticed to the big boys in London, the fat old blokes with the permanent lunch tables at Soho restaurants. You had to go through the mill and you had to obey.

Rock 'n' roll, with its electric guitars and amplifiers and maybe a few horns, seemed, at this point, rather inaccessible and expensive. You had to have flash; you had to be in movies and on TV.

But, almost at the same time as the arrival of the American rock giants, there sprang up in Britain a musical style that required little capital outlay, little musical ability, and much team spirit and enthusiasm: skiffle. It could well have been part of the Boy Scout movement, a fitting end to a jamboree, a nice singalong around the campfire, but actually skiffle had its origins in the British revivalist jazz movement, which had arisen in the 1940s as a reaction to the dull commercial dance band music of that time. The jazzers sported beards and pipes, blasted hot, New Orleans-style jazz in their suspenders with their shirts hanging out, and believed that in their resurrection of old sounds made by even older black men lay The Truth.

As already noted, the man directly responsible for starting the skiffle craze was Lonnie Donegan. He'd been a banjo player for Chris Barber in one such revivalist band and, during breaks when the other players were sinking pints of beer, Donegan entertained the customers with his library of American folk songs culled from record and songbook. His taste was wide, ranging from Leadbelly's field hollers and the dust bowl experiences of Woody Guthrie to 1920s novelties like "Does Your Chewing Gum Lose Its Flavor on the Bedpost Overnight?" One of the Leadbelly songs, "Rock Island Line," was released on a jazz EP and rapidly rose to the top of the charts, starting a craze for skiffle group music. Nobody outside of jazz circles knew or cared about the origins of the word "skiffle." What was really attractive was that this music could be made easily and cheaply and played in ensemble.

To start a skiffle group, all that was necessary was to buy an acoustic guitar (skiffle guitars were being advertised for as little as £5) and learn no more than three chords; the bass was effected with a tea chest, broomstick, and string; the rhythm was scrubbed out on a washboard. After "Rock Island Line," skiffle groups and clubs mushroomed all over Britain. The early British rock stars—Tommy Steele, Marty Wilde, Cliff Richard, Adam Faith—had mostly started their careers as skifflers. The fad was at its height in 1957, but it faded pretty fast, since the music was extremely limited and most of its fans were lured into the brighter and more contemporary picture of rock 'n' roll. And it was in London that the more promising skifflers were nurtured into stars by the pop music establishment.

Teddy Boys, rock 'n' roll, skiffle, and general antisocial behavior had all been observed carefully from up North in the land of the jam buttie, tripe dinner, and cloth cap. In Liverpool, the youths were to steer teen entertainment on a course that was eventually to transcend the island's boundaries and transform Britain from an occupied country into an Invader. Two of the main reasons were *isolation* and *the rough life*.

Though they were isolated from London, the Liverpool lads had adopted the crazes of their Southern brothers. Those who could afford it bought Teddy Boy suits; the rest made do with bolo ties made from shoelaces. They went to see "Rock Around the Clock," hoping for a riot but finding serenity instead. The young John Lennon was all prepared to do some seat-ripping but, as nobody else seemed keen, he decided against it. Like his friends, he formed a skiffle group. The country-and-western buffs sneered at these rank amateurs with their cheap guitars and lack of spangle and spur. "They'll not last long," they said. "They'll soon be back to their brick-bashing and gang warfare."

But, as is often the case in isolated areas, the skiffle fad lasted much longer in Liverpool than in London. Far from being just another passing novelty, it was taken quite seriously by certain boys who were musically inclined but couldn't read music. Many of the songs, like "Last Train to San Fernando," were no different from any of the cherished country songs. Liverpool itself contributed a folk song, "Maggie May," which got on the B side of a hit by London's Vipers.

But by the late fifties, even Liverpool's skifflers were finding that old folk songs, whether American or Liverpudlian, weren't enough. Elvis and his big guitar had presented a challenge and a quest. So the Alan Caldwell Skiffle Group became Rory Storm and the Raving Texans and then, finally, Rory Storm and the Hurricanes. The Gerry Marsden Skiffle Group became Gerry and the Pacemakers; the James Boys lost their folk/cowboy image and changed their name to Kingsize Taylor and the Dominoes. The Blue Genes expanded into the Swinging Blue

Jeans. Eventually, the Quarry Men, John Lennon's skiffle group, went slick and Yank with their new name, Johnny and the Moondogs, but local rockers didn't dig them at all. Musically, very fake.

At first, the Liverpool rock groups took material from the song classics of the wild men—Elvis, Little Richard, and Jerry Lee—but they soon found that these songs didn't stand up when removed from the drama of the recorded performance. For example, "Whole Lotta Shakin' Goin' On" is really a reflection of Jerry Lee's personality; it hardly exists without him. To separate these sounds from their originators was like doing "Mammy" without Al Jolson. The singer was the song.

But one thing the Liverpool groups weren't about to do was copy the smooth pop star professionals from Down South. There were several reasons for this.

The Northern groups might admire the musical skill of an act like the Shadows and the power and presentation of a Billy Fury, but while in London rock 'n' roll was being organized into a manageable business that could be safely termed "pop" by 1960, in Liverpool the lads were left to their own devices. There were no managers or record companies to underwrite the purchase of electric guitars and amplifiers and drums. There were no A&R men to supply them with the hot new releases from America or material from London publishers that might pass as rock 'n' roll; no one to provide ballads that could be beefed up with a light beat.

The Northern rock 'n' rollers were free agents in a setting of oppression. High unemployment, a high crime rate, vile slums, and viler food left the kids with one way out: music. And one of the sources of music was the ocean liner. From the seamen came stacks of American 45s: rare ones, obscure ones, records that had never been near a chart, never been played on overground radio. R&B and rockabilly and sounds you couldn't categorize from companies nobody had ever heard of. The enterprising seamen who brought back these gems were called the "Cunard Yanks" by the Liverpool locals. Of course, records weren't the only treasures brought back from abroad. They brought American cigarettes like Lucky Strike ("It's Toasted"), real Levi's, and American *Action Comics*. Like the Irish, the younger Liverpudlians looked to America as their adopted motherland. There was certainly no place for them down in the Home Counties.

So it was that the rock boys found a rough, tough music that not only fit their life-style in dirty old Liddypool but also gave them a sound that was far removed from the polite, high-stepping pop/rock of London's Shadows and the industry-controlled sex rock of, say, Billy

Fury (who hailed from Liverpool but had been metamorphosed by Rock Svengali Larry Parnes).

Who were the American recording artists that helped forge the Northern sound? Above all others, King Elvis. Then, of course, every R&R group owed a debt to Buddy Holly and the Crickets, the first self-contained guitar group—they played it all themselves and they wrote their own songs. Also, the wide-open spacing of the Everly Brothers' vocal harmonies appealed much more than the rather cloying, close-voicing of, say, the Platters. And even on otherwise run-of-the-mill pop/rock records, such as those by Connie Francis and Ricky Nelson, there were very often knockout guitar solos by unidentified players that were worth a painstaking copy job. Every now and then, a simple guitar-riff instrumental would show up in the charts—like Bill Justis's "Raunchy." All of these were simple and easy to play, with plenty of emphasis on feeling. Not dauntingly technical like modern jazz, they were good models on which to build an identifiable style.

But all of these artists were obtainable on vinyl at local record stores. At the NEMS record department in Liverpool ("The Finest Record Selection in the North"), the manager, Brian Epstein, took pride in the store's ability to fill special requests. And the fact is, that a good deal of American ethnic music was getting released in Britain by 1960. On the blues front, there were locally pressed albums by Champion Jack Dupree, Memphis Slim, and lots by Big Bill Broonzy and the ubiquitous Sonny Terry and Brownie McGhee. Together with Muddy Waters and Howlin' Wolf, those exemplars of country-cum-big-city-blues, these were the sounds studied and re-created by the largely London-based R&B bands. In fact, these R&B scholars could be termed classicists because they took care to duplicate the hallowed black originals—and sometimes the contrast between sound and picture was amazing.

The middle-class taste of the Southerners was not echoed by the less-fastidious Northerners. They had no time for preservation. There were too many decaying, sooty buildings around Liverpool without introducing more museum pieces, besides, that's what the jazzers were about. No, the young Liverpudlians were pragmatists, taking the music that they needed for their current circumstances. They adapted American music to their locale.

And the American music they took as their coal was brought in by the "Cunard Yanks." They favored hard-driving, bass-heavy, up-to-date black rhythm and blues and it's amazing from how far afield their fave rave 45s came. They liked the revivalism of the Isley Brothers ("Shout"), the New Orleans yarn-spinning of Benny Spellman ("Fortune Teller"), the "Hippy Hippy Shake" as described by a Chicano from Montana, Chan Romero, and especially that Detroit hymn to the bottom-line necessity of "Money" by Barrett Strong. The latter was on the Detroit Anna label, a prototype of the new Tamla/Motown sound, and the Liverpudlians were on to that style long before the rest of Britain.

Oddly enough, there were local groups who were attracted to black-girl vocal acts like the Marvelettes, the Shirelles ("Boys"), the Orlons, and the Ribbons. In particular, Johnny and the Moondogs (now calling themselves the Silver Beatles in homage to the Crickets) did a good deal of these songs in tremulous falsetto, which seemed pretty drippy to some of the local fans. Anyway, the Moondogs/Silver Beatles weren't really in the running in 1960. They didn't even have a regular drummer—and drums were the essence of what would soon be called the Liverpool sound. The groups were Beat Merchants and what they took from their imported American models was that pounding beat. Not for them the poetry of the blues or the rhythmic cross patterns of black drumming; they laid down their beat like a pneumatic drill, pounding with almost military precision and almost on the beat, rather than the subtler offbeat. The *whump* and *thud*, like work boots on city cobblestones, were faster and heavier than the American style. There was competition on Merseyside to be champion long-distance drummer, to bang hardest, loudest, and longest. Ringo Starr of Rory Storm and the Hurricanes was a pretty thick thumper, but Johnny Hutch of Cass and the Casanovas could claim the title for endurance: he said that if they removed his brain, his body would continue to beat on, regardless.

So Merseybeat was hard and fast and relentless. Filling in the chords was a *chunk-chunk-clog* made possible by two or even three harmony guitars. One, of course, took the lead lines, but the others provided the essential rhythm sound, thick and starchy and solid as a North Country dumpling. Providing a rudimentary bass was a bass guitar, usually plodding along on root notes. There was a demand for louder and weightier amplification and local boffins came up with tall gadgets called "coffin amps."

The beat groups needed the stodgy beat and the extra power because, pragmatically, they had to make themselves heard above the din of the burgeoning Liverpool beat scene. By the turn of the decade, the most unlikely places had become beat clubs. At first, it had been small cafés and cellar clubs, but now even the once-jazz-proud Cavern had given way and was booking beat groups, as was another jazz castle, the Iron Door Club. Dance halls, like the Rialto, Riverside, and Orrel Park ballrooms, allowed the big beat alongside the quick step. Litherland Town Hall put on beat bashes, as did the Avenue Cinema—and the groups were even allowed to set up shop in ice rinks like the Silver Blades.

By the summer of 1961, the beat scene was big enough to support its own newspaper, *Mersey Beat*. Its editor, Bill Harry, chronicled the comings and goings of all the name groups—Faron's Flamingos, Lee Curtis and the All Stars, the San Remo Four, Ian and the Zodiacs, the Searchers, etc.—and, by so doing, he gave the scene a sense of cohesion and identity that it had hitherto lacked. He also gave a disproportionate amount of space to the Beatles, probably because he was an old art school pal of the group's leader, John Lennon.

Spotted throughout the early *Mersey Beat* was the quirky writing of John Lennon. His pieces sat uneasily between the hard news and the handouts concerning the comings and goings of the Beat Merchants. His writing would have been more at home in the pages of some little arts quarterly or experimental writing magazine. But editor Harry admired the Lennon style for its "Englishness" and "pure rustic wackiness," springing not only from the Lennon imagination but also from a long tradition in Britain for wordplay and punning. Practitioners who'd inspired Lennon included Edward Lear and Spike Milligan, scriptwriter for the "Goon Show." *Mersey Beat* was perhaps just the right outlet for a native writer responding in his own tongue to the weird and wacky outpourings of America's Beat Generation (so admired among the avant-garde of Liverpool poetry cellars and clubs).

In volume one, number one of the *Beat*, there was a column headed "A short diversion on the dubious origins of the Beatles, translated from the John Lennon." Apparently, the pun name had come in a vision—a man appeared on a flaming pie and said unto them, " 'From this day on, you are Beatles.' 'Thank you, Mister Man,' they said, thanking him." Fans and friends recognized John's poetic, potted history as very funny and pretty accurate. The column covered their progress from vision to reality, noting the need for bass, amps, and drums; the Teutonic apprenticeship in Hamburg; and the return to Liverpool Village, where they found a scene slick with gray-suited groups. "Why have you no gray suits?" demanded Jim, a beatster who was playing the game in the middle of the tracks.

"We don't like them, Jim."

In the new beat trade were quite a few Jims who considered these Beatles to be living on cloud nine. Sure, the girls squealed and followed them home, but were these Beatles really serious about making it nationwide? About getting onto BBC radio and maybe TV; about getting as big as the Shadows or Cliff? Or were they just an extension of the art institute crowd, using beat music as a means toward an artsy-fartsy "happening"? These anarchic free-form "happenings" were the "in" thing among the modern art mob. One year the art students were taking up skiffle, next year it was trad jazz, and now they were muscling in on the beat scene. Dabblers, it was suggested, should get back to dabbling and let the other lads who've paid their dues earn their bread and butter in this business. . . .

Bob Wooler thought otherwise. A local club disc jockey and announcer (notably at the Cavern), he wrote a perspicacious article for the *Beat* in August '61, pronouncing the Beatles the number-one group. He knew his music—the imported sounds that formed the bedrock of the Liverpool beat—having amassed a large collection of rare R&B records from the "Cunard Yanks" and others. In fact, it was he who had introduced that remarkable record by Chan Romero, "Hippy Hippy Shake," at a Cavern disc session.

The Beatles were the best, wrote Wooler, "Because they resurrected original-style rock 'n' roll music, the origins of which are to be found in American Negro singers. They hit the scene when it had been emasculated by figures like Cliff Richard and sounds like those electronic wonders, the Shadows. Gone was the drive that inflamed the emotions. This was studio set jungle music purveyed skillfully in a chartwise direction by arrangement with the A&R men." And Wooler was canny enough to realize that the Beatle appeal wasn't solely due to their music. How they looked was an important ingredient: they were "unmindful of uniformity of dress." No gray suits here. They were "unkempt, liked long hair. *Rugged yet romantic, appealing to both sexes* [my italics], with calculated naïveté and an ingenious [perhaps "ingenuous" is what he meant] throwaway approach to their music. Effecting indifference to audience response and yet always saying 'thank you' . . . I don't think anything like them will happen again."

Also contributing articles to the *Beat* was Brian Epstein. Every week, he wrote up the new releases and, on the same page as Wooler's Beatle rave, Epstein recommended a new recording by the "superb" jazz singer Nina Simone; he also noted the "increasing popularity" of the Shadows and that they were now going Hawaiian with their record "Kon Tiki." He foresaw a large turnout for the George Mitchell Singers when they played Liverpool that Christmas. The Mitchell Singers were part of a popular TV series, "The Black and White Minstrel Show," a revival of the burnt-cork minstrel shows.

Epstein sold a lot of copies of the *Beat* at his record store. He approved of the way Bill Harry had given the local scene a voice—and a neat and well-organized voice at that. He liked to leaf through the paper and note the groups he'd had record requests for. He made inquiries of Harry. Were such-and-such under a recording contract? Was so-and-so reliable? He spoke in a polished and plummy upper-class voice; he shot his cuffs a lot; he picked lint from his smartly tailored jacket. An unlikely follower of the beat scene. Nobody'd ever seen him at any of the clubs. One of his employees, Gary, said that Sibelius was more to his taste.

Gary often found Brian gazing at a certain photograph in the *Beat*. "He seemed captivated by it," he says. "It was one taken when the Beatles were in Germany and they were standing in a dirty industrial area which had a sign saying HANNOVER. The lads were in their leather-gear stage, all James Dean-moody, all holding their instruments. They were tousled and grotty and dangerous, but they still looked like runaway schoolboys. John was in the center, cradling his guitar and looking even meaner than the others because of his slitty, almost Far Eastern eyes."

Mongolian eyes, scheming dreams. An erotically shaped guitar, pointing suggestively. An armed wolf. When Brian noticed Gary watching him, he blushed furiously. It was a habit and Gary knew some of Mr. Epstein's habits. For a long time, the fantasy photo was not seen around the store. It was in an out-of-date issue anyway. Then, one day in October 1961, Epstein asked Gary in that clipped and slightly distant accent: "What's all this fuss about the Cavern and where exactly is it?"

Two different worlds were about to meet.

Though he was a Liverpudlian, Epstein had been raised far away from the hurly-burly of working-class life there. The son of a prosperous furniture dealer, he had had a well-protected childhood closeted away from the Liverpool of the Great Depression, safe among all the comforts of a luxurious home and doting parents. As a child, he was fond of sagely reviewing his mother's costume prior to her departure for an evening's entertainment. He loved it when they took him to the theater because he loved romance and fantasy and the gorgeous costumes. He kept all the theater programs neatly stacked in his room. He loved style and refinement in the world-at-large and he drew satisfaction from the textures and surfaces of objets d'art.

He despaired when he was sent away to a boarding school for a privileged education. The rough-and-tumble, the lack of order, the anti-Semitism, the camaraderie; none of this was his style. The next boarding school was no better, but he did well at art and design. He begged to be taken away and, at fifteen, his wish was granted. A difficult, sensitive soul, but our boy just the same. Perhaps he'd find his feet in the family business.

But Brian shocked his parents by informing them that he wished to go to London to be a dress designer or to study art. They proposed National Service, which they hoped would straighten him out. He was discharged on "medical grounds." He was accepted, however, by the Royal Academy of Dramatic Art, but he never finished the course. So he returned to the family fold, joining the furniture business as a privileged executive. Here, at last, he showed promise. He proved to be an excellent salesman and an imaginative window dresser. He couldn't relax until things were just so. If a picture was even slightly askew, his life was in disarray until it was straightened.

Then, in 1959, his father appointed him manager of a new NEMS record store right in the city center. Brian ran a tight ship here—and a happy one, too. Though some of his employees found his temperament rather mercurial, they all agreed that he was meticulously fair and always well mannered. To most people, he seemed a very eligible bachelor—rich, stylish, Public School accented, and passably good-looking in a corrugated-hair and slightly milksop manner; an upper-class fifties' look. As he whizzed off for the evening in his smart-looking car, there were many girls at NEMS who wished they were his Miss Right.

But there was a night world in another Liverpool that sometimes drew him in. He had a taste for quick and violent sex with strange men. His preference was for "rough trade"—truck drivers, servicemen, oiks and yobs and riffraff who could be solicited only in the seedier parts of the city. It was a dangerous game in which blackmail often played a part and getting beaten up was inevitable. The working classes had many names for homosexuals and one of their favorite sports was "queer-bashing."

The immaculate executive with the fastidious taste in art saw beauty in the beast and drew pleasure from brutal humiliations.

When he saw the photograph in the Beat, it was John Lennon—wild, butch, and wolflike—who attracted him. And business—legal business could take him to the Cavern.

He was at a crossroads in his life. No signposts helped him, only a nagging urge to be creative, to do something in the arts. A challenge was needed, some project to absorb his restless energy and give him dreamless sleep, to put his talents and drive to full use, so that he would rise above the pygmies of Northern middle-class life.

John Lennon was looking for ways to escape, too. He'd more than fully stretched himself—he'd lurched, staggered, fallen down, and gotten up again to continue his frantic barge through life. Like Epstein, he was unfulfilled, but his background was very different. Lennon's blood and bones were Liverpool-Irish with a touch of the gypsy and he came from a broken home. Yet, even in his working-class circumstances, he'd had a good share of warmth and comfort. His Aunt Mimi had raised him in a nice house in a quiet residential neighborhood. Below his window were fields; from not far away could be heard the cries of golfers. He liked reading, particularly about the schoolboy escapades of Just William (a sort of British Huck Finn). At school, he wrote and illustrated comic books for his friends.

But when the Teddy Boy era arrived, he became an instant convert and was soon reputed to be among the worst of the winkle-pickered, razor-toting hoodlums. Some demon drove him howling through the city streets, instigating many a punch-up and more, bearing a heavy load of chips on those ever-hunched shoulders. His Aunt Mimi was perplexed. She'd always given him the best she could afford and had instilled in him the virtues of honesty, politeness, and decency. But he refused to stand up when the national anthem was played; if he was told not to smoke, then he took to smoking; if sex was taboo, then he had to try it. He was a born rebel.

Fortunately, rock 'n' roll and then skiffle came along to capture his imagination and energy. Razor and brick were exchanged for guitar, singing heroes took the place of hooligans. First he wanted to be Elvis, but Elvis came from Harmony Heaven, U.S.A. Next he formed a skiffle group, the Quarry Men. A name close to home. There was never any question about who the leader was. Not that he was ever a real organizer in the sense of attending to details like punctuality and planned practicing. John operated more mysteriously, providing a *spiritual* leadership in everything he got involved with.

And there was an abundance of spirit in that first group, more spirit and enthusiasm than actual musical ability. None of the members knew how to tune a guitar. They were John's gang, in for a laugh, carried along by the idea of commanding attention, creating a "happening." Who cared about loyalty to the skiffle folk canon? Just howl and shout and jump for joy! Leader John was as likely to suddenly burst out with a garbled version of "Blue Suede Shoes" as to sing solemnly of troubles for blacks on the old cotton plantation. In fact, he never had much time for the real folk stuff, American or British. He hated research; he liked fast music that was all dressed up and ready to go. He didn't bother to learn the proper chords before performing in public. As for lyrics—if he couldn't remember them, he'd make them up as he went along.

Paul McCartney was Liverpool-Irish, too. But some Celtic Twilight had stained his soul. He'd preferred reading *Rupert Bear* to *Just William*. He liked the wistful and nostalgic songs his dad strummed out on the parlor piano. His dad had played in a dance band and knew lots of the sturdy standards of the twenties and thirties, four-square melodies with ice-cream-brick harmonies. Paul developed a good ear for chords and their more sinuous changes. In the skiffle era, he took to the guitar, learning all the basic chords from *Play in a Day*. A stickler for studying a subject till he'd mastered it, he soon learned to whoop like Little Richard and to sing as high as the Everly Brothers. He'd also learned the correct words to a heap of rock 'n' roll songs, including Eddie

Cochran's "Twenty Flight Rock"—an accomplishment that impressed John Lennon when they first met at a garden fete.

Paul's all-around musical ability and his ambition (well concealed behind a fetching smile) won him a place in the group. John, though perpetually at sea and dead proud to be journeying without maps, must have recognized the need for solid anchormen: Paul was permitted to bring in his school friend George Harrison, a rather dour personality streaked with earnestness and possessed by a grim determination to play decent lead guitar. Blessed with little innate musicality, he had by this time learned some of Arthur "Guitar Boogie" Smith's tricky runs, as well as the five-note blues riff on the hit single "Raunchy." Biting his lip till it bled and frowning all the while as he grappled with his craft, Harrison provided Lennon with some much-needed solid guitar work—and also a butt for John's often cruel humor. Stolid and serious, George posed no threat to the leadership. Paul was a source of constant musical discoveries: "Come on over, John. I've found a smashing chord!" Increasingly, John and Paul would ensconce themselves in the McCartney house to put together their own songs, written around current hits and utilizing their latest harmonic discoveries. Even then, John tended to specialize in the words, while Paul came up with strong diatonic melodies.

Gradually, the Quarry Men's founding members—the schoolmates who'd been in it for the larks and giggles—dropped out. The gigs were getting serious, but serious in the wrong direction as far as Paul's show-business designs were concerned. There was too much of the vagaries of art college in the air. In particular, the Quarry Men desperately needed a regular drummer—how could they rock without a beat?—and yet John let that mystical abstract painter Stu Sutcliffe into the band. Stu might know what to do with a paintbrush, but he certainly hadn't a clue about bass playing. Rock 'n' roll was for him a defiant stance, a kind of living sculpture. Its promise of wild abandon performed with sulky looks fit well with the James Dean persona he'd carefully created for himself. John was beguiled by Stu's style—his dress, his slouch, and his commitment to art. Through Stu he'd come across Van Gogh, the perfect example of the rebel artist doomed to be misunderstood in his lifetime, painting for the hell of it. A heady brew. Of course, all this was airy-fairyland to Paul: the point was, Stu couldn't play bass worth shit.

The boys hung out at the Jacaranda coffee house, one of a myriad of operations run by a feisty Welshman named Allan Williams. To him, this group was no more than "a right load of layabouts." Sketching, yarning, and rapping, watching the workers and students go by outside, they could kill a whole day quite happily. However, Williams did admit they had some talent as artists. They painted a marvelous mural in his cellar and, when he casually turned impresario, he commissioned John and Stu to design and build the floats for his Liverpool Arts Ball, a copy of the real London affair.

By now, the boys had abandoned the skiffle-sounding Quarry Men name and taken up a faster one, Johnny and the Moondogs. In return for their services (which had included odd jobs around the Jac and serving the occasional jam buttie), Williams agreed to let them audition for visiting impresario Larry Parnes—*the* Larry Parnes, Mister Rock 'n' Roll from London, the Rock Svengali with the stable of working-class lugs he'd groomed and greased into shiny sex objects for all persuasions. Mr. Parnes was Up North to get cut-rate backing groups for his Furys, Powerses, Prides, and Wildes. Word had reached the South about the rising Liverpool beat scene, particularly Rory Storm and the Hurricanes. Rory's incredible stage leaps had become legend.

For the audition, John decided they needed a slicker name, something to prick up the ears. Stu came up with "Beetles" after John had given him the Crickets as a model name. John laughed and liked "Beetles" but couldn't resist changing it to "Beatles"—a pun on the Mersey "beat," something to ponder. Everybody else on the scene thought it was bloody stupid and typical of art idiots who'd never make the Big Time.

There were to be other more established and more competent groups at the audition—like Derry and the Seniors and, of course, Rory Storm. Cass, of Cass and the Casanovas, generously suggested to John that it might be more commercial to call his group Long John and the Silver Beatles. John vacillated, then compromised on Silver Beatles alone.

At any rate, names didn't matter because the Silver Beatles weren't very impressive, what with Stu playing with his back to Mr. Parnes and an ageing, hired drummer staggering in halfway through their performance. The more likely groups were engaged. But later, because he still needed cheap backups, Mr. Parnes used the Silver Beatles behind one of his lesser lugs, Johnny Gentle. The band performed satisfactorily on a Scottish tour and Allan Williams, surprised and pleased, started getting them more bookings and soon drifted into becoming their ad hoc manager.

The Silver Beatles now began the slow-but-crucial process of winning their spurs in the ghastly arena of the local beat game. Dance dates had become a cue for the gangs of thugs and Teds to come together and rip it up. Bike chains whirled, switchblades flew, eye-gouging was not unknown. There were a couple of murders (one at a Silver Beatles gig). The birds were no better behaved than the boys— scratching and tearing rival Judys and flinging themselves onto the stage for a grope at their idols. Later, in the ladies' lavatory, they liked to list on the wall the sexual attributes of their fave musicians, for in the alleyway and in the back of the group van they'd done exhaustive field work.

The most notorious spot for gang violence was the Garston Baths, better known as "the Blood Baths." The musical entertainment was very much a background factor here. In order to combat the rampant thuggery, management organized flying squads of tanklike bouncers. Clad in siren suits with black-leather accessories and armed with heavy oak clubs, these bouncers came to be more feared than the gangs. Pitched battles between gangs and bouncers had all the blood-spilling and bone-crunching of Arthurian times, with none of the romance or chivalry, but it must be remembered that the standard had been set by their fathers and forefathers. For at least a hundred years, Liverpool had been second only to Glasgow in violence.

John Lennon was not known as a wallflower. He enjoyed picking a good brawl and was an expert at the traditional art of "butting"—charging in, head down, like a furious goat. But at places like "the Blood Baths," he held his peace and the Silver Beatles retreated when the fur began to fly. But it was a testament to their growing popularity, especially among the Judys, that gangs would sometimes waylay them after a gig. One night, after appearing at Litherland Town Hall, they were attacked. Stu Sutcliffe was kicked in the head but, despite considerable loss of blood, he refused to see a doctor. His death a few years later was probably caused by this incident.

The Silver Beatles now had devoted fans; they were becoming a cult. The early fans remember having to hold up broomsticks with microphones attached in the days at the Jac when the Silver Beatles didn't have mike stands. Even at this time, they had no regular drummer. A colorful mess.

Just as they were getting fed up with the bloody gigs and the odd casuals (they'd backed up a stripper named Janice with such numbers as "Sabre Dance" and "The Harry Lime Theme"), they got a chance to break away. Allan Williams had chanced upon a German club owner who was looking for rock 'n' roll bands for his Hamburg club. Williams dispatched one of the more accomplished bands, Derry and the Seniors. The reports back were excellent. The Germans, used to stiff Teutonic bands with a march-time complex, were very impressed by these wild and crazy English boys who could swing and "mak show." Williams was asked to send more of the same. He pushed for Rory Storm's group, but they were committed to a holiday camp summer season. Gerry and the Pacemakers, a droll-looking group but well drilled and spanky smart in their blazers topped off with serrated hankies, didn't want to leave the homeland. A pity, because the Germans would have lapped up their moving version of "You'll Never Walk Alone."

So Williams, as a last resort, unloaded the Beatles, who had dropped the "Silver" from their name, onto Hamburg. He was getting tired of their constant demands for better dates anyway, but Derry Wilkie, the Seniors' lead singer, was furious. Writing from Hamburg, he protested adamantly, saying that the Beatles were a bum group and would ruin the scene for everyone.

The Beatles left in April 1960 for the first of what would be four trips. They had gotten themselves a drummer by the name of Pete Best, who made up for his lack of solid technique by his conventional, dark good looks and general reliability.

Hamburg, like Liverpool, was a dirty old seaport. But it was closer in ambience to Sodom and Gomorrah. In the Reeperbahn pleasure district, where the British bands played, the joys of the flesh weren't furtive and concealed as they had to be in Liverpool. No cloak of Victorian guilt hung over Hamburg and the Beatles responded like any red-blooded working-class males abroad for the first time: they went overboard. The frauleins were more buxom and more prone to sexual delights. The German audiences were easy to please, provided the group "mak show" and bounced high and stomped out a steady beat. They might have to play for eight hours at a stretch, but they were coaxed on with pep pills and crates of cheap champagne. Chuck Berry, Little Richard, Jerry Lee Lewis—the repertoire of those warhorse boogie bluesmen did the trick for the Germans, although the music sometimes sounded like one long, demented screech note backed by a Chinese-torture *thump*.

The more outrageous the bands were, the more the Germans seemed to like them. John used the stage as his theater of attempted shock, addressing the customers loudly as "fucking Nazis," *Seig heil*ing merrily, coming on in only his underwear or with a toilet seat around his neck.

Back at their lodgings, the free-form life continued. John urinated from his window onto passing churchgoers below; excrement was deposited quite often on the floor rather than in the lavatory. Yet, during all this muck-spreading, the Beatles were also learning to play many kinds of pop music, building up a large repertoire, watching other British bands, and putting down a good stomping beat sound that was eventually admired by Derry and the Seniors, especially by sax player Howie Casey. They kept other groups awake at their lodgings with their continual late-night practicing.

Even the stage loutishness had a creative result: the band began talking to the audience onstage almost as much as they played and they developed a winning way with wisecracks, comebacks, and antiheckler one-liners. American servicemen, used to sharp and fast comics at home, were much taken by this ability. And the Beatles were beginning to attract elements of the German intelligentsia.

As far back as the Gymnasium movement of the early nineteenth century (a root factor in German nationalism) and notably in the pre-World War II years of the Children of the Sun, the Germans had taken a sharp interest in the beauty of the male physique. Britain's pederasts had flocked to Germany during the thirties because, in the words of author Christopher Isherwood, "Berlin meant boys." Street boys, rude ones with slight flaws, were much in demand among artists, but now the Germans and certain visitors were finding a hitherto-unsuspected surly sexiness in these British boys. Especially in the Beatles, with their look of fallen angels and their style that lifted them above the lumpen.

German youngsters, no less rock-inclined than the rest of the world's youth, joined the homoeroticists in their admiration of the Beatles. Other intellectual fads had left them cold: the itchy travels of the mindless American Beats, the dense word puzzles of the French existentialists. But the visual appeal of the Beatles excited them and fit snugly into German history.

Among these thoughtful admirers were Klaus Voorman and Astrid Kirchherr. She photographed them in a cold, austere, artistic manner and designed their wardrobe, taking them out of the mauve jackets, black shirts, and crocodile-gray shoes they so liked and putting them into a uniform of black leather. Leather jackets *and* trousers—very sexy, very kinky. Astrid also persuaded them to have their hair cut in a greaseless pudding-basin style, which had become popular with German boys as a reaction against the short brutal cut of the Nazi years.

Astrid had fallen in love with Stu, who became her first model, and the others followed suit. Gradually but inevitably, Stu pulled away from the gigging and settled down in Hamburg to a life as a painter, supported by Astrid.

But now the Beatles had a look and a sound. They were no longer a bunch of rowdy lugs. Each time they returned from Hamburg, their reputation and following grew. The Hamburg gig hadn't done the other groups much good professionally, though the fun had been great, and soon more and more Mersey groups were to journey out there. But the new leathered and coiffured Beatles startled the Liverpudlians. Many believed them to be a German outfit. The Cavern, now a beat center, booked them regularly and, in that stifling, sweaty, rat-infested cellar, they looked terrifying and terrific as they ran the gamut from classic rock to corny country and even Latin-American. They also threw in a lot of oddball numbers they'd learned off B sides from the Bob Wooler record collection. Though they all wore the leather gear, they otherwise had no uniformity. No timed dance steps, no neatness or cleanliness, and no current pop pap. The only tie with pop norms was the handsome and athletic Pete Best. Allan Williams and Bob Wooler considered him to be the group's strongest commercial asset. Some people thought the drummer should be moved right out front.

Liverpool and Hamburg, birds and booze and butties. The Beatles seemed to have it made. Except that John and Paul had a strong urge to break out big, to get on the national charts. To be as big as Cliff and the Shadows and for that they had to have a record. While they'd been in Hamburg on their first trip, they'd performed on a Polydor record, backing British singer Tony Sheridan as the Beat Brothers. Back home, they spread the story about how they'd made a hit record as the Beatles and they urged their fans to go out and ask for it.

At NEMS, Brian Epstein certainly had requests for this record. He diligently researched it and found it was called "My Bonnie." He now had a reason to go down to the Cavern and face that photograph. He made sure his visit would be official, ringing Bill Harry, who in turn called the Cavern's owner, who instructed the tough doorman to let the big man from NEMS in for free.

So it was that at lunchtime Thursday, November 9, 1961, a dark-suited businessman carrying a briefcase was ushered down the Cavern steps to meet a fantasy head on. Epstein witnessed a typical Beatles Cavern show—the chatting to the kids, the private jokes to each other, the stream of four-letter words, the smoking, eating, spitting, sweating, and the hard-driving, hypnotic music. His eyes kept coming back to the wild red Indian, narrow of eye, slim of hip, and cruel of mouth—John, the obvious leader.

Afterward, after two whole shows, Epstein introduced himself to Paul and George. He didn't dare speak to John.

Brian Epstein had found a way of escape and a reason for living in the Beatles. Though their world was in back alleys and cellars similar in seediness to his own night world, he had no intention of fusing this exciting discovery with quick trickery. Far from being lads of the one-night stand, these Beatles were potential brand leaders of beat. First a little window dressing was necessary, a little trimming and sewing and cleaning up. There was to be no fooling with the merchandise.

Two hundred copies of "My Bonnie" were quickly ordered. Polite inquiries were made about the ins and outs of beat group management. Allan Williams was approached and he advised Epstein not to touch the Beatles with a ten-foot pole, as they'd recently done the dirty on him by breaking their management agreement. If the tough, street-wise Welsh hustler couldn't deal with these punks, what chance was there for a genteel Public School man still wet behind the ears? No well-bred educated middle-classer had yet shown any interest in this netherland of pop, with its shrill shop girls and daft crooners and slimy managers.

Though late, the Beatles kept their appointment with Brian at the NEMS shop. Brian was already fantasizing that he would make them number one in Britain. Would they agree to let him manage them? Paul asked him to agree not to interfere with the music. No intention. John stared him straight in the eye and said, "Right, then, Brian. Manage us."

The pact was made between Brian and John and, with missionary zeal, Brian set about his task. His doubting parents were calmly but firmly informed that his boys were going to be the greatest entertainers in the world. From now on, Brian would not tolerate a word against the Beatles. Only he could scold them, sometimes strongly—with his voice high and clipped, his face bright red, and his foot stamping.

Brian was as good as his word. NEMS Enterprises, a limited company, was formed in order to get proper bookings for the group and to insure prompt payment. A management contract was drawn up and signed by the boys. Brian himself forgot to sign.

The local bookers, a tough bunch, saw Brian as a million-pound note in Penny Lane. They were amazed by his gentle but firm approach, his fairness, his invitation for them to come around to NEMS to discuss details over sherry at an exact hour. Details—these were the stuff of his operation. And they would lead to the realization of his dream. Details, not about contracts and percentages, but about being punctual at a gig. The boys were lectured long and severely on this and other items: a song order must be drawn up for each show and it must be kept to; friends from other bands must not be allowed to sit in casually; no eating or drinking or smoking or joking onstage; and they must learn a decent stage bow. Also, the leather outfits must go. They were not "rough trade." Not even rough diamonds anymore. Brian designed them a uniform: gray suit with velvet lapels. John balked, remembering his opinion of gray suits, as expressed in *Mersey Beat*. But Brian had a way of dealing with John. Didn't John long to get out of Liverpool and conquer London? John went along with the suits and then with the boots and the regular hair trimming.

One can get an idea of Epstein's meticulousness from this typical

schedule for Monday, June 25, 1962, presented to the Beatles on a
typewritten sheet:

Midday: Cavern Club (as usual).
Plaza Ballroom, St. Helen's.

Neil will call for you between 6:30 and 6:45 P.M., in order to arrive
at St. Helen's not later than 7:20 P.M. This is our first engagement
for the "Whetstone Circuit," who control sixteen venues in the
Northwest. There was some difficulty in obtaining your fee for this
booking and the directors of the Company concerned are watching
these four Monday bookings most carefully and have assured me
that, if successful, they will be pleased to use the group at other
venues on their circuit. For this first night, at least, programme con-
tinuity, (as always) suits, white shirts, ties, etc. One-hour spot.

Brian had not, however, forgotten the golden key—hit records. "Operation London" must be started. He liked calling projects "operations,"
as if he'd carefully planned them and was fairly confident of success.
Actually, he dived into such things with plenty of energy and little
knowledge, relying on instinct. "One did this, one did that. One
shouted from the rooftops," he wrote in his autobiography, *A Cellarful
of Noise*. He was hardly the man for that sort of behavior, but London's A&R men were soon to be astonished at the perseverance of this
rosy-cheeked, posh bloke from the provinces. Fancy claiming his group
was going to be bigger than Elvis! Didn't he know groups were out, except for the Shadows—and they were a national institution, were all-
arounders who could dance, too. Anyway, look at the demo material he
was touting! A hodge-podge tape of slackly played standards like "The
Sheik of Araby" from the Roaring Twenties, "September in the Rain"
from the Tired Thirties, and "Your Feet's Too Big" from Fats Waller's
repertoire. All rottenly sung and played.
    The selection reflected Brian's cautious middle-of-the-road taste.
Decca turned him down, but they did at least allow the group a test
session. The other companies wouldn't even consider that. What about
John and Paul's own songs? They seemed even worse—rough-edged
and substandard. And the drumming was decidedly pedestrian.
    However, Parlophone (one of giant EMI's many labels) needed a
stake in the pop/rock scene. George Martin, the A&R chief, was looking for an act with staying power, "a fireproof act," whose records, once
they took off, would just keep selling on the strength of the last release. Like Norrie Paramour's act, Cliff and the Shadows. There was
Norrie, bespectacled and respectable, sitting back at Columbia while

the hits rolled in. And Columbia, like Parlophone, was part of the EMI conglomerate, but Parlophone was the giant's jokey label, a Christmas cracker of novelty items: brass bands, Scottish dance bands, girl pipers, pseudo-Latin American orchestras, and the famous "Goon Show" records. Once in a while, a single might click, but they were one-of-a-kind novelties with no chance of a follow-up. Martin longed for good songs and a good musical vehicle. His talents were being wasted because he was a well-schooled musician and a fine oboist. He showed musical taste, if not commercial acumen, in having turned down the raucous Tommy Steele in favor of the more melodious skiffle group, the Vipers. Steele, of course, had gone on to become a big star. Martin had transformed the Temperance Seven from a noisy bunch of art school amateurs into a decent approximation of a twenties dance band—and he'd managed to reach number one with them. But follow-ups were hard and the novelty didn't last.

So he was hungry for a group. Maybe, just maybe, he could find a group and mold them into another Cliff and the Shadows. When Epstein appeared with his acetate (cut at an EMI shop and highly recommended by the engineer), George Martin was prepared to listen seriously. Here at least was a gentleman from roughly the same class as himself. No overt pushiness, a man who talked about "artistes" as he did and who took his own graceful time getting to the point.

Martin confessed he knew little about groups. But after he heard the acetate, he told Brian he thought he "had something very good here." He sensed a fundamental musicality and an originality that was sorely lacking in the pallid pop produced at that time. On the other hand, these Beatles weren't as troglodite as the classic rockers. Paul's voice struck him as smooth and commercial. Perhaps he had here the genesis of a group that could stack up against Cliff and the Shadows: Paul and the Beatles. He thought the group was "worth a shot" and he agreed to give them a test. At the test, they pinned great hopes on their own compositions, especially "Love Me Do," which they hoped would be an A side. Martin wasn't exactly ecstatic and he thought "Love Me Do" rather tuneless, but he still felt there was something there to be mined, so he signed the Beatles to a contract. In September 1962, they recorded their first sides.

The Beatles had done their homework and now "Love Me Do" was tighter, brighter. John had added a catchy harmonica lick, inspired by Bruce Channel's recent hit "Hey! Baby." At the test, Martin had privately expressed to Brian his doubts about Pete Best's drumming. And lo! At the actual recording session, Pete Best was replaced by a new drummer who resembled Dopey of the Seven Dwarfs; he couldn't execute a drum roll, but he was certainly a better beat-keeper than Best.

Ringo Starr, an ex-member of Rory Storm and the Hurricanes, had been on the point of emigrating to America in order to find work as a cowboy. Martin knew nothing about the furor among Best fans in Liverpool when they learned of their fave's sacking. Was it jealousy because of his popularity and sex appeal? Or was it that the taciturn Best simply wasn't a Beatle, hadn't their sense of fun, didn't complement the picture?

Certainly, Epstein now had a group with something for everyone: the brutish and canny John (with that hint of vulnerability), the cherubic and almost-pretty Paul with his smile and diplomacy, the handsome and serious George, who anchored the music with his lead guitar, and the bovine Ringo with his funny-paper appeal. The whole deal meshed, like the four Marx Brothers. Brian had the Beatles on pop tours now with big American names like Roy Orbison and Bruce Channel—and the band's acceptance outside Liverpool was more than heartening. It was slightly spooky: the audience would start to scream before the boys even started playing. The feeling was spreading and no amount of Brian's precision planning could arrange this kind of groundswell on the part of the mysterious masses.

"Love Me Do" was released on October 4, 1962, without any fanfare. George Martin's EMI colleagues thought this must be another of his comedy records (like Roland Rock-Cake and His Wholly Rollers on that Goon record). When they heard the record, they dubbed the group "Martin's Folly." But NEMS ordered ten thousand copies and this was enough to get it into the lower rungs of the charts. Eventually, by dint of natural popularity, it reached number seventeen in England. Music paper reviews were quite encouraging; the Beatles were praised for their bluesy sound.

Martin needed a follow-up and, playing it safe, pitched the boys on "How Do You Do It?", a surefire cheerful little confection by a real pro, Mitch Murray. He was amazed when his group showed no enthusiasm, putting in a grudging recording of his find. Instead, they persuaded their master to let them go to town on one of their own tunes, "Please Please Me." After some musical carpentry, Martin emerged with a strong chart contender. The church-bell descent on the opening verse lines was attractive and there was a touch of gospel excitement in some of the chord changes and harmonies. A good, lightly punning title, too.

In March 1963, "Please Please Me" was listed as number two in *Melody Maker*. In the musical context of 1963, the record was refreshing but certainly not revolutionary. It was perfectly acceptable. But a mania for everything Beatle had already started to spread, a mass conspiracy in which only the killjoys didn't participate. Beatlemania was to be a phenomenon of its times—created by special circumstances in which the actual music played but a small part—and outside the control of any organization. Certainly no one man could catch this wind.

Brian Epstein, having achieved his ambition of reaching the Big Time, felt that he could fashion more hit acts from the same source. He set to, building a Northern stable of stars along the lines of Larry Parnes. A Parnes with class and tact. Already he'd signed Gerry and the Pacemakers, commending them into the capable hands of George Martin. The easygoing Gerry went along with "How Do You Do It?" and Martin's belief in the song was proven correct: on March 23, some twenty days after the Beatles reached number two, Gerry and the Pacemakers topped the charts. On April 27, "From Me to You" by the Beatles, a rather lackluster effort with the "me" and "you" line wearing thin, was at the top and had sold half a million copies. The race was on. Next Brian signed a hulky, handsome Liverpool lad named Billy J. Kramer, who couldn't hold a note. But after some Martin tape wizardry on a workmanlike Lennon/McCartney song, "Do You Want to Know a Secret?", Billy J. Kramer (backed by a top instrumental group from Manchester, the Dakotas) reached number two in June. Soon afterward, Kramer reached number one with another Lennon/McCartney song, "Bad to Me." But Gerry, an ex-railway employee like Kramer, had already sailed to the top again with "I Like It" and later he did it again with his club-tested "You'll Never Walk Alone," the old Rodgers and Hammerstein standard. The Liverpool Football Club adopted this song as their theme.

Brian also signed up the Fourmost, the Big Three, Tommy Quickly (as a ballad singer), and even the Cavern cloakroom attendant, Priscilla White. As Cilla Black, she was groomed very carefully to be a top star of stage, screen, and record. Of course, the Beatles were the flagship of the NEMS Empire (now with offices in London, complete with a press officer).

But the Northern gold mine was not to be Epstein's alone. Liverpool was deluged with agents and record scouts. Allegedly, some even signed each other up. Tony Hatch of Pye Records went to the Iron Door Club and got the Searchers, a plum for any A&R man with an ear for the well-tailored professional. They may have been from Merseyside, but they sounded all-American and looked clean-cut. Their high harmonies were crisp and pleasing, their demeanor was full of self-confidence, and their taste in songs was excellent: they covered records by the Drifters, Jackie De Shannon, and the Orlons. Their rhythm guitar strumming was rich and jangling. Some locals reckoned the Searchers to be better and at least as popular as the Beatles. "Sweets for My Sweet," their very first single, went number one.

Other top Liverpool Beat Merchants to be given record contracts included Rory Storm and the Hurricanes, Derry and the Seniors, and Faron's Flamingos. And when they ran out of local potential—by this time there were over five hundred groups to pick from, and not a few with Beatle copycat names like Grasshoppers, Bugs, Toads—the A&R men trekked to other North Country cities. The prevailing opinion was that it was the locale that had produced the Beatles, that they were not an isolated phenomenon. A BBC-TV documentary team made a film called *The Mersey Sound* and Radio Luxembourg started a series called "Sunday Night at the Cavern." Meanwhile, in Manchester, George Martin's assistant, Ron Richards, discovered his very own Beatles in the Hollies (what a huge influence Buddy Holly had in Britain!). Like the Searchers, they showed a good knowledge of lesser-known U.S. records and their version of the old Coasters number "Searchin'" made the Top Twenty in 1963. Also from Manchester came Freddie and the Dreamers, as homely a bunch as ever made the hit parade, but with an appeal that had the children laughing at their stage antics and their mums and dads smiling with relief that here was knockabout comedy in the old tradition. Who could not rejoice in Freddie's amazing scissor leaps? The ex-milkman, with the publicized taste for a hot milk as his nightcap, was on EMI's Columbia label and, before the year was out, he had two big hits in "I'm Telling You Now" and "You Were Made for Me."

The South responded to the Northern Invasion. Decca, who had rejected the Beatles in favor of Brian Poole and the Tremeloes, were somewhat vindicated when the group's version of "Twist and Shout" went to number four. Poole hailed from Dagenham, not far from London, and Decca's thinking had been that this nearness would facilitate company and group communications. Unfortunately, Poole, a Buddy Holly fan, had a rather clerkly appearance and lacked great appeal onstage. On the other hand, Columbia felt they had London's answer to the Beatle challenge in the Dave Clark Five. Their military-bash beat and macho shouts (similar to a football crowd in full throttle) were complemented by soldier-boy good looks and a dedication to physical jerks and gym lore. "Glad All Over" made number one in November, allowing several newspapers to claim that the Tottenham sound had "defeated" the Mersey sound.

To many, including myself, the Beatles were simply the spearhead of this Northern Invasion. But there was much more to it than mere records. Print and pictures played a large part in the Beatle phenomenon of 1963 and it was the media, encouraged by a demand from the masses, that transformed it all into a true "happening." Why did the media choose this precise moment to embrace these soft toy gods?

In retrospect, it appears so simple. The summer is usually a "silly season" for news, but in 1963 there had been a thunderstorm of hard and shocking news: the Profumo scandal, involving corruption and sexual license in high places, had forever destroyed any national respect for Top People setting an Establishment example to the lowly rest. Cabinet ministers had been caught, literally, with their pants down; there were dukes, duchesses, and prostitutes involved. The Establishment was cracked forever and the image of the discreet (and thus sexless) upper-class Britisher was destroyed. A new Britain was already forming, ready to take its place. And, as if this scandal weren't enough, hard on its heels came the Great Train Robbery. Where was the silly season; where was the light-relief news?

Over the past three years, it had become apparent to the leisure industry that the teen market had become extremely lucrative—worth over £100 million a year. The kids of the baby boom years (which had started in the forties) now had money to spend and one of their chief pursuits was pop music. Rock 'n' roll hadn't gone away but had metamorphosed into pop—and this pop wasn't merely music but was also a pair of jeans, a way of walking, a hairstyle, and a way of talking.

Enter the Beatles at exactly the right time. They were a fun topic for a delayed silly season; they could be marketed as cuddly toys; they spoke in a funny Northern working-class dialect, just like the old radio comedians and the music-hall stalwarts before them; they could be pictured as four bouncing haircuts (or lack of haircuts). They were perfect media fodder. They appealed across the board.

Common but not ashamed of it, lively and active but not banging on about social deprivation like the Angry Young Men in the social-reality films, the Beatles were in it for the laughs and the money. They could send up themselves and their industry. The barriers between Them and Us, between the star and the audience and between the cat and the Queen, were down. A pop group, like a royal event, could unite the entire nation and provide a momentary escape from grim reality. Everyone—from babies who burbled about "Beakles" to the *Times* music critic who wrote of their "pandiatonic clusters"—was enthralled by them. Even Field Marshal Montgomery wanted to examine them. There had never been this universal interest in Tommy Steele or Cliff Richard. Working-class fun and frolics were about to become everybody's chic.

By Christmastime, "She Loves You," the "Yeah! Yeah! Yeah!" anthem that Paul and John had knocked off in a few minutes when they needed a new single, had sold 1½ million copies. In Dora Bryan's Christmas hit, "All I Want for Christmas Is a Beatle," she admitted not caring which Beatle she got as a present. To her, they were *all the same.* She'd hit the nail right on the head: the Beatles were *all the same,* four carefree, happy-go-lucky, moptopped, cuddly toy-boys. Beatle was royalty, was above criticism, was a national institution. But would the world take Beatle to its heart? Would they make it in America, the world center of show business? What need had people over there for such an insular phenomenon, a rocking revival of British music hall?

I felt like Scrooge. I was told I was a snob, but I didn't believe in the Beatles. In fact, I hated them because they were tearing down the proscenium arch and, from another angle, their R&B wasn't close to the real thing. No, I saw more hope in the Rolling Stones. Maybe there would be a breakthrough for authentic blues—in white face, of course. Mick Jagger certainly had more sex appeal than any of the Beatles and I had a personal stake in Jagger: already I was being mistaken for him in the streets and alleys of Dublin.

I was back at Trinity for the Easter term. It was, as usual, bitterly cold in Dublin: the fact that it was January was neither here nor there. The "eejits" (idiots) were out in force—the Witch Woman wrapped in her old newspapers, the Hanging Judge (a Trinity graduate) in his tatty judicial robes. And now I was to join them as a fellow "eejit," for, constantly, strangers would stop me on the street to ask me whether I was "that Mick Jaggers." Usually they wouldn't stay for a reply, but wend on their way with a curse, or a shake of head, or even a sign of the cross.

At first, I felt a certain amount of indignation. I felt I was better-looking than Mick Jagger, at least in the conventional sense: the rubber lips, the snake hips, the sneer—I had none of these. And I usually went out of my way to be polite to the natives, remembering past wrongs done in the name of Britain.

However, my blues band, Bluesville, was in the doldrums. We needed a shot of excitement, something to kick against. Mick Jagger and the Rolling Stones were getting a reputation as the bad boys of pop. They snarled and looked cynical, they didn't wear band suits, and they were often getting thrown out of posh hotels for not wearing ties. Mick Jagger's luxuriant hair curtained his face when he sang and he looked more like a latter-day Just William than John Lennon did. The Beatles were goody-two-shoes compared with Jagger and his Stones. Jagger's music was just right for his surly stance. Maybe now the real R&B would bust through and shake up British pop! What a pity it was a Beatle number, "I Wanna Be Your Man," that had propelled them to their current place in the Top Twenty.

Musically, I was also much more attracted to the Stones than to the Beatles. The Stones were closer to home, having sprung from the London R&B scene with a repertoire of numbers drawn from the same black blues bag as Bluesville. Socially, Jagger and Brian Jones (and maybe Keith Richards) were from a class not far removed from my own. I could empathize. My historical studies, particularly of nineteenth-century French revolutionary movements, told me that the Stones' antisocial behavior was a new version of *epater le bourgeoisie*: annoying the middle class. It was a great and safe game to play in Britain because everything was so sweetly reasonable and tranquil—and the Age of Frivolity was beginning to dawn, as we shall see.

So I decided to take a few pointers from Jagger and his band. New life might yet be breathed into Bluesville—and the blues in general. And though the older Dublin folk held me in contempt as an "eejit," I was finding that some of the colleens were offering me their favors as a result of my Jagger resemblance. It was, in fact, at this time that I received a note from one of our band followers which read: "Ian, I would like to have sexual intercoarse [sic] with you at your own convenience. Yours, Moira."

The rise of the Stones had occurred shortly after that of the Beatles. What the Cavern was to the Beatles in Liverpool, the Crawdaddy was to the Stones in Richmond and, in both cases, a canny manager played an important part as an image-maker. But here the similarities end. The Beatles, working-class lads to the bone, were like Elvis and all the pop heroes before him: they desperately wanted financial success to lift them out of the awful slough of despond into which they had been born. The three key Stones—Jagger, Richards, and Brian Jones—were middle class and not in real need of a square meal. Like Marie Antoinette and her court, they were playing at being peasants. But they took their music very seriously.

It was a seriousness not shared by the older blues aficionados. Most trad jazzers liked a bit of blues, but the older and more rural the better. What they couldn't stand were the raucous teen themes banged out by such modern black jukebox heroes as Bo Diddley and Chuck Berry. This was pandering to the children's tastes. Chris Barber, trad-jazz leader and crusader for true blues, banned the Stones from the Marquee, a London R&B stronghold. They were, he said, "unauthentic."

Mick Jagger and his sidekick Keith Richards quickly grew to hate trad jazz and its moldy old jazzers. Their up-to-date music was down to earth and they made no attempt at being commercial—no toothy smiles and rehearsed bows, no matching ties and hankies, no choreography. No bloody concessions. Only the blues! Their music was the real thing and they were just being themselves. Their music was just as authentic as the fetid field hollers uttered by the tired old blues traddies up in London: actually, the Stones were more real, more relevant—because whereas the traddies mostly held safe, clerkly jobs and journeyed home

after a gig to a hot milk and a nice family, Mick and Keith had opted
to suffer for their sound, like real artists. Already they'd lived the bohemian life by inhabiting a cold-water matchbox flat on a seedy street in
Chelsea, home of the arts—but only a few miles from the London
School of Economics, where Jagger was a student. In the flat, the blues
boys lived off naught but potatoes and Jagger, in particular, lost the
rippling muscularity he'd achieved as a teenager when he'd scaled
mountains with his physical education instructor father, Joe. I once saw
Mick and his father scaling mountains on BBC TV.

When Brian Jones first joined the group, he balked at this ascetic existence. A childhood of tender, loving care in well-to-do Cheltenham
(county town retirement spot for Empire-builders) had softened him.
He looked positively beatific, a choirmaster's delight. He was also quite
well schooled in melody and harmony. Unfortunately, he'd once played
in a trad-jazz band, but had at least appeared onstage with Blues Incorporated. Mick and Keith soon sorted him out—with the potato diet and
the aural lashings of Slim Harpo, Jimmy Reed, and Elmore James.
Soon Brian was hooked on the neurotic crybaby slide guitar of Elmore
James.

The "unauthentic" Stones eventually found permanent residence
and a sympathetic following at the Station Hotel in Richmond, a
sleepy riverside town near London. The three blues boys were backed
by some very reliable blokes, sturdy working-classers: Bill Wyman on
bass, Charlie Watts on drums, and Ian Stewart on piano. A stolid support and thin on looks, but at this stage of the game who cared about
looks? Certainly not the Stones.

However, looks—or, at least, *image*—was a most important matter to a
close-knit clique that took to descending on the Station Hotel to experience the Stones' shows: the New Aristocrats, later to be a key part of
Swinging London. The group was linked by their classlessness—cockneys mixed with earls—and by their uninterest in the past and anything
to do with Britain's glories. They lived life lightly, taking it on the
wing, and this was easy because another thing that linked the New
Aristocrats was that they had plenty of cash. Which they'd earned
honestly. There was, for example, David Bailey, the cockney fashion
photographer fabled for his luck with the ladies ("David Bailey makes
love daily" went a current folk rhyme); he would bring along his latest
flame, probably Jean Shrimpton, the skinny fashion model. In tow
might be Mary Quant, a fashion designer specializing in what she described as "sexy" clothes. She and her friends were madly attracted by
the Stones' earthy glamour.

In a wider view, the members of this image-conscious group were
denizens of the New Britain that was being celebrated—perhaps even

created—by the Sunday newspapers' latest sales promotion: the color supplement. On the creamy pages of these magazines were gritty, real-life looks at, say, starving blacks in a Third World country juxtaposed with artful spreads of fridges, furniture, and fashion. So one could see Them going without their cake, while We at home ate ours ravenously.

The Rolling Stones, a Home County band with Darkest American rhythms, were perfect putty for somebody with an eye on the main chance.

Dehem's Pub in Soho had been a writer's hangout in the twenties and thirties. Evelyn Waugh and his peers were frequent visitors, but by the sixties the pub had become a center for the new breed of pop journalists, who were joined by publicists and managers and even road managers. R&R was building a large support army. During one long, liquid lunchtime, Peter Jones of the *Record Mirror* was singing the praises of the Rolling Stones to all who wished to hear. He said they were a group to be reckoned with; they were putting out the real stuff. In this pub that same lunchtime was a teenager named Andrew Loog Oldham, who cocked an ear to Jones's eulogy. At the moment, Oldham was in the employ of Brian Epstein's NEMS Enterprises as a publicist, but he'd heard about these Stones before from Mary Quant, an ex-employer of his. He decided to take a look at this group. Like Epstein before encountering the Beatles, Oldham was restless and hungry for action, for something to engage him. He hated stuffy middle-class England because he'd been raised in it and had even attended a very minor Public School.

Beware of those who hang precariously onto the rungs of the upper-middle classes! They feel very bitter, they can be very dangerous. They can even be revolutionaries.

Oldham caught a Stones gig and at once saw the potential in the front three. Jagger could be deviled into a real sex object, Jones looked like "soft gay trade," and Richards was suitably street-thuggish. The bass player chewed a lot and looked bored, but he had a function. The drummer stared blankly into the far horizon and that was OK, too. But the pianist was too simian; he'd have to go.

Oldham brought along his financial aide, an old show-biz hand named Eric Easton, whose stable of acts included Mrs. Mills, the fat lady pianist of honky-tonk fame. Easton was impressed, but he thought Jagger's offhandedness and petulance would be too much for Auntie BBC. "He'll have to be replaced," he said solemnly. Oldham thought he must be mad. Still, Easton had the money.

Oldham went into action with a speed that befit the times. He soon had the Stones signed and recorded, choosing as their debut A side a safe Chuck Berry number, "Come On." Then he got them a spot on

"Thank Your Lucky Stars," a network lip-synched pop show televised from Birmingham. An important plug. For this appearance, he put them all in jackets and ties—except Jagger, who wore slacks and a sweater. But the surliness was still there and many viewers called in to complain. These repercussions upset the band, especially Jagger. But Oldham, who was gathering his star material ever closer under his wing, reassured Jagger that this sort of irate reaction from the stodgies was just what was wanted for success. He encouraged his star to lay on more of the pouting and the bottom-waggling and jackknife marionette movements (in the style of James Brown). Jagger agreed. Even so, he waited till success was more certain before quitting the London School of Economics.

"Come On" only made the Top Fifty, but it did get the Stones much-needed national visibility: a tour on the same bill as their idols Bo Diddley and Little Richard. The latter, a connoisseur of "camp," immediately spotted star potential in Mick Jagger, just as he had in the Beatles. But it was "I Wanna Be Your Man," surefire Beatle material, that did the trick. Naturally, to their loyal Richmond club fans, it seemed that the Stones had betrayed their R&B roots for the glitter of pop.

In February 1964, they released an exciting reworking of Buddy Holly's "Not Fade Away." Bolstering this insipid, patsy number with the Bo Diddley "shave-and-a-haircut" trademark beat, the Stones had come up with a creation that was a real commercial concoction. They were certainly onto a potent brew!

Over in Dublin, meanwhile, I had decided to cash in on my resemblance to Mick Jagger. I refused haircuts, went on a diet, and got my tailor to take in my trousers at the hips and thighs. I took to studying the pop papers again, to see what was making it on the charts. Things hadn't changed as radically as one would imagine. Ballads were still the rage and the only thing that separated them from ballads of the fifties was the new deep, chugging beat on hits such as: "Little Children" (Billy J. Kramer), "Needles and Pins" (the Searchers), and "Candy Man" (Brian Poole and the Tremeloes). And Tin Pan Alley warhorses "Diane" (from the twenties) and "I Believe" (from the fifties) had been barely altered for their entry onto the charts (by Ireland's own group, the Bachelors). Another point about these current hits: they were all American songs recorded by British acts. So had there been a revolution?

Revolution was on my mind because this school term we were studying "Working-Class Movements," with special emphasis on Karl Marx and his action disciple Nikolai Lenin. I realized that, in order to change the world, I would have to infiltrate the system. No use howling outside the Establishment's gates. This I was learning from my studies—and now I determined to apply my newfound knowledge to pop music.

"We must cut down on the ethnic blues stuff. We must aim for the charts," I told Bluesville. But they were shocked at my betrayal of our blues ideals. Besides, where do you record in Dublin? Forget it and come and have a jar of ale. Still, I knew that recording was the key and, some way or another, I was going to get us down on tape.

The band let me insert some Roy Orbison numbers; they also quite enjoyed playing "Not Fade Away." I noticed that our hard-core blues fans were falling off, but instead we were attracting intellectual types, bluestocking girl undergraduates and clean-jeaned men in quasi-military wear. They were all Beatles and Stones fans and none of them had any interest in early Elvis or indeed any of the real rock 'n' roll heroes. Still, an audience is an audience. I, of course, had the support of my political science lecturer, who continued to sing my praises in Trinity magazines, growing more eloquent each week in his analyses of what he saw as my "innate revolutionary stance, couched in a cunning cloak of flippancy."

But one night, I discovered the greatest pop weapon of all: pure sex. It happened when Bluesville was appearing for a charity function at a church in Mount Merrion. We seemed to be always playing in churches and monasteries, since the big ballrooms were still spurning R&B and R&R, preferring to stick with the Celtic all-purpose show bands. Bluesville was now surrounded by electrical devices. Amplifiers to the right of us, left of us, and behind us; covered in suitcase crisscross material, glowing with red lights, studded with chrome lettering spelling: FENDER SHOWMAN. Guitars of many shapes and colors, even a gleaming sax with a player in dark glasses, and me at the battered church-hall piano, its innards stuffed with clumsy chrome mikes complete with grill. When the electricity was switched on and we played, we could amaze the welkin, waken the dead, and bring an end to the Celtic Twilight. Electrification! As exciting to us as it had been to Lenin after the Revolution. At the flick of a knob, we humble, ordinary folks could summon up roaring blue devils. And we did that night. Fueled by jars of ale and stout, we gave the assembled audience of punters, guerriers, biddies, and slags great chunks of rhythm and blues without racism and ghettos and suffering. I sang about having the blues around my bed every day and felt reasonably authentic because it was cold in Dublin, bitterly cold, and I had a runny nose and chilblains. So we hadn't really lost the seriousness of the blues; we were just applying it to our everyday lives—like the Stones—and I was really getting into the songs, really feeling mad, when WHAAM! I fell into a city of black-coffin amplifiers and the amps and I all collapsed together onto the stage floor of Mount Merrion. What a mess! What a foul-up!

But wait. While I lay on the floor, I heard a scream—a girlish one—then more, excited with sexual anticipation. My bottom touched a loose amplifier wire and the shock sent me into the air, jackknifing in the Jagger manner. A huge howl of ecstasy from the audience. After that, I limped around the stage in agony (and ecstasy) while the band played on, though their instruments were now acoustical. But the *thump-thump* of the drums was enough to accompany my agonized dance and the crowd joined in with claps and yelps. I realized that I had happened upon my innate sex appeal and I wished Moira (of the note) were there so that I could take her up on her offer of sexual "intercoarse." It was a revelation—this newly discovered sexiness. I determined to work on it and, after the gig, I returned to my rooms at the college and went to bed—after tossing out the usual comparative strangers I'd found there. There was to be no more missing of the boat, I decided. I was going to seize fortune and make it do my bidding. I knew I could be a star. The call of the wild, the journey to greatness in America could come true. But first I would have to conquer Britain. America would never accept our carrying coals to Newcastle. America had produced the music, had produced everything in the pop arts. What did they need us for? Certainly they'd never go for the Beatles!

From the moment Brian Epstein first experienced the Beatles in person —having a St. Pauline revelationary flash in that Cavern dungeon—he had told everybody that those boys were going to be the world's greatest entertainers. Having captured the charts and hearts of Britain, he set his sights on the conquest of America. He liked to say it could be done in a single gulp. He called his plan "Operation America." But what exactly was this plan? Where were the details? Pearly words tripping from the silvery tongue of Epstein were all very mellifluous, but lots of grizzled old record-biz people laughed at such daydreaming.

First, America was still clearly the pop capital of the world, its product flowing freely into its colonies, like Britain. Elvis was still the King and Roy Orbison kept coming up with monster melo-ballads that stormed Britain and the world. It was a one-way traffic in records: the precious few British acts to hit in America had been isolated successes, freaks. Mantovani, Vera Lynn, Lonnie Donegan, and Laurie London made no lasting impression but had only brief moments as exotic items. Cliff Richard, our most successful recording artist in the teen field since 1959, had never made much impact in America. The music was enjoyed all right, but there was little identity to it. Where was the tie with Harris tweed, Scotch whisky, and the Queen? What was England anyway—apart from some luxury goods and a bunch of eccentrics? Brian Epstein wanted the world to love his Beatles—their music and also their way of speaking, laughing their outlook—and the only way to achieve that objective was to conquer America, the place where the music came from. Also, the place with the most potential customers.

In November 1963, he had made a reconnaissance trip to New York with Billy J. Kramer. NEMS artists didn't mean a thing in America. As for Beatles records, they'd had to be leased out to minor labels. Capitol (EMI's American subsidiary) had bluntly stated that they didn't "think the Beatles will do any business in the American market." So "Please Please Me" and "From Me to You" had been released by Vee-Jay, basically an R&B company in Chicago; "She Loves You" was out on Swan of New York. None of these releases made any kind of impact. Why should they? Without the flesh, blood, and character of the Mersey boys, the music, thus far, was trifling ting-a-ling. American pop by this time was pulsing with deep bass and tummy-thumping drumming. Motown was starting to make itself heard.

Epstein and Kramer were installed in an expensive hotel. They looked good—full of British phlegm and iciness—but they had little ammunition. They had a lot of British newspaper clippings, an enormous amount of blind faith, and British cheek masquerading as charm. That was all.

On the other side, in the skyscrapers of New York, the record moguls saw Epstein as a pygmy. A very polite one, admittedly. Capitol Records, though owned by EMI, realized that it was at the nerve center of world show business. Its executives—middle-aged veterans of big bands and crooners, men who had walked with Sinatra—were well aware that they controlled a well-oiled music-making machine that could encircle a disc craze as a cowboy lassos a horse. They could jump on a craze and ride it till the poor novelty collapsed and died of exposure. Then they'd move on. They had worked twisting, hootenanny, and surfing in this way. It was called "marketing" and their machine was a complicated one, involving radio stations, newspapers, TV stations, and talent agencies. The whole deal. This was the real three-ring circus and it was a sacred one; no Limey was going to tell them what to do. Now if he had a good product, that was another matter.

Epstein had been studying the current American hits and had realized that Beatles records needed more funk and less clink. He went to the Capitol people with a demo by John and Paul of a song that, according to Epstein, echoed America's own native spirituals. The veeps didn't need to parlay anymore. "I Want to Hold Your Hand," with its depth-charge *clank* guitar and scouse spiritual singing, appeared to have a chance. They'd give it a shot. The record was set for American release in January 1964.

Sid Bernstein, concert promoter, didn't need persuading. While employed as an agent at the mighty General Artists Corporation (GAC), he'd taken a course in British culture and had visited Britain. While studying Shakespeare at Stratford-on-Avon, he'd run across Beatlemania and now he was convinced that America would go for it. He took the extraordinary step of booking the renowned Carnegie Hall—shrine of classical music and the occasional tasteful jazz concert—for a Beatles display on February 12, 1964. This showed as much blind faith as Epstein. A good working relationship was immediately established between the two seers.

Ed Sullivan, host of the star-making TV variety show, had also been caught up in British Beatlemania when he and his wife had been trapped in a fan crosscurrent at Heathrow Airport. He reckoned there must have been fifty thousand girls there and the crush of fans had prevented the Prime Minister, Lord Home, and Queen Elizabeth from taking off. "Here is something," he had told his wife. He remembered the Presley days. He remembered the groundswell before stardom and he remembered that it had been a single appearance on "The Ed Sullivan Show" that had made Elvis a household name. Maybe his personal tastes didn't run to rock 'n' roll, but as a onetime journalist he knew his duty. These Beatles were a news phenomenon and he might just be able to help create news in America. He and Epstein began talking figures and Epstein insisted on top billing. Sullivan gave in, but insisted on the group doing two shows. He also hedged his hunch by making the first appearance part of a theme package, an all-British show (cockney singer Georgia Brown and uke-playing comedienne "Two Ton Tessie" O'Shea were also booked).

Epstein went out of his way to woo the press, knowing from past experience that print people found his boys to be excellent copy; they were the special darlings of egghead writers keen to catch onto the new trend of reporting on pop-culture phenomena. Stories appeared in *The New Yorker* and the New York *Times*. Brian returned to England, in his own words, "excited and delighted." The seeds were sown, but even he didn't realize he was about to reap a whirlwind—otherwise he'd have taken more care about the finer print in Beatle spin-off merchandise.

By January 1964, "I Want to Hold Your Hand" was number one in Britain. Advance orders had been just under two million copies. But, amazingly, the record shot to number one in America before the month was up. Amazingly—because there had been hardly any hype thus far from Capitol. It was what was in the grooves that had made "I Want to Hold Your Hand" a hit. The demand had even preceded the release:

several key radio stations had been playing imported tapes and press-ings of the record and receiving terrific response—switchboards twin-kling like Christmas trees.

Capitol moved fast. America was to be baited into Beatle madness. First, $50,000 was allocated for a "crash publicity program." Time was of the essence, since the Sullivan shows, plus Carnegie Hall and a Washington concert, were coming up quickly. Sixteen press agents were hired and press kits, complete with Beatle wigs and a four-page Beatle newspaper, were sent to every disc jockey in the country. Five million stickers proclaiming THE BEATLES ARE COMING were spread about and managed to find homes not only on the usual telephone poles and fences but also on lavatory walls and in offices and even boardrooms. Intense concentration was applied to the Beatles' hairstyle, as this seemed to be the most startling aspect of the Limeys—the "mop-top" or "pageboy" or "Prince Valiant" or even "feather-duster" look. This was decadence, but friendly, *fun* decadence and Americans could all join in as they had during the hoola hoop era. Capitol's press corps tried to entice celebrities into being photographed in a Beatles coiffure. Janet Leigh, the film actress, agreed. Billionaire Paul Getty had a Bea-tles wig plunked on his scalp. Within Capitol, it became *de rigueur* to don a wig at least once, with upper management setting the example and lower employees being offered free Beatles haircuts. Lapel buttons were an absolute standing order. Years afterward, a Capitol veep admit-ted, "There was an awful lot of pure *hype*."

But hype—or salesmanship—is what the Republic is all about and has always been about. The land of the Big Deal, the eternal game of confidence trickery, of the continuing spirit of Barnum. Even the Church endorsed the great chase for the dollar: hadn't adman Bruce Barton proved in his 1920s best-seller, *The Man Nobody Knows,* that Christ Himself was the first Great Salesman?

Anyway, America has always loved a parade and, in early 1964, she was ready for a big one. A proper bit of fun after the traumatic shock of President Kennedy's assassination. Camelot had vanished in a mighty gloom and what was needed was something silly and simple and having nothing to do with politics or current affairs or even America. So here, as if handed on a plate, was the perfect diversion—four cuddly dolls from a tight and funny little island full of Disneyland castles and so many miles away across the foam.

The die was cast. The teams divided—into hustlers and hustled. American business and media were ready. So was the public.

And on February 7, B-Day arrived. The Beatles and their entourage landed in America and the group themselves and some of the British journalists were not at all certain that conquest was inevitable. Phil

Spector was on board because he was certain the Beatles were going to make it in every way. Because of their blessed aura, momentarily he had forgotten his fear of flying. Like so many, he wanted to catch some rays of their reflected glory. Others on board, manufacturers and the like, wanted to catch the spin-off dollars, but Epstein, up in front, refused every approach—politely. They must go through the proper channels, namely his franchising company, Seltaeb (Beatles backward). Three properly franchised factories were ready to make the T-shirts and then there would be dolls, edible discs, ice cream flavors, lunch boxes, tennis shirts, pajamas, boys' underwear. Brian drew the line at sanitary napkins, though. And, of course, later, when Beatlemania was epidemic, merchandising got out of hand and there were many unlicensed products. Eppy was never that astute at the money details. He was big on fantasies.

Could this be a fantasy at New York's airport? Or had Capitol and Seltaeb done a magnificent rent-a-crowd job? Three thousand vociferous fans and not just girls but plenty of boys, too, with their hair brushed to the front. There were the first U.S. Beatlemania faintings and the first police requirements for ID in order to be in Beatle presence. And there was the first press conference, right there in the arrivals building.

This was a reporter's dream. Here was no "Yes, sir—no, sir—ask my manager" guff. Here was a comic routine full of wit and charm. The Marx Brothers? No, British music hall: cheeky chappies cocking a cheerful snook. Parents felt relieved that these rockers were harmless comics; their children loved the Beatles for putting on the straight world. Everyone was happy. Here's some of the exchange, if you'll bear with repetition of what has become folklore:

STRAIGHT MAN: Will you sing something for us?
COMIC: We need money first.
STRAIGHT MAN: How do you account for your success?
COMIC: We have a press agent.
STRAIGHT MAN: Do you hope to take anything home with you?
COMIC: The Rockefeller Center.
STRAIGHT MAN: Are you part of a teenage rebellion against the older
          generation?
COMIC: It's a dirty lie.
STRAIGHT MAN: What about the campaign in Detroit to stamp out the
          Beatles?
COMIC: We've a campaign of our own—to stamp out Detroit.
STRAIGHT MAN: What do you think of Beethoven?
COMIC: I love him—especially his poems.

That last crack was from dear, lovable, Simple Simon Ringo, the one who listed his ambition as "to be happy." Ringo we were sure about. We weren't so certain about the others. But for the time being, the product seemed just right and the media went to work. A woman reporter grabbed an airport phone and told her editor: "They are absolutely too cute for words and America is going to *love* them. In fact, they'll eat them up!"

From that point on, the Beatles were confined to that special, rarefied, unreal world that Elvis knew so well. From bubble to bubble, surrounded by guardians, well-wishers, exploiters, and sycophants. The fans started climbing the drainpipes, storming the limos, mailing themselves in packing crates. Soon there would be the wheelchair armies of cripples waiting to be blessed. Meanwhile, on February 9 there was "The Ed Sullivan Show." Seventy-three million was the official viewing figure—or 60 percent of U.S. viewers. As to the music, who cared? Well, George did and was to continue to hate Beatlemania because it was musically destructive. Anyway, this Sullivan show got a higher rating than the 1957 Elvis appearance. There were far more kids, for a start—they were about to reach a national majority. Everybody, it seemed, watched. Even Billy Graham broke his no-TV-on-Sunday rule. Elvis and his gang watched and the King said, "They've brought it on home, boys." Jerry Lee Lewis aimed a gun at his set, then relented and admitted that "They got every angle figured out. I mean, they're good, but good!" Little Richard was sequestered in church at the time, but he said he knew they were righteous because he was in touch with God.

Carnegie Hall, the Washington concert, even the rudeness at the British Embassy party—they handled it all superbly. The New York *Times* bent over backward to out-intellectualize the London *Times*: "They have a tendency to build phrases around unresolved leading tones. This precipitates the ear into a false modal frame that temporarily turns the fifth of the scale into the tonic, momentarily suggesting the mixolydian mode. But everything always ends as plain diatonic all the same." In other words, the Beatles were steeped in country music as much as in good old Alley tunes and they weren't bound by the moribund strictures of classical music.

The folkies surely appreciated the fifth of the scale used as a tonic and they certainly worked in modes. But the folk outposts—entrenched in Greenwich Village, in San Francisco, and in the college towns—were sharply split about the Beatles. Was this more R&R hype or was it a musical breakthrough? Had the rock machine triumphed again, destroying the advance into public consciousness made by the folk movement? Would urban acne despoil the apple cheek of those who had wandered the highways and byways of the real American music? Later that year, *Hootenanny* magazine published an article by Robert Shelton, in which he made the following criticisms of the British Invaders:

"Beatlemania is the shrieking of hysterical girls; it is fans lined up for hours for a glimpse of a quartet of shaggy Teddy Boys; it is jelly beans tossed onstage; it is a demand for discs that has made a major record company suspend all other popular and classical releases. . . . 'Tom Dooley' was a time-steeped ballad of an actual episode, while 'I Want to Hold Your Hand' is a souped-up, over-engineered love song. The difference between them speaks volumes about the merits of folk song and the Merseybeat. The Kingston Trio started something very constructive in American music. If the Beatles end it, we'll all be the losers."

But, somewhere on the road, Bob Dylan caught Beatles songs on his car radio. He was staggered; he started laughing with glee. They had made him come home to the music he'd started with back in Minnesota, when rock 'n' roll was young and pure and sassy and honest. They were serving him up a rootfest, raw. And not only that, but they were flinging their own bits and pieces onto the festal board. Their chords, for example, were "outrageous." He told his colleagues that these guys were "pointing to the direction the music has to go." And, twiddling his radio dial, he found that the Beatles were leading the way for other groups of substance—like the Animals. With the gravelly voice of Eric Burdon shouting black hurt, it was hard to believe that these people hailed from the British North, too—the Animals from Newcastle carrying back to Bob Dylan his very own coals with their own number-one smash "House of the Rising Sun," that public-domain New Orleans folk ballad that *he* had laid down back on his first album. That had been an acoustic-guitar record and now here were the Animals electrifying the ballad with rolling guitars and organ and transmogrifying the thing. Dylan realized that this was where it was going to be at and that he must go there at once. "I just couldn't bear to be Mr. Jones, man," he later said.

The Animals bellowed into the U.S. charts in the summer, preceded by waves of British Invaders and welcomed in by the young natives and even their parents. Of course, the Beatles were still the spearhead and, by April, Beatles records held the top five positions in the charts. BRITANNIA RULES THE AIRWAVES bannered *Variety*, but they hadn't reckoned on the other hordes Britain could produce. Hard on the heels of the Beatles came the Dave Clark Five with their Tottenham sound, the military stomp of "Glad All Over." Clean-cut and athletic, they fit in much more with the American norm and were a perfect choice for "The Ed Sullivan Show." In April, they reached number six and, by that time, they'd done their first tour and had been truly mauled by their mostly female fans. The DC5 were to go on to more hits and to be the joy of promoters, parents, and the general public. They were always on time and their shows were well lit, well performed, and always ended right at the appointed time. Many in the trade reckoned the DC5 to be industry stayers and a better bet than the Beatles. Their fans screechingly agreed.

Other Merseybeaters broke in, though not as big as the DC5: the Swinging Blue Jeans with "Hippy Hippy Shake," bringing back to America her own Chicano rocker; Billy J. Kramer with "Little Children," a song from New York's Mort Shuman; Gerry and the Pacemakers with "Don't Let the Sun Catch You Crying," a reflective ballad and an odd one with which to crash the charts. From Manchester came the Hollies, a discovery of George Martin's assistant, Ron Richards, and they hit with "Just One Look" in May. Another group from Manchester, Herman's Hermits, didn't make it in America until December, with the American song "I'm into Something Good." But while the Hollies were a record act, Herman had a lot going for him in his appearance. Buck-toothed, square-jawed (in the Kennedy fashion), and blessed with a winningly goofy smile, he was soon gobbled up by the teeny girls and pix of Herman and his pals were to be teen mag fodder over the next year or so. Herman's Hermits quickly became known as "Pop's Boy Scouts." They could act, too, and Herman himself had started his career as a child actor in Britain's long-running soap opera "Coronation Street."

Mickie Most, a very clever record producer, had spotted Herman when he was on that show and using his real name of Peter Noone. Most quickly signed him and, with the help of studio musicians, started shooting out the singles. Never an album man, Most firmly believed in the two-and-a-half-minute ear-catcher. He saw a group called the Nashville Teens when they were backing Bo Diddley and he matched them with an American country-blues tune called "Tobacco Road." Amazingly, the single hit big in America as an example of the British sound.

The Nashville Teens were from Surrey, near London, and were steeped in the local R&B music. Playing live, they could blow the blues merrily, but on record they had to be molded by craftsmen like Most. The same applied to the other R&B groups. Manfred Mann forsook the narrow blues/jazz path for safe Brill Building pop like "Do Wah Diddy Diddy" (by Phil Spector's champ team of Barry and Greenwich). The nonsense song established the group in America. Also from London—Muswell Hill in grimy North London, to be exact—were the Kinks. Like Manfred Mann, their beginnings were in the R&B movement, when they were known as the Ravens. But the Davies brothers, Ray and Dave, had always delivered their blues with plenty of cockney spike. Larry Page, like Mickie Most a onetime would-be singing star, was eagling around for likely fun groups to manage and he at once twigged to Ray Davies' art school muggery and the Ravens' potential as tearaway pop anarchists. He signed them, changed their name to the Kinks (after the currently "in" word, "kinky," referring to perverted sexual practices) and dressed them in pink hunting jackets. The effect was oxymoronic: an acute conflict between the lumpen loony faces and the upper-class-twit uniforms they were wearing. The Kinks were placed in the hands of American producer/hustler Shel Talmy, a fortunate choice. Talmy had arrived in London in 1962, armed with acetate records—Beach Boys and Lou Rawls tracks, impressive stuff—he claimed to have produced but which had, in fact, been produced by Nick Venet. He'd scored with versions of oldies like "Charmaine" and "Diane" by Ireland's own Bachelors, a housewife-pleasing vocal group with a harmonica folk sound. In the wake of the British Invasion, even the Bachelors (with "Diane") made it big on the U.S. charts, which showed an addiction to anything vaguely Britannic. After two so-so singles of R&B material (e.g., "Long Tall Sally"), Talmy went with a Ray Davies composition called "You Really Got Me."

Ray Davies' eerie singsong gamin voice, with its almost Jamaican inflections, coupled with a crashing blues jump tune and thickened by steel shafts of clanking distorted guitar riffs, made for a catchy and dangerous record. Very nicely crude, very garagelike. In November of 1964, "You Really Got Me" climbed as high as number seven on the U.S. charts. They were never to reach number one, but the Kinks were to establish a strong cult following among serious rock 'n' roll fans in America.

But the Invaders were not all drawn from the Other Ranks—some of them came from the officer class: the Zombies (taking their name from the popular horror film genre, just as the Searchers had taken theirs from a John Wayne Western) had originally gotten together while students at St. Albans, a minor Public School. Colin Blunstone, ghostly voiced, joined them later as vocalist and Rod Argent composed the songs. However, they came to national fame when they won a newspaper contest with their version of Gershwin's show tune "Summertime." The prize was a Decca recording contract and the gist of the resulting publicity was that the Zombies were a brainy bunch, with over twenty "O" levels (academic diplomas) to their names. They became known as Thinking Man's pop stars, which may not have endeared them to British record buyers. "She's Not There" reached number twelve in Britain, but in America the record went to number two. Their subsequent popularity on record was largely in the States, where they were much better appreciated and where they gained near-legendary status.

From an even grander background came Peter and Gordon, but they were never rockers. Instead, they featured spongy, two-part harmony, with a nod to the Everly Brothers. The two had met while attending Westminster, a great British Public School in the heart of London. After they left, they got a gig playing at a quite chic West End club called the Cromwellian, doing oldies and folk songs, but pretty soon they found a marvelous song source: Peter's sister, Jane Asher, was being ardently courted by Paul McCartney. In fact, he'd become a member of the Asher household, even having his own room in their Wimpole Street flat, where Paul and John Lennon used to dream up songs for imminent recording sessions. The stuff came pouring out, all kinds of pop genres and much that they couldn't use. One of these was "World Without Love," a real old-time Alley shmaltz song. It always made John break up when Paul sang the first lines. Just right for Peter and Gordon, thought EMI after they passed the boys on their audition. Geoff Love, a veteran orchestra leader (he was also Manuel of Manuel and his Music of the Mountains) was assigned to back them and he did a creditable job, oozing out just the right amount of bass-drum *thump* and rockish guitar. In June of 1964, "World Without Love" hit the number-one spot in America.

Chad and Jeremy had a strange start. They'd met at drama school and had played the folk clubs, performing their relaxing ballads strummed to acoustic guitars. Ember, a small British label, signed them but had no local luck with "Yesterday's Gone." However, World Artists in America released the single and eventually the song reached number twenty-one. They scored an even greater success with "Summer Song," which hit number seven in September. Chad Stuart was of good Northern stock, but Jeremy Clyde was from the very upper crust and a rarity in show business: his grandfather was the Duke of Wellington, descendant of the man who'd won Waterloo.

The girls played their part, too, in the first year of the Invasion—though the rocking wasn't much in evidence on their records. Lulu was originally Marie Lawrie from the tough Scottish city of Glasgow. With her band, the Luvvers, she cut a version of the old Isley Brothers' hit "Shout" (this song was a staple with the British beaters and the Beatles featured this as part of their stage act). Mickie Most produced the record, achieving a very vital sound. Most was first-rate at matching the right number with the right backing—he'd also produced "House of the Rising Sun." He seemed to denigrate his work, though, claiming in the press that he treated pop much as a salesman would treat the manufacture and sale of soap.

Dusty Springfield, once part of the successful Springfields pop/folk group, had a U.S. hit in 1964 with an up-tempo beat ballad, "I Only Want to Be with You." She was known for her vulnerability and her volume of pancake makeup. Sandie Shaw was famous for her slinky sexiness, for mothering an illegitimate child, and for not wearing shoes during her performances. She hit in America with "Always Something There to Remind Me," an American song. Cilla Black, with a thin, squarky voice similar to Shaw's, joined the girl chart Invaders that year with a grandiose, beefy ballad from Italy, "You're My World." Not exactly the kind of song you'd expect from an ex-Cavern cloakroom attendant. George Martin had done a good job, though, on the production.

Finally, some real oddities made it in with the first British wave. We've mentioned the Bachelors with "Diane," but there was also Julie Rogers and "The Wedding," George Martin and his Orchestra with "Ringo's Theme," and lest we forget, Cliff Richard, the much-maligned singer that every Merseybeater seemed to be reacting against, had three records in the American Top One Hundred in 1964. Nobody seemed to notice that achievement and nobody remembered that he'd actually made the bottom chart rungs back in 1959 with his "Livin' Doll," an English number-one hit.

However, 1964 was to be the year of the group, not the single singer. It was the boy gangs with guitars, cheeky grins, and funny hair and lingo that were the chief Invaders and, in time, the revolutionaries.

At Trinity, I had been following the progress of Beatlemania and the Invaders with enormous interest. I'd never dreamed the Beatles would mean a thing over in America. Of course, I took particular interest in the Stones' progress. How would Americans take to their coarseness? Or would Oldham tame them for U.S. consumption? I filled my rooms with pop newspapers and trades and I read and read: "Not Fade Away" managed to scrape onto the charts by June, when we at Trinity were preparing for the Trinity Ball, in which Bluesville was to appear by request of the provost. On the strength of their press trailers, the Stones were booked on a U.S. tour. It turned out to be a patchy affair, with empty stadiums in some cities and devoted fans in others. So far, word was only getting to the hip people who were in the large cosmopolitan centers. But in San Bernardino, the band got a surprise when they were greeted by thousands of Stones fans creating scenes like those back in England. The Stones fans were noticeably more sloppy in dress and more shampoo-shy than Beatles fans. On the West Coast, the Stones met their nemesis on a TV show called "Hollywood Palace": the host, Dean Martin, a hangover from the Sinatra rat-pack days, didn't like the group one bit. He was more respectful of the baby elephants, another guest act. With a glass permanently in his hand, he kept tossing out slurred insults about the group, like "Keep me away from them," and "Don't leave me alone with them." His performance won millions of young fans over to the Stones' anti-Establishment posture. The story was much talked about in the press. Oldham must have been jubilant. For the rest of the time, the boys enjoyed taking in the sights and sounds of Lotusland, California. They were amazed by the surfer Adonises and kept a stream of derogatory jokes running to their assigned promotion man, George Sherlock. To them, Sherlock epitomized the sun-worshiping fools of the beach culture and if there was one thing the Stones hated, it was surf music. Their day began at night; sunshine was a real headache. Jagger dubbed George—with his deep tan, display of hairy scrubland chest, and habit of continual finger-popping—"Surfer Baby." He immortalized him in a song, "The Under Assistant West Coast Promotion Man." Later, George Sherlock was to play an important part in my own pop life.

After the electrification incident—when I had discovered my sex appeal—and after the American breakthrough by the Invaders, I decided I really should go all out for the brass ring. If this wide assortment of British boys could do it, so could I. While others sat in the Trinity library (home of *The Book of Kells*) and studied dull texts, I sat in Samuel Beckett's favorite library seat writing pop songs: ballads of unrequited love, of girls floating Ophelialike down Pre-Raphaelite rivers of no return, of teen harassment within the urban stress area. I stopped for a breather because I could see that the academic air was clogging up my brain processes. Simple songs were the answer, but how to be simple in this heady atmosphere?

The vacuum was broken by an invitation from Roger Question, left-wing head of Trinity's drama group, to record "something evil and revolutionary" for that summer's college revue. Like so many student efforts, it had an ostentatious title of high-sounding meaninglessness: "Pall Me Mantle." I obliged by calling in Bluesville's harmonica player and a friend of his who usually played tuba. This particular afternoon, I asked him to bang a big bass drum, which happened to be lying in a corner of the studio I'd selected. Well, it was really a damp basement with a tape recorder and piano (and odd bass drum) on Merrion Square, opposite the house where Oscar Wilde was born. Better days had been seen by this basement, but now we three settled down to sling together "something evil and revolutionary" for the drama group. I knew they meant R&B.

We selected a Chuck Berry riff (which he in turn had borrowed from the deep folk fund bag) and, after awakening the engineer and helping him stave off a visit by the bailiff's men, off we went.

"Pall Me Mantle," the theme, was well received by the student audiences. During quests for *The Book of Kells* (or *Kelly's Book,* as the treasure was often called), American tourists often strayed into the college theater, intrigued by the silly revue title. One night, a gray-haired and sharp-looking tourist approached me and said he'd really gotten a kick out of my theme music and so had his son. Was this tune available on a recording? After the run of the revue, I reclaimed the tape, now a little crinkled, and packed it in my bags. A chance had come for it to win me fame and fortune in America!

The reason for this summer's trip was a telegram from the 92 Yesler Club, where I'd worked the previous year in Seattle. They wanted me back for a summer stint and this time they'd pay me properly and I wouldn't have to make the pizzas during the break. Quickly, I returned to London in order to buy the right gear—Beatle boots with Cuban heels, a leather jacket, and lots of turtleneck sweaters. I prayed for my hair to grow and grow—and it did, except that, after a few inches over the collar, it did an about-turn and curled up, making me look like a demented peasant from the Dark Ages. Back in Eire, the Dubliners scorned me as an "eejit." But I grinned and bore it and began the arduous journey by charter plane to New York. This time, only two forced landings were made, in order to eject drunken Dubliners.

In New York, I braved the peat-thick heat in my leather jacket and made it across town to the Port Authority Bus Terminal. The cross-country trip took three solid days, but this time I knew the ropes. I availed myself of the comfort station, especially when neighbors got too friendly with their hands. I pulled out my Marx and Lenin textbooks when I wanted to sleep. Usually, these books did the trick. In Idaho, I was accused of being a Communist; in North Dakota, I was a faggot; in Montana, I got off the bus for a shave at a local barber, who told me how his business was going bust since the coming of the Beatles. He started wielding a vicious pair of scissors after his Sweeney Todd-style shave, and I tried to calm him by asking whether he'd just style my hair slightly. "Hell, I'm a barber. I ain't no sissy coiffure artist!" he replied.

In Seattle, at the coffee house, they had made a huge banner to greet me: IAN WHITCOMB—DIRECT FROM LONDON VIA LIVERPOOL. The whole scene had changed. There were no longer any questions about bowler hats, umbrellas, and tea and crumpets; it was all "fab," "gear," and long hair and Beatle talk. Some of the kids complained that I didn't sound as British as the Beatles. What an irony! All that money spent by my parents on my education at an expensive Public School in the heart of Dorset! And they wanted me to speak common and Northern! I obliged by slurring some words and clipping a few gs.

However, I did realize that I'd better reap while the reaping was good. Britain called the tune and I was out to exploit. The first free moment I had, I looked up recording companies in the Yellow Pages. These turned out to be record distributors, but, as I learned, one of these distributors had his own label. He was Jerry Dennon of the Jerden label, the King of the Northwest sound, currently riding the crest with his discovery, the Kingsmen (of "Louie Louie" fame). I made an appointment to see Mr. Dennon, dressing carefully in my best Beat Merchant outfit. He was a busy man, with telephones ringing, but he had an admirable air of calm about him, too. Very reassuring. I told him quite candidly, and in so many words, that I was going to be the next Mick Jagger, a huge hit. Already I'd been mistaken for him, I said. He was very polite and asked me to leave my product with him. I produced the tape, much more crinkled since its journey across sea and land. He would let me know.

I returned to life in the coffee house. Now I could play rock 'n' roll to my heart's content and there would be no folkies to contend with. They had all mysteriously vanished, but I missed Billy Roberts, my Dinkytown pal, and, in his memory, I started fooling around with an old folk song from the skiffle era, "The Sporting Life Is Killin' Me." I rolled it with arpeggios and, behold, it sounded very like "House of the Rising Sun." A visiting jockey from the local big rocker station, KJR, told me I should record that mother and fast.

"All work and no play . . ." I took time off to pursue some of the local girls. Whereas last year they had thought I was from another planet, now it was simple to win their attention. In fact, they approached *me* and spoke a sort of pidgin North Country English with much body language employed. These gorgeous creatures with their ponytails and Dutch-girl hairstyles, shorts and halters and patterned pants, were mine for the having. All fresh, deodorized, ready, willing, and able. Over here there was none of that Irish teasing, no excuses for not being allowed to unclench the teeth during kissing because "'Tis mortal sin." I was on a couch late one night when one girl's parents were out and she was lying on top of me in the American manner. She purred, "Talk pretty to me. You talk so vurry pretty." I had stopped talking because I was planning devilish fun. Then: "Ian, baby—you're turning me on!" What a vivid phrase! You turn on a tap, a television, a stereo—but a person! Was this a metaphor for American life in general? Whatever—I rushed to the nearest pad and pencil without delay. Suffice it to say, the girl was nonplussed, but later that night we did get back together as Johnny Carson flickered bluishly in the background.

In no time at all, I discovered that over here there were certain rules of the game. There were girls who would do this but not that; girls who drew the line at the upper thigh; girls who'd fuss and fret when you tried to unbutton their blouse but would let you go ahead in the end. There were plenty of willing players around the coffee house. Eventually, though, I settled on a "steady," an eighteen-year-old with real "come-hither eyes" like neon ovals. Her body undulated seductively and was clad in what I learned were "preppy" clothes. She was a rich girl named Debbie. We struck up a good partnership: she let my hands stray farther than most other dates and I, in return, laid on the Beatle routine with a trowel. Her parents lived on Bainbridge Island, an exclusive neighborhood and, after I'd stated my credentials and returned to my real accent, I was warmly welcomed into the family fold. Her father, a big oilman, said I reminded him of Prince Charlie— which I wasn't sure how to take in terms of my personal vanity, but I certainly partook of the oilman's hospitality. The home was a super-house in neo-Tudor but with more than enough of the modern conveniences, especially "wet" bars. I was allowed to stay very late with Debbie on the den couch—in fact, her father appeared to enjoy our petting sessions, interloping near the imitation climax in order to offer me a nightcap. He was forever winking at me. The mother eyed me up and down a lot and had a habit of pursing her lips tight even as she smiled along.

But I was inhibited at their house, despite the parents' connivance. I was certain there must be hills and dales, groves and deep forest clearings where we could tryst in natural splendor. So on weekends, after my shows, we went cruising in her Mustang. For hours and hours, we toured the leafy suburbs of Seattle looking for a good place to park. It was bloody frustrating—I had no idea there were so few public places for private petting in God's Own Country. On all sides were estates with electric fences and chain links and floodlights and barking dogs and uniformed security guards with sawed-off shotguns. Private property ruled around these parts. Where were the great lakes and echoey forests; where was the romantic snow-capped mountain on the Rainier beer can? Gone was the Wild West, except at Disneyland.

One advantage to our long hauls through the Seattle environs was that I got to hear a good deal of pop radio via KJR, the local big pop/rocker station. And I was heartened to realize that American pop was far from dead, that the Arthurians hadn't slain that big, slick processional that had been creaming along since the days of ragtime. The sound, currently concocted more and more on the West Coast, made the Beat Merchants seem very rough and rude. Our faces appeared spot-grotty compared with the sun-kissed crooners like Dean Martin, smooth as Scotch as he sailed through his current Top Ten'er "Every-

body Loves Somebody Sometime," and Bobby Vinton, who I thought
had vanished with the other Bobbys of those "American Bandstand"
days, had reached number one with "Mr. Lonely." Even heroes of the
Jazz Age were topping the charts: Louis Armstrong, virtual inventor of
jazz trumpet, had sold a million of his "Hello, Dolly!"

On the rock 'n' roll front, Roy Orbison, always a favorite of mine
with his unique crying falsetto and pop opera epics, reached number
one that fall with "Oh, Pretty Woman." This was a perfect pop record
from its *tramp-tramp-tramp* beat and catchy ninth chord riff to its
Spanish tinge in the middle and climactic finale when the seemingly
eternally spurned Orbison is surprised to see the pretty woman turn on
her high heel and head his way. I cheered for the fandango man with
the black helmet hair and loser look. What a relief after "It's Over"
and "Only the Lonely."

On the distaff side, but on the same station, Motown was turning out
splendidly simple bangalong R&B pop via the Supremes. With their
sexy baby voices, they put me in mind of the Barbie dolls I'd seen on
my U.S. travels and their "Where Did Our Love Go?" had a light-
chocolate, on-the-beat rhythm that was as attractive as Orbison's and
much less vulgar than Dave Clark's. From the sidewalks of New York
came the street-corner harmony (filtered through an Italian nightclub)
of the Four Seasons (featuring Frankie Valli of the astral falsetto).
"Rag Doll" told a touching story of ghetto love and the high notes were
heart-wrenching. There was a lot of falsetto in the air that summer.
Could this have been the influence of gospel? At any rate, the charts
reflected a wide range of pop and it was all very healthy.

I was glad to hear that the surfer singers were hale and hearty and
hadn't been chilled by the Invaders. Jan and Dean were "riding the
wild surf" as usual and chirping in the high register, too. Though their
boogie-chug busy beat and thick waves of Spectorlike sound were not
helped by rather similar tunes, they did come up with a sly slice of
humor in "Little Old Lady from Pasadena." As for the Beach Boys,
they were at the height of their powers with the double-sided hit, "I
Get Around"/"Don't Worry Baby." The former was a first-class production and, lyrically, a quintessential exposition of the hedonist "on-the-
move" beach mentality. There was the assertion of gang territorial
rights, as well as plenty of male exclusivity. It seemed to me to be terribly American and "Don't Worry Baby" was a perfect complement: the
caring and considerate heart that lay like a marshmallow beneath the
hard shell of every macho American male.

With pleasant memories of my bath in surf culture the previous summer, I was disappointed to find a distinct decline in the rugged masculinity of West Coast youth this year. Many of those macho jocks with

the close-cropped hair and muscles were now letting their hair grow and were trudging about with sloping shoulders and fallen stomachs and arches. This, of course, was the insidious influence of the British Invaders, most of whom came from underprivileged backgrounds and had been raised on chips with everything (Spam being the major staple in their diet). I was not of this ilk; I was an ardent admirer of American physique and diet (especially hamburgers and malteds) and I lost no time in telling my Seattle friends that I regretted their imitation of the British slouch. It affected their attitude toward life, too.

My friends, though, would simply point to pictures showing quite clearly Brian Wilson's large "corporation" belly. His brother Carl was fast catching up. The Invaders were "cool"; the Beach Boys were now increasingly a group for girls to admire. The male allegiance was shifting to the British.

Brian Wilson, a very sensitive soul, was aware of this change and he called a Beach Boys conference to discuss the whole threat. Were his richly textured harmonies and lilting tunes to be thrown out the window? Should the Beach Boys go the crude route? His answer was to sit up late at night and write even more lovely songs, songs that got more and more into the realm of art. Eventually, the tug-of-war between beauty and beastliness became too much for him. In December, with Capitol at his heels demanding singles, singles, singles, and more of the same surf sound, and with the pressures of a national tour weighing on his mind, Brian Wilson suffered from acute nervous exhaustion. It first showed itself in a fear of flying and a spate of crying spells. The session guitarist Glen Campbell replaced him for the rest of the tour.

Wilson's great inspiration had been Phil Spector. Both were sensitive souls who were pushing their craft closer and closer to art, stretching the fragile and ephemeral pop form to its limits and beyond. And both developed a fear of flying. Before the year was up, Spector conducted his famous plane incident. He was on board a jet with songwriters Jeff Barry and Ellie Greenwich when he decided the plane wasn't going to make it. He exited—together with the songwriters and fifty of the other passengers—while the plane was still on the ground. Jeff Barry later speculated that Spector probably wasn't getting enough attention.

He certainly got attention from a single he produced at the end of the year. Considered a masterwork, it was that rare pop animal—a record that pleased aesthetically and sold by the millions. "You've Lost That Lovin' Feelin'" was a great song in the first place, written by Barry Mann and Cynthia Weil especially for the Righteous Brothers and characterizing frigidity in a nutshell. The Righteous Brothers had been knocking about as a "blue-eyed soul" duo and had had a few chart nibbles when Spector decided to immortalize them. They fit well into his black stable and Philles Records needed something big and noble because last year's triumphs were a long time ago in pop history. Spector had to surpass his previous efforts.

The record was many months in the making. The result was a monumental wailing Wall of Sound—and a sound impervious to analysis. Instruments melted into each other in the ghostly mix, the Brothers traded wails, the bass plunged deep in a cavernous ocean. And pop had been stretched almost beyond radio acceptance—three minutes and forty-five seconds. But the song burst through and, by Christmas, was heading high, reaching number one in February 1965. In Britain, the record beat out Cilla Black's cover version and, early in 1965, an admiring Andrew Loog Oldham bought space in all the music papers to praise his idol: "Already in the American Top Ten, this is Spector's greatest production, the last word in Tomorrow's Sound Today, exposing the overall mediocrity of the music industry."

Eventually, Debbie and I settled for drive-ins and it was there, during a lecherous tangle in the bucket seats, that I saw *A Hard Day's Night*, the Beatles' first film. It was directed in frenetic style by Dick Lester, who had previously given us such speeded-up, zany films as *The Running, Jumping, Standing Still Film* (starring two of the Goons) and *It's Trad, Dad!* The Beatles seemed to be involved in one long chase reminiscent of the Keystone Kops. Debbie's interest was as much in their antics as in mine and I felt a keen sense of rivalry. Afterward, while at the concession stand, some girls heard me asking for a hot dog and broke into tears. I asked them why. "Because you come from the same part of the world as Paul McCartney," they replied. This was reflected glory indeed and the power of pop was burgeoning so much that I determined to demand a decision from Jerry Dennon at Jerden Records the very next day.

I told him I was fit to explode as the next Mick Jagger. Dennon consulted some trade papers, played the crinkled tape again, and asked me what I had for the other side. If he turned over the tape, he'd find "Bony Moronie." "OK, you win," he said. "We'll give it a shot." I signed a mass of paperwork. I was so pleased that my signature was required. I now had a record contract and was one of the grand stable of Jerden recording artists. I would have to provide a biography. This was fun.

The next day was my birthday and I celebrated by allowing myself to be picked up by a gypsy-type girl at the 92 Yesler Club and taken to her apartment, where one thing led to another. The whole matter was over in seconds and then came the dawn of regret: this was a first for me. Would she have a baby? Who could I confess to? Should I convert to Catholicism? And, saddest of all, childhood was now behind me.

For the rest of that Seattle summer, I buried myself in my club work and in my history books, banning all thoughts of sex. I treated Debbie like a lady. I talked golf and finance with her father. Then, just before I had to leave to get back to Trinity, Jerry Dennon called to say he had a box of pressings for me. That night and all the next day on the journey home, I gazed at the flimsy plastic thing with its blue label and its legend:

JERDEN RECORDS
"SOHO"
IAN WHITCOMB
(Recorded in Dublin)

Thoughts of Debbie's tears and her father's winks and hearty handshake were banished by this wondrous gift. Now it was "all systems go." Soon I would be on the charts with my fellow Invaders.

Semifinals were over. I had produced a fat sheath of papers full of waffle about "The Place of the King's Signet Ring in Constitutional History" and I had argued that early Irish society was certainly *not* "tribal in nature." While my colleagues rushed off to relax in drinking and fox hunting, my mind turned to my contract with Jerden Records. There had been no word from Jerry about any progress on "Soho." Nor had it appeared in any of the American trade papers. It wasn't even "bubbling under" the Top One Hundred.

But I did have a contract, I was a Jerden artist, and I was determined to forge a smasheroo. "Soho" (née "Pall Me Mantle") had not been conceived as a hit platter. I would go Spectorian and create a smash from scratch.

By this time, people around Dublin were getting fed up with having "Soho" flashed under their noses. I had become the Ancient Mariner of pop. "Grow up!" said one. "Piss off," said another. Bluesville was impressed but wanted to know where their credit was? I said I'd rectify that matter on the next platter.

For the next few weeks, I sequestered myself away from lectures and band activities. Determined to put together some hit songs, I decided to start by studying the Lennon/McCartney oeuvre at the piano—note by note, chord by chord, line by line. I took their songs apart as others would a car or a watch. I remembered reading some advice by Raymond Chandler that the only writing school necessary is to "analyze and imitate."

At first sight, Beatles songs appeared ultra-simple—little love songs with no greater message than love from him to her. Almost simplistic and with nursery-rhyme tunes. Somebody in the music department told me that the Beatles employed neglected medieval modes, but I didn't know about that. I *did* know that their tunes were often oddly spaced, melodically journeying up and down strange paths not frequented by the old Tin Pan Alleymen. The plangent fifth note of the scale was much favored, one single word would be given several short step notes, and they liked to break out of the Alley thirty-two- and sixteen-bar prison. Outside they'd hop about on tonal leaps (like the C to B flat to C harmony in "A Hard Day's Night"), giving their songs a folksy quality. There was a fetching mountain-music sound to their two-part close harmony that reminded me of the Everly Brothers and their song shapes had the same simple compactness of Buddy Holly. Much of their material was blues-based and some of the songs were country, so that altogether I could see that their musical influences were eclectic. However, I found no evidence of British music hall, that influence they expressed in their interviews. Altogether, though, their songs were, in the end, all their own—and I could find little to imitate.

I was not good at the "I-me-you" song formula and modes weren't my forte. Lyrically, that damned Pre-Raphaelite imagery kept butting into my song efforts—Ophelia and King Arthur—and when Celtic laments started to intrude, I cursed Trinity's famous treasury of literature.

The common touch was needed, some street lingo. Then, while walking down Grafton Street in search of a pork pie, I was bumped by a drunk whom I recognized as a former history lecturer since fallen on bad times. Gambling, girls, and Guinness had taken their toll on this scholar—the sporting life was killing him. That was it! I'd almost forgotten the advice of that Seattle deejay: I should utilize the old skiffle/folk song, tricking it up with pop clothes in a way that would rock the charts, as well as satisfy my academic and folk leanings—not to mention my friends and colleagues.

Alone at the Drama Society's piano, I thought about the Animals' recording of "House of the Rising Sun." I too should have the drums crashing in six/eight time, but I would also employ a great, swirling organ, arpeggiated guitars, and my piano. Piano and organ—a traditional gospel sound. And I, as vocalist, should scream and growl about the rough times on the wild side of life, but in my expensive accent? No good for the searing seriousness I was hearing in my mind. No—I would sing the song in a voice of the people, in a cockney accent. It would be the sound of the suffering forever paying their dues.

I was taking no chances: I also altered the song title to "This Sporting Life," since there had recently been a tough and well-received film with that title. *Newly familiar* material is a pop secret.

Like a Dublin Spector, I worked on the number all that winter. Eventually, I cajoled Bluesville into the Merrion Square basement studio and we tried a version. But there wasn't the necessary *angst*. Also— no organ there. I located a Trinity student who not only had a small Farfisa organ but also was working part-time in a professional studio in downtown Dublin. He suggested that we make a demo tape for the studio owners. They also controlled a string of Irish ballrooms and clubs and a stable of racehorses. Dangling temptations of fame before them, I again cajoled Bluesville into recording. We got a passable version, though the organ was terribly thin and shrill. But in the last chorus, I had the brilliant idea of jumping to a higher register and screaming with real pain. This was a hook, an ear-grabber.

The studio owners turned me down, but asked if I'd like to invest in a chain of Sino-Irish takeout restaurants. Oh well, I had my tape and only a little doctoring was necessary before its launching. By this time, Christmas was almost upon us and the term was over. I didn't trust the mails with my precious tape. Like a fine artwork, it needed careful accompaniment on any journey. Then, on the radio, I heard a hit by a group new to me, the Shangri-Las, who sang lustily of their love for the "Leader of the Pack" in a dramatic Spectorlike production. When I saw a picture of the lead singer, Mary Weiss, in her black boots and plastic short skirt and blond hair, I lusted madly for Debbie. I put two and two together and decided to make a trip to Seattle. Yes, Debbie's father told me on the telephone, they'd love to have me spend Christmas with them, especially since their eldest son, Haxell Jr., was getting married again. I would add a touch of class. Don't forget the ukulele.

Quickly, I joined an Anglo-Swiss nursing group, thus qualifying for a seat on their Christmas charter trip to San Francisco.

I was staying at the family's neo-Tudor ranch-style home on leafy Bainbridge Island and I was being charming to the parents and servicing Debbie well—but my mind was on my tape and Jerden. While the family was intently dressing the Christmas tree and Debbie was safely in the kitchen running up a batch of sponge fingers with my favorite passion-fruit topping, I slipped away to Jerden to play Jerry the tape. Even at that evening hour, Jerry was in his office, phoning distributors, radio stations, pluggers. He nodded and tapped a foot as we listened to the tape. I said it needed more organ swamp to make it hitbound. Jerry said, "Whatever's right." He did some quick calculating and gave me another nod. From one of his many Northwest rock groups, an organist was summoned and, in the studio around the corner, as the snow fell in tons outside, the kid and his Hammond threw a great fog over my original recording. As a final commercial touch, like the olive pinned to a club sandwich, I rattled some maracas.

The tape was then mixed and later packed off to be mastered and pressed. This time, it would say IAN WHITCOMB AND BLUESVILLE. Now I had another excruciating wait—until January of 1965. To take my mind off it, I threw myself headlong into the traditional American "White Christmas"—decking the halls with holly, rocking around the tree, and stacking the yuletide albums by Perry Como, Bing Crosby, and the Hawaiian Hula Boys on the family stereo system. I even went for a mechanical sleigh ride with the family. On Christmas Day, I managed to hold down that vile mixture of candied meats and gooey cakes and jams that Americans consume at this time. It was all very alien: for me, Christmas takes place in Europe. At last I felt I was in the Wild West, right on the frontier, but I plugged on, irregardless and with much hypocrisy. I kept servicing Debbie and she responded rather too intensely, talking of love and future baby-making.

"A double wedding would have been real dandy," said her father as we sipped Napa Valley champagne after Debbie's brother's wedding. I got another wink and also a nudge. The combo was playing the Notre Dame fight song and I had just danced with Debbie's mother, who had clutched me very tight. I knew I had to get out of this place pretty soon. Exploitation time!

So it was back to Dublin, back to lectures, back to playing the grubby engagements. Back to wait for the next assault on the American Dream. . . .

4

1965: "EVE OF DESTRUCTION"

October, 1965:

A tragic encounter at a Trinity party. A silly party full of high seriousness, raucous laughter, and smoke, and thrown by two chinless wonders and attended by gray men and skinny women. Competing with the human noise was a drone of Beatles, Stones, and Dylan after Dylan after Dylan. Acoustic and electric. People were dancing to the electric Dylan. Overall, the sound of the party was a petulant whine to the beat of the slow drip of cant.

What was I doing here on Upper Mount Street among the cream of the new urban folk rockniks? I fancied the distant Ffiona in the knee boots and wire glasses and I was dying to raise the fire that I knew lay dormant beneath those multicolored wool knits.

Suddenly and astoundingly, the Man in Black arrived: Roy Orbison! I'd seen him earlier that night at a concert at the stadium, but I never dreamed I'd see him in the flesh. He was a mysterious stage figure, dark and gloomy and yet magnificent and godlike, gliding from song to song with never a word in between, stark still while all around him moved and shook. But what was he doing here among us mortals?

He had fallen into the company of a notorious personality collector, the "mad" Earl of Ballsbridge, a perpetual Trinity student, now aged forty or so. The Earl, clutching a bottle of Bollinger, was remonstrating with a chinless host. Then said the host: "I'm sorry, we're fed up with you and your silly pranks. It's not Halloween yet and I don't know your friend's face." The door slammed against both the Earl and Roy Orbison.

But even if this ignoramus had never heard the soaring bel canto voice of the "Big O," even if the fool had never heard "In Dreams" or "Oh, Pretty Woman," he surely couldn't turn away such a striking presence. Clad in black from top to toe, from the black helmet of hair and black shades down through the black matador outfit to the shiny black Cuban boots, Orbison resembled a heavenly stygian being, a man in perpetual mourning, a creature from another world, the antipode to O. Stoppit of the pier show—and here was a door slamming into a slice of pop history!

In the nick of time, I dashed across and interposed my body between door and doorway. I wised up the host, who gleefully rushed away, announcing that the entertainment had arrived. The "Big O" rewarded me with a smile, a "thank you," and a handshake. Yes, he knew my name and my hit record. Then he faded into a gloomy corner with a mulled fruit juice and a plate of cheese that a bluestocking girl had handed him. Some members of his entourage managed to squeeze through in Orbison's wake and I soon got into conversation with a man who appeared to be a combination rhythm guitarist, road manager, and co-songwriter.

I asked how things were going. "Oh, we love the North of England and the South of Ireland. They never forget. But it's tough in the big cities this year. Seems there's a mood against Roy's *singing*." I said that there was a mood against singing, period. And what a shame when Orbison has raised himself up from his humble hillbilly origins to stalk the skies with his resounding bel canto. "I've lost you there," said the cohort, "but I do know we're just not making the charts like last year. We sold thirty million units up till now and, oh Lord, 1965 was to have been such a banner year. Roy's bursting with great songs that two-and-a-half minutes of vinyl just cain't hold. Know what I mean?" I suggested that Orbison should write a Western opera starring himself as the Lone Avenger. "We got our feelers out, but I'm tellin' you, it's hard times ahead. Roy just cain't talk a song. Now, we're not knocking the protesters and such, but it's so hard for Roy to sing gutter bad. He's raised himself above that gritty dust bowl hobo stuff. We did so look forward to 1965. . . ."

Our talk was interrupted by the intrusion of the chinless host: "I say, look here—is your friend with the Adam's apple going to oblige us with some mountain ditty, something reeking in dissatisfaction with the whole fabric of modern society? Something we can dance to? And has he got his banjo to strum?"

1965: A year with a certain ring for me: this was to be my Annus Mirabilis—the year in which I joined the great brotherhood of rock 'n' roll stars. More importantly, I suppose, it was a watershed year for pop music, the year in which the sixties, as we came to know them in all their opinionated noise, began. Before 1965, we were still basking in the last glows of the Golden Age of Rock 'n' Roll.

This archaic term was to be replaced by "rock"—austere, hard-staring, all-questioning, and all-embracing "rock." True, there would be cloaks, and beads, and flowing medieval locks, and flowered shirts and incense and peppermints—but all this finery would have deep purpose and meaning. Current affairs and pop music were to come together, the highbrow would mix with the lowbrow. Film-makers, journalists, poets, and soldiers would contribute to the rock consciousness. Eventually, even the Vietnam War would be known as the "Rock War." The era of jelly bean fun was to disappear forever in this extraordinary year of racket and high visibility, of tumult and shouting, and, finally, screaming.

This was the year in which America recovered from Beatlemania and the British Invasion. This was the year in which she hit back with her more meaningful and relevant music, the folk rock of the Byrds and the music of the master, Bob Dylan, who recorded protest songs about poverty and fighting that one could sing to. Current events provided fuel for the songs: America took off its Clark Kent costume and super-soldiered into Vietnam, upping the number of troops from twenty thousand at the start of the year to over two hundred thousand by the end. On the home front, President Johnson declared a billion-dollar war on poverty and pushed through ninety major reform bills—a record. At the same time, America was supposed to be enjoying the greatest prosperity in her history, but this private and public plenty seemed to have eluded, yet again, the blacks and the poor. Their weapons were anger, frustration, and, ultimately, violence. There was fire in the streets. Watts was torched.

For the young middle class, the moneyed majority, this was the time to get up and go. Drugs were there to be discovered. LSD was still legal. There were dozens of other highs, both chemical and natural. The world held infinite possibilities and there was a scurry among would-be pacesetters to be the leaders of those young millions who now owned it. The Beatles, most notably, could no longer churn out the cute one-liners of Learlike nonsense, nor could they rush around in any more self-indulgent whimsies like *Help!* They needed substance like Dylan and, at the end of the year, they emerged triumphant with their answer to the New Consciousness, *Rubber Soul*. Also from Britain came the Who, with their dazzling display of autodestruction, a comment on our violent age and an articulation of Mod inarticulateness, "My Generation." The world is such a mess it makes me stutter, it blocks me, the album declared.

Everyone of any importance was contributing to the new rock. Poets who had studied English lit. and had come away full of literary imagery appeared and actually made the charts. Simon and Garfunkel—a name that should have been kept for legal firms or upholsterers— explained that there was such a thing as "The Sounds of Silence." What next? At least the Invaders had introduced a revitalized American music with a British music-hall flavor. But these new intruders were bringing in a high seriousness and a musical news commentary. For that, I needed only to go to lectures and the library and read the newspapers!

But, "In my beginning is my end," wrote T. S. Eliot and, wisely, he didn't stay for question time. He also wrote, "In my end is my beginning," and still the world was none the wiser. Especially not in 1965 and the rest of the sixties. We were entering into a strange astral era of planets in and out of alignment and of minds in and out of synch. The only people in the way of this new progress were those who were *irrelevant*. For example, Ian Whitcomb, teen idol for a week or so.

And yet, as 1965 began, I was poised on the brink of amazing America and the pop world with a record that combined folk music, ragtime, social commentary, and rock 'n' roll: "This Sporting Life." A record that was to be the triumphant end of my love affair with American music and the British music hall, an affair that had begun way back in the summer of 1949 when I had rejoiced in the Tannoy music at the seaside—American pop—and then, later that night, experienced the extraordinary mixture of laughter and tears that was O. Stoppit, the end-of-pier comedian. Both American pop and O. Stoppit constituted my great escape into a new and personal reality.

All through the subsequent years, I had yearned to contribute to those exciting rhythms already shunting, clattering, clip-clopping, stomping, ragging, boogie-ing, swinging, rocking around the world. But most of all, I wanted to put my rhythm on the rails of America—the country that was forever on the move, on the road, on the up-and-up, on the make. Where problems were settled with a swift left to the jaw —and then one moved on to the next town, the next state, or just faded away into the sunset. Freedom! Of course, I loved my friends and family and, after a spot of freedom, it's great to come home again.

So I was ready to contribute to American popular culture: some finely wrought yet unpretentious work that might appeal to the masses. And what happened? The American people elevated me to fame with a trifle, a piece of piffle knocked off in a fit of absence of mind:

"COME ON NOW, BABY, YOU KNOW YOU REALLY TURN ME ON!"*

Sir Winston Churchill died in January 1965, but the Great Britain that he had supported in word and deed had died during World War II. Ideas like duty, service, manners, noblesse oblige, and patriotism were gradually reduced in importance and, by 1965, weren't even currency for satire. Britain was to become a decorative and quaint background for the swingers of the world. Of course, my class and I had been on a growling retreat for years. Most of my colleagues and relatives lived in walled estates in the still-lovely English countryside.

Bursting with bombast and energy was the newly elected Labour Party and in their leader, Harold Wilson, they had a crafty trimmer who immediately identified himself with pop. Perpetually dressed in his utilitarian Gannex raincoat and continually making points with his pipe, Wilson never tired of telling us that he was a member of Parliament for Liverpool, where the Beatles came from. He liked to be photographed with them. John Lennon called him "Mr. Dobson" to his face, but Wilson smiled on, regardless. He knew which side his bread was buttered on. He was "with it." He ordered up fast-moving slogans in the street pop lingo: "Let's Go with Labour!" His people talked of "The New Egalitarianism," "The New Classless Society," of speed and action. "Dynamism" became a trendy word.

Of course, the media responded. They had been told that the economy was on a huge upswing (it was, in fact, in irreversible decline)

---

and that now was the time to spend. The Sunday newspaper supplements were crammed with full-color ads for all the material things of life; article after article informed us of our new heroes, not only the Beatles but also fashion designers, hair stylists, bistro chefs, antique shop owners, gambling casino impresarios. These were the Pacesetters (another key word). They had drive and they loved money and all of them went to the same clubs as the Beatles and Mick Jagger. But were there enough rock stars to go around? The search was on for more of the same. There must be more Lennons and more Jaggers around.

The frenetic speed of the times was reflected in ITV's popular rock 'n' roll show, "Ready, Steady, Go!" On the screen, we saw a jumble of dancers in the very latest gear, actual TV cameras and lights that flooded and blinded our picture momentarily, and then, somewhere among the scrimmage, our star—Marianne Faithfull. I remember her mournful rendition of "As Tears Go By," her big eyes circled with makeup, her clothes from granny's era, yet sexy in that current casual manner.

I had sensed the quickening pace of the times. *Dynamism.* I wanted to be part of the race, but I also wanted to capture it on paper. Nothing was real to me unless written down on paper.

I bought myself a legal-sized journal.

I took out subscriptions, not only to *Billboard* but also to *Cash Box* and *Record World.* All these were "trade" papers and written in special trade lingo. I particularly enjoyed *Coin Operator,* which reported about jukeboxes and their world. Here I seemed not far away from Philip Marlowe and Mickey Spillane. Records in the review section were "comers," "hot slices," "smasheroos," "stone foxes," and, just before they made the Hot One Hundred, they were "bubbling under." On the British charts, I studied (and enjoyed) the new Beatles record, "I Feel Fine," a pleasant, jogalong song. From deep in the London R&B scene, where he'd been a resident at the very Mod Flamingo Club, came Georgie Fame and the Blue Flames with "Yeh, Yeh." This was a real breakthrough for the scene, but made at the expense of the singer's fine North Country origins. He'd been born Clive Powell and hailed from Lancashire—Larry Parnes had rechristened him. Also from the London R&B scene came the Moody Blues. They'd been holding the fort at the Marquee and there they might have remained, deep in the ethnic groove, had they not recorded a version of an obscure black American R&B record called "Go Now" (originally recorded by Bessie Banks). A funk waltz, this sprightly little record shot up to number one in England and hastened the Moody Blues into an image befitting the Regency perambulatory rhythm of their hit: ruffles and frills and enormous lapels. They also posed for the press with moody looks and stances.

Still, there was nothing of their Birmingham background in their work. At least Gerry and the Pacemakers sounded Lancastrian, summoning up a truly romantic picture of Liverpool and its waters in "Ferry Cross the Mersey."

Much fuss was made about the emergence of a beefy new beat balladeer, Tom Jones from Wales. "It's Not Unusual" was certainly a meaty number with an infectious Latin rhythm and Jones had great pipes, but I preferred and cheered Del Shannon's "Keep Searchin'," which went high on both sides of the Atlantic. A welcome return. But where was Orbison? "Oh, Pretty Woman" had been an enormous success last year. I got so engrossed in seeing what my competition was doing that I even found myself trying to complete the pop crossword in *Beat Sounds*. And all the time I was watching and hoping that my record would jump into the Hot One Hundred or at least "bubble under."

I was watching and waiting and reading when one day I received a summons to see my tutor. He said he spoke for all my teachers when he admitted that my pop preoccupations were getting out of hand. "Could you not show an equal interest in, say, the Fenian movement in relation to Parnell? Or, perhaps, in nineteenth-century working-class movements?" At that moment, due to a gulped lunch of Galtee processed cheese with brown sauce, washed down with a pint of Guinness, the only movements of which I was aware were in my bowels. But, instead, I answered that I was going to have a bash at the study of communism during this coming term. "With special emphasis on the use of the barricade in nineteenth-century street fighting?" Yes. "Good fellow—it's not that we frown on your extramural activities, it's just that we at Trinity want to produce the well-rounded gentleman."

It was true that friends and faculty had been getting mighty tired of seeing me flash my record contract and little blue disc. Many had advised me not to take this sideline too seriously, while others (deeper into English well-bred backgrounds) told me not to "show off." They were right: exhibitionism was for foreigners.

I addressed myself to academic studies and kept my journal. . . .

February 25:
Gratified to have rooms in college at last (Oscar Wilde had rooms on this same block), but it's really very irritating when they're used as a club by professional students, some of whom are well into their forties and comparative strangers to me. Clearly, they're lured by the merry coal fire and its pot of mulled claret. Certainly, I set the fire, but where

the claret came from I have no idea. Came home late from a clandestine Bluesville gig last night to find a clutch of these strangers feeding my fire with my furniture. When I complained, I was breathed on heavily by one of them and told to, "Give us some rhythm and blues." Too tired to show them the door and, besides, one of them was wearing the uniform of an IRA sergeant.

March 12:

Bitterly cold still and I must admit that the warmth produced by the tangle of bodies sleeping in my rooms is most welcome. Some of these strangers are beginning to seem like old friends and one turned out to be a degowned history professor (buggery), who has been most helpful on my history research. In fact, he's turned me on to Trotsky. But the Big News is this: early this morning, I returned from a gig at Sound City, Dublin's own Cavern (where I've been having great success shouting the slogan "You Turn Me On" to a serious blues riff that the band plays). A Seattle girl taught me the slogan, as I recall. Anyway, I returned to find a telegram waiting for me. In Gaelic, of course, but I got one of the strangers—the IRA chap, I think—to translate: RECORD OUT NATIONALLY VIA TOWER LABEL, SUBSIDIARY OF CAPITOL RECORDS. FANTASTIC REACTION HERE, IAN. I FEEL THIS CAN BE A LEFT-FIELD SMASHEROO. REGARDS, JERRY. This was an excuse for all and sundry to celebrate with cups of mulled wine and start throwing my bedroom furniture on the fire.

April 2:

Am trying hard to repress my excitement and vaulting ambition but it's difficult. I *so* want to show off! Trying to keep a straight face during lectures about "Descartes and his Candle" but wanting to shout out loud. Jerry has sent me a mass of clippings about my record. E.g.: "This Sporting Life" reported at number ninety with a bullet in *Record World* ("Newcomer stretches the blues out into a taut performance. Slice is a worker.") The Fenway *Reporter* says, "Like, it's weird. Definitely a record. Requests should be coming in after a few days' play." *Cash Box* has me at 22 percent airplay in their "Radio Active" chart. And it's on the playlist at loads of stations throughout Good Old America—KJR (Seattle!), KFWB, KRUX, WAPX, WBIG, WMAC. . . .

Another telegram just arrived: PLEASE GET BLUESVILLE IN ACCORD, AS I WILL BE OVER TO CUT ALBUM BEFORE YOU CAN SAY PHIL SPECTOR. REGARDS, JERRY. Trinity has produced Edmund Burke, Oscar Wilde, Samuel Beckett, J. P. Donleavy—and now another artist! Break out some more claret!

April 12:

Jerry Dennon arrived today from Seattle, looking very businesslike, rather solemn. There's a "money potential quotient" at stake and it seems I'd better shape up and start to take this record biz seriously again. I'd booked him into the ethnic Royal Hibernian Hotel, charmingly Edwardian, but he quickly changed to the Intercontinental, where they have iced water and *The Wall Street Journal.* That evening, in their restaurant, I was punishing a T-bone while Jerry was toying with fresh Boston prawns *de Wolfe Tone* when a phone was brought to our table. After the batteries had been changed and the machine cranked, Jerry learned that the call was long-distance *from Hollywood.* An agent from General Artists Corporation (GAC) (Jerry wrote this in cablese on a napkin) had just "caught this fantastic disc" on his car radio and he had to pull off the freeway and call around to see if this "Irish lass" was signed. Jerry dealt with the call in honeyed words, committing us to nothing, and later in his suite we signed a heap of papers. I felt so important due to all this paperwork. I signed and signed. Even later, a deputation from Bluesville arrived to demand contracts too. I hid in a closet. After doing all the lonely spadework, I now find everybody trying to get into the act. Every man a star. Jerry dealt with them beautifully, never losing his temper and never granting anything. They went away happy, with little model Indians from the Great Northwest.

April 13:

A busy, red-letter day! First off, I was surprised to see a suntanned adult in a turtleneck and cream slacks drop in on my medieval history class—and try to get off with Ffiona, one of the better-endowed bluestockings (in fact, he succeeded in making a date with her, which *I've* never managed to do!). Later, this brazen fellow followed me into my rooms, whistling, "We're in the Money." In he came, if you please, and plunked himself in the easy chair usually reserved for comparative strangers. At this stage, I thought I'd better ask him his business. "Come Fly with Me," he replied. I busied myself with making some toast while he explained in normal language that he was Hal Shaper, my publisher for Britain and the world, excluding the U.S.A. and Canada. He doodled copyright signs on my notepaper. But how had he heard of me? All through an old chum of mine, Denny Cordell-Lavarack, who had been at Public School with my brother and had later played one-string tea chest bass in one of my many bands. Denny was now, apparently, making something of a name for himself in the London pop scene, involved with the Moody Blues and Georgie Fame and Brian Epstein and God knows what else. "You should come over and see us in the hopping, popping, and swinging world of London," said Hal. Then, from his cream slacks pocket, he fished out a manuscript, which turned out to be an antiwar protest song called "No Tears for Johnny." This sounded like excellent Thinking Man's material and might well elevate me into the American college folk league. I was aware that Bob Dylan and Joan Baez had both made the British charts with straight, unadulterated folk songs. But I knew that Americans—my people—preferred their messages with a dose of beat.

Hal gave me a rendition of the protest number in the Johnny Mathis dulcet manner, rightly suggesting I record it in my own inimitable cockney/ragtime/rock 'n' roll style. Then he excused himself with a couple of soft-shoe steps and, as he flew through the doorway, brushing against an arriving gang of professional students in search of hot buttered toast, he sang loudly: " 'Got a Date with an Angel'—Ffiona!—so it's 'Softly, as I Leave You.' " I later discovered that he wrote the lyrics of "Softly as I Leave You." Clever fellow. South African, too.

Later:

Rushed around to the Intercontinental to show Jerry the song and get his approval. He was awash in a sea of paperwork—more contracts on yours truly! I sang him the song and he offered me a mint and said, "Whatever's right, Ian, whatever's right."

Even later:

We've just finished cutting the LP at the cubbyhole studio where we did "This Sporting Life." They're charging a high price now, but Jerry *talked to them.* During the recording, Jerry paced the control room nervously, but Hal smiled and snapped his fingers. After we'd laid down all our serious numbers, including "No Tears for Johnny" (which came out well; I kept Joan Baez in mind as I sang it and Hal put his copyright signature on the tape box at the end), the band went into a boogie-shuffle jam. Oh Christ, I thought, here they go showing off! I joined in on the piano, but it was painful because the drummer's cymbal dug into my back due to his excitement and the smallness of the studio. And after a few bars of this Chuck Berrylike blues riff, I reckoned the effort a write-off because there was a great *thud* as a hefty ashtray, powered by the music, slid off my piano and onto the floor. Forget it, I thought. So, for a lark, I got close to the massive ex-BBC talk-show mike and began whimpering a chorus about being "turned on." I was remembering that Seattle girl, the way the Dublin girls reacted to my singing "You Turn Me On" at the clubs, and the little-girl voices of the Supremes. Apart from that, I wasn't thinking of anything. I knew we weren't doing this for real.

But we were. Jerry had left the tapes running. He played it back and we all agreed it was frightful, though Hal said he'd better put his copyright on the thing. Then we split.

Much, much later:

Jerry and Hal are here in my rooms, poring over contracts and agreements and also discussing my future. So rarely do I get this kind of attention—normally I'm treated like a doormat, speaking of which, I'm at last free of the uninvited student guests, thanks to Hal. He's a black belt in karate and he threw them all out—shellalaughs, bottles of stout, fishing rods, and all. So while Hal and Jerry mold me into a "product," I'm going to settle down to some work on Bakunin, the anarchist, who's even more fascinating than Trotsky or Marx.

April 24:

Jerry has flown back to America with our tapes, anxious to play them to the executives and pop pickers at Tower Records, Hollywood. I expect they'll choose the protest song since it's so like "This Sporting Life." The latter has bogged down on the lower rungs of the Hot One Hundred. With "No Tears for Johnny," I'll be able to make my statement to the American people and establish myself as a sensible star. Just received a telegram from Jerry, which reads: WILL KEEP YOU APPRISED. He's more eloquent in cables than conversation. But no matter—Americans really understand the business of business and I for one will gladly leave them to handle such matters.

Today I locked up my rooms and flew back to London with Hal Shaper (and Ffiona, who has unaccountably taken up with Hal—I always suspected she was part colonial because of her pronunciation of her *as*). Hal said I should come to London, in order to "come out" as he puts it. Rather like a debutante. "No no," says Hal. "All that's gone in this new era of the Swinging Sixties. Come to Swinging London and take your pick from the supermarket of sex, drugs, and rock 'n' roll. Whatever's your color or taste, we've got it."

Though on the brink of economic disaster, the Britain that I returned to was enjoying a night-and-day party. While the oldsters bought TVs and other electric appliances, the youngsters went out on the town and raved. The center for raving was London, that run-down, peeling, blackened, geriatric accumulation of past glories which was to be dubbed "Swinging London" by a group of American journalists in search of a story. The serious swinging went on at night around the West End to a backdrop of historical monuments, statues of Empire-builders, huge Victorian piles of art galleries, the Houses of Parliament, and Buckingham Palace. In the clubs and bistros and all-night rave joints, the swinging set lived their dream in a whirl of pure hedonism.

All classes mingled and all emerged with the same dreary suburban-London accent. No trace of excitement, except in the language, which was all superlatives. Everything was *fabulous,* in a monotone. Most fab-ulous were the clothes and, if Swinging London meant anything, it meant gaudy and multicolored clothes. One dolly bird might be wear-ing plastic on her thighs. Her boy friend might be dressed like an officer from the Crimean War, though his father had only been a pri-vate in World War II. Britain's glorious past was raided unmercifully and laughed at. Dozens of little antique-clothes shops dotted the back streets of Chelsea, selling everything from Raj pith helmets to Battle of Britain air ace helmets. What a laugh to mix all the periods up into one hilarious cocktail ensemble. And then to talk like a common coal-heaver. Maybe you *were* the son of a coal-heaver or maybe you were the heir to a dukedom. Everyone was the same, everyone dis-sembling, in this Mad Hatter's tea party that was *Swinging London.*

Working quietly behind this mad whirl was a new group: the Public School Mafia. These gentlemen were the new breed of pop entre-preneurs. Some were even performers, like Peter Asher, Jeremy Clyde, and a group straight from Public School called the Bunch of Fives, but most preferred to keep a low profile, wheeling and dealing, with kid gloves and "blah" accents, *behind the scenes.* But though they may have given the impression of being effete and perhaps even P. G. Wodehousian, when it came to hard cash and tough deals these gentle-men could give the roughest spaghetti-eating Chicago jukebox operators a run for their money. Brian Epstein, a minor Public School man, was not typical of this Mafia, but he was a charming and very safe figure-head, being truly innocent when it came to squeezing the most dollars from the Yanks.

Traditionally, the great Public Schools had been training grounds for Empire administrators, boys who would become wiry, muscular, goal-directed men, skilled at superintending natives in every corner of our far-flung possessions. Now the greatest of those possessions was gone and yet the schools remained. For the blacker sheep of the student body, the gleaming pop sixties presented a ripe plum. The public were the new natives.

So the days of the British Alleymen were numbered—those incredi-bly aged men with bulbous, gin-soaked noses and fat cigars and presen-tation pen sets on their desks. Many moved out of records and shows into the quieter pastures of music publishing. Dick James, once a top crooner via records like "Robin Hood," was content to run the Beatles' publishing company and watch the money roll in. Andrew Loog Oldham, Denny Cordell-Lavarack (who was soon to produce Georgie Fame, Procul Harum, the Move, etc.), Kit Lambert (manager of the Who), Chris Blackwell (of Crosse and Blackwell), and Simon Napier Bell (who became associated with the Yardbirds) were among those who formed the new Invaders. They were to prove a good match for the Americans.

I was now to be introduced into this world of Swinging London and crafty Public School men by Hal Shaper.

April 27:

A hectic round of clubs and parties, as part of my initiation as a burgeoning pop star. Bought a pair of hipster trousers, but they're most uncomfortable: they either want to slip off or I'm always tugging them up in a vain attempt to get them above my waist in the old style. The man at John Stephen's said I had an unfashionable hip size. Nobody has any hips these days, apparently.

At the Scotch of St. James, a trendy club decorated in Scottish baronial, big pop names laze around in murky corners, sipping Scotch and Coke mostly. I saw George Harrison looking gloomy, but I'm told he's always like that. Something about feeling inadequate regarding his guitar expertise. Was about to introduce myself to Mick Jagger when Hal warned me off: I was wearing the same hipster plaid as Jagger and he likes to be exclusive.

We moved on to another part of the club, where the Afro-Cuban band wasn't quite so loud. Here Hal introduced me to Kit Lambert, who manages the Mod group the Who. He was very well spoken and I felt quite at home and thus rather inhibited. He was wearing a Guards Brigade tie, which I thought a bit dubious. Still, the Who are pretty hot right now—"I Can't Explain" is at number twelve on the British charts—but in America they still haven't broken through. Perhaps too closely associated with the local sociological scene, Mods and Rockers and Op Art, etc.?

"Wait and see," replied Kit Lambert. "We have carefully planned ways and means. The Who aren't going to *follow* any trends; we're going to *set* them."

A lumbering figure like me, Kit Lambert was originally attracted to pop because of its potential for instant fame, excitement, and action. As he also said, "It's a field where it's possible to make a great deal of money very quickly." We had each separately toiled as assistant directors in the dying days of the well-bred, well-tuned, suit-and-tie British cinema. Genteel stories about an ordered society. But films took a tiresome long time to make and the old Ealing-type subjects were goners.

Lambert met a kindred soul in Chris Stamp, another assistant director, and together they decided they'd make a short movie about a vital, contemporary happening: the pop group. Beatlemania was at its height and, though they'd have dearly loved to have acquired a bona fide proven hit outfit, they hadn't the necessary cash, so they decided they'd go out and find some unknowns and build them up into stars for their film project, some group that was wild, noisy, and dangerous. They'd do an Epstein.

One night, ferreting around, Lambert found himself in the drab and unfashionable northwest part of London, at the Railway Tavern at Harrow and Wealdstone. Onstage were the Tuesday night regulars, the High Numbers, with their guitarist Pete Townshend.

Kit Lambert had chanced onto the Railway Tavern at exactly the right moment. Pete Townshend had only recently discovered guitar-bashing and -smashing. It had all happened by accident a few weeks ago at this same Mod hangout. . . .

Since their first days as the Detours, the group had run through many pop styles: Beatles songs, Dave Clark marches, a Tamla/Motown binge, and heaps of Buddy Guy, the great Chicago blues guitarist. Blues—that was their best form. Their own numbers (Townshend's, actually), were based on blues because blues' simplicity and clean-slate framework allowed freedom of expression. No complex chord changes and bridge passages, plenty of feeling. But even here, in this musical child's garden, Pete Townshend was frustrated because, although he had these tremendous feelings, they came out deformed when he played them. When he'd been at art school, self-expression had been a swift matter of splashing paint straight onto the canvas or a handy wall. Brushes, pencils, pens—no technicalities standing between artist and work. But this electric guitar was like a rented horse—it wouldn't gallop. It wouldn't fire out that feeling inside him, a feeling welling up so giant and so Today, so much more Here and Now than old-fashioned canvas-dabbing. But he hadn't had the time or patience to study any Chet Atkins guitar instruction book with those diagrams on proper fretting, fingering, and bars. It was OK for Loony Moony—enthroned at the back like a rear gunner, assaulting the skins, deep into his own crazy world—and Entwhistle looked stolidly content with his lot as he picked out the notes on his bass. Very steady and reliable compared with raver Roger Daltrey—prancing and preening and strutting like a Jagger parody, stalking the low-ceilinged stage, kicking up the dust of ages, and always staring down angrily at the self-obsessed narcissists bopping in oblivion. Roger was lucky because he could tear away like mad at the blues, shout till he was purple, even spit on the out-sized collars of passing Mod sissies.

Maybe Roger was expressing a general, vague anger at the hide-bound, claustrophobic atmosphere of England? Kit Lambert loved this anger, relished it. Such deafening, wonderful noise, too! The louder they played, thought Pete, the more they could cover up their technical deficiencies—and he was really having trouble with his blues feelings now. The runs were coming out crippled, damn them, but he took it out on the guitar by shaking, throttling, and whacking the thing down like an ax and windmilling with his arm as he crashed onto the chord, as if this violence would make the music scream and thus achieve that deep inner feeling he wanted to express.

And if the scream feeling wasn't achieved, if it was just a nasty din— well, at least they were making visual expression. Visual arts, animated graphics he understood. So Pete was struggling with his guitar—axing, throttling, windmilling—and he became so frustrated that he raised the machine high in order to crash down on the constipated chord, but the ceiling was so low that *bong! craack!* the guitar stem smashed. An expensive guitar, busted and splintered just like that. But worse, those dumb, conceited, drugged Mods paid not a bit of attention. So to get that attention, he stomped around the stage with the wounded guitar, strings and splintered neck dangling. When he found the head and other bits on the floor, he threw the lot into the crowd—and then they paid attention. In fact, they loved it and wanted an encore. Well, they got more and how! Keith Moon accompanied the guitar-smashing by destroying his drum kit. It was all very exciting and bloody expensive, but nobody dubbed the exercise "autodestruction" just yet.

Kit Lambert said, "Bingo!" He knew that in the High Numbers he'd found his mass art form. He had noted the noise, the violence, the electricity. He noted Daltrey's sexy body and he didn't mind Townshend's big hooter because his whirling-dervish act more than compensated. And, of course, Moon was Bakunin, the anarchist, visiting the Modern Era. Yes, he had it. But he noted also the tremendous rapport that the group had with their audience. Oh, the group didn't smile and smarm like old music-hall hacks. They shot at the crowd from rock guns and the kids ate up the bullets. The kids were clapping along and bobbing fast on up-tempo numbers and smooching on the slow ones. The question was whether this Mod movement—which appeared to Lambert to be more intelligent and advanced than those of the Beatles or Stones—

could be spread into the big lucrative pop mainline? Could the cult movement have mass appeal?

Lambert broke the good news to Chris Stamp and together they went to view the theatrical spectacle at a gig in Watford, another horribly drab and unfashionable part of London. They knew they'd have to lift the High Numbers out of this small-potato circuit and into the West End, into a decent recording deal, and onto some network TV—if they were to start a whole new scene and make them big stars and big money.

A meeting was arranged. Lambert and Stamp described their plans, their visions, and their cash guarantee. If the group signed to this management deal, they'd be assured of a thousand pounds a year, even if they didn't work at all. Robert Stigwood, a hungry Australian, would act as their agent. Pete Meadon, their present manager, would have to go. He'd worked hard, but his vision was limited: too parochial, too outer-London. Meadon was a real Mod, a self-conscious one and too committed. Yes, he'd gotten them a record with Fontana, but "I'm the Face" was too obvious, a shopping list of Mod talk and Mod gear, as though it had been gleaned from a handbook on the wonderful world of Carnaby Street. The record had flopped.

The High Numbers agreed to sign and Lambert and Stamp raced to work. First off, their previous group name was restored: "High Numbers" was culty, cliquish, obscure. The public might think the group was dream-wishing to be high on the charts—and how amateur a wish that was! But the name "The Who" was perfect: noncommittal, impersonal, suggestive of lost identity, of Mod Made Universal. Kids could identify with the name and others would be mystified. It would make great copy for journalists, who always love word-play. "The Who." "The Who?" "The Who." "The What?" "No—the *Who*."

Next priority was apparel and hair. "Appearance is the most immediate concern with the kids," said Lambert. He'd been watching them carefully from the back of Who appearances; Townshend, in turn, had been watching them from the stage. The two minds met and mixed Mod fashion with Pop Art fashion. Andy Warhol in America and Peter Blake in Britain had popularized the term "Pop Art" by using everyday commercial objects like soup cans, Coke bottles, and national flags as the subject matter of fine art. Why should painting be restricted to still-life fruit arrangements, peaceful landscapes, or lifeless abstraction? There was beauty to be found in modern ugliness. But, while Pop Art was confined to galleries and magazine spreads, the canvas of the Mods was *real life*. They were walking, talking, finger-snapping *works of Pop Art*. And now the Who organization was to take this a step further by introducing Mod Pop Art into pop music. In 1964, the chicest area to be involved in was pop music, thanks to the Beatles and their followers.

Wardrobes of clothes were purchased from Carnaby Street; expensive hair stylists were employed. Pete was persuaded to have the Union Jack tailored into a jacket; muscular, thin Roger Daltrey was dressed in sausage-skin hipster trousers and a tight white sweater on which he would spell out various slogans using adhesive tape. Keith Moon wore a T-shirt with a bull's-eye and the legend: POW!

After clothes, the next detail was attitude. The boys were encouraged to be as rude and nasty as possible—in print. They were to issue statements that the world had had it. They were to brag and bluster, to out-Jagger Mick Jagger. Daltrey told the press that his best friends were criminals. He'd also gotten a large chip on his shoulder about the upper-class snobs. The general ambition of the group was to be expressed like this: to get fucked up on pills and booze, then to fuck the world for money and women, ending up with a large mansion in the country. Moon could do without the peaceful ending—he'd probably opt for a stupendous explosion, detonated by himself.

But the media wasn't going to aim its spotlights until the Who had made their chart mark and, at the least, appeared at the "in" West End clubs. The horses must be led to the water and then that water must sparkle. Lambert and Stamp were making sure that there would be *flash, crackle,* and *pop.* One thing they didn't have to plan: a built-in hostility within the group. They could hate each other's guts onstage and it made a hell of a show. "The band with the most hate." What a catch phrase!

After months of gigging around Shepherd's Bush, mainly at the Goldhawk Club, the band finally busted into the West End. They got a gig at the Marquee late in 1964. It was a hollow triumph, though: huge bills were outstanding—for handbills and posters and all the clothes and hairdos, plus a movie short, and, of course, a horrendous guitar casualty list. As 1965 began, the Who were £60,000 in the red.

They needed a record. They needed a George Martin. They got Shel Talmy, the American with the hit-single touch, the all-arounder who'd produced hits for a disparate collection of acts, ranging from the Bachelors to the Kinks. Talmy agreed to produce a demo on the Who and, hearing them as an edgy, hard-sounding rock 'n' roll ensemble, fit them into a Kinks mold: rough, jerky, dressed-up R&B, with plenty of teen raucousness, padded by seasoned session men if necessary. Talmy wanted some original material and Townshend came up with "I Can't Explain," a short stabbing statement of Mod inarticulateness. Decca, searching for a new hot beat group for both sides of the Atlantic (they

160 ROCK ODYSSEY

were called London Records in America), signed the Who because of the Talmy track record.

In the studio, Talmy became the sound chef in the Spector manner. Other ingredients appeared: a vocal backing group called the Ivy League, a pianist named Nicky Hopkins, and a guitarist named Jimmy Page. Talmy had used Page on his Kinks sessions, though that fact had remained a trade secret. After all, these Mod fashion plates might look good onstage, but maybe they couldn't cut the mustard in front of a cold mike. Townshend was horrified. And Page didn't play on "I Can't Explain." The others stayed and the Talmy production turned out to the satisfaction of Decca and Lambert and Stamp. Townshend would wait and see. An artist, seething with a need for self-expression, was struggling inside that Mod suit.

The record made a slight impact but didn't exactly set the Thames on fire until, as luck would have it, the Who landed some vital TV exposure. "Ready, Steady, Go!", inheritor of the zippy excitement of Jack Good's TV rock shows, gave them a break. Then "Top of the Pops," a more conventional BBC-TV show with a more general audience, booked them as a last-minute replacement and generously captioned them a "Tip for the Top."

Network television appearances had clinched the stardom of Elvis Presley and the Beatles. The Stones were greatly aided on their way to becoming household names (and curses) by appearances on "Thank Your Lucky Stars" and even the Dean Martin debacle worked in their favor, publicity-wise. A mere seven days after their BBC appearance, the Who's "I Can't Explain" entered the Top Twenty. They were well on their way—and now Lambert and Stamp could start firing off their salvos of spleen flakkery: quotes from the nasty lads. The Pop Art sound had arrived and the Who were that sound. The press was ready and eager for some outlandish stuff. . . .

By July, the Who's "My Generation" was getting written about at length in the papers. It turned out to be the anthem of the Mod generation with its singer-spokesman's wish to die before he grew old (over thirty?). Anathema to me: I'd just bought a chest-expander in readiness for my own stardom. One must bow to success, but I read the press reports with horror. "It's a more up-tempo number," Townshend was reported as saying in *Disc* (I hadn't yet heard the record, as I was on tour —more on that later). "Talks about old people and young marrieds. Fellow telling story can't really express himself properly and stutters. In a way, I'm trying to stop the group getting old. It's the one serious thing we're always talking about. . . . The group sound has changed— we've got a rougher, more vicious approach now." And then later: "I wouldn't mind growing old in a Picasso sort of way or like Charlie

Chaplin." John Entwhistle was reported as showing his rebellion by "sending up old ladies" because "that gets me vicious." Keith Moon said he liked "parties with sandwiches and cream cakes and party-type birds." But Daltrey's words were the real shocker, making me go into a choke: "We like money because it raises us above the hated upper-middle class. . . . I want to walk into a place and see this conservative geezer standing at a bar all poshed up with a big car and I want to be just as well dressed and have just as big a car so that I can look at him and say, 'Look at you! You're going bald!' And he won't be able to say anything back at me! I'm halfway there now. I've got a flat in Belgravia and I like to spit out of my window if I feel like it."

However, behind all the bombast, brag, and commercial cunning was solid support from the kids. True, the Who was leading them by late 1965 but, in turn, the Who organization was also reflecting an important and influential movement. Musically, it may have sprung from the London R&B movement but the Mods had gone on to postulate a response to life in modern urban Britain. These kids, with plenty of pocket money and a reasonably good education, were a far cry from the Teddy Boys of the 1950s. As rockers, the sixties' Teds appeared Neanderthal. Style in every detail of life was the key to the Mods—from coiffure down to the bottom of the trouser crease. Leisure time was no longer seen as spare time—grabbed hours in between the drudgery of work—but as Real Time, Life.

The only thing the Mods lacked was a solution to the world's problems. They were apolitical. The Mods didn't march for any worthy world-caring causes; they strutted for themselves. They were their own works of art and art offers no prosaic solutions. The Mods simply *were*. Unfortunately, this apathy toward current affairs doomed them as the sixties spawned more and more polarized political camps. Young Americans, spurred on by crafty older ones, were now to take the lead in an age of protest, complaint, finger-pointing, and generational warfare.

British dominance in rock 'n' roll—pop fun and frolics—was about to end. The serious Americans were coming. Dylan was already on the British charts and Baez was following in his wake. I, on the other hand, was preparing to bring my contribution to America, in grateful thanks for all the popular art she had given me. I knew nothing of the gathering storm; I only knew I wanted my time in the sun. All I lacked was a work permit visa.

Recently, there had been a crackdown on British acts working in America. Now it was necessary to get an H-I permit and this entailed proving that your act was unique and of exceptional artistic quality. American labor groups, especially the Musician's Union, had put pressure on the Department of Immigration. What was wrong with Ameri-

can musicians? As a result of these tactics, tours by such groups as the
Nashville Teens and the Zombies were canceled. The major ports of
entry shut their gates to all British acts, except for the super money-
makers (and taxpayers) like the Rolling Stones and the Beatles.

How on earth, then, could I get in? But Jerry Dennon, quiet, polite,
and a big fish in li'l ole Seattle, managed to wangle me an H-I by telling the local authorities that the producers of "Shindig," that nonstop
rock songfest on ABC, craved the services of Ian Whitcomb, Jer-
den/Tower recording artist. Why did a big show like "Shindig" want
an obscure Britisher, the toast of Seattle? Read on. . . .

May 9:

Summer term at Trinity is a drag—can't get into strawberry teas,
cricket, and girls in summer dresses. Eyes glued to *Billboard.* Amazingly, the Tower execs have released that "Turn On" junk! I can't believe it! I'd put my *all,* including sincerity, into the protest song that
Hal had given me. Here I was, poised to conquer Amerikan Kulture,
and I'm saddled with this panting effort!

June 1:

Wonders never cease! the "Turn On" junk is cracking the national
charts as "You Turn Me On"! It has a bullet on all charts. It's getting
banned, too. I got a telegram from Tower's West Coast promotion man,
one "Jumpin' George Sherlock": WE'RE SHIPPING 50,000 OF YOUR
MOTHERS A DAY! ARE YOU READY FOR THIS, IAN BABY?!? And in Seattle,
Jerry had not been idle: JACK GOOD AMUSED BY YOUR RECORDS. WANTS
YOU ON "SHINDIG" SOONEST. HAVE OBTAINED H-I FROM MY UNCLE-IN-LAW.
PLEASE COLLECT FROM EMBASSY. REGARDS, JERRY.

On the crest of all this excitement, Bluesville and I played the Trinity Summer Ball. Luckily, the band has little desire to come to America,
as they've heard that tea comes only in bags and stout is hard to come
by. Besides, Jerry couldn't (or wouldn't) get them permits. The ball
was pure pixilation in Pixieland as we crashed into our numbers.
Gleaming at the front of the bandstand in the provost's garden was my
political theory professor, with wine glass in hand, shouting out, "Yes, I
helped teach him that!" whenever I yelped a loud Afro-American blues
note coupled with protest words. Peering out into the night glow, I
spotted Mr. Anangoola, the African student to whom I'd introduced
jazz and the blues. He was swaying in a festive pinstripe suit, as he
waved to me and screamed gratefully, "Thanks, Ian—I've got *it!* I've really got *it!*" He meant the Big Beat. Later, I was asked to come and
meet the Provost of Trinity himself, a great honor since I'd never set

eyes on him before in all my years at the college. He was in a tent, drinking black velvets (champagne and Guinness). Swaying to the beat, perhaps. "Ye've done well, McWhitcomb," he said. "Are ye Irish? At heart, I'm sure. I'll wager you've made a few shillings and now ye'll be away over the water like so many of us before ye! What can I do?" I replied that I'd love a lectureship after my star had fallen. "Don't forget your mother or your college," he replied, chucking me under the chin. As dawn broke in that fairyland of twinkling lights under a ceiling of real Irish stars, you could hear the angels sing. We all linked arms and sang a rousing version of the great wartime song "We'll Meet Again." A splendid send-off.

June 9:
STARDOM AT LAST! Today, I was mobbed at L.A. International Airport—my first mobbing—and it was delicious. If no special person adores you, then it's nice to have the world adore you. You're not obliged to give anything in return, except a smile and a wave, and these I did—in the manner of the late President Kennedy, whom I had seen in a Dublin street all those years ago.

Let me backtrack to detail my glory: I spent a few quiet days in Seattle, signing papers with Jerry or sequestered high up in a Best Western hotel room. Jerry said it was wisest to keep a low profile, as I was on the verge of a solid hit. "Turn On" is selling in large quantities. It's now known as a "unit": i.e., so many *units* have been shipped. I got rather depressed in the hotel room—counting the waves on the flickering blue TV screen and tasting the bitter air conditioning. I called Debbie, but her father curtly informed me that their "princess" had found Mr. Right, a real estate developer from Spokane.

So I was relieved to enplane for the trip to L.A. "Shindig" was waiting for me. At last I would meet my hero Jack Good. During the plane trip, I enjoyed the plastic tray spread of Salisbury steak, potatoes *au Neuilly*, pastry from Belgium, and coffee from Brazil. I also enjoyed the Al Jolson selections on the "Memory Lane" channel of the stereo headset. Frequently, our bass-voiced pilot would interrupt Jolson to point out fabulous sights below us or to announce the baseball scores. My neighbor, a bullet-headed, seersuckered businessman, regaled me with tales of his years in Britain during World War II and his current venture in tropical fisheries as he downed screwdrivers. He never inquired as to what I did for a living. I suppose many Americans imagine that English gentlemen do nothing. All the while, stewardesses, deep-frozen and metallic, freshened our drinks and tolerated the constant goosing of their behinds.

As we were deplaning at L.A., the chief stewardess, beehive quivering, marched up to me and announced loudly: "Hold everything! Get the kid off first!" My fellow passengers were amazed, especially my seat-mate. Flanked by airline personnel, I was guided down a concertina corridor and suddenly emerged in a vast arrivals area. A barrage of flashes and lights and a shrill, demented chorus of *"Eeeee"* and *"Oooo"* and the like. Peppered with things like "It's 'Mr. Turn On' himself." Very young girls—children, actually—snatched at my madras blazer and thrust things at me: gift-wrapped boxes, furry toy animals, biscuits, squidgy cakes, Bermuda shorts, etc. I smiled and waved, thinking of Prince Charles. A policeman, toting a gun and a nightstick, pushed me through a side door. "You shut down the en-tire section, boy," he growled. I told him I was merely a cog in the leisure industry. Un-impressed, he lifted me into a police car and conveyed me to a regular car, whose driver I noticed was in plainclothes. This was no policeman, as I soon discovered.

Off we roared, with a fleet of teen cars in hot pursuit. "We'll give them a run for their money, but stay tuned to their beam, if you get what I mean, old bean," said my driver, shaking my hand as he negoti-ated turns on two wheels. He was a silvery-haired adult in a lustrous suit (no tie), a shirt with an enormous collar, and a broad-brimmed preacher's hat. A briar pipe stuck out of his mouth at a jaunty angle. "Hi, Ian! Say hello to Jumpin' George Sherlock, in charge of West Coast promotion for Tower Records Corp. Let me ask you a personal question: do you need any bread?" George had a soft *Gone With the Wind* accent and a relaxed manner. As to bread, I told him I'd enjoyed the jet meal but could always put away the odd burger. "Correction, old man," he said, swerving off the freeway and shooting down into the depths of the city, shaking off several of our teen pursuers. "I mean, like *greenbacks*, folding money." I replied that I was quite comfortably off, having a family trust fund, and that I wasn't pursuing pop as a full-time career. I felt rotten about saying this, right after I'd said it. Maybe I was suffering from jet lag and culture shock all at once. George said, "I read that bio. we got from Jerden—about you being re-lated to the British aristocracy. No doubt, you dwell in a castle. *MMMmmmm*—but I just *love* that ancient Britain." His voice had sud-denly taken on a curious clip and, after a few moments, I realized he was attempting a British accent. Rather embarrassed, I turned around and saw that we still had a few pursuers and that one girl was leaning out of her car window, waving a pair of panties. "Know what? We gotta strike quick. You're a hot property right now and let's work that sizzle till it turns to a frazzle and embers out." Then George filled me in on his long history as a promotion man, how he went back to the days of 78s and Nat "King" Cole, how he'd "broken" Bill Haley in

California with "Rock Around the Clock," how he'd ridden the surf craze with pleasure, and, finally, how he had spent a long time promoting the Stones for London Records and had pictures of himself with Mick Jagger to prove it. "Why, he even wrote a song about me. It's called 'The Under Assistant West Coast Promotion Man.'" I offered my compliments, but he waved me off. "Hey, man, you're the star—and, what's more, I'll show you how." He janked the car into a side street, causing the closest fanmobile to imitate but fall short. I heard a deep *whuuump,* followed by an eerie silence and then a sort of banshee wailing. "We're in Darktown—Watts—but tune in to the sound of money music!" And he switched on the car radio and started punching buttons: *"Huh-huh-huh-huh"* came out of one station, "Come on now, baby, you know you really turn me on" came out of another. Then: "British chanter Iron Whitcomb, high-screech wimp 'Turn On' lad, was mobbed at L.A. Airport today when he arrived in the Southland for personal appearances. In other news, the arrival in Vietnam of Marines and paratroopers of the First Infantry Division boosts the count of American servicemen out there to seventy-five thousand. You heard it first on KFWB hit radio, the rock of the ages where the hits roll night and day!" I was flooding the airwaves. He went on to inform me that I was banned in Portland, Oregon, by special order of the mayor on account of "suggestiveness." In other towns, my record was being accused of promoting drugs and cheap sex. "They also say you're a fag." He explained, on inquiry, that this meant a *back-passage boy.* "But don't worry—a lot of Americans think all Britishers are fags—and, anyway, you know you've made it in this business when people call you a fag. The point is, you're causing a stir and you're selling records. You're what's happening right at this moment in time!"

June 10:
I am actually living in legendary Hollywood. How long till I get my star in the pavement? I'm not staying at the famous Knickerbocker or Roosevelt, but it's very kind of George to let me crash on the wall-to-wall pink-and-burgundy pile carpet in his cozy apartment in the Voltaire-Cherokee Garden Court, just off Hollywood Boulevard. We're a stone's throw from John Boles's star in the pavement. Speaking of stones, this part of Hollywood has quite a few, as well as broken bottles and other rubbish. It appears to have seen better days. The dinky swimming pool is crowded with goldfish and other rare tropical specimens. Some of them bite—as I found out this morning when I went for a dip and got badly bitten.

George heard my cries and dashed out to my aid, his hair in a hairnet. He sets great store by appearance and spends, he says, at least an

hour a day fixing his silvery hair. After he tended to my bite, he gave
me advice on appearance. "Remember, you're a star now," George told
me as he slowly mashed a breakfast of mixed fruits in an electric
blender. "And you must dress like a star. Pull up your collar. Let your
hair grow a tad over your ears. Get some *velour*." This "velour" word
was a mystery that would have to wait, for after our healthful breakfast
—George is a health nut who will only tolerate eggs or milk in pow-
dered form—we settled down to some *record routining*. "When you
sing your hit, you gotta visualize it with special actions so that you leap
outta the TV tube like gangbusters." He choreographed my moves so
that I'd start off with my back to the audience for six bars, followed by
a slow spin around in what he called "The Mersey Style"; next came a
spot of sidling around into a chorus finish of hands cupped "sexy-
British" for the gimmick *"Huh-huh-huh-huh"* break. I entered into this
with the best will in the world, but not without slight regrets for the
passing of my serious pop side. Still, it's great to be in *Hollywood!*

After an hour of this routining, George's face was glistening brightly
and I must have started to smell a bit—because George suddenly produced a can of deodorant and sprayed me fiercely. Next he produced
another can and lacquered my hair so that it became frozen into a helmet. "You're almost ready to meet the media," he pronounced proudly
as he stood back to admire his work. "Now to get some velour."

Hollywood Boulevard was a hive of activity. Everyone appeared to be
going somewhere at terrific speed. I felt the sense of urgency—and yet
the denizens glided or swayed ("sashayed" was how George put it)
rather than gallumphing awkwardly like we so often do in Britain. I
spotted several cowboy types leaning against the fronts and sides of
plaster shacks shaped like orange crates. One of these crates said:
MUSSO & FRANK'S GRILL—OLDEST IN HOLLYWOOD, SINCE 1919. I was
puzzling over the sign when George apprehended a customer exiting
the grill. "Hi ho!" he said. "What's happened, man? Lost your gig and
on the skids?" The man certainly looked shabby and down and out, yet
exotic and dashing as well. He was stocky and had hair almost to his
shoulders, like an out-of-work medieval page. His clothes were furry
from vest to boot. An Ostrogothic look. He replied in a lazy but irritated tone: "Whaddya mean? We'll be on the charts next week. You
out to lunch or what?" "Say hi," said George unflinchingly. "Say hi to
Ian Whitcomb, Tower's own British sensation. And now, Ian, say hi to
Sonny Bono, fellow promotion man." "You're wacko," said the Ostrogoth. "I dropped the promo gig a long time ago. I been with Caesar
and Cleo since then. And now I'm Sonny of Sonny and Cher, so
there." And with a growl, the barbarian slouched off, slicing the flash-
bulb air with his impressive nose. "He's off to see the boys at Martoni's.

We'll take a peek in there later—after we've purchased your velour," said George.

Sonny and Cher had met at a Phil Spector recording session back in 1963. At that time, she was an occasional backup singer on Spector epics—she sang on "Be My Baby," together with a cathedral-full of vocalists—and Sonny was a general factotum for the Great Man, Spector. Sonny had already knocked about the L.A. record scene for a number of years. Born Salvatore Bono in Detroit in 1935, he had moved with his family to L.A. after World War II and, for a time, Sonny had worked alongside his father at Douglas Aircraft. In the late fifties, he got a job as staff producer at Art Rupe's economy R&B label, Specialty Records. Rupe had done an amazing job for art and commerce by releasing the classic rock records of Little Richard, Larry Williams ("Short Fat Fanny" and "Bony Moronie"), and Jerry Byrne ("Lights Out"), all on a shoestring budget. Bono had written some songs for Specialty artists and, after a time, he got along well with Rupe and landed himself the staff producer job. But Rupe decided to stop original recording and rely on his past catalog after a series of frustrating episodes with recalcitrant artists. In other words, he'd had enough of the R&B game. Razors, wine jugs, and processed hair—they could keep 'em. Art Rupe was going to be in bed by ten in a safe suburb. Bono kept scraping on in the local record scene, forming his own independent labels, writing songs (like "Needles and Pins," which Jackie De Shannon recorded and the Searchers hit with), and doing a spot of record promoting, which is where he met George Sherlock. But George was a "surfer baby" and Sonny was a man not used to sunlight. Their paths didn't cross much; hence George's faux pas outside Musso & Frank's Grill.

Cher was born Cherilyn Sarkasian LaPier in 1946 in El Centro, which is a dusty sprawl in California close to the Mexican border. However, Cher was not Mexican: she was part Armenian and part Cherokee Indian. The redskin part was to be much stressed after her record success with Sonny. In 1964, after their courtship during Spector sessions, Sonny married Cher and, a little later, the couple was making records for the local label Vault as Caesar and Cleo. Nothing took off, but in 1965 Sonny managed to get a contract with Atco, a national label, and it was decided that the couple would record under their real names, Sonny and Cher. Their first releases were nice singalong songs, but nothing to excite the nation, though L.A. kids loved them and they got onto the local charts. They were such a lovable couple, not like normal parents at all. They wore funny clothes, furry things. They didn't try and force their opinions on the kids. They were gentle and never said no. They didn't have to preach because they were a living example of love and peace and goodwill. Yes, the L.A. kids loved them. And Sonny and Cher always stopped to sign autographs—from their chauffeur-driven Cadillac. Even without a national hit, they had all the trappings.

As Sonny pointed out to George, the happily married singing duo were about to broach the national charts—and, indeed, were at number nine on some local L.A. charts with their song "Just You." And they were about to release a recording that would zoom them right up to the very top of the national charts: "I Got You, Babe." This charming and disarming folksy song of married bliss swayed along back and forth, a nickelodeon band organ on a horse and cart. A bit of Dylan, some Spector, lots of tambourines, a harpsichord, batteries of drums, an oboe, and lashings of love. Later, I learned that my younger brother, Robin, had been chief tambourine shaker. How on earth? While I was attending summer term at T.C.D., he had dropped in on L.A. for a holiday, having just completed a working stint with the family oil company in Oklahoma. Sonny and Cher had adopted him and he had also endeared himself to many other record people, as I was to find out. He even made some records for Tower, their angle being that, as one Britisher was very much like another, the American teens might well mistake Robin Whitcomb for Ian Whitcomb, which would be useful since Ian had a habit of studying at remote universities.

"I Got You, Babe" was to emerge as one of the harbingers of a new trend in pop: folk rock. But, at present, I was so tied up with the process of star-making that I could no longer see clearly.

June 10 (continued):

The *velour* that George was so hell-bent on getting for me turned out to be a plush carpetlike material fashioned into trousers and sweaters and very current. George topped me off with a deerstalker hat, backed off to admire his creation, and said, "Groovy! Now we're ready to meet the industry."

I followed George around the corner and down the street and finally in through an unimpressive red door which announced itself in flowing script as MARTONI'S. Suddenly, from the outside blaze of harsh light, I was plunged into a cave of gloom. A sense of furtiveness, of illegality, of playing truant permeated all.

It was only about noon, yet hunched along the bar were a dozen or so assorted shapes nursing drinks. George led me down the line, introducing me to the wraiths one by one: "Tower Records sensation," etc. I met some of the key disc jockeys, who were caught between shifts in a state of utter relaxation. They had names like Big Jack, Johnny Dark, Wayne Mountain, Emperor Jones. They all spoke in deep bass voices, reeking of masculinity and after-shave. One or two hadn't the time for me, clearly. But I certainly had time for them. They fascinated me, these captains of the airwaves. Did they talk in this echoey boom even when in the bedroom? I felt a bit silly in my deerstalker hat. And they, in turn, had qualms about eccentric British Invaders. I didn't blame them, for I knew from their overall age that they had been around in the days of Patti Page and Frankie Laine and Sinatra. They had jock-eyed in the Golden Years. Their appearance told me this, too. Their hair was neatly trimmed and often lambent. Some were still in uniform —gold-trimmed blazers emblazoned with letters, like KFWB, instead of the usual mottos. George led me over to a dingy corner, where a fat man with a shiny bald head sat sucking noodles at breakneck speed. "Hey, hey! Hello, Rockin' Rex. And say hello to Ian Whitcomb, currently at number eight on your Top Forty and climbing. Boy, but that pasta looks copasetic and, as for the sauce—it's outta sight!" "Yeah," said fat Rex, "so I suggest you trot over to the waiter and get him to bring me another batch, plus a heap of clam juice." George quickly complied, disappearing into the ink. "And what can I do for you, boy?" I chatted about the weather and my history course, frankly rather out of my element. Rex flicked a noodle off his greasy cheek, thrust out his chins, and demanded: "What's the hat for?" I was caught off-balance and replied that I wasn't sure. "What's the plush for?" He prodded my velour sweater. "I'll show you," he went on, "how the useless can become the useful." He proceeded to wipe his hands on my new velour, getting clam juice on me and blue dye on himself.

I might be a star on the ascendant, but this barbaric behavior was too much for me. I'm slow to explode, but when I do. . . . I jerked back my elbow and clenched my fist in readiness to give the bovine wretch a straight left to the jaw. Fortunately for my future, George was right behind me and the result was that my elbow knocked his bowl of Rex's clam juice down the front of his Hawaiian shirt, onto his exposed chest, and over much of his dangling jewelry.

Still, a crisis was averted. I must watch these explosions. I want to make it big, but I also must stay true to my upbringing.

June 11:

George says what I need is a girl and he'll fix it. This morning, I went up the Capitol Tower to meet the executives at Tower Records, an amiable bunch, though they looked and acted much like businessmen anywhere and could as easily be marketing oil as pop records.

It's strange that I've met no young people yet. I wish I'd had a chance to chat with those fans who mobbed me at the airport.

"The reason the Tower boys looked so serious," George told me later as we munched date-nut bread in a health food store, "is that they're worrying about your follow-up to 'Turn On.' Tower caught a nice wave right on the curl with 'Turn On' and now we gotta ride another with you." It's terrible to realize that homes, families, and new cars depend on my coming up with another fit of absence of mind like the one that produced "You Turn Me On." Jumping jellybeans!

Tower Records is a curious company. Operating out of the Capitol Tower, it's supposedly independent of the big brother company. Capitol has the Beatles and the Beach Boys, as one is made well aware of at each bend of the tower. Down in the basement, there are studios where mostly country acts record, though I did spy Sammy Davis, Jr., there when I was being shown around. He raced up to me, wreathed in smiles, and gave me a bearlike embrace. And I don't even know the fellow. Tower doesn't seem to do much original recording. Their releases come from tapes supplied to them by outside companies (like Jerry Dennon's) and from British releases rejected by Capitol. In this latter way, Tower has obtained Freddie and the Dreamers, as well as Brendan Bowyer and the Royal Showband of Waterford, Eire. I'm shocked about the Bowyer purchase because one of the reasons I wanted to be a star out here was to escape from those dreadful, dreary Irish showbands! Anyway, Tower started operations at the end of 1964 and until my arrival they'd only had one small hit—with a group called Davie Allen and the Arrows, sort of latter-day Shadows stuff. I got Tower their first hit and right now "You Turn Me On" is racing into the national Top Ten. While I was meeting the Tower executives, a very boyish chap raced up to me and shook my hand as he gave me a perfect-toothed smile. Though he'd dashed across the length of Tower's main office (a circular dash), I noticed that every hair on his long-haired head was perfectly in place. I wondered how he did it. And how he kept it so thick. I've been noticing that lots of my hairs come out in the shower. Maybe George's water is polluted. The breezy boy's name is Mike Curb and he's the producer of the Arrows. He's much admired around the Tower offices and knows every secretary's first name. I like him.

June 12:

My record continues to climb, while the sun continues to shine in a blatant manner. The question is, how do we follow up? I suggested the folk-protest song, but the Tower execs informed me, through George, that folk music was from 1963 to 1964. When I protested, George put me on the line to Tower's president, a very avuncular gent named G. "Bud" Fraser. He was charming but firm and told me he'd been in this business for twenty-five years. So we'll have to think of some other number. Have to dream up a gimmick.

Meanwhile, George drove me out to meet the deejays at KRLA in Pasadena. This is the most important rocker station in the area and it's strongly associated with the Beatles. All their activities are reported and the latest news, hot on the air today and direct from London, is that the group has been slated to receive an MBE each: Membership of the Most Excellent Order of the British Empire. Apparently, this is for services to British exports. KRLA is ecstatic. But I'm ambivalent: I mean, I love rock 'n' roll and the business and I also cherish the memory of our Empire days, but I've never linked the two worlds together and I'm not sure I want to. I have trouble seeing Rudyard Kipling and Ringo Starr as fellow Empire-builders.

As the excited deejay rattled on about the MBEs, I turned my attention to the landscape rushing past us as we rode along the freeway: velvet hills, plush as velour; a large flowerbed to the right of us, spelling out in riotous colors WELCOME TO PASADENA. I thought of the Temperance Seven's hit song about that town and I also thought of Jan and Dean's hit. And I imagined little old ladies scurrying about in a 1920s town where grass was greener and honey bees hummed melodies.

But George turned up the radio and the harsh sounds of hit music shattered my reverie. "KRLA—the sound of today!" The jock screamed cracks about the songs and singers, the weather, the contests they were currently running, the fact that KRLA now had the Beatles' ex-publicist, Derek Taylor, working exclusively for them, and that KRLA was the first station to be playing the brand-new, not-yet-released *Beatles VI* album. "Thus, boys and girls, KRLA maintains its perfect record of being the first station to broadcast every major new Beatles disc. . . . And remember, lads and lassies, that we never impose upon our very own personal friendships with John, Paul, George, and Ringo." Then—cut!—we were into a Coke commercial and then—cut!—we were into news about Vietnam escalation and then—zap!—we were into "Wooly Bully" by Sam the Sham and the Pharaohs, KRLA's current number one.

George impatiently punched other stations in and out after only a few minutes of KRLA. They all seemed to have an "exclusive" on the new Beatles album. George explained that he was *monitoring*. "This is work, real work," he added. But he was pounding the wheel to the music, as well as doing "jerk" dance movements with his elbow. He was happy in his work. A contented worker in the right job— unalienated. As I thought about Los Angeles, with its nonstop sun, boundless activity, host of perfect bodies (which so far I'd only spied briefly from car windows), and unalienated workers, I concluded: "This is the Millennium! This is Marx come true!"

George told me to cool it and we pulled off the freeway and down leafy lanes into the environs of KRLA. I was expecting a great edifice with a tall tower and aerials—an air giant's castle. But KRLA is a concrete block tucked away behind an old hotel. Unimpressive. There was a collection of small girls milling around the doorsteps. A cry went up: *"It's the Emperor himself!"* Emperor Jones, whom I'd met briefly the day before, had stepped out to take a breather from his radio shift and was about to effect a small "walkabout" for his fans. Neatly dressed in station blazer with matching tie and hankie, hair gleaming and nicely sculpted, he descended the final doorstep and, all at once, pulled down the corners of his mouth, crossed his eyes, mussed up his hair, and screamed: *"Who's crazy?"* *"You're crazy!"* answered the girls. *"Who's the one who likes to eat roller skates with Thousand Island dressing?"* *"You do, Emperor!"* Then he beckoned to some minion behind him and out was trundled a trolley loaded with cartons.

George hiked me over to the scene, pulling up my shirt collar and straightening my deerstalker. I felt like a right idiot. "Hi, Emperor! Say hello to Ian Whitcomb, currently on the 'KRLA Tunedex' and redhot." The Emperor's answer was to hand me an ice cream cone. George took me aside to explain that the Emperor was doling out to the kids his latest station sensation: a new ice cream flavor personally invented by the Emperor himself—"Scuzzy." It was a mixture of nuts, toffee, fruit punch, cream caramel, maraschino cherries—much odder than Conway Twitty's famous "Twitty Burger." The girls were wolfing down this vile concoction and, from their butterball shapes, I gathered they were no strangers to leisure and fun foods. This group of fatties rather spoiled my image of Southern California girls as perfect physical specimens.

Eventually, we were granted a short audience with the Emperor in his office. He kept calling me "Iron" and, when I finally plucked up the courage to correct him, he merely shrugged and said, "Hell, Iron's more masculine." Mostly he wanted to talk about the recent trip he'd made to the Bahamas: "With a fellow countryman of yours who, I'm proud to announce, has joined our station, exclusive." He was referring to Derek Taylor, the ex-Beatle publicist. He and the Emperor had interviewed the Fab Four at the Nassau location where they were shooting *Help!*, the latest Beatle frolic. "Let me tell you," said the Emp with a frown on his tanned face, "beneath those little-boy haircuts are some man-talking adults. To quote Derek—and the guy's got a way with words—'We better watch out, these guys could take over.' Meanwhile,

KRLA, the *only real Beatle station in the world,'* is presenting the moptops at the Hollywood Bowl. Congratulate me, George." George hugged him. And shortly afterward, George presented him with a stack of Tower's latest releases. The Emp didn't seem too pleased. And before George could slip the new Brendan Bowyer record on a nearby turntable, the Emp was off, excusing himself by saying that he had to prepare for a big Hollywood Boulevard parade tonight. Apparently, he will be seen boogaloo-ing on top of a Rolls-Royce, which he will exchange for an elephant after he's changed into his ermine.

George retreated from the office, offering me a tour of the station. Nothing fancy, KRLA. A small, compact, and practical operation. I had to say hello to some more jocks who George said were important. However, the most important person of all, he informed me, is the program director—and we didn't get to see him. His secretary, generously built but ice-cold, smilingly told us that her boss was "in conference." Said George: "But I just saw him swinging down the hallway." She replied: "In that case, he *stepped out.*" And her mouth and smile snapped shut, thus closing the matter.

Undefeated, we wandered on, with George stuffing 45s into the jocks' pigeonholes and singing snatches from Tower's latest releases to passing KRLA workers in a distinctly Sinatran voice. Pointing to a playlist pinned to a passing wall, George whispered: "Look at your mother—right up there with the stone foxes!";

KRLA TUNEDEX

This Week	Last Week	Title	Artist
1	1	"Wooly Bully"	Sam the Sham and the Pharoahs
2	2	"Help Me, Rhonda"	The Beach Boys
3	4	"Back in My Arms Again"	The Supremes
4	5	"You Turn Me On"	Ian Whitcomb and Bluesville
5	9	"Mr. Tambourine Man"	The Byrds

I was irritated to see that Bluesville was still being tagged on to my name. I had hoped I was plain Ian Whitcomb by now.

I wondered who these Byrds were. What an antiquated spelling! Like Ye Olde Tea Shoppe. Perhaps they play medieval rock. "The Byrds are hot, man. You'll meet all these hot cats on the shows we got lined up for you." George fished out a piece of legal paper and rattled off: "We got you on 'Hollywood A Go Go' this afternoon. 'Shindig' tomorrow. Then 'American Bandstand,' and sandwiched in someplace we got to meet the press, and after all this ballyhoo you're slated for a West Coast tour from San Diego to Seattle—the stars include the Beach Boys, Sam the Sham, the Righteous Brothers, the Kinks, Jan and Dean, and Sonny and Cher. After that, are you ready for a 'Dick Clark Caravan of Stars' which will cover this whole United States? And after that —who knows? The movies? The moon? Maybe you're a new Peter Sellers!"

I thought I'd calm him down by explaining that I had to prepare for my college finals. Well, I tried to, but it only made him more excited. He told me we'd discuss these finals at a later date. "Meanwhile," he said, "there's a heap of competition coming up and we must keep on our toes." He handed me the latest issue of the *KRLA Beat* and pointed to an article about Bob Dylan. "He's a college type, same as you." I was staggered. I knew about Bob Dylan from my folk music experience back in 1963—but what was Dylan doing in the pop/rock field, in the never-never land of Technicolor dreams?

This is what the *Beat* wrote: "Everybody's going to be talking about this strange and sensitive young man who uses bad grammar to make beautiful poetry and a rough-edged voice to sing spellbinding songs. At present, a lot of acts are recording Dylan songs and finding that they appeal to youth. Dylan is achieving the impossible: bridging the gap between the folk and rock worlds—bringing intelligence and maturity to the scene."

What had brought Dylan to the attention of the world of rock 'n' roll radio? I should have been consulting my music trade publications more closely: "Subterranean Homesick Blues," an up-tempo electric blues number with some wild and loose jamming from the raunchy and rocking backing band, had put Dylan onto the charts in April. By the end of May, he'd reached number thirty-nine. This record was the first time the general public became aware of Dylan's change from folk acoustic to a special kind of acerbic rock 'n' roll. In "Subterranean Homesick Blues," he hurled out a slew of images about a seemingly explosive population waiting under the city for a time to pop up and stagger the straight world. It was a warning that the Children's Army was coming, for a man was mixing up a concoction in the cellar and you didn't need a weatherman to tell the wind direction.

To radio execs, the record was a good and gutsy beat number. No more. Maybe a novelty fluke. But Dylan was sticking with electricity, inspired by the example of the Beatles, the Stones, and the Animals. Much as he might admire them (and they admired *him* greatly), he was never going to imitate. He was too much of his own time and of his own country. The style he was brewing in the studios that spring was all-American in origin: blues, country, folk, and rock 'n' roll—plus his own unique waterfall of word pictures. Tom Wilson, his producer, agreed with Dylan that the organ and guitar sound on the Animals' "House of the Rising Sun" was worth building on. In turn, he liked the secularized gospel backing of my own "This Sporting Life." He'd heard it when the L.A. airwaves were full of that sound in the spring. Forget the cockney accent—the organ swirl, combined with the piano and the obligatory R&R guitars and drums, made a useful model. The British were only pointing out to Americans the worth of their own urban folk music. From now on, Dylan was to leave the broadside balladeering he'd been famous for in folk circles. He'd done his share of editorializing on political matters, he'd provided enough marching material, teach-in singalong stuff, even an anthem for the civil rights movement ("Blowin' in the Wind"). Now he wanted to concentrate on the "I-you-me-and-us" of popular song. He was going to address personal and social matters, using a current idiom as his vehicle. His eyes and ears were tuned to the changing times.

"Like a Rolling Stone" was recorded and arrangements were made for the Paul Butterfield Blues Band to accompany Dylan at the Newport Folk Festival in July. A storm was about to break, roughing up traditionalists in both folk music and popular music.

And where was I? Intent on becoming a rock star, while retaining my scholastic dignity. Taking a worm's eye view. . . .

June 12 (later):

George could see my shock at the Dylan article and to divert me, I suppose, he invited me to come and meet my fans out in the parking lot. Their attentions made me feel better—but I was aware that they hadn't screamed at me when we'd arrived at the station. However, George told me to grab the moment while it was cooking, and especially while the Emp was otherwise engaged.

So I met Bernice and Jeannine and Sharon, in their Bermuda shorts and white high-heeled shoes and T-shirts reading WE LUV THE BEATLES. Bernice told me she hated Ray Davies of the Kinks because Ray told the *Beat* that he didn't like Bermudas. She showed me the article to prove it. I perused the page, while George handed out free copies of Tower 45s. The Dylan chart entry became stranger to figure out when I read this:

"*Fashion Tips:* Don't wear earrings unless you're also wearing high heels. *Etiquette:* What to do, seriously, when your boy friend orders a "hamburger with" at the drive-in—and you want to kiss him good night. *You order garlic toast for yourself.*"

That afternoon, I taped "Hollywood A Go Go," a syndicated TV rock 'n' roll show that's allegedly seen as far away as Rhodesia and Finland. The set was sparse—cameras, lights, and a few rostrums. The empty spaces were filled with boys and girls who danced or gazed. All the acts had to lip-synch their records. Chubby Checker (the Twist King) was on the set and, when he heard my record, he pronounced it "bitching." Bobby Vee was a special guest and looked every inch a star in his sheeny silk suit. He really had his hand movements and head turns down to an art. We chatted during a break and I brought up the subject of Bob Dylan and my concern about him. To my amazement, Vee told me that Dylan—before he got into the folk kick and when he was plain Bobby Zimmerman back in Minnesota—had played a few gigs with Vee's band—as pianist! Vee said Dylan was very good, in the Jerry Lee style, but that he could only play in C. He said he knew a lot about country music, too. As it was hard to find pianos at their gigs, Dylan didn't play with Vee for long. But Vee has fond memories of him and said he was really well versed in current rock 'n' roll at the time of their meeting. He had the impression Dylan was very hip to whatever was happening. I wondered if the young Zimmerman had ever been a Bill Haley fan. That was my real acid test. I was by now longing to meet Dylan.

The other guest act was the Byrds. Their recording of "Mr. Tambourine Man" was high on the KRLA chart and, of course, it was a Dylan composition. During the rehearsals, I listened carefully and found their *clank* and *clang* quite pleasing, the twelve-string Rickenbacker guitar sounding like an electrified Elizabethan lute. But I couldn't hear much rocking in the number, nor could I fathom much sense in the words of "Mr. Tambourine Man"—a minstrel entertaining with only a tambourine must be extremely monotonous.

Anyway, soon it was time for me to mime to "You Turn Me On." I'd dressed in a suitable Shetland sweater, but my corduroys looked in need of a pressing. George agreed. With Chubby Checker, Bobby Vee, and the odd Byrd standing around watching, I felt like a real idiot pretending to sing, mouthing out an intensity and gyrating my hips in an attempt to look sexy. For variety's sake, I slid my hand up and down the microphone, which I felt was an interesting touch. The director thanked me through the loudspeakers overhead, but later, when I overheard him in the control booth, it was obvious that he was more pleased with what he called his "boob shots." I must admit that the dancing go-go girls, regulars on the show, were extremely attractive. One in particular had been giving me the eye during my taping and I made mention of this to George. He went over to her rostrum and gave her a 45 and my compliments. I had started to sidle over to her when she suddenly rushed to another rostrum, whinnying like a pony and shaking her lovely flaxen hair at—the Byrds.

Certainly, their performance got enormous reaction—and respect—from the kids. A lot of these kids looked as if they were part of their entourage. The girls wore long dresses with elaborate needlework and some wore big floppy hats—a Victorian, almost Pre-Raphaelite appearance. The boys looked like the Byrds, which is to say that they wore rumpled jeans, fringed buckskin "frontier" jackets, and cowboy boots. All these clothes had led what appeared to be a fast past life. They could well have been hand-me-downs or purchased in a thrift store. But the Byrds and their followers smelled most fragrant—a kind of exotic oil, I learned.

Although I and my fellow artists had been trying to do as good a job as possible on the lip-synchronization, the Byrds made hardly any attempt to match lips to record. Some of the time, I could have sworn they were having a chat among themselves. They weren't playing the game. And Bobby Vee played it so beautifully, so skillfully.

After "Mr. Tambourine Man," they did a British song from World War II called "We'll Meet Again." I was surprised that they should know this, as it had never been a hit in America and was very much identified with Vera Lynn, the "Forces' Sweetheart," during her long-running wartime request show, "Sincerely Yours." The song had always given me goose bumps—until now. The Byrds had altered the chords and underlaid their jangling guitars so that the old straightforward tearjerker became, in their hands, a sly put-on. And then I realized where they'd probably run across "We'll Meet Again": Stanley Kubrick, the film director, had used Vera Lynn's recording at the end of *Dr. Strangelove,* over the mushroom cloud of an H-bomb—giving the recording a heavy dose of irony.

I approached the gathered Byrds and told them how much I'd enjoyed the old version of "We'll Meet Again" and did they realize it had helped us through the war? Their spokesman, Roger (née Jim) McGuinn, a rattled-looking character in wire spectacles and with an owlish face, replied: "We know little of such a war, good sir. We just believe it to be a curious old relic of a song." I spluttered something about remembering the Battle of Britain and having respect for the past. The spokesman cut me off: "I trust everything will turn out right." Before I could retaliate, George hustled me away for press pics with Bobby Vee. I was quite distressed to discover that World War II, so ingrained on our European minds, was neither here nor there to these Byrds.

The Byrds were the first manifestation in the pop music world of the fusion between folk music and rock 'n' roll. As we have seen, since the early sixties folk music had been attracting the educated young—the students and college graduates. In the protest and social comment songs of the traveling campus and coffee bar singers (like Tom Paxton, Phil Ochs, Len Chandler, and, of course, Bob Dylan), the New Young found a song form that was relevant, that spoke to them about pressing matters such as civil rights, the poor, war, and H-bombs. The linking of light music with heavy causes had, of course, started in Britain with the CND movement of the late 1950s, but over there the music that accompanied the marches and demos was merely background music, merely a carrot to attract people's attention: trad jazz, old campfire folky songs of the jollier variety.

In America, the heavy causes were to be underlined by an equally heavy music. Sometimes it got positively ponderous. In the songs of Phil Ochs, for example, the screaming yellow journalism often swamped whatever music lay underneath. But, at any rate, the folk music movement, which hitherto had been the preserve of the Old (and getting older) Left and which was becoming rigidly doctrinaire about what could be sung about and with what instrumentation and amplification, was getting younger and more in step with the times.

Rock 'n' roll, though, was still anathema to the folkies—commercial junk for the pimple-faced, illiterate lumpen proles; tool of rampant capitalists—until the Beatles . . . and the British Invasion. After that, many young folk fans realized that it was possible to be intelligent and to play rock 'n' roll. And they were made to look around at the great and living tradition of fine Afro-American music in their own country. It had taken foreigners to put them onto their own culture! Dylan saw the light. So did the Byrds.

The group consisted of Roger McGuinn (leader), David Crosby, Chris Hillman, Mike Clarke, and Gene Clark. Between them, they could boast many years' experience within the folk field in both its pure and commercial manifestations: McGuinn had worked in the Limeliters and the Chad Mitchell Trio, two easy-listening folk groups, and had actually played lead guitar with Bobby Darin when the star inserted a folk spot into his nightclub act. The others had variously played in the New Christy Minstrels, Les Baxter's Balladeers, and the Scottville Squirrel Breakers.

In L.A., where one can never forget the present and its pressures and inspirations, they came together as the Byrds. McGuinn had this sound in his head—of jet planes, of folk ballads, of Beatles, of Dylan. Wasn't it possible—it *must* be possible—to combine the pelvic pulse of rock 'n' roll with the street poetry of the new folk music? "House of the Rising

Sun" was an ancient folk song galvanized with rock life via electrification and syncopation. Dylan had dented the charts with "Subterranean Homesick Blues." The next step would be to take a really heavy, heady slice of Dylan—a ballad normally sung to the plain accompaniment of an acoustic guitar—and rock it up and serve it up as a delectable dish, acceptable to the millions who bought pop records. Art and commerce would both be served.

This clear and level-headed thinking was the work of the Byrds' manager, Jim Dickson. With immense skill, he managed to get his group contracted to Columbia and produced by Terry Melcher, a veteran of the California surf 'n' sun scene when he'd made records as Terry of Bruce and Terry. The piece of material that Dickson selected for their first Columbia session was a rocked-up remake of Dylan's "Mr. Tambourine Man." No chances were taken: at the session, only Roger McGuinn was allowed to play, while Hal Blaine, Leon Russell, and Larry Knechtel—tried and true sessioneers on surf, Spector, and "Shindig" recordings—played the rest of "Mr. Tambourine Man." After all, truth is truth and beauty is beauty—but it's what's in the grooves that counts with the music directors of Radioland. The sound must fit the format. It fit like a glove: by June of '65, the record was at the top of the charts.

Personal appearances were another matter. Here the Byrds were allowed to go their own whimsical way. Let them dress in buckskin and boots and talk mysteriously about Jet Age music. Let the mystique spread. The clubs of Sunset Strip like Ciro's no longer were the preserve of the dancing, sun-kissed featherbrains go-go-ing away to endless retreads of "Louie Louie." Now it was dance, shake, and get some food for thought from the Byrds! If you were really "in," you went to see them at the Crescendo Club—on a weekday. Never on weekends—that was tourist time, when those overweight girls from Orange Country came in to feel dangerous and claim that they were from Hollywood or some nearby deep canyon.

It was so bizarre to sway with Byrds music within the decor of the Crescendo or Ciro's. These places still retained vestiges of the old days in the thirties and forties when they were swell nightclubs where the cream of the film colony wined and dined and danced to moon-in-June or swing bands and every so often Bogart would take a swipe at a headwaiter. Nowadays, the old folks stayed away from the Strip, leaving their old caves to the youngsters, the New Barbarians. Or were they? Byrds fans seemed strangely quiet. They nodded and smiled a lot. They giggled at private jokes. Buffalo Bills in the court of Queen Bess. It was all perfectly harmless and perfect for a party.

Meanwhile, Bob Dylan was having a rough ride on his transformation track, but he was a sticker. In April, he had made the British charts with a song from his pure folk period, "The Times They Are A-Changin'." This was the first time he'd made a pop chart and he was excited. He started reading the British pop papers. He probably skipped the news that Roy Orbison liked to rent cinemas to see Westerns and also liked to eat peanut-butter-and-jelly sandwiches before retiring to bed. Also, that Gerry (of Gerry and the Pacemakers) had confessed to being a keen golfer and to taking up pop psychology. But he couldn't have helped noticing the emergence of a Dylan clone: Donovan. While "The Times They Are A-Changin'" lay at number fifteen, this boy Donovan was up there at number seven with his own composition, "Catch the Wind." A good lullaby of a folkish song, neatly strummed and sung in the Dylanesque nasal style but with much greater tunefulness. Of course, the number wasn't about anything of any consequence—like "Blowin' in the Wind" or "The Times They Are A-Changin'." But one couldn't ignore Donovan. The press was making a meal out of the similarities between the two folk bards. . . .

Donovan Leitch came originally from Glasgow, Scotland, a tough city, but lately he'd been living with his parents in the pleasant town of Hatfield, just north of London. His big break had come on "Ready, Steady, Go!" when he'd appeared in his faded denims and his little Dylan cap, wielding a big guitar that said THIS MACHINE KILLS. Pete Seeger's guitar had said THIS MACHINE KILLS FASCISTS, but Donovan replied to his critics that these days there weren't any fascists around. None that *he* knew anyway. He was a nice minstrel, with a gamin sexiness and a winning smile. He claimed Woody Guthrie as his main influence, same as Lonnie Donegan (the Skiffle King). Roving was what made him happy and to rove one didn't need a suit so he didn't own one. All over Britain, and parts of the Continent, he'd roved and rambled with his sidekick Gypsy Dave, whom he'd met at an Aldermaston "Ban the Bomb" march. Later, in their ramblings, they'd lived for a while in a World War II pillbox in Hastings. They knew the beaches of Southern Britain very well. It was painful trying to read Kerouac and Samuel Beckett on those hard and often tar-coated stones, but they found a haven of rest and contentment in Devon and Cornwall. Nature spoke to them there and the message was: be gentle and courteous and knightly. They lived this message, spreading universal love through soft music. They set an example to their legion of followers: the two shared the same jeans, boots, and even women.

Now, in May, Donovan was a star and thinking of moving to a luxury flat on Baker Street. Not far away, at the Savoy Hotel, the Bob Dylan entourage was stationed. They were in London for some concerts and they were flush with Dylan's unexpected chart success. He'd never made a chart in America, although "Subterranean Homesick Blues" was now making a bit of noise over there. However, in Britain, "Subterranean Homesick Blues" was bounding up the charts—to finally land at number twelve. Hey, the tasteful Britains were ready for the new, all-electric Dylan!

But *no!* At the Albert Hall, they booed and hissed when Dylan revealed his new music. They wanted the old folkie. "I don't believe you!" he cried to the audience. But the Brits had a point: "Subterranean Homesick Blues" fast skiffling was fine, it was that kind of song —a word-tumbler, a song of urban hustle and bustle. But mucking up ballads of rich imagery so that the words were lost in the god-awful voodoo hillbilly racket—that was unforgivable. Lyricism and body beat just don't mix.

Dylan went into a muck sweat, then into a stew. He took it out on a poor bugger of a reporter, a local stringer for *Time.* The man became a "Mr. Jones." Dylan spilled more bile on veteran pop journalist Laurie Henshaw from *Disc,* who visited him in his Savoy suite: "Can you tell me where and when you were born?" "No. You find out." "What are your present plans?" "Building a rocket on my plantation in Georgia where I have a Cadillac. . . . The people that listen to me don't need your paper. . . ." "Why be so hostile?" "Because you're hostile to me, man. You're using me. I'm an object to you. Why should I have to go along with something just so that somebody else can eat? Just say my name is Kissenovitch." "Let's talk about clothes." (*Appearance is everything, according to Andrew Loog Oldham and Kit Lambert and the tailors of Carnaby Street.*) "I wear drapes and carry an umbrella." The interview ended when Dylan called for his bodyguard. MR. SEND-UP headlined *Disc* when they ran the exchange.

It was a rehearsal for press interviews to come. Later, in San Francisco, where they understood this kind of talk, Dylan was to announce himself as "just a song-and-dance man." Allen Ginsberg and Ralph Gleason were to smile knowingly. They were *in on the joke:* grow with the music or it will grow without you. But that was later, after a debacle similar to the Albert Hall experience: the Newport Folk Festival.

The acoustic folkies should have known what they were in for. If they'd listened to pop radio, they'd have heard the sound of things to come in "Subterranean Homesick Blues." If they'd listened to what their leader was saying, they'd have known that he was plunging into the noisy chaos of twentieth-century urban life: "I accept chaos—I am not sure whether it accepts me. My poems are written in a rhythm of unpoetic distortion, divided by pierced ears, false eyelashes, subtracted by people constantly torturing each other, with a melodic purring line of descriptive hollowness."

There it is, all laid out as plain as a pikestaff. The songs of today must sound like today—with bombs falling on Vietnam, faces getting lifted by the thousand, blacks hurting for change in fetid ghettos, and amps turned up so high they'll burst your eardrums.

At Newport in July, the Paul Butterfield Blues Band came on to accompany the new Dylan. They plugged in and all hell broke loose. The folkies went bananas. Backstage, pacifist Pete Seeger, apoplectic with rage, grabbed an ax and threatened to cut the electric cables if this sacrilege didn't stop. Of course, he stopped short of action—in the pacifist-liberal tradition. Outside, in the darkened chaos of the audience, not a few souls said, "Right on."

Gone was the Greenwich Village cheerleader. Present was the Pop Star. In September, "Like a Rolling Stone," the social chronicle of the New Generation, reached number two in the U.S.A.

But we must return to see the Indian summer of another world. End-of-pier in sunny California. . . .

June 16:

What a relief to get back to normalcy! To meet such an *anchor* as Jack Good, Oxford University man! I taped "Shindig" today, the nonstop rock 'n' roll TV series that Jack set up himself out here and which he has fashioned into a howling success on the ABC network. Like his British show "Oh Boy!", it's one of the fastest shows on TV. In fact, it looks a lot like his other work, except that the acts are 1965. I was very lucky to be picked because lots of British acts (like Sandie Shaw, for instance) are being denied visas since their names aren't well known enough to American viewers. It was whispered to me that Jack only hired me because his young ex-Public School assistant, David Mallet, thought it might be a "wheeze" to have such a tweedy Old English upper-class idiot like me on such a rocking show. George denies it. However. . . .

The dancing girls are even more luscious than those on "Hollywood A Go Go" but are much classier and more stuck-up. And what a wonderful bill! Dick and Deedee, Cilla Black, the Shangri-Las—and *the Beach Boys.* I was glad to see that they lived up to all my expectations: suntanned, wind-blown, hair frozen into great waves, clad in striped beach shirts and white trousers. Polite yet distant—exactly right for stars. Wholesome and sunny, like their latest hit, "Help Me, Rhonda," which they sang on the show. It's a shuffle number and not specifically about surfing, so it appears they're diversifying from their narrow field of beach life—probably as a response to the British Invasion. Everyone was very careful with Brian Wilson. He had a case of nervous exhaustion a few months ago and is in a delicate condition. I must say they were very amused by me and quite polite.

On the other hand, Cilla Black hardly said a word to me—but that's understandable: you don't come all the way from sodden England to Lotusland to see a fool in a deerstalker hat. George keeps adjusting this blessed hat, but I'm glad that Jack Good has decided to dress me as a leather boy for the number I do with the Shangri-Las ("Give Him a Great Big Kiss"). After that, I remove the leather jacket and, in my regulation black turtleneck sweater and tapered jeans, I sing "This Sporting Life." The censor for the series, a dear old lady (possibly from Pasadena) has forbidden me to sing "You Turn Me On." Too suggestive for family audiences.

One of the joys of "Shindig" was that it was like being in a school play. We are all amateurs as far as acting and dancing are concerned, but Jack made us dramatize our routines and he linked up each song in a theatrical manner. The ghost of Shakespeare hovered in the air and Jack was everywhere bellowing instructions. For instance, I had been quietly going through my routine in front of the cameras when an Oxonian bellow came through the hanging studio speakers: "No no no, dear boy! Put some more *ooomph* into it. Make believe you are a real dangerous bike boy with a dagger—like Gene Vincent after I got hold of him!" Suddenly, Jack materialized from the shadows, leaping onto my rostrum in his costume of baggy pants, red suspenders, and bowler hat. He proceeded to rehearse me in every movement, down to the flicker of an eyelid. We might have been doing *Richard III*. I asked which camera to peer into. "Haven't the foggiest," said Jack breezily. "I leave all the electronic gadgetry to Rita." He'd brought his trusted "Oh Boy!" director Rita Gillespie all the way over from England with him. Very reassuring. Then we broke for tea. "No tea bags here—the real McCoy for me," said Jack.

When the house band, the Shindogs, began to rehearse a number, Jack cast aside his teacup and started bouncing around to their beat, occasionally whirling like a dervish and shouting "Whoopee!" It was all very infectious . . . for me, at least. But the musicians, the top session players in town (some of whom had recorded with the Byrds and other hit acts) stayed cool, calm, and collected. Being from L.A., I suppose they had to "relaxayvoo" (as they say out here). However, the music they pulsed out was devastatingly good, as if they'd been born with rock 'n' roll coursing through their veins. Never for a moment did they

appear to be carried away and yet the most heart-wrenching cries came
from their chromed saxes, their lumpy wooden guitars, even from their
polished, hideous electric organ.

An advantage to "Shindig" is that we sing our music *live*, so we don't
have to wrestle with that embarrassing charade of lip-synching. Most
of the songs were joined into a medley, which made life quite difficult,
so by the time we were ready to tape that evening, I was nervous.
Would I come in on cue, let alone on the right note? But Jack was
there to comfort and cajole. Just before the red light went on and while
the audience girls and boys were being rehearsed on their screams and
claps, Jack assembled us all backstage and delivered a pregame pep talk.
Standing on a box and sounding like a headmaster before a key rugby
match, he said:

"Now look here, Shindiggers, we've got to buckle down and put on a
ripping show because all America and her mothers and fathers will be
judging us. We're going to go out there as stars and come back as
superstars! Right?" *"Right!"* we all responded as one. "Yes indeed?" *"Yes
indeed!!"* This was Jack's equivalent of a brimstone gospel service and
it was very effective. After the exhortation, we dashed to our marks and
the tape rolled. Whoopee! Even Brian Wilson was filled with zeal.

It's odd how in moments of high drama one notices insignificant details—or maybe they're symbolic of their times? Anyway, I was aware
that George's trousers ended well above his ankles. But no time to
ponder—dressers put me into the leather gear and floor directors placed
me in the middle of the rough-talking, street-wise Shangri-Las. I was to
be their "Leader of the Pack" as they sang the hit. The blonde, Mary
Weiss, looked very provocative. *I* felt slightly foolish. After their number, the stage was mine and I whipped off the leather to lie down on a
ramp and deliver "This Sporting Life." The girls screamed on cue. Immediately afterward, Jimmy O'Neill, the beaming and immaculate host,
asked the girl in the Stridex medicated pad commercial to go wash her
zit-covered face with the special pad. "Is your face really clean?" "I
think so," blushed the girl. "Go rub the Stridex pad across your face."
After that, we had a close-up of a blackened pad: "Living proof that
Stridex medicated pads clean dirt and grime from your face better than
soap and water." George and some of the other industry people floating
about backstage considered this to be a very hard-hitting commercial.
Got straight to the point—a very American habit.

My attention was immediately diverted from these business considerations by the Beach Boys—archetypal and simply wonderful, spiffy
and keen in their stripes and whites and ocean whiffs. Memories of '64
came flooding back, making me misty-eyed. How long could this good

1. My father and I on the ocean promenade at Brighton, Sussex, England, the World, the Universe, around Easter, 1950. A weekend vacation from the dreaded boarding school nearby; a chance to go on the pier and drive the American Dodg'em cars, eat American doughnuts, and wallow in the crash and clatter of American music. My parents were very understanding.

2. In 1955, on the eve of rock 'n' roll, I pour some fizzy lemonade for my brother Robin, on the left, and my best chum, Speedy, on the right, at Battersea Park Fun Fair, London. Robin later drummed for Sonny and Cher.

3. At boarding school, private and pricey, in 1957. Rock 'n' roll had already struck a sleeping Britain and here I am cracking a joke at the expense of a history textbook. "He seems to have a fund of endless frivolity," my headmaster wrote in the school report.

4. Ostensibly an honors history student at Trinity College, Dublin, I spent most of my time in music of a sort. Here we are in 1964 and I'm lead singer in Ireland's only rhythm and blues band, Bluesville Manufacturing. I've Beatled my hair, dressed in searsucker, and am about to fall over in a tipsy state and evoke screams from the girls. We're on the eve of a U.S. hit with "This Sporting Life," which we've just recorded for Jerden Records of Seattle. It's Autumn 1964 and my love affair with America is continuing apace.

5. The same gig. The location was a church in Mount Merrion, just outside of Dublin. We were not asked to perform there again.

6. Inside Tower Records, April 1965, I pose in what was to become my quintessential rock 'n' roll outfit: the deerstalker hat and herringbone suit.
PHOTO BY GEORGE GERMAN

7. On the set of the rock 'n' roll TV show "Shivaree" in L.A. in July 1965, where I sang my only social protest song, "Too Many Cars on the Road." Standing behind me are the Ronettes. PHOTO BY GEORGE SHERLOCK

8. In July, I was part of a fantabulous bill at the Hollywood Bowl, the like of which will never be seen again. What a pity the sound system broke when I appeared and I had to resort to loudly told jokes.

9. Meeting the stars: The original caption of this clipping says we *were* at this party, but I'm damned if I can remember the thing, nor can I remember being with Mike Love. He says he can't remember it either. What conclusion should one draw from this?

10. Armed with my first Tower album, Dick Clark interviews me on his classic show "American Bandstand" on July 3, 1965. PHOTO BY GEORGE SHERLOCK

11. A publicity shot taken in late 1966 when I was being handled by Derek Taylor, who had me grinning more, dressing better, and generally having a good, healthy time. PHOTO BY CYRIL MAITLAND

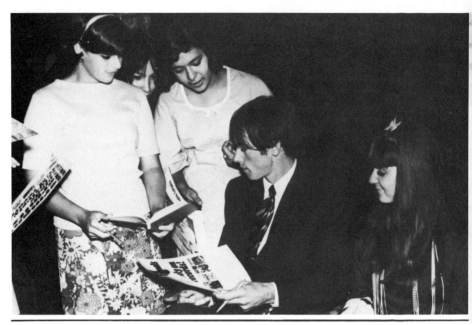

12. The price of fame: In 1966, my first appearance on "The Dating Game" when it premiered and I was a guest star in that very first show. My prize was a charming Valley Girl and good seats at a Herman's Hermits concert. On my second appearance, I won a trip to the Bahamas.

13. Disc jockey jamboree: While deejays Tommy Vance and Rhett Hamilton IV rave about my new Tower release, I look on gratefully. KOL was a major rocker in Seattle and it was always worth keeping in with the radio folk. I speak as a present-day deejay (KROQ, Los Angeles).

14. At the end of my career with Tower Records, I persuaded them to let me attempt a re-creation of the energy of the original rock 'n' roll of the fifties. Hence this picture session in Griffith Park, Los Angeles. The executives at Tower felt that this concept was not trendy and so my final album with them bore a more traditional teen jacket.
PHOTO BY GEORGE GERMAN

15. Caught between gigs in late 1967.
PHOTO BY ROBIN FROST

16. The high point of my R&R career came near its end when I produced Mae West's album *Great Balls of Fire*. It was a joy to make and my friendship with Miss West, star of stars, continued until her death. In this picture, we are seen outside the Mayfair Music Hall, Santa Monica, where I'd just performed such songs as "Where Did Robinson Crusoe Go with Friday on a Saturday Night?"

17. Here I am in 1983, feeling well and with all of my faculties intact, looking forward to becoming a "responsible senior citizen." It was a "learning experience" living through the sixties and one that I'm glad to share with you. I wish I could say that I did it all my way. PHOTO BY JIM SHEA

thing last? Already there were whispers that Brian was spending more and more time "in his room," getting introspective, getting away from the camaraderie, the team spirit of the old surf days.

But at least for tonight, on that sound stage at ABC where once (I was informed by a stagehand) Al Jolson had made *The Jazz Singer,* all was well with America and the world (which, to my mind, is the same thing). The Beach Boys surfed smoothly through all their hits, climaxing with their latest, "Help Me, Rhonda." On the grand finale, the entire cast—even Cilla Black—clapped along to an inspiring spiritual about a camp meeting sung by the black duo Joe and Eddie. Afterward, I felt I'd done a decent day's work and that I was truly a professional.

George whisked me off to Martoni's, where I shook hands with more disc jockeys and "key" program directors. There George spotted Frank Sinatra and followed him around the room like a bloodhound. "My main man, he's my man," George kept saying. He also said "hi" to Phil Spector, but the legend, surrounded by a phalanx of bodyguards, didn't reply. Meanwhile, I met a fellow Britisher, a disc jockey from a San Diego station called Lord Jeremy. He was wearing a deerstalker and smoking a Sherlock Holmes pipe—and laying on the "what ho" and "pip-pip!" a bit thick. Is he copying my act? From his accent and manner, I'd say his upper-class credentials are dubious. I also chatted with Derek Taylor, the ex-Beatle press agent who now works for KRLA. I made a joke to the effect that we were both "professional Englishmen milking the Yanks." He didn't seem to appreciate my remark. His wife looked daggers at me. Of course, they're North of England, which may explain things.

June 17:
Had a meeting this morning with the Tower executives about my future. Much talk of "goals" and "positive thinking." The execs all looked rather glum. Seems that "Turn On" has peaked at number eight nationally and is slipping down the charts rapidly. Tower needs a follow-up and needs it fast. In the office, there and then, I couldn't for the life of me dream up a suitable song—my mind was more on my history finals. Anyway, "Turn On" happened by chance, without thought. Still, I am now a cog in this "industry of human happiness" (as Andrew Loog Oldham put it) and I must take it seriously, particularly as so many lives and cars and pools depend on me. The meeting was cut short by the arrival of Mike Curb with a bunch of hot tapes from new groups he'd assembled. He flashed me a very winning smile and mentioned how nice the weather had been lately. I backed out and set myself the task of continuing my pop life. I phoned up David Mal-

let, the well-bred Public School boy who assists Jack Good, and I asked him for suggestions. He's as self-assured as Mike Curb and even breezier.

David and I got together over a cheeseburger and fries. Eventually, we decided to re-record one of the numbers I'd done with Bluesville in Dublin: "N-N-Nervous!", a blues song that I sort of "borrowed" from Willie Dixon, the rotund black blues singer and writer. One can't really copyright the blues because they're basically all the same, but I must admit that the theme was Dixon's idea. Still, he's lucky to have me giving his idea a wider audience. Ethics, ethics! David told me to shut up and said he'd produce the new version and make it more "funky" and "in the groove" than the Bluesville version. I shall be glad to get rid of Bluesville, for they've been nothing but trouble, according to Jerry Dennon: pestering him about getting a cut of my record royalties, claiming it was *their* sound that made me a star. Apparently, everybody at Trinity, including the postman Julian, is boasting that he had a hand in my hit. Everybody's cutting in on the act!

Later:

Amazing how fast people out in Hollywood work. David roped in some of the "Shindig" musicians—James Burton (late of Ricky Nelson's group) on guitar, Jim Horn (yakety sax man of the Duane Eddy records), Delaney Bramlett on bass, and Mickey Conway (a genuine New Orleans bluesman) on drums—to the RCA studios and we've cut the new "N-N-Nervous!" in under two hours. In the control booth sat the Tower executives, frowning and shifting in their seats. After we played them back a rough mix, one of them said that the song is "interesting" but that time would tell whether or not the cut "has legs." Still, said another, "We'll give it our best shot." Pity George wasn't there to boost their enthusiasm, but he's on the road with Mike Curb, helping Mike to push a group that sings about Honda motorbikes or something. Also, Tower's just landed a Freddie and the Dreamers track and they're aiming their big guns at the top of the chart with that. "We'll run it up the flagpole and see if anyone salutes it," said one of the executives. David didn't seem at all worried, just wished me a "toodle-oo" and dashed off in his MG to confab with Jack Good.

Afterward, I managed to contact Gale, one of the "Hollywood A Go Go" dancers whom I'd met at a party, with the excuse that I wanted to discuss some Dylan with her. At about 2 A.M., lying with me on her Murphy bed, she told me she's in touch with aliens from outer space and that they know of me as "Eloi." She's developed some odd welts on her otherwise milky face.

San Diego, The Holiday Inn:
   So looking forward to this tour. What a cast! the Beach Boys, Sam the Sham, the Righteous Brothers, the Kinks, Jan and Dean, and Sonny and Cher. Latter duo are another Jack Good discovery—they bugged Jack to get on "Shindig" until he finally admitted that Cher is very pretty and let them do a spot. With their crazy furs and hair and folk-rock songs, they're really making it, hitting the charts with "I Got You, Babe." Now they're regulars on the TV show. Before the tour, Sonny advised me to be considerate to fans but never to get too close to them, as they can turn nasty. He and Cher go out of their way to sign autographs, though.
   They gave me a ride down to San Diego in their super chauffeured Cadillac, complete with phone and TV. I was worried about getting to the gig on time, but Sonny said to be a star you should never care about being on time. At the gig, which was an enormous gymnasium, Sonny introduced me to Sam the Sham. This was a great thrill because I've grown to love "Wooly Bully," a quintessential pop record: mysterious words and a catchy voodoo chant. Sam is really Domingo Samudio of Dallas, Texas, and specializes in what's called "Tex-Mex" music. His group hardly says a word, but they appear to be nice Southern boys. For their act, they dress up in Eastern garb that looks like it's made from the curtains in my motel. Sam wears a beard, a gold tuxedo, and a turban. However, despite this exotic vaudeville appearance, Sam turns out to be an educated gentleman and he and I discussed the philosophy of John Locke while waiting in the locker room of the school's gym.
   In a far corner, I noticed the Kinks, keeping to themselves. Mostly they muttered expletives, played cards, or ran nervy licks up and down their guitars. The chords they play seem to be always the same: G/F/B flat—round and round and round. Eerie and disconcerting. I long for a safe old cycle of sevenths. Their sound reminds me of Roman epic films. And when they dress up in their jolly huntsman costumes, the effect is bizarre, especially when one of Sam's Pharaohs is nearby.
   One of the Kinks' road crew, a fearfully common cockney runt, kept demanding cups of tea and/or "blow jobs" from the vivacious college girls who are acting as our usherettes. Perhaps the fellow was suffering from culture shock. I've noticed that the lower classes fret terribly while abroad and need constant reminders of the homeland to reassure them —tea, pork pies, jam sandwiches, etc. Whereas my class, used to being posted to boarding schools and having foreign service in the blood, as it were, are quite at home in alien climes. The Kinks refused to appear onstage until they had been paid in cash. Eventually, a bag of cash appeared.

I had a most unfortunate experience. Just before being announced, I was approached by the show promoter and told: "Sitting out in the audience is a good friend of yours from England who's now a disc jockey out here. His name is Lord Jeremy, so won't you please mention his name onstage?" Merely to oblige, I did this. But no sooner had I spoken the name than a spotlight hit this Lord Jeremy, as if on cue. He stood up and took a bow in his deerstalker and heavy tweeds. Then he kicked up his heels, waved a Union Jack, and yelled, "Tallyho and let's go with KLAP, the station of sockeroo!" After exiting the stage (to loud applause, I might add), I was tackled by a man with an "Abe Lincoln" face and beard who snarled, "You asshole! Lord Jeremy is with our archrival station. *We're* presenting this show, not them. I oughta slug ya!" Pulling in my chin and standing up rigid, I replied, "How dare you speak to me in that manner. I ought to tweak your beard." Which I attempted to do—but Sonny Bono restrained me. Afterward, he took me aside to explain that this "Lincoln" character is a very important "key" program director. Oh God! He'll probably order my records blacklisted.

Seattle, Washington, The Edgewater Inn:
Here it is, my birthday—twenty-four today—and I'm on the verge of hysterics. It came about in this way—and I'll have to backtrack to explain the chain of events: Seattle is the last leg of this Beach Boy-led super package tour. After San Diego, we did the fabulous Hollywood Bowl. How I wish I could have savored the glory and basked in the balm of applause. But no sooner was I onstage than I was off. I do remember that, during my act, the sound system broke down. So I kept the show going, in the grand old manner, by telling Max Miller music-hall jokes and also some pier stuff. Afterward, backstage, the local jocks said I did a "helluva job" covering up the problem and that I was a real "pro." But the Los Angeles *Times* review the next day said I was not worth the trip from Dublin. I was on the point of calling up the reviewer, a certain Charles (Chuck) Champlin, when Sonny Bono again restrained me. He certainly knows the ropes.

After the Bowl, we were supposed to play the Cow Palace in San Francisco. I'd never been to San Francisco before, somehow getting sidetracked to Nashville, L.A., and Seattle, but all my English friends said it was the most beautiful and tasteful city in America and hellishly artistic. The night before the gig, George reappeared and escorted me to Martoni's, where he left me at a table with Sonny and Cher. Cher is very beautiful and smiles a lot. One forgets about the rest of the entourage, the chauffeurs and bodyguards and so on. I was amazed to hear Sonny ask Cher, during dinner, whether she felt like making the

Cow Palace gig, and to hear Cher say she wasn't going. Yet contracts had been signed. Obviously, I have much to learn. Phil Spector was eagling around, but nobody was paying him much attention. Apparently, he's not very hot at present. During dessert, George reappeared from somewhere in the gloom and said he had bad news: he was buying a Scotch on the rocks for the program director of KHJ, a new and important rocker station in L.A., when the program director mentioned that all Ian Whitcomb records have been *blacklisted* in their chain. So that San Diego "Lincoln" man has had his revenge! Oh well, honor and dignity are worth sticking out one's neck for. "Manners maketh man." Still, it's bloody annoying—and poor old George looked most upset. But Sonny bought George a special house drink and introduced him to Frank Sinatra's bodyguard.

The Cow Palace gig went OK. Didn't see much of Frisco—except that I learned from a local inhabitant that they hate having their city called "Frisco." That put me slightly on my guard. Saw the cable cars and the hills, which were exactly as they are in the travel films. I don't remember much about the Cow Palace performance itself. This work is getting to be a blur, just a job. I remember the usual high-pitched screeching. A contagious disease: they scream at the Beach Boys because they're stars, but they scream at me, I think, because I come from the same country as the Beatles and the Beatles come from God and maybe by being near me they can catch some reflected grace. I must say that, onstage, Dennis Wilson, the drummer, looked very scared and, when a teddy bear hit him in the face, he downed his sticks and rushed off. Overreacting, I thought. But he was followed by the rest of the Beach Boys and, on their way out of the Cow Palace, they grabbed me and we all bundled into their getaway Cadillac with one-way glass. No sign of Sonny and Cher on this show. Sam the Sham kindly gave me a copy of Thomas Hobbes's collected works before I went on. The Kinks continued to scowl and say not a word to me, but then I didn't say anything to them either.

In Seattle, the tour was even smaller in cast. The Righteous Brothers had somehow dropped out, too. Something about flying or contracts or drummers. In Seattle, I should have been at my happiest because here was where I began so many years ago in the halcyon Kennedy days. But right from the start, there was violence in the air. The police were truculent and jeering. Jan (of Jan and Dean) wasn't recognized by one of the cops guarding the sports arena artists' entrance. Unable to get in, Jan socked the cop. I can begin to understand this kind of violence: when you're hyped up for an explosive rock 'n' roll performance, any little detail can detonate you. And after the show, after you've wriggled and shaken and gotten the girls excited and you've been told viscerally that you're godlike and yet you know in your head that what you sang was awful and that the band was terrible, that the mikes weren't working properly, and that the piano was just a matchbox—after all this cold realization, *still* the girls twitter and screech. It's beginning to piss me off, this complete lack of any artistic discrimination. I feel like the Kinks. In fact, backstage, I smiled sarcastically at Ray Davies and he smiled crookedly back. We agreed that the whole game was a silly farce and that we would be Dadaists together.

So, full of rage, I returned to our tour hotel, a swank new place called the Edgewater. All day, a mother had been imploring me to autograph her daughter's cast and meet the girl. Finally, right after the act, I relented and followed the well-fed mother along the corridor to the suite. I was signing hard on the plaster cast on the girl's broken thigh when there was a commotion and, looking up, I saw a cop and a security guard. "OK, everybody *out!*" ordered the cop. "No adults in a juvenile's room." There had been a few tour gophers chewing the cud in the suite, but they immediately vanished. Being American, they knew the score. Calmly, I continued to sign the plaster—until a stomach blotted my view. "Hey, punk—you better *git!*" Through narrowed eyes, I regarded the fat blue officer. I said, "Don't you *ever* speak to me in that manner, my man. Remember you are a *public servant!*" "Wise guy, huh?" He and the security guard laid into me with punches, while I defended myself as best I could with my hardbound British passport. Within moments, they had me up against the wall and in handcuffs. The mother and daughter and other assorted fans were shrieking and carrying on. Where was George when I needed him? Luckily, Jerry Dennon was around and he sorted the matter out with some well-chosen words, a few albums, and a spot of folding money. Is this the sort of thing that happens to Connie Francis? And it's my birthday, too. The feel of handcuffs is quite horrible, filling one with all manner of guilt for mysterious reasons.

Omaha, Nebraska, At the Sign of Ye Holiday Inne:
I'm in the middle of a month-long tour with the "Dick Clark Caravan of Stars." I met Dick Clark sometime earlier—I'm losing a sense of exact dates—when I was on "American Bandstand." A very personable man—and solid. Later, we chatted in his office and I noticed he has a taste for turn-of-the-century Americana: wind-up gramophones with horns, cuspidors, and old Coca-Cola mats and trays. The sort of bric-a-brac one doesn't associate with Chubby Checker or Fabian. Clark has *roots*—and I like to keep this fact in mind as we rootlessly pound the highways of America in our Greyhound bus, bringing the good news of

R&R, long hair, and general liberation to the inhabitants of the mashed-potato circuit.

I've played all around the South and Midwest and I've been through all those towns with names from movies and old pop songs, those ringing names that sound and rhyme so well. Played 'em all, sometimes in high school gyms, sometimes in National Guard armories, sometimes in sports arenas, once on hay wagons. I've seen America—and yet I've seen little outside of the homogenous motel rooms with the same stormy TV reception, Impressionist wall prints, and Gideon Bibles. At least American Youth has seen us and rejoiced.

When our dirt-streaked bus rolls up at our Holiday Inn (always the Holiday Inn), having taken us all through the night after our previous gig, across prairies where no buffalo roam, through Laramies and Cheyennes and Tombstones where no outlaws lurk but where the Big Macs are stacked, frozen, ready for the next rush—when we grubby, horny, weary rock stars arrive at our next bed stop, the local teeny-boppers are there to greet us. Around the foul machine they press, autograph books and cameras at the ready, anxious to see real-life sex symbols up close—while I sit inside the bus, anxious for any sign of real old-time romance, of the Old West, of the dust kicked up by the thundering hoofs of a gang hell-bent for the butte they call Robber's Roost, where they can be safe from the hot pursuit of the sheriff's silver-mounted posse jingle-jangling behind them.

As the underaged girls gaze in at us stars, we in turn leer out at them, choosing the ones we want to take to our rooms. "The smiley ones up front are no good," says one star. "They won't do a thing. Look for the straight-faced ones hovering in the background, pretending not to be fans. They're the ones you can fuck till their eyes pop out." Our guide is a veteran of R&R package tours, so his words are noted, for apart from food and sleep, sex is the only thing on our minds. I really can't take much more of this life-style.

The beat goes on—drone, drone, drone—while the boring Midwest slides by with its prairie, silo, prairie, silo, billboards, silo, Howard Johnson, prairie. . . . So I usually try to escape by dipping into my history textbooks. The finals are in October and some of this stuff is very dense. I wish Peter Asher would talk to me; he's supposed to be brainy, a member of Mensa. Neither Peter nor Gordon have talked to me yet, but I heard from Tom Jones, the friendly Welshman, that they've cold-shouldered me because they consider "Turn On" to be absolute trash without any redeeming social value. They say I am giving pop a bad name by perpetuating the shlock of the past. Since the Beatles and Dylan, there is a New Consciousness, a new maturity in R&R, but I'm as well educated as Asher and Waller and Dylan. Why the hell don't I speak to Tower and get them to release some more thoughtful material? "N-N-Nervous!" will never do. . . .

This is too much! One of the lesser acts, a bass guitarist, is pulling his trousers down to waggle his bottom at a passing family station wagon.

I must do something about my hair—it's coming out in handfuls. Perhaps a result of the water pressure in the Holiday Inn shower. The length of one's hair is frightfully important in this pop world at present and I intend to hang onto my stardom for a while. But I will also try to keep that stardom within the confines of a certain morality, even though the world—as we know it—is falling apart at the seams.

Columbus, Ohio:

Here I am, on another tour package, but this time I'm the only star, which I suppose isn't saying much. The others are unknowns, groups with pudding-basin haircuts and a couple of chords and a record that sounds as though it was made in a garage. Prince Valiants of the South. Why is it that they all seem to come from there and they're all overweight? Their greatest thrill is to go out "snacking," traveling from store to store, filling up on cakes, jelly babies, pecan pies, beef sticks, etc. Why does the Southern accent make them all sound like idiots when they're not really idiots? We're based in Ohio for the next dates of this tour, "Shindig '65" (I'm the only act that's ever been on the show) and it looks like anyplace else in this godforsaken country. Same old choice of baked potato or french fries; thousand island, blue cheese, or french dressing on your salad. Can't get any fruit or fish. My hair is still coming out and I'm getting fed up with this obsession about sex.

The other night, a "gang bang" was arranged at our hotel and I was invited. In a huge suite, decorated with the usual Impressionist repros, lay a homely fan, on a double bed which still was covered with a flower-pattern bedspread. Waiting in line were members of our tour with their sex machinery out: some primed, others priming. One after the other, they jumped aboard the fan girl with shouts of "Eureka!" and so forth, while a guitarist accompanied the action with the riff from "Louie Louie." A rich, blood-red dawn was bursting through the windows behind the silhouetted queue, making the whole thing almost painterly, but as the last performer, a grotesquely fat road manager, lumbered up, I thought: "This is a very violent scene, akin to a scene on the lines of the French Commune fighting of 1871 or Berlin in 1918." Staggered and disgusted, I retreated to my room to chat about Dylan with one of the girl's friends, a quite attractive redhead. We had been getting along famously for an hour or so, when in reeled one of the chief orgy-makers, a lead guitarist sporting an enormous engine. "Hi, gang!" he screamed. "Say hello to 'Roger'!" He pointed to his monstrous engine. "Come along, 'Roger'—don't be shy. Up, up, and fight fiercely for Mississippi U.! Who d'ya wanna fuck next?" I bundled the bugger out and, as he left, he accused me of being a "fudge-pounder," whatever that means. The girl and I resumed our talk. Shortly afterward, there was a sharp knock on the door, which I ignored. A few seconds later, the door was broken down by two burly police officers. They stood looking at us with folded arms. I asked them if they required anything. One said, "You, kid—for cohabitation with a minor," banging a notice which was attached to the back of my door. "Me an' Charlie've bin listening to your spiel in the connecting room and you can't fool us with all that junk about getting your lumbago massaged!" I wished George could have been there. I wondered how Elvis would have dealt with the situation. I desperately needed someone with the qualities of leadership, a Field Marshal Montgomery of Rock 'n' Roll. I had to do something, so I gave them several copies of the *You Turn Me On* album. They accepted these tokens after I'd signed them to their children.

"N-N-Nervous!" has been released and I see that it's hovering on the lower rungs of the *Billboard* Hot One Hundred.

Fort Lauderdale, Florida:

Disgustingly hot and humid. I'm sure this sort of weather encourages violence. The heat has brought out the demagogue in me.

I'm on a package tour with Freddie and the Dreamers and the Dave Clark Five. The DC5 arrived by chartered jet, had their equipment set up by trim men in track suits, and were on and off the stage in a flash. Mind you, they gave a well-oiled show and included all their hits and smiled healthily. Saw Clark himself backstage performing push-ups and tossing barbells around in a very discriminate manner. Freddie & Company were another matter. Mad as March Hares, they leaped all over the place and squirted water pistols and threw cakes at everybody. Onstage, Freddie giggled and cackled and did his leaps. As a grand finale, he hurled all the microphones into the audience. This was much appreciated.

I opened the second half. This is how I got into trouble: for days I'd felt a cold coming on, so I'd unsuccessfully tried aspirin. Then I learned about Contac and, just before this Florida show, I fortified myself with two Contacs and a glass of sherry.

The minute I got onstage, I felt groggy yet bold. The cheers egged me on, so I scaled the piano and, from that height, I invited the kids to charge the cops and mount the stage to join me in a party. The next thing I knew, I was being manhandled and dragged off by a squadron of officers. Handcuffs again. Yet they felt quite good this time, quite warm. The police captain lectured me about responsibility and the dangers of crowd excitement. "I could get you for inciting a riot, but you ain't worth it 'cause we won't get any press coverage. Now, Presley was different. *That* was worth it. And wouldn't I love to land that Jagger 'fudge-pounder.' Beat it, kid. You fags are tiring me!"

San Jose, California:

I've been reliably informed that "You Turn Me On" is all the rage in "fag" bars. Apparently, the "fudge-pounders" have taken to the number because of the high-pitched ambisexual nature of my singing. What began as a college lark is ending as the anthem of a new liberation group called the Jolly Boys of America. They've written to Tower, who forwarded their letter: the gay boys think I'm gorgeous and promoting "the Cause." Today, I got a demo tape from them of a song called "I Want to Ask You a Personal Question, Aubrey Dear (Can I Borrow Bobby Tonight?)." It's quite amusing, in a Noel Coward manner. I've sent it off to the Tower executives as a possible follow-up to "N-N-Nervous!" Anything goes in modern-day pop.

Portland, Oregon:

Just passing through here, en route for a Seattle show with the Rolling Stones. Although I'm banned here by order of the mayor, I couldn't resist stopping to buy one of their delicious pecan pies, individual-sized. Tower, in a turmoil, has cabled me thus: IAN. TWENTY-FIVE YEARS IN THIS BUSINESS. HAVE WALKED WITH SINATRA. PLEASE DO NOT—REPEAT, DO NOT—ATTEMPT TO WAX SONGS OF A HOMOSEXUAL NATURE AT THIS POINT IN TIME. GOOD LUCK AND KEEP KOMMERCIAL. REGARDS, GORDON "BUD" FRASER, PRESIDENT, TOWER RECORDS CORP.

Seattle, Washington:

A meeting with Mick Jagger backstage in Seattle has exorcised all the demons from my last experience here! I was hanging around, waiting to appear, when I heard this Dartford, Kent, accent and, looking below me, I spotted a little fellow in a white cricket shirt and checked trousers. The trousers startled me because they were exactly the same pattern as the ones I was wearing. I'd bought mine at John Stephen on Carnaby Street. I was remarking about the similarity when the tousled head interrupted me, politely and quietly:

"You're Ian Whitcomb, aren't you? Andy Oldham and I are fascinated by you and your records. Like what inspired you to record that

'Turn On' song, and where d'you record it, and who was playing? Oh, and where d'you go to school?"

For the next fifteen minutes or so, the little schoolboy with the full lips and tiny hips engaged me in questions about my background. He seemed genuinely interested to find out *where I was* at exactly. He shook his head a lot and smiled and nodded. He seemed pleased with my answers. At one point, I did remark, "You're Mick Jagger, aren't you?" He waved the question away. He even stood back and relaxed as a boy asked me for my autograph. After filling Jagger in on the details, I felt a desire to pour out my heart to him. He seemed so strong and self-assured—and relaxed. Perhaps *here* was the Field Marshal Montgomery of Rock 'n' Roll!

I told him my troubles, about the excesses of touring, about the tainted stardom, about the fragile pop dream. He listened, a bit quizzical. Then he said: "Look, mate, you've got to see this business from a bird's eye view. You're getting too *wormsy*, know what I mean? You're taking the thing too seriously and for the wrong reasons. This business has little to do with music, but a lot to do with the Big American Con Game. They love it; they love being conned. Anyone with a bit of luck and a pretty face and a lithe body can have a hit record. *You* did it. But if you want to stay ahead of the game, be a businessman. Exercise all you like when you're onstage, but when you're off let the curtain down and turn off the rock—or you'll kill yourself. Me, I'm a cricket buff and I don't mind a good Trollope to go to bed with—the book variety. But I let 'em have the bumps and grinds onstage and I run the corporation off-stage. . . . It's funny you should be asking me about all this stuff— 'cause Andy and I were admiring you for appearing to be so removed from all the crap. Cheer up and smile. You don't think I want to be singing '(I Can't Get No) Satisfaction' when I'm forty, do you? Christ on a bicycle, I'd rather be dead!"

"Satisfaction" remains one of the great rock records of all time. It's not my cup of tea, but then, as is apparent, my pop dreams were evaporating as the new regime adumbrated itself. Nothing was ever going to be as clear as "Be-Bop-A-Lula" again—at least not for me.

Nevertheless, it's clear to me now that "Satisfaction" expressed pithily the Sound of Suckland, as in "It all sucks, man. Everything *sucks*." All over this dissatisfied Boy's Town of Suckland was grievance, pain, discontent, alienation, fed-uppedness, resulting in complaints and more complaints, and then petulance, insolence, peevishness, querulousness, resentment, and then words become meaningless and the whole great complaint takes flight in one monstrous *whine*. . . .

That's how "Satisfaction" begins. With one long fuzz-buzz, chain-saw guitar whine. And the trouble for me was that I couldn't identify with this national teen malaise because I wasn't a teenager and, indeed, I'd never really been one. I had never felt a truly long-lasting, transcending, superterrestrial COMPLAINT—beyond my trousers riding up my thighs when I was a fat boy, or getting occasional constipation, or being thirsty, or slightly hungry for a pork pie. But all these irritations lasted for but a moment and needed no existential "Satisfaction." Jagger's lament was much greater than somebody stepping on your blue suede shoes or threatening to knock the rock. Jagger's lament was a moan that the whole fuckin' world was messed up because *we* weren't getting any satisfaction out of it.

So the very first lick of the record registers the mood of complaint. The fuzz-buzz persists through the whole song, nagging and whining like a runny-nosed, urine-soaked little brat, hitting those all-hallowed three notes back and forth, back and forth: fifth to sixth to flatted seventh and back and forth—surefire hit notes, as used in a trillion R&B, R&R hits like "Can I Get a Witness," "High Heel Sneakers," and "You Turn Me On." The safe blue whine is set up and into this whining wind (or is it the whine of a bullet?) insinuates the voice of the Prince of Wails himself. At first, that voice is soft and reasonable, close up and well mannered. Little Boy Blue sidling up to Bo Peep—but then the voice hardens and gets grating and adds a stridency to the bash-bash military beat that had up till now been almost Orbisonian or, anyway, Dave Clarkian in its friendliness.

But now out roll the complaints mercilessly—about the radio man full of useless trivia, the TV man ranting about an equally useless shirt, and then, more to the point, those wretched, recalcitrant girls who won't let you get anywhere with them.

Curiously, the last bars of the tune are almost identical to the last bars of that classic British march, "The British Grenadiers"! This was an amazing discovery for me at the time. Perhaps Field Marshal Jagger and his aide-de-camp Oldham are sending me a message that, though the rest of the world is *on the blink,* all's well at home and always will be—forever England! Turn over the 45 of "Satisfaction" and, lo and behold, there is a song about Jumpin' George Sherlock himself! "The Under Assistant West Coast Promotion Man." I know it's about George because Jagger told me himself during our Seattle meeting. George is rightly thrilled.

But all this "in" stuff was of no interest to the kids of America. The point was that "Satisfaction" needed no analysis. It summed up how they felt most days—when they didn't know exactly what they wanted but they were going to get it—whatever it was. As in Dylan's rambling whines, the imagery floated by in a blur and you filled in your own personal details, your complaints.

It was just not enough anymore to cruise up and down the strip; the sea and surf and sand and sun were no longer hip. "Summer Means Fun" the Fantastic Baggys had sung—what did they know? P. F. Sloan, one of those Baggys, was hip to what was happening and he was determined to do something about the matter. He changed his image and wrote a song called "Eve of Destruction."

Flip Sloan was a West Coast Alleyman, a Boardwalk Busker, and he could really turn 'em out for the market. As a teenager, he'd been signed by Lou Adler, professional manager of Screen Gems-Columbia Music (West Coast), as a writer and had immediately been teamed up with Steve Barri. Their "Kick That Little Foot, Sally Ann" had charted in the Top Sixty for Round Robin; they wrote for Connie Stevens, Shelly Fabares, Betty Everett, and Ann Margret. In their surf period, their songs included "Swimtime U.S.A.," "This Little Woodie," and "One Piece Topless Bathing Suit." By early '65, Lou Adler had formed Dunhill Records and the surf sound was continued with their first release, "The Surfing Songbook," with Sloan and Barri providing backup vocals.

But one day, Adler had rushed up to Sloan with a hot dub, a demo of Dylan's "Like a Rolling Stone." Adler was convinced this song was going to revolutionize the trade. No more mindless dance records; instead, concentration on the gray matter. Phil had better put on his thinking cap and come up with something in this protest vein. Sloan, actually, was already wearing a little Dylan cap. He genuinely identified with the guy. Into "Eve of Destruction" he poured a pile of universal wrongs, a bubbling mess of the current-affairs blues. Something was very rotten in the world—or was it in Flip's mind?

The song came on folksy in the Dylan manner, with plenty of G-clippin'. So much ground was covered, so many trouble spots were pointed out. In the Eastern world bullets were loadin' and in the Jordan River bodies were floatin', while in Washington a bunch of useless senators were passing equally useless laws, and in Alabama there was as much hate as there was in Red China. No good escaping into space because on your return the world would still be the same old mess, as, for example, when we zero in on domestic life and find folks hating their neighbors yet blithely saying grace before meals. All the while, the writer sits in a cataleptic state, unable to move a muscle and contemplatin' in a blind fury, so much so that his blood is actually coagulatin'. Verdict: This whole crazy world is too frustratin'. Echoes of "Satisfaction."

Thus spake Cassandra Sloan. Now comes the vinyl trick. Sloan, Barri, and Adler had run across a folk singer named Barry McGuire while they were making the rounds of the Sunset Strip folk-rock clubs. This cuddly, shaggy sheep had good upbeat folk connections, having been a New Christy Minstrel (he'd growled huskily on their 1963 hit, "Green, Green"). "Eve of Destruction" needed lots of raspy rage and this McGuire provided, getting real low down and snarling and almost spitting when he got to the part about hating your neighbor but not forgetting to say grace. The excellent Dylanesque accompaniment was by seasoned session men—slice-strummed acoustic guitars, wide-mouthed and full-blown harmonica, tumbril drums, and a marvelously ghostly background organ line.

The message was clear: since everything is such a mess and beyond correction, we should all eat, drink, and have a jolly good time—because tomorrow we die. This was far more accessible than Dylan. This made sense. This was an immediate hit. This was—Loot Music!

Hollywood (September):

I have returned from touring to find a changed world. Everywhere is the sound of folk rock and protest. "Eve of Destruction" by Barry McGuire is at number one and Dylan's "Like a Rolling Stone" is at number two. "Eve of Destruction" I can understand but don't like. "Like a Rolling Stone" I can't understand. Dylan sounds like a tetchy old curmudgeon and the band sounds a bit like Bluesville on an off night. Still, I must lay off the *sour grapes.*

"Eve of Destruction" is on all the local rocker stations and even on the other ones—at least, the announcers discuss the record on news-item shows. Some of the rocker stations preface the record with a disclaimer. One "Good Music" station (specializing in Johnny Mathis and Frank Sinatra) issued an editorial: "We play entertainment, not propaganda." To prove it, they've been playing all manner of arrangements of the ex-traordinary new Beatles song "Yesterday." The "Good Music" lovers, the adults, are pointing to this song as an example of how nice rock can be. It is amazing to realize that the Beatles have gone from the simplis-tic rock-a-chug of "I Wanna Hold Your Hand" to this quasi-baroque chamber music tune with the mystifying word poetry. The string ar-rangement is beautifully done, but the trade is now wondering just how big a part arranger/producer George Martin plays in Beatles artis-tic endeavors.

"Yesterday" was a turning point for the Beatles' musical image. Stick-ing out like a pair of old corduroy trousers in a pile of Carnaby Mod gear, the sound of the song did indeed owe a lot to George Martin. As he says himself, he put his "hallmark" on this track and it's very much in his style of conservatory-schooled "easy-listening" music with a touch of class. The use of a string quartet had hitherto been unheard of in pop. Never before had Beatles records used other instruments and other musicians, and never before had the old pop generation—the Alley publishers, writers, and crooners—felt so comfortable with the latest fashions. Now, at last, the older set could identify with what was happening. They were in touch—because the Beatles were in touch with them, with their sort of relaxing, restful, tuneful, nostalgic music. Few bothered to realize that "Yesterday" was a McCartney/Martin work and, more importantly, marked the beginning of an artistic schism in the writing team of Lennon and McCartney. "Yesterday" (originally a piano sketch that McCartney called "Scrambled Eggs") legitimized the Beatles; solid singers of the old school flocked to record it. By December, Matt Monro, the ex-bus conductor currently recording for Martin's Parlophone label, was in the British Top Twenty with his version. In the ensuing years, there were to be well over three thousand versions made, ranging from highly orchestral to slack-key Hawaiian ukulele. Only one other ballad challenged and beat "Yesterday" in the winter of '65: a version of "Tears" by the Liverpudlian comic Ken Dodd. It was to sell more records in Britain than any other recording of the entire year. The song had been written in 1931. The wheel turns and is forever still.

Hollywood:
   This folk-rock protest stuff sounds like something produced by the Trinity College Socialist Club in conjunction with the Folk Club and the junior freshman poetry class. I made this point today while making the rounds of the radio stations with George, trying to hustle my "N-N-Nervous!" record (which, I must confess, appears pretty redundant by today's standards). At KRLA, a disc jockey listened to my folk-rock comment and, in reply, handed me a photocopied slip which I later read in the car as George drove us back to Hollywood. I had to read it in between George's lectures to me about staying cool and not bad-mouthing the new music. The slip read: "Our listeners set the music policy. We play whatever records they indicate a preference for—so long as they are not morally offensive. If they decide they want to hear Chinese music, then that's what KRLA will play." George continued to talk—about how I should adopt fur and high boots as a sort of Sonny and Cher folk gesture—so I buried myself in the current *KRLA Beat*.

Full of protest news: P. F. Sloan, writer of "Eve of Destruction," is only nineteen and used to have very bad acne, but "it cleared up—and so did his mind," says his mentor, record producer Lou Adler. Adler is well into the protest biz, although until recently he was riding the surf trend. Dunhill, his record label, is by all accounts a "protest factory." Meanwhile, the rest of Hollywood hasn't been slack: a group called We Five claims: "There is a definite social change because the kids are more aware that there are social problems in this world which have to be spoken out against." Dylan, the High Priest himself, is quoted as saying: "I don't write controversial songs. I write facts. If you can't look in the mirror, that's your problem." Warner Bros. Music, who publishes Dylan's songs, boasts that there are sixteen singles and twenty-eight album tracks of Dylan material in current release, including Dino, Desi, and Billy's "Chimes of Freedom," and David ("The Stripper") Rose's "Mr. Tambourine Man."

With some relief, I read that the president of MGM Records has ordered dancing lessons for his acts: the Animals, Herman and the Hermits, and Sam the Sham.

From foreign correspondents come tales of defensive action by the authorities against the new folk-rock look: Donovan has been turned away from "hundreds" of hotels due to his jeans; "Ready, Steady, Go!" TV announcer Cathy McGowan was turned away from the Savoy because she was wearing a fashionable trouser suit "full of holes"; the Rolling Stones continue to be banned from everywhere. Up in Scotland, the oppression is worse: a youth was up on a charge of wanton window breaking when the magistrate remarked: "Do not be carried away by the complete morons of the pop field with hair down to their shoulders and filthy clothes." This prompted a rebuttal from Andrew Loog Oldham: "What gives him the right to assume that long hair goes with dirt? Doesn't his wife have long hair? As far as I and the Stones are concerned, the man is dead—part of a dead generation." The long hair controversy caught even me up during one of the tours when I was changing from plane to bus in Dallas and a cowboy-hatted man with a huge, overhanging belly grunted as he passed me, "Why ain't you in Vietnam, punk? Git in there and git yer hair cut!" So at least I can feel some anger about social details. Maybe I can feel strongly enough to write some protest songs? But I feel I cannot go as far as "Georgie Porgie" Leonard of Attleboro High School, who is going to have his case heard by the Massachusetts Supreme Court because his headmaster won't let him attend school with his hair at its present length. His attorney has been quoted as saying, "Long hair, as worn by Beethoven, Liszt, Washington, and General Custer, did not carry the presumption of uncleanliness and school authorities have no power to dictate how students should wear their hair or to what length it should be cut."

While all this pop business had been going on, there had been a civil war in a suburb of Los Angeles called Watts. Between August 11 and 16, rioters in this ghetto set fire to their neighborhood, looted shops and businesses, and fought the police and soldiers. There were thirty fatalities. But I didn't know where Watts was and none of my friends ever went there, nor did I associate its black residents with the ebony heroes who sang R&B. Once upon a time.

Hollywood (later that day):

George said that, as Roger McGuinn wears Pickwickian glasses and David Crosby wears a cloak, then I should nix the velour and go all the way with a Sherlock Holmes costume or perhaps go Dracula. I ignored the whole question as we walked into Martoni's for drinks and dinner. On a newsstand was a paper showing a picture of Lyndon B. Johnson displaying his flabby old belly and the scars of his recent gallbladder and kidney stone operations. It was so revolting that I was almost put off having any dinner at all.

Even inside Martoni's, the folk-rock protest world wouldn't leave us alone. We met the manager of Freddie and the Dreamers (who have achieved a number one for Tower with their record "I'm Telling You Now"). The man greeted us dolefully and told us in a very thick British North Country accent: "It's that Bob Die-lon man. The bloke's really killing our Freddie." Freddie, you see, is basically a sunny chap and it's going to be hard for him to get with the new fashion for finger-pointing and complaining. We moved on because people in Hollywood don't spend time around those on the verge of failure.

We ran into Sonny Bono, who has really adapted to the new scene. Indeed, he and Cher have, to a certain extent, set that scene. They have recorded Dylan songs and they've done their own; and tonight we saw the makings of an actual protest song. We were chatting with Sonny at the bar, waiting for a table. Sonny was giving me pointers about my pop future. As I recall, he was wearing his normal three-quarter-length leopard-skin pancho with his fur-trimmed moccasins, green cords, and golf-checked socks. Cher arrived wearing horizontal-striped bell bottoms in canary yellow—that was all I could see of her clothing, since her hair covered the rest. Sonny was rubbing his hands and saying how much he was looking forward to the stuffed veal parmigiana in clam sauce, with a rare chianti of his choice to wash it down. He was rubbing his hands and licking his lips, while George was saying he'd order exactly the same—when up strode the maître d'. In sotto voce, he ordered Sonny and Cher to leave at once because they were "incorrectly dressed." A short altercation followed (with George in a quandary—not knowing which side to take and constantly saying, "You're so right," with his head jerking left and right like a Wimbledon spectator). Finally, Sonny and Cher left in grand style—with the show-biz crowd agape. Later, I heard, Sonny had dashed off a protest song in the heat of hurt, a song aimed to "arouse the conscience of mankind." Within hours, he had it on disc as "Laugh at Me" and, as I write this (next morning), grateful stations are already airing their dubs.

Honolulu (October):
"Shindig" has come to Hawaii and I have been asked along as a special guest. Tommy Sands, who lives on the islands, is the star and I admire him for his star presence—very aloof, sleek, and shiny. Didn't even say hello to me, but, as I say, I admire him for that. The cast and crew keep their own company for the most part and that's fine with me because I have developed the most awful toothache. Saw a Hawaiian dentist who told me I had "trench mouth" and, when I asked him what caused this illness, he cheekily pinched me, winked, and said, "Nooky, nooky—worse to come!" Eventually, I found out that this "mouth" is caused by overdoing it sexually. I tried calling Gale, the dancing girl, but her roommate told me she's upped and gone to live in San Francisco in someplace called "Hate Ashberry."

I'm sharing a room with Len Barry, the singer who currently rides the charts with "1-2-3." He harbors no great love for British Invaders, but I told him I don't come from that part of the country. Right now, I'm lying on my bed with a toothache, trying to think what I shall sing on the show. I know no Hawaiian songs. "Aubrey Dear" doesn't seem right. I've been reading lately about our old, great days of Empire in a book titled *Jottings from an Active Life* by Colonel Weston-Jarvis. Stirring stuff. I may consider recording some extracts from this book for a spoken word track. I will do it in evangelical Southern preacher style and back it with gospel music. I'll cable Tower about this idea. I wish Len Barry would stop braying blue-eyed soul phrases; he sounds quite demented and it doesn't help my pain. He should be more considerate— after all, I lent him $15 yesterday.

IAN, STOP AND I MEAN STOP. TWENTY-FIVE YEARS IN THIS BIZ. WALKED WITH SINATRA, ETC. WHAT I SAID ABOUT HOMOSEXUAL SONGS GOES FOR

SPOKEN WORD. EVEN SIR LAWRENCE OLIVER [sic] COULD NOT GET AWAY
WITH IT. KEEP TRYING. REGARDS, G. "BUD" FRASER, PRESIDENT, TOWER
RECORDS CORP.

Pittsburgh (late October):
Trying to save "N-N-Nervous!" by going on the road hitting the
local radio and TV shows. Not much hope, I fear. Tonight, I did a TV
show with none other than Barry McGuire. We had dinner beforehand
and he turns out to be a perfectly charming man, very warm and gentle, not at all like his hate-filled song. We both had a bit too much to
drink and, when we went on the air, we were in the "Sweet Adeline"
stage. In fact, that's what we sang. He knows all these old songs and
we went on to do a very forlorn version of "When Irish Eyes Are Smiling" and a spirited version of "Coming in on a Wing and a Prayer."
Everyone was in tears at the end. All very therapeutic, as Bing Crosby
would say. Why doesn't the world know the real Barry McGuire?

Santa Rosa (November 5):
Armed with promo copies of "N-N-Nervous!", George and I assaulted a rural rocker station up a dusty road somewhere near San
Francisco. We are on a "hyping trip"—wholesale plugging in a last-
ditch attempt to save the poor little record. The station was a red-tiled
bungalow with touches of thatch. Outside the temperature was near
ninety degrees, but inside a gale of air conditioning was blowing. The
program director, Swinging Swallow, kept us waiting for what seemed
like hours while he organized a listener contest to find out which kid
had the fattest lips. What rot! Then, when at last we were allowed into
his inner sanctum and George had swiftly managed to get "N-N-Nervous!" spinning on the audition turntable, all this Swallow did was lay
back in his expandable swivel chair, sip a beer, and talk about last
night's game on TV. George played along gracefully, but Swallow, a
hatchet-faced man in his late forties, banged on about the game and
kept picking up the record player arm in order to skip grooves on my
record—the 45 on which my pop future depends. Finally, he dropped
the sports and turned off the record player. Spinning his chair vaguely
in my direction, he asked: "When you gonna make another record,
son?" "But you just listened to a smash, Swallow," said George with a
boogaloo swing of his hips. "Naw—I mean one I can play." Before I
could answer, Swallow continued with: "Have you guys heard this
'Eve of Destruction' mother? It's a stone fox smash!" And to emphasize
his point, he burst open another can of beer, soaking my record. "A lot
of the lyrics I can't make out, but what I can is goddamn *treason!* Can
you believe a guy who knocks our Draft, our senators, our church, our

H-bombs—and all on a pop record?" "So I take it," said George with a dismissive click of his fingers, "that the disc is negative as far as your big boss playlist is concerned?" "Not on your Hollywood scalp doily! It may knock the U.S.A., but I don't knock success. I grab it by the balls and hang on tight. That 'Eve' disc is Dylan made commercial. It's gonna open up a whole new area. It's a new kind of *loot music* under the title of *protest,* remember that! Now, Whitmore, you got something I can play, something that fits the times and our format—and I'll spin it like crazy. But until that time, it's so long and have a happy day. *Out!*"

That winter, back in Dublin, I sat for my finals. Somehow I managed to write my heart out, filling page after page of wonderful waffle on Marx, Engels, Bakunin, and Lenin, plus all the other ghostly historical figures who had ridden beside me during those months on the road. The Trinity authorities were kind and considerate. They awarded me a second-class degree in modern history. I received a letter from my tutor:

My dear Whitcomb,
You'll be glad to learn of your reasonable pass, no doubt. Under the circumstances—I mean your success in America—we all feel that you performed remarkably well in the exams. I speak for all of us on the faculty when I say, "Well done and good luck" in whatever you decide to do in your future life. We hope you will come and strum your banjo to us at some future date.

Saoirse!
J. D. O'Hill

The British Invaders stayed mostly in the homeland for Christmas. The Yuletide spirit is best caught in Western Europe. Somehow Father Christmas, no matter how expensively rigged out, doesn't come to life in America, and certainly not in the acrid air of Hollywood Boulevard. Many of the Merseybeat groups took up residence in Christmas pantomime shows like *Cinderella* and *Puss in Boots.* A great future was seen for Freddie (and, perhaps, his Dreamers) in this traditional form. In December, the Beatles returned to Liverpool for the first time in a year, playing the Empire Theatre to an audience of five thousand. There were only seventeen cases of hysteria and many seasoned Beatles watchers pronounced Beatlemania to be dead. The Beatles were now musical artists and would have to take their places beside the other contenders. While the group was appearing in Liverpool, it was announced that the Cavern was to be closed for sanitary reasons.

In the Christmas edition of *Disc,* the music paper, the stars offered seasonal thoughts. A new and outrageous R&B group called the Pretty Things sent this message: "May all our fans get stoned out of their minds on Christmas Day." Mick Jagger said he couldn't stand Christmas, as it's so phony. However, he'd rather be at home than in America, where "life is too fast with everybody rushing around like a lot of idiots. All the food tastes prepacked. British fans are more polite and appreciative. Besides, they let just about anyone into hotels over there!" He was already looking forward to the next year's cricket season.

The main pop topic was the astounding success of comedian Ken Dodd's recording of the ancient song "Tears," which had sold millions and had eclipsed the sales of all other records that year. Pop fans were divided, the traditionalists accepting the choice of the open marketplace, and the spokesmen for the New Consciousness, for rock, condemning the record for sticking in the mud of Tin Pan Alley. Said John Entwhistle of the Who: "I leave the room when I hear 'Tears.' They should have two charts—one for real teen music and one for mums and dads and teens who go to church." What was the point of all the Who's breakthrough guitar-smashing if antiquated rubbish like "Tears" was going to top the charts?

The perpetrator of "Tears" was unabashed. "The Nut from Knotty Ash," a proud Liverpudlian from the grand tradition of Northern drolls, spoke from his dressing room at the Birmingham Theatre, where he was appearing in *Humpty Dumpty*: "Like the Beatles, I'm Liddypooly all the way through and I'm feeling tattifalarious about my success. As for my knockers—well, they're just not professional because no real pro would risk professional suicide by knocking another artiste's performance."

And with that he closed the interview and put on his tall and very funny hat. Then he clambered onto his stilts, adjusted his joke teeth, and walked onstage waggling his tickling stick. He was also armed with a list from which he read the names of parties celebrating birthdays, weddings, and mother-in-law funerals.

In Dublin, Roy Orbison was trying to enjoy a Trinity party. And in Belfast, the Who, having come off-stage in their Union Jack coats, were warned that these coats would not be acceptable when they played Dublin. The suggestion was made that they wear jackets made from the Eire Republic colors, which could easily be run up by tailors in Dublin's only boutique. The Who agreed. The show would go on. . . .

5

1966: "THE SOUNDS OF SILENCE"

Ken Dodd was no doubt King of the Comic Court, but there were plenty of courtiers making a busy living around and about Christmas-tide, 1965–66. Freddie and the Dreamers, Gerry and the Pacemakers, Herman's Hermits, the Rockin' Berries, plus many more groups from the Beat Merchant days were finding a niche in the traditional British urban folk art of pantomime—putting on the grease paint and the fancy panto costumes, some climbing into horse outfits, others learning the old jokes and the surefire chorus songs, all keen to get out on the stages of Great Britain to entertain once again the mums and dads and of course the kiddies. Why, the Barron Knights had actually burst into the Top Ten with their seasonal greetings, "Merrie Gentle Pops"!

But apart from this theatrical jollity, there hung over the land a quietness, as if Harold Wilson had cloaked the once-rocking Isles with his dreadful, practical Gannex raincoats. Perhaps a respite was needed after the heady years from '63 to '65. Perhaps the chugging beat had temporarily run out of steam. Or perhaps all the crannies of Afro-America had been explored, exploited, and processed through the pop refinery, bringing to an end progress and adventure as far as the syncopation story was concerned. From ragtime to rock 'n' roll: full stop, period, *finis*. About-turn and recycle! Everything in the garden was lovely; we all had plenty of money and leisure time. All we needed was lulling, loving music.

This last thought was a terrifying one, the kind of theory that landed like a black crow on my fevered brain in the living-death hour before dawn, usually after I'd overeaten the lamb curry or—at Christmas—the rich, iced, and marzipanned fruitcake.

Whatever the reasons, the British charts were decidedly stodgy in January 1966. In general, the rocking had stopped. The Seekers were high on the charts with "The Carnival Is Over" and the Beatles were at number one with their placating and hymnlike "We Can Work It Out." Farther down were Beatle bits by David and Jonathan and by the Overlanders—two of the more successful of the many versions of Paul McCartney's ballad "Michelle." Peter Sellers put some humor in Beatleland with his Richard III impersonation on "A Hard Day's Night" (number thirty-seven). Straight music was well represented by the Toys' homage to Bach, "A Lover's Concerto" (number nine), by P. J. Proby's Brobdingnagian rendering of "Maria" (number ten), followed closely by big balladeer Vince (King of the Working Men's Clubs) Hill and his "Take Me to Your Heart Again" (number thirty). Newcomer Crispian St. Peters was grabbing pop paper headlines by claiming to be better than the Beatles and as good as Elvis, but his record was a limp wimper in soft folkish rock, "You Were on My Mind" (number thirty-one). It was nice, in a nostalgic way, to see Gene Pitney back with "Princess in Rags" (number sixteen), as well as Cliff Richard and the Shadows, now two separate acts.

But only the Who, the Kinks, and the Spencer Davis Group were keeping the rock pulse running. Roger Miller summed up the mood of the Isles in his "England Swings"—it swings like a pendulum.

As was his wont, Elvis, the King of Rock 'n' Roll, lay at home in Graceland over the Christmas season. Not only were his traveling clothes in the closet, but it seemed he had also hung up his rock 'n' roll shoes. Ever since he had been discharged from the Army, Elvis had been cooling the hot rock and settling his voice more and more into deep crooner tones, treading in the footsteps of Russ Colombo, Bing Crosby, and Frank Sinatra. He even clambered into a tuxedo to appear with Sinatra on a TV special. He was being touted as the new Bing Crosby, a once-rhythmic singer who could also put in a decent day's work as an actor, serious or lightly comedic. The image and sound were now of a rather doughlike, ordinary American—dull and square and law-abiding. In fact, he had become the reverse of the lean rebel rocker of the 1950s: he was now the all-around entertainer.

This, as we now know, was all the fiendish plan of Colonel Parker, the William Morris Agency, and the Hollywood producers. Elvis was a product to be canned, bottled, frozen. In 1964, it had been decreed that, henceforth, the only Elvis releases would be movie soundtrack albums. And these movies were ground out like franchised hamburgers— always the same standard but always tasting *beige*. Most of the songs were fluff rock whipped up by an obscure Alley hack named Ben Wiseman. Most of the plots were set in some exotic resort. Elvis himself squirmed inside the stifling packaging, pronouncing the songs "shit" (off the record) and his new movie as "my latest travelogue."

Jack Good tried his best to get the King back on the old rocking tracks. Jack got a bit part in one of the Presley movies and between shots he begged Elvis to get low down and raunchy. How? Very simple: Jack would produce his records, perhaps direct the films. Elvis was excited. The idea got no farther than the Colonel.

Parker reasoned that there were 250,000 diehard Elvis fans around the world and, as they bought every record and saw every film at least three times, good rocking didn't matter. It was as simple as that—the old Army game, the Great American Con Game—serving the suckers, soaking the "marks."

But real rock 'n' roll was bigger than that. It had loyal supporters who felt betrayed by the Elvis machine. They were wise enough to know it was the System (not the Star) that was to blame. But they showed their dismay by swearing off Elvis records and the result was that, though the King shipped "gold," he came back by the hundreds of thousands as "returns." By 1966, Elvis was not a hot disc property.

In Britain, we loyal fans retained the image of the early, hungry, rangy Elvis and we kept that image alive via the Official Elvis Presley Fan Club, run by one Tod Slaughter. We knew Elvis was never going to perform in our country—due to fear of flying, fear of fatness, or his Colonel's fear that the Colonel might never get back into the U.S.A. because he was a Dutchman. We all knew about these drawbacks. But we nurtured and cherished the Old Elvis. Print the legend, ignore the facts. So, in his stead, a fleet of Elvis impersonators sprang up in Britain—youngsters with keen, lithe limbs and slicked-back hair and sideburns, kids with all the jerk-off fantasy appeal that Elvis once had. Muswell hillbillies, Suffolk cowboys, Scottish bandits, all of whom resembled the hillbilly cat more than the fleshy fellow laying up at Graceland that Christmas.

In America, there was a definite cooling toward Elvis which I experienced firsthand in December of '65. I found myself onstage in Memphis, Tennessee, during yet another lightning package tour. Trinity was over with, I was a B.A. (an M.A. if I paid the college another ten pounds), and I had been twiddling my thumbs as a hitless star, unrecognized in my own land. So I had jumped at the tour. Onstage in Memphis I felt thrilled to be in a city where so much of the purest, unrefined rock 'n' roll had roared from. The home of Sun Records! I said so to the audience. I mentioned Roy Orbison, Jerry Lee Lewis, Carl Perkins, then Elvis. When I said *Elvis,* they booed and hissed. They actually booed and hissed. Those stupid little pimple-faced teenage cretins! I was thunderstruck.

Afterward, I was approached by a genial man named George Klein who told me that he was a local deejay and school friend of Elvis. After thanking me for my gracious tribute to his pal, he assured me that Elvis was well up on what was happening on the pop scene and was certainly aware of me and my record. He added, "He's thinking of you." I had barely recovered from this extraordinary revelation when Klein offered to sign a chit allowing me a bundle of maple leaves from the Graceland lawn.

Playing Memphis and, later, visiting the famous Sun studio put me in mind of the good old days, so when the tour had ended and I found myself with a few free days in Hollywood, I ventured up to Tower Records and told them of my plan to bring back the good, hard rock of old. "As long as it sounds new and is playable, we'll give it our best shot, promotion-wise," said the head of marketing, a dark-suited man whose name I can't recall. With this qualified approval, I contacted David Mallet. He assembled some of the "Shindig" boys, including James Burton and Jim Horn, and we went along to the studio where Elvis had cut some of his best rockers, Annexe/Radio Recorders, and with that same engineer we cut a host of numbers, including "Hound Dog," "High Blood Pressure," and one that I wrote as a sort of salute to the old days, "Good Hard Rock." I prefaced that track with a spoken piece about the seeming banishment of R&R: "It was the morning after the 'Eve of Destruction'. 'Shindig' had gone and all the rock 'n' roll shows, but suddenly I heard this voice. Mankind had pulled through!" Then the pounding drums began and I went into some pretty brainy stuff about R&R: "Springing like Minerva from the head of Jove came good hard rock/fully armed and belching beat and flashing daggers—Rock!"

Sadly, "Shindig" had been given the ax. I had the honor of being on the very last all-rock "Shindig" show and of singing the last song, my version of "Hound Dog." I removed my sweater and thrashed around a lot and pounded three pianos. It was all very moving for me, as I adore farewells. Jerry Dennon sent me a telegram advising me to stay more in control of myself.

As it was near Christmas, I persuaded David Mallet to go into the studio again and cut a quick novelty song, something in the vaudeville/ragtime vein. I had been running across marvelously decorative old sheet music covers and, on audition, had recognized a mine of fresh old music, full of wildness and fun and history, too. One of these songs I chanced to hear performed on an album by a ragtime crusader named Max Morath, and I determined to rock it up a bit and record it: "Where Did Robinson Crusoe Go with Friday on Saturday Night?" I strummed hard on my ukulele, Jim Horn honked away, James Burton put in some appropriate strokes, and Chuck Berry's old drummer did a soft-shoe shuffle on the drums. The result was—charming. And we forgot about it as a commercial proposition. But I felt I was branching out into fresh fields, for man cannot live by beat alone.

I needed to branch out because my latest release, "Good Hard Rock," stiffed out (as they say in the trade) very fast on both sides of the Atlantic. But back in England, in the bosom of the family, deep in the snug Home Counties, I got a real New Year's treat when I read the following in the "Readers' Letters" column of the *Record Mirror*. A headline in bold print said: LET'S HAVE MORE ROCK! Then—

An R.M. reader asks for more rock 'n' roll
"Why don't record companies release more rock 'n' roll records anymore? Apart from Sam the Sham, the Sir Douglas Quintet, and Ian Whitcombe [sic, but what the hell!], there's nothing. You can keep Tamla/Motown, soul, and folk music trash—give me good old-fashioned rock 'n' roll any day. Long live Freddie Cannon, Sam the Sham, and all rockers!

Yours,
Fred Hobden,
Church Farm, Cowbeech,
Hailsham, Sussex

I was touched and flattered and I made a note of the name and address. Investigations proved that there were pockets of staunch rockers tucked away in the depths of the countryside and every bit as loyal as the urban members of the Elvis Fan Club. They were waiting for the Second Coming.

However—just as I was about to embark on a trip to meet these fans in the flesh, I was overcome by doubt. Was I really true to rock 'n' roll? After all, I had recently cut the "Where Did Robinson Crusoe Go with Friday on Saturday Night?" novelty and I was itching to widen my music. I took my foot off the westbound train and retreated home to ponder.

But I was not alone. For during this same holiday season, the Beatles, lying in state at their various mansions, had already launched out into a wider world of more meaningful, less accessible music. *Rubber Soul* had been the first example of their departure from the tried-and-true grooves of normal pop. Nor was the album in the old R&R vein. John Lennon, who had always been a natural for the black-leather gear and whose attitude toward life had always seemed to echo that of the average Teddy Boy, maintained that "Whole Lotta Shakin' Goin' On" was the greatest R&R record ever made. Yet here on *Rubber Soul,* he seemed to be under the influence of Dylan. Far from his previous public-property songs, John's songs were autobiographical now: "Norwegian Wood," at first hearing a sardonic and tastefully suggestive love song (given mystification and an edge by the sinuous waltz tune and the whine-nag of George's new toy, the sitar) turned out to be an artistic diary of an extramarital affair. The woman in question sounded quite "with it" and moneyed: she could afford to buy Norwegian wood and she probably had contemporary tastes, read the quality papers, but liked a bit of Northern rough stuff on the side. "In My Life" was less cryptic and more gentle—and strange (for the normally tough John) in its nostalgic look back on such a short life.

While John was publicly acknowledging the influence of Bob Dylan —the stress on the personal reflection and the de-emphasis of the omnibus song—Paul told the press that "Yesterday" was so far, "the most satisfying thing for me." It was apparent now that the Lennon/ McCartney team was split and that there was a world of difference between John and Paul's work. If John edged toward the outer limits, stretching the bonds of popular song, then Paul was making himself a nice niche within the old boundaries—and yet giving his music fresh twists and turns and bringing in influences from styles not usually found in Alley pop. For example, "Michelle" owed much to French cabaret *chanson* with its bittersweet harmonies (stretched minor chords and diminisheds) and sad-to-be-glad tune. But it was also novel in its sudden change of key, which moved the listener up and down the musical structure. Very invigorating—and this lifted it just above being sugary.

Rubber Soul, which had been released in December '65, was a departure, both musically and lyrically. The very title was a change from the earlier straightforward album titles. What did *Rubber Soul* mean? And how did the group get all these odd sounds and voicings? Producer George Martin was pleased to be playing a more creative part in the musical and electronic layerings of *Rubber Soul*. No longer was he an executive who got the tapes turned on and off, watched the clock, and hoped the boys would get their songs in the can within one working day. He was now an important part of the team creating magic from multitrack tape recording, with its snipping, overdubbing, and sel-synching, wonders that could boggle lesser minds. The artists were in control of the machinery, a far cry from inmates taking over the asylum.

Rubber Soul was a puzzling title, but there was no sales resistance. The next single, "Paperback Writer" was even weirder lyrically. No "I-me-you" love stuff, no singalong romancing for the jellybean crowd; instead a desperate plea from a married man who wants to be a paperback writer. Was John and his *Spaniard in the Works*-type word-play becoming dominant? How many American record buyers knew who this Lear man was or what the *Daily Mail* is? Yet these puzzling references didn't appear to bother Beatles fans in the slightest: the record whizzed to number one on both sides of the Atlantic. We were entering an age of mystification, complete with crooked smiles and knowing smirks and lots of giggles. The great game was to work out what the Beatles really meant, the secret message unknown to squares.

A great change in pop had been wrought. The short holiday of togetherness was over. Pop was splitting into streams: records for the teenyboppers, records for the heads, records for the mums and dads. The Beatles had lifted pop from being pap for shop girls or dead-end kids; from 1963–65 their music had joined pop in one joyous celebration for the world. Everybody loved the Beatles. But in 1966, the Beatles were going their own way; they were no longer content with being public property. The America/Beatles honeymoon was over.

Anti-Beatle sentiment began to show itself. The eruptions came during a long, winding, and tedious tour—as it turned out, the last tour they would ever make. In Europe, things had gone smoothly if boringly. Frankly, they were going through the motions; their hearts weren't in the business of grinding out the old yeah-yeahs. Of course, Brian loved it all because that was all he had now and it was his lifebelt to be with his boys. On May 1, they'd appeared at the Empire Pool, Wembley, as winners of the *New Musical Express* poll, their last appearance onstage in Britain. Then they returned to Germany to play Hamburg at the vast Sports Arena for a short half hour. They couldn't visit the Star-Club because it had closed, but they did see Astrid and other old pals. John advised his German friends to stay clear of their shows, as the group was rotten these days. Next they hit the Far East, playing an efficient concert at the Martial Arts Hall in Tokyo.

So far so good. In the Philippines, they noticed the gleaming sky-scrapers and hordes of Westernized Orientals with their burgers and fries and Beatles cuts. All the New East looked alike—and it was Holi-day Inn America. There was an invitation to some garden party or lunch or something—and if the Beatles entourage knew about it, they certainly didn't intend to turn up.

The next day, all hell broke loose: the invitation had been issued by the wife of President Marcos, local dictator, and she was furious. BEATLES SNUB PRESIDENT screamed the headline in the English-lan-guage paper. There were minor riots and even death threats; at the air-port, the boys had to run through clusters of enraged customs officers, who shoved and kicked them. Brian, ever the diplomat, had issued an abject apology over Philippine air waves, but John, honest as always, told the international press that he didn't even know the country had a President.

In August, they were in America again and the reactionaries were waiting. Regular Americans, the God-fearing, bullet-headed variety, had particularly disliked some of the Britishers who'd invaded in the Beatles' wake: those Rolling Stones and Animals. Where were the smiles that tell you to have a nice day? And what could have possessed the once-lovable moptops to produce an album cover showing them as butcher boys holding decapitated dolls and joints of bloody meat? What had this got to do with fun pop? Or anything? John said the cover was "as relevant as Vietnam." His explanation went unheeded; radio stations in the Midwest and South were up in arms. The cover, which had been released on promotional copies of the album, primarily to deejays, was changed. *The Beatles—Yesterday and Today* became *Yesterday,* with a nice pic of the lads leaning against a large steamer trunk.

Next came the "more popular than Jesus" fuss. Here the chasm be-tween American and British society became violently apparent. Months before, John had had a relaxing interview with his friend Maureen Cleave of the London *Evening Standard.* The chatting drifted around, hitting many subjects as John had a lively and unorthodox mind. They touched on organized religion and here John's reaction was fairly ex-pected: he wasn't for it at all; he didn't mind Jesus but his disciples were "thick" and that's what ruined religion for him. "Christianity will go. It will vanish and shrink. . . . We're more popular than Jesus now." A comment on the mixed-up values of the times; he went on to say that both rock 'n' roll and Christianity would go. Quite so. Nobody in Britain was shocked. Churches were always half-empty and if John wanted to shock people he was certainly off the mark on this subject. Knocking the Church of England had gone out with the fifties.

But the "bigger than Jesus" quote got excerpted and headlined on the cover of a vapid American teen magazine called *Datebook*. I'd been featured in this mag once and I knew their coverage was important to Tower but that the topics would be confined to hair and food, faces, and the like. The *Datebook* headline created a furor in Middle America: Beatles albums and merchandise were burned in ritual bonfires; some radio stations banned Beatles records (for a short while, until rating drops forced them to change their minds); the Ku Klux Klan and fundamentalist clergy backed many of the more virulent demonstrations. But the group that appeared to be most upset by John's casual comment was the press.

Again, Brian Epstein stepped in to cool the outcry with his soft tones. Appearing on a network TV show, he gently explained in commonsensical language that the offending interview had been given to a good friend of many years and in the atmosphere of his own home: "This is what he said and, to a certain extent, he meant it. He did not mean to offend or upset anyone." He went on to say that the good thing about the boys was that, "they do, in fact, mean *quite* honestly what they say. I never try to influence what they should say. They've always spoken outright and honestly and, you know, this is the way everybody should be." But then in stepped one of the other guests, who quite heatedly supported John's statement, explaining that the singer—who had never sung a suggestive song or done anything in bad taste—had simply voiced the truth. John wasn't responsible for the truth that religion was on the decline and that Christians were in the minority. Here the host broke in: he knew the facts and they showed that there were 500 million Christians worldwide, which was more than even the Buddhists could claim. But it boiled down to a fuss confined to America, specifically to Birmingham, Alabama, where the first anti-Beatles demonstration had occurred. "What didn't start in Birmingham, Alabama!" jeered the guest and the host quickly went to a commercial. When they returned, Brian said emphatically that the core of the whole Beatles thing was not the hair or the clothes but the music. "Yes," said a woman guest, "I use their songs in my nightclub act, but nothing rock 'n' roll—you can do it as a ballad, just the music alone is beautiful and so are the words."

But beautiful music was not in evidence on this tour and the Beatles knew it and were frankly fed up with their fans, the ones who only came to scream and sing along. George hated the musical disharmony and said so; John was thoroughly disenchanted with the whole shebang: "Show biz is a little bunch of red-nosed people who live together and call themselves 'Show Business.' We know some people in that club, but we don't belong to it." And as to crass Americans: "I think we're showing them that we're not all jolly John Bulls or happy-go-lucky cockneys." Ringo and Paul, closest to show biz, played the game, but it was a treadmill.

The final concert of the tour was on August 29 in Candlestick Park, San Francisco. Brian turned to an associate and pronounced: "This is it. This is the last one ever."

I was there. I happened to be in San Francisco, appearing as a live exhibit at the Teenage Fair, a traveling market of goods for the young set. As a come-on for the customers, minor acts and local groups were hired—rather like in the old medicine shows—to make noise and show. The going had been hard for me and I had been reduced to selling my kisses at one point, so I jumped at the chance of being a guest of station KYA at their Beatles concert. I got in as escort to Miss Teenage World, a pretty enough girl but one who had no time for me, as she was hell-bent on meeting the Beatles. We sat in our box, we heard the shrill choir of teenyboppers, we saw four dots, and the girl got to meet the boys backstage.

Rejected and dejected, I made my way to the parking lot. Suddenly, a group of girls recognized me and raced over to pour their tears all over me. Why? Again the same old story: because I came from the same country as Ringo, John, George, and Paul. Then a cross-eyed boy staggered up to me with a death threat, thinking I was a Beatle. The cops were called. Finally, I went back to my motel to have a deep think about my career. Later on, I managed to contact Gale, the go-go girl now living "the Beat life" in 'Frisco.

Back to Britain:

"Flowers on the Wall," the first national hit for the Statler Brothers, was very appropriate for my mood in January 1966, with its chirpy, chin-up singing to clever, sarcastic words about a hero having lots of fun alone in his room counting flowers on the wall, playing solitaire, chain-smoking, watching "Captain Kangaroo," and dressing up in tails with no place to go. If this was an example of the new intelligence in song lyrics, then I was all for it. But no such luck, "Flowers on the Wall" was just another example of slick country-and-western writing in the Nashville manner. A novelty hit, I'm sorry to say.

I sat at home and thought about "goals," a word I'd viewed anew in America. It had nothing to do with soccer but a lot to do with aiming one's life in a definite direction and rocketing there fueled by gallons of *positive think.* I was determined to hang onto my star for a while, even if there were no long-distance calls or cables from Jerry Dennon,

Tower, or George Sherlock. After the past year of excitement, my world appeared very flat, even depressing—yet my worries were trivial, compared with the state of the real world. Vietnam and all that was too much to contemplate. . . .

Turning toward my own country, things looked pretty murky, too. The number of suicides was up enormously at the start of the New Year (usually suicidal persons effect their exits *before* Christmas). Pundit Malcolm Muggeridge had an article in *The New Statesman* called "The Great Liberal Death Wish," warning of the doom and wrath to come; the latest best-selling book was a piece of "faction," *In Cold Blood,* in which two murderers emerged as quite sympathetic characters and one forgot about the victims. There was a new magazine, *Art & Artists,* which was to focus on "Auto-Destructive Art." The magazine would be treated with a chemical, so that after a few days your copy would disintegrate. Would there be a feature article on the Who? They were forging ahead, boasting to *Melody Maker* that they now had a total of forty-eight twelve-inch speakers onstage, totaling six hundred watts of power. All told, they had £3,000 worth of equipment in their show and it could deafen you in only a few minutes. Already, Townshend had lost a good deal of his hearing. Other bits were lost: their producer, Shel Talmy, was dumped for telling John Entwhistle to keep his *drums* down. Fancy this geezer not knowing what John played! *Out!* They'd produce their own records from now on. The important thing was road management, not creative direction: three roadies were now employed. And there were accountants to tote up the cost of guitar-smashing. Each guitar wrecked was £175, making a grand total of £3,000 per year. Such round numbers. No one in the group was making a penny for their art, except Pete Townshend, who wrote the songs. He'd gotten himself a block-long American car and an American hearse. But the bread would come in for them all soon: they were poised to storm America.

Though the Who's sartorial splendor was still something to behold, the Mod world that they had reflected was dying. The peacock days were dwindling and, as for Swinging London, it was soon to be just a memory. Many of the original clothes designers were bankrupt and many of the boutiques in Carnaby Street were going over to cheap imported clothes from Hong Kong and India.

In April, *Time* published its discovery of Swinging London, a year late, but this didn't worry young Americans. They now swarmed over the dead area buying all the imported junk they could find. A hot summer was to bring in the mini-skirt. Up in Liverpool, the scene was grim, with no fancy dress provided by foreign entrepreneurs. The North had reclaimed its position as "the Arsehole of England," though concrete was covering up much of the drek. Those Beat Merchants not in panto or waiting for summer season by the seaside or on the Working Man's Club circuit were making ends meet as butchers, bakers, milkmen. The Cavern stood silent, but there were plans afoot to reopen it for the booming pilgrimage business. Of course, it would have to be spruced-up, washed, and disinfected. Reality ends here. Harold Wilson was keen on this idea.

As if to put the final nail in the coffin of the Northern comedy, the Fab Four themselves submitted to in-depth interviews with the London *Evening Standard*, in which they let it all hang out, trying to destroy the myth that they were gods, indeed, that they were "bigger than Jesus." Wouldn't Beatlemania just fade away? No. Beatle hagiology was under way.

The Rolling Stones, however, continued to tramp the same ground, crushing flowers and everything else under their boots. They trailed darker clouds than the sweet sadness of "As Tears Go By" through the story of the poor bitch on her "19th Nervous Breakdown," to the apocalyptic vision of "Paint It Black." No need to be afraid of their sitar—it was as much icing on the cake as the electronic-bass bubble shooting down to ocean depths at the fade of "19th Nervous Breakdown." "Look," said Mick to *Melody Maker*, "I just went *da-da-da* into a tape and then the sitar player came into our L.A. studio and did what I sang. A jazzman in pajamas, actually. He made a *g-doing* noise and we liked that because it went well with Bill's piano going *b-jing*. Simple as that, see."

What with new instrumental sounds and electronic feedback and all the overlaying one could do with tape, it was no longer a simple matter of recording. Pop musicians were concerned more and more about their sound, which must be different. Of course, the Who had always been in the vanguard, but now this new bunch, the Yardbirds, had come up with a Gregorian chant, can you imagine? John Pavey of the Fenmen announced, "We are getting a Jap called Koto and we'll all be working on electronic music from now on." A group from Birmingham, the Move, claimed to have invented "Brum Raga" while playing at the Marquee Club; and the dear old Merseys, not to be left behind, were working on what they called "China sounds."

What about the Americans? Could they be far behind, now that they were having their revenge via the Byrds? The latter were well into their Space Age sounds via "Eight Miles High" (which was, as we shall see, to cause them to be much misunderstood) and they would soon be dropping names like Bach, Coltrane, and—Ravi Shankar. It had been David Crosby of the Byrds who had turned George Harrison on to Shankar, the Indian sitar expert. And Crosby was into a whole new scene, for protest was gone—and good riddance. Negative vibes. What the Byrds were saying, according to Crosby, was "Hey, love somebody." They were into "positive things, like saying UFOs are real." Not far behind the way-out sounds of the Byrds was Nancy Sinatra in her kinky footwear ("These Boots Are Made for Walkin'") and her extraordinary opening bass line that slithered down the scale to hop about on blues ground. Nor must we forget the Beach Boys with their introduction of barking dogs and train noises into their recorded work.

Ken Dodd, the "Tears" man and bane of the New Music, welcomed this experimentation: "Beat groups are a colorful addition to the entertainment scene. . . . Eccentrics are always welcome."

But the man who had inspired the most characteristic sound of 1966, Ravi Shankar, doubted whether East would ever really meet West. He saw the interest in the sitar as a "passing fancy." If the popsters went on seriously to study the instrument, that was fine. But the Occidentals were a notoriously antsy lot. "Ours," he said, "is a very disciplined music, a classical tradition, a philosophy—not in a superficial way, but from deep inside us. Western musicians haven't time or patience to study for the years necessary. They just borrow a flavor. We think it very childish."

Donovan was inclined to agree. He said he'd started on the blessed sitar six months before, but he was giving it up because too many people were using it as a gimmick sound. Anyway, he said, there were "beautiful things happening in America," on the West Coast, far away from the mysterious East. Instead of the usual books, his fans had started sending him flowers via Interflora.

Bookishness was very apparent in the work of a new and popular group called Simon and Garfunkel. When I first heard their names, I thought they must be a firm of lawyers or perhaps kosher butchers. How could they hope for fame and fortune in pop with such an unglamorous group name? So . . . *dour*. Surely they could change their names? But no—"The Sounds of Silence" established them at the top of the charts and their gentle Everly Brothers-inspired harmonies and English lit. lyrics made them the darlings of schoolroom and campus. I noticed that frail souls—especially bluestocking student girls who might not care for the visceral music of the Stones—enjoyed Simon and Garfunkel songs. Here was a way to be in the swim of things and yet not have to pretend to be a zonked-out street urchin. The lyrics were studded with literary devices and allusions, while the beat was feather-light. This rock encouraged self-composure.

Paul Simon and Art Garfunkel had grown up together in Queens, New York. In 1957, they had made the charts as Tom and Jerry with

"Hey Schoolgirl" but failed to follow up this success. Here they might have naturally ended their story as one-hitters who had lucked out. But Dylan altered their thinking and, in the early-sixties folk boom, they managed to land a contract with Columbia. Their first album was a mixed bag of Dylan and Simon songs, accompanied by acoustic guitar. Nothing sensational and sales were dismal. Garfunkel went back to college and Simon went to England, where he played the folk club circuit. But canny producer Tom Wilson, who had worked the electronic wonder with Dylan on "Like a Rolling Stone," learned that one of their album tracks, "The Sounds of Silence," was getting a lot of action in Boston. Wilson overdubbed the standard folk-rock instrumentation and the single was released without the knowledge of the singers. The mixture was just right for the market, even though it was a bit like slopping mayonnaise on pastrami.

The lyrics stood out in stark relief, however, and they tapped the feelings of the gentler college crowd, who were literate and attended class but who nevertheless felt there was something wrong—right now—with the human condition. They felt alone in an increasingly impersonal world. For example, the singers see a horrid Kafkaesque city of neon signs splitting the night and showing people bowing to neon gods, making the *sounds of silence*. Very clever literary contradictions which, in sum, made up a relevant truth. Could the neon gods be Elvis and the Beatles? *Whatever*—Simon and Garfunkel were soon to join that same neon world and, hopefully, would better it. Simon told the *New Musical Express* that he meant serious business. The duo were bringing to the public an "untranslatable encounter with truth." But he didn't take his pop fame as seriously as he did Life. "Very little in rock 'n' roll is creative," he told the reporter. In a couple of years, Simon said he would quit the game to go write the Great American Novel.

Maybe that's what I ought to do, I thought, as I surveyed the noisy scene and agreed that it was mostly the *sounds of silence*. A fellow star on the "Dick Clark Caravan of Stars" had told me that one could get two years of gravy—and no more—from one Top Ten hit. So maybe when that time was up, I should retire and teach—or write the Great British Novel, except that that had been done many times. The trouble with Britain, for me, was that I felt redundant. Every position in the arts was filled and everything in the arts seemed to have been achieved. The burden of culture, high and low and pop, was heavy—Shakespeare, Dickens, the Beatles. So it was with some relief that, one bitter March day, I received a telephone call from Paris asking whether I would like to play at the Olympia Music Hall—the place where Edith Piaf had often sung. I was thrilled and agreed at once. Who had suggested me? Monsieur H. Shaper, *mon editeur*.

March 15:

In preparation for my Paris trip, I journeyed up to Carnaby Street to get some new duds. The place is ghastly now, full of tourists from America and quite a few East Indians. Ten-inch checks are "in" for jackets and slacks; shoulders are much narrower and hipster trousers hang almost to the crotch. Not right at all for my rather hunky Empire build. As I perused some Dylan caps (in scarlet and lilac), I cocked an ear to the music being piped in through huge speakers on the walls. So loud that the clothes actually waved in the aural breeze. It was my old colleagues, the Kinks, with their social comment hit, "Dedicated Follower of Fashion."

Right after the Kinks record came the thin and scratchy voice of a distant radio announcer. "You're listening to wonderful 'Radio London,' with nonstop music twenty-four hours a day," he said in a cheeky North Country accent with transatlantic touches. I've lost track of how many pirate stations there are now. But they're certainly a help in getting one's records played. The BBC has such a narrow playlist and those few records are picked by a panel of a half a dozen old ladies and cardiganed queens. And you don't, as I thought, have to sail out surreptitiously to a storm-tossed rusty ship in the North Sea and effect a boarding in order to get airplay. You simply stroll into one of the pirate company's offices in and around Mayfair and invite the boys out to lunch. They're very accommodating and many are ex-Public School boys.

The boutique assistant appeared with what he claimed was exactly right for me. To my amazement, he was offering me a perfectly ordinary, indeed *drab,* pinstriped banker's suit, the kind that are ten-a-penny in the High Street. "This nostalgia gear is becoming very 'in,' sir," he said. "Victorian cloaks and top hats are popular, but I see you as more of a forties figure, dancing to Glenn Miller." Before I could think of a suitable comeback, he handed me the tie he'd selected. It was exactly the same as my old school tie. Amazing how yesterday has become part of today's *camp* craze.

By the middle of 1966, the days of pirate radio were numbered. A bill to outlaw the pirate ships and forts, beaming their wonderful stream of pop from just outside the three-mile territorial limit, would be passed in Parliament shortly. The BBC, holder of a government monopoly on broadcasting, was preparing its own answer to the pirates: Auntie BBC would copy the pirate format and establish its own "Radio One," which would dole out pop music with jingles and placebo commercials (for

"BBC One"). Already they had hired "Radio Caroline's" Simon Dee to host a new late-night show.

Pirate radio had been pioneered by Rohan O'Rahilly, an Irish businessman, in April 1964, when he established "Radio Caroline" aboard the good ship *Caroline* (named in honor of JFK's daughter), which was moored off the southeast coast of England. Local businesses in Kent and the Thames Estuary soon started buying advertising time when they learned that Caroline could command an audience of up to 9 million. O'Rahilly's success led to the proliferation of other pirate stations: "Radio City," operating from a fort on Shivering Sands; "Radio 390" in an antiaircraft tower near Whitstable, "Radio England" and "Britain Radio" sharing the same ship three and a half miles off Frinton, backed by unnamed Texans. American money was also behind the most successful pirate: ritzy "Radio London" moored next to the Texans. Five hundred thousand pounds had been spent equipping this ship and many of the deejays sounded American or at least midatlantic. It soon became the "with it" station. Other ships were also established around Britain near large urban areas, like Liverpool and Glasgow.

For the inland traders the pirates were a tremendous boon and for the pop-hungry audience they were a source of new music. The BBC had always been very mean with their pop ration. Truth was, that the elitist BBC governors didn't approve of giving the people what they wanted. When R&R had first struck Britain, it was actually banned on the BBC.

By 1966, the paternalists in Socialist Britain (and the Socialists were more against commercial broadcasting than the Conservatives) were ready to rid the seas of the radio pirates. As a bill was prepared, the BBC moved to steal the pirates' thunder and expertise. Something of the outlook of the high-culture establishment can be gleaned from these extracts from an article written by Stuart Hood, an old BBC hand, and published in the learned news magazine weekly *The Spectator* in July 1966:

"There are nine pirates in all, strategically placed, making no attempt at public service but beaming their programmes and commercials at the thickly populated areas where the wage packets are fat and an advertising spot at the end of the week can have an immediate effect in the local supermarkets on a Saturday morning." So far, so factual. But then Hood strides on to the slippery ground of artistic judgment, of what is good and what is bad for the people. The old paternalist game, the headmaster who knows what's best. But I must confess that although only a free society like ours could produce all the many manifestations of pop—a colorful and often garish supermarket—there are times when the omnipresent outpouring of pop from radio, record, boutique, dentist's waiting room, and especially transistor got to be so oppressive that I, too, wished for a taste dictator. Hood's relevant paragraph is worth quoting in full:

MORAL INDIGNATION

Some people feel strongly that a stream of "pop" music is in itself reprehensible. They point, rightly, to the increase in noise in our transistorised civilization, to the use of sound (any sound) as an aural stimulant, and to the neglect of silence. They find the beat of the groups distressingly monotonous, the lyrics—with few exceptions—banal and repetitious to the verge of illiteracy. It is no doubt a reflection of some kind on our educational system and way of life that so many people should have a hunger for this mass-produced noise; but like it they do—not so much the teenagers, surprisingly, but housewives, commuters driving to work in the morning, commercial travellers, lorry drivers. There seems no reason, short of some sort of aesthetic dictatorship, why they should not have it.

The most telling point here is that, in 1966, it's not the teenagers who are using pop as an "opiate." It's the working adults who are using pop music as a background drone to fill the void of their dreary lives. Their jobs are sheer monotony and they cannot bear to be alone with their own thoughts. With the introduction of the cassette and the coming of age of the album (and, in America, the blossoming of free-form FM radio) the rock aficionados are beginning to desert the pop/pap stream of AM radio and to see their music as an experience integral to their lives. For them, music is no longer wallpaper. Rock fans would rather die than take their music for granted.

But, in the meantime, the last days of the radio pirates were at least giving exposure to records that would not otherwise have received airplay. The pirates also introduced a myriad of regional accents, ranging from perky, no-nonsense Northerners, to singsong Welshmen, glottal-stop cockneys, and creamy-voiced pseudo-Americans. These were accents never heard much before on BBC (except on comedy shows), but within a year or so we were to hear on the BBC not only our records announced by these exotic voices from far-flung counties, but also our news bulletins. So strong were some of these accents that it was at times hard for some of us to understand just what was going on in the world.

So the cultural revolution wrought by the Beatles and their provincial confrères was not confined to music, clothes, and hair. It was to affect the whole picture of the traditional Britisher. The rest of the world, not only America, was to eagerly embrace the music and the messages brought by the now high-and-wide-flying Britishers, youths whose fathers had seen life only from the bottom of the social ladder. But, as we have seen, these rocking youths were financially controlled by the same old Public School class. So, as yet, I wasn't all that worried.

Paris, France (March 12):

Very excited about playing The Olympia Music Hall. I want to renew my friendship with Mick Jagger and get his advice again. And I will see a dream come true: the mixing of modern rock 'n' roll with the traditions of music hall and cabaret, thus bringing together the zip of the Super-American Fun Palace and the old-fashioned ribaldry of the end-of-pier show—those two seminal experiences from my summer of '49.

Apart from the Rolling Stones, I was sharing the bill with the Moody Blues, Wayne Fontana and the Mindbenders, and the delectable Marianne Faithfull. My gleeful anticipation was marred the night before I left for France by the discovery of a mysterious lump on my left thigh. Convinced this was cancer, I immediately checked into Emergency, only to discover that the lump was a large boil. The Indian doctor rather rudely told me I could have easily popped it myself. I told him I'd rather have a burnished Bengal Lancer—which I thought was a good joke, but he considered it "racist." The world *is* getting very touchy.

I had brought along my ukulele on the off-chance I might meet up with some Parisian *chansoniers* and get into a jam session with them. Very fond of accordions and *triste* French saxophones. Waited an awful long time at Le Bourget Airport before being collected by the promo man from Pathe Marconi, Tower's distributor over here. Felt rather foolish standing there with my uke and the French beret I'd decided to wear for the trip. When at last the promo man found me, he said he'd been nearby all the time but hadn't recognized me at first because I don't look at all like my pictures. I asked why and he replied that my hair was much "skinny." Must do something about this hair loss. I'm sure it's due to the shower spray. Thank goodness there are precious few showers in Britain—and, of course, none in France.

As we had a few hours to spare before the Olympia show, my escort, whose name was Claude and who resembled George Sherlock in appearance and style, asked me what I'd like to do. I tried to reply in French that I'd like to sample some of the native cuisine and I began with, "*Je désire . . .*" He immediately suggested we get some "jig-a-jig," outlining hip curves with his hands and shaking his ass. Eventually, he understood and we jumped into a passing taxi. Hoping for some *pâté de campagne* in an offbeat *ouvrier's* bistro, I was disappointed when he took me to a garish and noisy hamburger joint called Le Drug Store. Claude claimed everybody who was anybody went here—and then he waved to Tom Jones, who looked very lost. Claude went over and talked to him about "jig-a-jig," which seemed to please Jones enormously.

Meanwhile, I tested my French again, but to no success: asking for butter (*beurre*) I got beer; asking for Belgian beer (*bière Belge*) I got a huge dollop of butter. They really are a cretinous lot, but Claude returned to save me—and seemed very amused by the whole thing. After several glasses of Pernod, he grew very expansive and started singing loudly in a semioperatic voice. Apparently, he used to be a well-known crooner. I expressed an interest in hearing some French popular music and Claude, stopping on a high note, said that there was no group as good as the Four Tops around Paris. No no, I said—I wanted to hear the real old *chansons* played by accordionists, etc. Claude shrugged and said he'd give it a shot. For the next hour, we raced around Paris in a taxi, Claude stopping every so often to ask directions —usually of some scantily dressed female. We seemed to be getting nowhere fast and, by 6:30 P.M. (and a great deal of alcohol), I grew worried about being on time for the Olympia show. By this time, Claude was strutting on top of a bar table singing tragic songs about rape and incest to the accompaniment of a man blowing into lavatory tissue wrapped around a comb—the closest I got to genuine French *ouvrier* music.

We made a mad dash to the Olympia, the taxi driver showing no fear of hitting women, children, or animals. In fact, Claude kept encouraging him to aim at dogs and cats, the mangier the better. It was pelting with rain, so I burrowed into my suitcase and pulled out my Gannex raincoat. I was longing to show off my Swinging London wardrobe to the clothes-conscious Froggies—and I hoped Mick Jagger would be impressed, too.

At the theater, Claude immediately got into an altercation with the show's organizer. Apparently, I was supposed to have gone on first, as I'm the least important act. Instead they'd had to put the second act on and, to my amazement, I saw from the wings that this act was an authentic medieval French street band, complete with tumbrils, nose flutes, and flagellants.

There was no time for me to change into my Carnaby gear, so I had to go onstage in what I was wearing: my dripping wet raincoat, trousers, and hair. And somehow or other, I was clutching my ukulele. I must have looked a strange sight, but "You Turn Me On" was greeted

with cheers and shouts of "Bravo, Wheetcoomb!" I followed with
"N-N-Nervous!", but the audience didn't know this number and grew
restless and talkative—so instead of my normal monologue in the instrumental chorus, I did a quick resume of French history from Charle-
magne to De Gaulle. Upon hearing the name "De Gaulle," there was a
terrible commotion and I was hissed and egged off the stage. Most unfortunate. Then the show's promoter started berating me in a thick *pa-
tois*. I beat a hasty retreat backstage to find Claude, but instead I met
Marianne Faithfull, who graciously offered me her hand to kiss. Then
I moved on to the Moody Blues, who were grouped in a corner of the
bar giggling a lot, probably due to fat-cigarette intake. I gave them a
quick impression of Brian Epstein and then, to tumultuous applause, I
went off in search of Mick Jagger. Eventually, I found him in a dark
corridor chatting up a very attractive girl. He was quite polite and gen-
tlemanly, introducing the girl as Anita Pallenberg "from Germany." I
was eager to pick up our Seattle conversation where we had left off, but
Jagger got very distant and cool, staring straight through me. Then he
jerked his head in the direction of the bar. I got the message and
moved along and he resumed his tête-à-tête with Miss Pallenberg.

Back in the bar, I didn't attempt to join Bill Wyman or Charlie
Watts, as they seemed very glum and not at all hospitable. There was
some mention about not being able to get any proper tea. Brian Jones
was a different matter, looking unnaturally bright and vivacious, his
eyes gleaming in an unearthly manner. He seemed to be talking to me,
although I was a long way across the room. So I went up and listened
carefully. Couldn't make out a word he was saying, but he was saying
it beautifully. Rooting around for a conversational topic, I hit upon the
fact that we were both wearing the same check on our trousers. This
didn't have much effect on him and I realized that the remark was a bit
gauche because it meant we both were patrons of John Stephen's shop—
which is now terribly déclassé. So I let the conversation die a natural
death, ordered a double brandy, and got directions back to the hotel.

As I got out of the taxi, who should I see but Tom Jones, the
warbling Welshman. We'd met briefly on one of the many Dick Clark
tours I'd done last summer and he seemed very relieved to see me. I
asked him, jokingly, whether he'd got much "jig-a-jig" this afternoon
and he replied that that was exactly what he was trying to fix at this
moment. Pulling a pert French girl from a parked taxi, he asked me
whether I spoke the lingo. "*Un petit peu*," I replied. "Well, ask her
about the *coucher* stuff," said Tom. I had a go, but I must have got my
grammar mixed up because she slapped me hard on the face, jumped
back into the cab, and ordered the driver to "*Allez, vite.*" Tom looked
crestfallen as we walked into the Louis XIV Sheraton. I told him to

cheer up and take a good Trollope up to bed with him instead. But Tom didn't appear to be amused by my little pun and we parted silently.

London, April 1:

I might get more response from Mick Jagger if I were a journalist. Reading *Disc* today, I learned a whole lot more about him—and something of his philosophy too. According to the article, he's always at posh restaurants these days, in the company of either David Bailey, the fashion photographer, or an assortment of barons and earls and dolly birds. I wish I could break into that kind of society! He has breakfast at lunch time and likes to wear old army battle uniforms with tarnished brass buttons. The Beatles, too, are getting into this old-clothes game. And Dave Davies of the Kinks is in the habit of wearing top hats. On the subject of personal philosophy, Jagger says this: "Sometimes, when I watch myself leaping about the place, I wonder what am I doing with my life, acting the fool like this, when I could have been a journalist or something?" Still, he's compensated somewhat by having a chauffeur-driven black Rolls-Royce with smoked windows. His ambitions, after getting his new flat decorated, are to learn to play the piano and to read more books.

In the photographs accompanying the article, he certainly looks very fit and healthy. I hear he exercises a lot. I wonder if he has a chest-expander, as I do? I very much doubt he partakes of the fat cigarettes and the variety of pills that some of the other rock stars need in order to be all-around entertainers.

I'd like to have spoken to Jagger longer and to have gotten some more advice. I'd like to have told him how many people mistake me for him. We do look alike, although I have a larger build. So many of the original British Invaders have lost their way in America, finally coming home to become lounge and club acts or postmen or pork butchers that I really admire Jagger for hanging in there and never letting managers or American hustlers and fans get the better of him. Listen to his healthy disrespect for Americans in general, as told to *Melody Maker*: "America would be great if there weren't any people there." He also believes that the young Yanks read much too much significance into Stones' songs. For example, he says about "19th Nervous Breakdown," "We're not Bob Dylan, y'know. The song's not supposed to mean anything. It's just about a neurotic bird, that's all. I thought of the title first—just sounded good." Most of these pop-star interviews are conducted in cheery, smoky old Victorian pubs over Scotch eggs, pork sausages, and oodles of lager and lime. In this sort of atmosphere, it's very hard to be pretentious.

But while Jagger's straight talking makes good common sense, the latest charts bewilder me. Lots of new names I know little about. I am being overtaken by events. How terrible to be last year's sensation and then become a lonely golden oldie when I'm still under twenty-five!

The April chart was full of British names surging in, some from the provinces, some from London, all with contributions to make toward the progress of pop. The canvas grew crowded but more colorful. From Salisbury, in Wiltshire, came Dave Dee, Dozy, Beaky, Mick, and Tich —a boisterous bunch of mates who had come under the wing of ace songwriters Howard and Blaikley. Using this gang, Howard and Blaikley were managing to produce some cheerful shouts like "Hold Tight," currently in the Top Ten. Fleet Street picture editors loved Dave Dee & Company because they were willing to act as clothes horses for the more outrageous Carnaby Street gear, posing in flower-pattern jackets full of contrasting colors, tissue-paper shirts, and tentlike bell bottom trousers held from slipping down the legs by eight-inch-thick vinyl belts with Long John Silver buckles. One fashion editor, remarking on the latest Dave Dee all-flower pattern suit, praised the designer for being wise enough to remove the curtain rings.

Pinkerton's Assorted Colours hailed from Rugby, home of the famous Public School, where they had been discovered by Reg Calvert, the same manager who had come up with the Fortunes. Reg was bringing a sweeter sound back to pop after the shouting of the Beat Merchant days. Pinkerton's, sporting pink jackets and the sound of an electric autoharp, had hit with "Mirror Mirror." From Andover, in Hampshire, came four country lads with a lumpy bumpkin crudeness endearing in its rocking rusticity, the Troggs. Their punk-classic creation "Wild Thing" was the bottom line in what R&R had been all about. Raw sex, dive-bombing guitar, crashing drums—there wasn't even any suggestiveness. The message was clear and crude: *We want it now.* The Troggs were Neanderthal and *great* and their leader, Reg Presley, had to be admired for his gall alone. Unfortunately, the effort to produce "Wild Thing" was too much and the Troggs could never keep that same momentum going. But "Wild Thing" became a worldwide smasheroo.

From within the dying Mod movement came the Small Faces, all onetime top Faces and all standing at less than five-feet-six in their stocking feet. Scurrying about from club to TV shot to radio gig, they resembled a band of midgets on the rampage and, one fine spring day on Portobello Road in Chelsea, I almost trod on them at the entrance to the old-clothes boutique "I Was Lord Kitchener's Valet."

This was becoming a very popular shop for the real McCoy *camp* or *nostalgia* or *period* clothes. It was all the same thing: history, the past, yesterday—what a laugh and great for raving it up at parties! Dave Dee & Company were trying on genuine cavalry officer's uniforms, breaking off for a quick duel with Crimean War sabers. Dave Davies looked sharp in gold-braid overcoat and high-peaked cap once owned by a captain killed at Cawnpore, India. Never mind that the Kinks had just released a dig at those upper-class fops with their record "A Well-Respected Man," these twits had *fabulous* clothes. Manfred Mann, an anti-Apartheid South African, had been in the other day to buy an admiral's topcoat. Paul and John were fond of browsing there, too, and rumor had it that they might deck out the whole group in old soldier uniforms.

One of the earliest patrons of "I Was Lord Kitchener's Valet" had been Eric Clapton. He liked to wear uniforms around the house as he ran blues licks up and down his fretboard at over 500 m.p.h. Blues was his survival food and he'd left the Yardbirds because they veered away from the basics and onto pop fodder like "For Your Love." Granted, they were now enjoying the limelight with their spaced-out rave-ups like "Shapes of Things" and "Over Under Sideways Down," but the fact was that their blues-blowing was caged in a pop-song prison. Even the interesting thirteenth-century Gregorian chant "Still I'm Sad" had to be forced into the same sappy, self-pitying pop-song mold. No doubt, American kids ate up this new Yardbirds music, but these same kids had very little interest in blues originals like Muddy Waters and Bo Diddley, let alone the blues Kings: Freddie, Albert, and B.B. From all accounts, the U.S. kids were using Yardbirds records as an accompaniment for toking up on mind-blowing drugs.

During the height of the British Invasion, the Yardbirds had been left behind. True, there had always been internal group differences, which hadn't helped their image, but the Yardbirds had pioneered such electronic ear-startlers as feedback, fuzz, and raga rock. (Of course, the effective droning on one interminable chord, or even no chord had sprung from the old black blues greats who simply ignored convention, since European harmony hadn't found a place in the African soul.)

As the Metropolis Blues Quartet, the Yardbirds had wrung out some solid revivalist R&B. When blues firebrand Eric Clapton joined them, they became the Yardbirds (prison geezers) and took over the Crawdaddy Club residency left vacant by the Rolling Stones. Also left behind by the Stones was their manager, Giorgio Gomelsky, and he quickly took on the Yardbirds. Pretty soon the group became the most fashionable R&B makers on the London club scene. But Gomelsky wanted the world and he knew it took pop hits for this. Graham Gouldman, who had written excellent hit material for both Herman and the Hollies, came up with the odd-sounding but very commercial "For Your Love" and, in April of 1965, the group's recording of this number hit very big in Britain. By June, it was number six in America and the Yardbirds were seen on both "Shindig" and "Hullabaloo" (TV copycat of Jack Good's original). On tour, the Yardbirds weren't very together as an act, their true environment being the free and easy atmosphere of a London club. Here, with the lights down low and the public pressure off, they could experiment with their guitars. Lean the thing against the amp and the note lingers on and on by feeding back; with a fuzz box, a sort of sax sound or even piccolo or oboe could be approximated. Some guitar solos went on for what seemed like hours and, since they were on the same chord, they created a hypnotic effect. *Blues trance*—what a lark! Then you had another swig of Scotch and Coke, grabbed your girl friend, and caught the last tube home.

But over in America, farfetched interpretations were being made of Yardbirds rave-ups. The long, squealing guitar lines seemed to lead the new "heads" in a transcendental journey beyond outer space, deep into the canyons of their minds. There was much, much more to "Shapes of Things" than electronic wizardry. American youth—hip youth—paid no attention when the new Yardbirds lead guitarist told *Hit Parader,* "I like using different effects and noises—it's one way of covering up bad playing!" Ha ha! Then drummer Jim McCarty told it like it is: "Americans are responsive, but they don't really know what we're doing. Whites over there know nothing about the blues." Overall the group's ambition was to clear away the negative protest music by bringing in "good-time music." Jeff Beck's ambition was to own a big American car. But manager Giorgio Gomelsky heard how his group was becoming a psychedelic wonder in Invaderland and he begged for more of the same —and more mystical, too. Don't miss the magic bus! Art for art's sake, but money for Chrissake! And who knows—maybe the twain will meet. . . .

London, April 5:
  Must get some new material and keep up with the trends. I wish hipster trousers would go out of style—they're bloody uncomfortable. No word from Tower Records about future releases, but I'm going to take a chance and go into a local studio and cut some sides. Called Denny Cordell, who's very hot now with Georgie Fame and the Moodies, and asked him to produce me for old time's sake. He's agreed! We're using the studio where the Stones cut their first records, Regent Sound in Soho.

To be in the swim, to be hip, or whatever they now call being fashionable, I've dashed off all kinds of songs. Each one took only a few minutes at the family piano and that's what most good pop should be: heat-of-the-moment stuff, or so I've read. Of course, the piano isn't the best instrument for writing rock on; it's too rigid and the notes look too arranged. Still, so far I've come up with a folk-rock song, a minidrama based on *In Cold Blood*, a self-pity thing about being left behind on the shelf, and a "You Turn Me On" imitation. Denny has already rounded up the musicians, so we're all set. I checked my bank account, too.

April 10:

What a grand collection of players! On guitar we had Jimmy Page, legendary session player for the Kinks and Donovan. He tells me he may be replacing Jeff Beck of the Yardbirds, as Beck's on the verge of a breakdown caused by the rigors of their current American tour. Page pulled out his fuzz box for my "Turn On" copy (which we now call "You Really Bent Me Out of Shape") and he slashed away with power rhythm chording on my self-pity number "Please Don't Leave Me on the Shelf." The folk-rock song came out so-so: "Lover's Prayer." May be a bit wimpy. And the *In Cold Blood* effort will have to remain a backing track for the time being.

Our bass player was John Paul Jones and our drummer was Mitch Mitchell—both seasoned sessioneers and pleasant fellows to boot. Denny, wearing a gargantuan Alaskan fur coat and a ring in his ear, bustled about placing microphones in every nook and cranny. He brought along his friend Georgie Fame, with one leg in plaster, and Fame made himself useful by conducting us with a crutch. All in all, a good session. I overdubbed some loony vocals and we sent off the tapes to Jerry Dennon, whence they'll get to Tower.

I realize now the importance of getting the right sound in the studio, which means right engineer, right padding on drums, right echo chamber, right amps, right lighting system. No longer can one simply waltz into any old studio and tape a live-type performance, as we did back in the Bluesville days in Dublin. It's the art of the studio and the record producer is the equivalent of a film director. He is an *auteur*. Mind you, I think Derek Johnson is cheapening the art of rock when he writes in *New Musical Express* that pop music is based largely on "novelty and gimmickry." He goes on to advise: "Come up with a way-out idea or a unique sound and chances are you'll have a hit. Dylan is cashing in on his eccentricity and good luck to him!"

I could perhaps have been forgiven for believing that a return to good-time vaudeville music was imminent. The wish was father to the thought: how exciting to hear the tinny old acoustical record of Harry Champion's "Boiled Beef And Carrots" in living stereo! And as spring turned into summer, a number of isolated hits, placed in medley, could point to a return to the Good Old Days.

The chief complainer himself, King of Random Word Selection Bob Dylan, had come with a rollicking, lolloping beer-bar hoot called "Rainy Day Women #12 & 35." Recorded in Nashville with a boozy band of shit-kickers, the record featured a tailgate trombone and a belching tuba. What lay beneath the martyr-stoning story I had yet to learn. The Beach Boys obtained a studio party atmosphere with their reworking of the old doo-wop hit "Barbara Ann"—a wee bit on the dumb side for me; they also rode high with a smooth-harmonied production of the decrepit folk song "Sloop John B.," which I remembered buying as a skiffle 78 r.p.m. in the fifties. From Greenwich Village came the Lovin' Spoonful with their lazy-beat, lopsided, grinning good-time music, which was certainly a change from the shrill protesters usually associated with that unsatisfied stretch of New York City. "Do You Believe in Magic" and particularly "Daydream" put jug-band fun to an R&R beat; I liked their sunny smiles and I liked the name of their American label, Kama Sutra. "Summer in the City," published by Faithful Virtue Music, brought their sound up to date and onto the burning sidewalks of New York. Traffic sounds were celebrated, as were nights on the roof gazing down on a metropolis a lot less elegant than Lorenz Hart's "Manhattan."

Escape from the mundane was adumbrated with a touch of poesy by Bob Lind, a troubadour who hit the British charts around this time. "Elusive Butterfly" turned out to be a butterfly of love glimpsed by an early rising maiden as it floated onto the horizon. The effect was very wispily romantic until the heavy breathing, and then I was reminded of (A) my big hit and (B) Mae West, whom I'd always admired.

Still, there was no progressiveness to be frightened of here and I learned that Bob Lind was managed by the Sonny and Cher management company. By chance, Denny Cordell had given me an advance promo copy of another Lind number very much in the good-time form, with the suggestion that I might consider covering it: "San Francisco Woman" had a ragtime feel, but it was about a world unknown to me—a penniless, homeless girl trudging up Stanyan Street (always those wretched hills!), all her belongings in one battered suitcase. Yet she has no problems because she'll crash with friends who drink wine and live on brown rice and beans. Denny told me this was a "happening" spot and, a few days later, I got a 2 A.M. overseas phone call from Gale, the go-go girl. She sounded lost in space, sailing the sky, but I did manage to decipher an invitation for me to come out to this "Hate-Ashberry" and join them because, in her words, "The vibes are high and so is the creation!"

On British soil, I continued my list of records contributing to the return of vaudeville/music hall. Herman's Hermits had scored the previous year with their revival of music-hall stalwart Harry Champion's "I'm Henry VIII, I Am" and now they were doing well with "Leaning on a Lamp Post," which has always been associated with George Formby, the Lancashire ukulele man. And I was glad to hear the Kinks' "Sunny Afternoon," a chugalong satire in the style of Formby's great "Fanlight Fanny, the Frousy Night Club Queen."

So it was with great enthusiasm that I accepted Denny Cordell's suggestion that I play piano on a session in which we were to record a new version of the comedy song "Right, Said Fred," which Bernard Cribbins, the actor, had hit with in '62. This clever narrative was to have a stellar band: Georgie Fame's Blue Flames, Mitch Mitchell on drums, Jimmy Page on guitar, my brother on tambourine, and me. The artist was Liverpool's own Tommy Quickly and his manager was none other than Brian Epstein. Would I get to meet the Beatles themselves?

Lansdowne Studios, London, May 2:

I was sitting at my grand piano among all these fine session players and getting ready to pound when suddenly an arrangement was plunked in front of me and I collapsed in jitters. Can't read those dots and squiggles, never could. Jimmy Page, kind soul, came to my aid by telling me what the chords were. And then Denny cast aside the chart and let me bang on in my usual Jerry Lee manner. The result was quite a meaty track, with the Blue Flames honking like hell.

Went upstairs to hear the playback and there I met the singer Tommy Quickly. In the Merseymania days, he had had a small hit here with "Wild Side of Life" and he was later sent out on tour with the Liverpool group the San Remo Four, another Epstein act. On this day, Quickly was rumpled and tousled and looked as though he'd been night-clubbing to excess. I'd hardly introduced myself when in strode Brian Epstein himself, though very silently, as his shoes are of the gentlest crepe and thinnest suede. He was dressed immaculately in a gray turtleneck sweater, dark blue blazer, and faun-colored trousers. His hair was neat and curly, his lips pursed, and his presence was immediately felt. Denny made the introductions and Epstein shook my hand, donating a short smile. Then he addressed himself to business, quietly but firmly ordering Quickly to go down and start his overdubbing.

I left for a pub lunch with Jimmy Page and the lads, but I couldn't resist returning later to see how things were progressing. They weren't.

I joined Denny and Epstein in the high up control room to find them
peering down below and grimacing. I peered, too, and saw an even
more disheveled Quickly reeling around the mike, waving a Scotch bottle. Epstein marched downstairs to the studio floor to deal with his recalcitrant act. His face purple with rage, he seized the bottle from
Quickly and showed him the door with a pointed forefinger. I split.

Later:

Got a call from Denny asking whether I was free to meet with Brian
Epstein tonight. Of course! He's stuck with this Tommy Quickly backing track and wants to know whether I'd be interested in putting my
voice on it. I'd certainly be interested in being in the presence of Brian
Epstein. . . .

His flat is in Knightsbridge, not far from Harrod's. I was told to be
there by eight-thirty sharp, but I arrived an hour too early, so I strolled
around the neighborhood. All very quiet, but it was even quieter at the
Epstein flat. The door was opened by an elegant black man, an ebony
Jeeves, who took my name and looked for my hat. Then he vanished as
if in a puff of smoke and I took stock of my surroundings. Walls of
white, off-white, cream, milk. The chairs and sofas were of jet-black
leather. There was some modern sculpture and a few gold-framed pictures. Everything was in its place and I scarcely dared breathe for fear
of shattering some priceless crystal that I felt sure was nearby. Presently, the ebony figure returned and ushered me upstairs to an oak door
upon which he knocked lightly. "Come."

Epstein was at his desk, cloaked in a silk dressing gown. He came
over, shook hands, and beckoned me to a chair. He asked my choice of
drink and I said sherry, medium dry. I felt at ease with this man. He
was my sort of person. We spoke the same language and in the same
accent. After a bit of small talk, he asked me what I liked in music.
I mentioned the essential R&B names, the old blues greats, and I added,
"Of course, I like your boys, as well." He wasn't impressed with this
latter remark and my eyes whizzed around the study to find some other
common topic. Spotting an oil painting of a Persian market scene, I
blurted out that I also really adored *In a Persian Market,* the descriptive
musical piece by Albert Ketèlbey. At once Epstein's eyes lit up
and, for the next half hour, we discussed light orchestral works from
Ketèlbey's *In a Monastery Garden* to Eric Coates's *By a Sleepy Lagoon.*
I waxed quite eloquently on the sad demise of the dedicated British
idealist, the kind of Public School loner who used to travel the world
spreading good manners and fine living—a vanishing breed since the
end of World War II. Epstein glowed and smiled and nodded.

Two bottles of wine later, he grew confidential. Seating himself in a chair nearer mine, he leaned forward and said with a piercing look: "I feel we've met before. I don't know what's come over me, but I want to tell you some things that have bothered me of late. My boys are getting away from me. They no longer take my advice. They have no patience for my schedules, my organization, my protection." I suggested it might be the rebellion of restless schoolboys against a headmaster. I told him that Jack Good had had the same trouble while trying to camera-direct Mick Jagger. But I felt I was interrupting a soliloquy, so I shut up and listened: "I loved it when I could dress them for appearances, arrange the running order, act as their spokesman. I loved the Liverpool days. . . . John and I made a pact to work together to beat them Down South—on Denmark Street—at their own game. Now the game's over—and not only is London conquered but also America and the world. But sometimes I wonder whether the world hasn't beaten us. I mean, have the Beatles become camp followers? What's all this arty stuff John's getting mixed up with? These avant-garde art gallery types, these poets, these fawning critics? He's believing his own press—but, what's worse, he's starting to write incomprehensible lyrics or else these autobiographical efforts. I mean, who is 'Dr. Robert'? And what is this childish stuff about a 'Yellow Submarine'? But it's 'Tomorrow Never Knows' that worries me most. That's too close for comfort for me. . . ."

There was an interminable pause. The silence was frightening, infinite-seeming. To bridge the chasm, I voiced a theory that "Yellow Submarine" was taken from an old World War I naval folk ditty called "We All Live in a Pocket Battleship" and that many other Beatles melodies were based on tried and true Tin Pan Alley molds. Why, I had heard that a lot of the songs were bought outright from a redbrick university student from somewhere north of Lancashire. . . .

Epstein's face suddenly froze and his hand stretched out to a buzzer on the wall. "I think," he said coldly and precisely, "that we will call a halt at this stage. The hour is late and I still have much business to attend to."

It was only when I was out in the street that I remembered the "Right, Said Fred" overdub.

Back in the U.S.A.:
Gerry and the Pacemakers, the Swinging Blue Jeans, the Nashville Teens—back at home where they began. But here was I, a lost Invader returning to a deafening silence. No fans to besiege me and to shut down the L.A. International Airport like last year. I had become redundant, a nonpopular pop singer; the fun in the sun had ceased. In fact, this bloody Hollywood sun had become oppressive, razoring down

rudely, attracting an unnatural number of tramps and persons of no fixed address.

Why wasn't George at the airport? Lugging my suitcases along Hollywood Boulevard, I searched for his apartment. Eventually, I trod upon the pavement star of John Boles, so I knew that I was near. Scratched across his name was the legend HOLLYWEIRD. Where were the flaxen girls in halters and bell bottoms? Then I thought I saw Sonny Bono approaching me, clad in the expected Ostrogoth fur cloak, knee boots, and floppy leather hat. But when the creature was up close, breathing hard and foul, I realized it wasn't Sonny. "Hey, man! You got any spare change?" He eyed my suitcases greedily and I moved away at a brisk clip.

Down Cherokee, I hastened in the gathering dusk, past wailing cop cars with waltzing red lights and rouged and rude old ladies pushing battered supermarket carts. Where was George's apartment building? It had gone—nothing left but an empty lot decorated with raped autos. I asked around, but the denizens kept moving or demanded money or drugs or drink. A few hundred yards farther along this ageing avenue, I found a spanking new apartment tower, the Tel-El-Pal, guarded by wrought-iron gates, into which I eventually gained entrance after an interview conducted by intercom. Greenbacks were produced and soon I was safely in a one-room apartment with two locks and a door chain.

I called Tower Records but got their answering service, which told me brightly that no one was there but that the new Tower smash was by the Sunrays and that I should request "I Live for the Sun," produced by Murry Wilson, father of the Beach Boys. Then I went out and bought a frozen Mexican TV dinner. But as I couldn't work the kitchenette oven, I had to settle for the Mexican dinner as frozen dessert.

* * * * *

Brian Wilson, spurred into action by the progressiveness of the Beatles, had decided to fashion "the Greatest Rock Album Ever Made." Working with a new lyricist, Tony Asher (who admired the loner's musical ability but not his promiscuous affairs with outlandish philosophies), he had shaped his total-concept, no-filler album in the privacy of his own hilltop home, using a full-sized studio recorder upon which he could lay his *Pet Sounds* and later get Asher to fit words as suitable topping. He was going to out-art *Rubber Soul*—it was his all-American duty. There would be not *one* concept but *many* concepts running into a multitextured whole, but sometimes leaping back to link up with a snatch of music from track one, like a snakes-and-ladders game only better, more like a tapestry of subtle layers of sound which prick up the ears and raise the eyebrows with the unexpected; and then finally the soul is reached on many levels, all mistily mysterious as in a dream and track-mixed so innovatively that at times the lyrics are buried beneath this glorious trifle pudding that, of course, must be taken seriously as the work of an artist. Day after day, night after night, Brian Wilson slaved at his tracks, stacking them with instrumental variety. Like Wagner, he was using music to express the turmoil in his inner galaxies. At some places on the tape, you could actually hear him talking in the background.

To many of his straighter fans, Brian had gone "weird." Why couldn't they hear the words on the first listen? To many radio program directors, *Pet Sounds* was "problematical," was not receiving "across-the-board demographic acceptance." Of course, reasoned Capitol promo men, that could be because the album wasn't getting airplay. The Beach Boys were becoming "communicators in a trick bag," *Catch-22* and all that. "Hell," said the radio men, "give us something in the usual grooves and we'll spin it." They got *Best of the Beach Boys* and all was well. Top Forty radio, the latest deal, dealt in the *newly familiar.*

Fortunately, the Beach Boys had decided to hire Derek Taylor as their publicist. With his suave leprechaun wit and a classy air that made him appear to float above the greasy graft of hit-hustling, Derek was the perfect man to spread the word around the media. Already he was writing puff articles for *Teen Life, Tiger Beat, 16,* and the other teenybopper mags. But he also had good contacts with the growing rock cognoscenti, which included editors of photocopied, inky publications that took rock seriously as an art form and spent pages closely dissecting the music as if in a biology lab, frequently veering off into torrents of consciousness. Dubbed "prozines" or "fanzines," these cottage-industry efforts were often pompous, tedious, and self-conscious—very keen to link rock stars with Hegel, Joyce, and any name they could hope to impress with—but they were single-minded publications produced with enormous passion and missionary zeal and they were an alternative to the mindless drivel put out by the glossy teen magazines. *Crawdaddy,* out of Cambridge, Massachusetts, was the daddy of the alternative rock press, having been started by Paul Williams in 1964. By the end of 1966, *Crawdaddy* was selling nationally and was about to go glossy. Around the corner was *Rolling Stone* and a whole pile of mags that would view rock as a whole scene—a life-style—rather than simply a fun sound to dance or make out to.

Right now, Derek Taylor was working within the established limits of teen mags, trades, and bio. sheets. But he was certainly breaking new ground when he issued the statement, for "immediate release," that "Brian Wilson is a genius." He spread the word to Britain via his weekly column in *Disc,* but he had no trouble persuading the British pop press: they fell over each other expressing their amazement at the riches in *Pet Sounds.* The industry joined in, too, with Andrew Loog Oldham stating that the album was comparable to Rimsky-Korsakov's *Scheherazade* and Eric Clapton considering it to be "one of the greatest pop LPs ever to be released. It encompasses everything that's ever knocked me out and rolled it all into one. . . . Brian Wilson is, without a doubt, a pop genius."

Satisfied that his message had been spread, Derek could now apply similar treatment to his growing, stunningly eclectic list of clients: the Byrds, Paul Revere and the Raiders, Captain Beefheart, Buffalo Springfield, and Mae West. He was also addressing himself to social matters concerning the kids and their culture, such as the hassling by those gun-happy, hoglike cops of the fun-loving weekend kids on Sunset Strip. Battle lines were being drawn and Derek would weigh in with his typewriter and his tongue. The artist and his audience—two species to be guarded and protected from the Philistines. Light up your pipe and bid the Man avaunt! Sunset Strip was not the right setting for the Artist in Hell. Or was it?

*   *   *   *   *

Sitting on the sick-green carpet in my one-room apartment with the wails of Hollyweird all around me, I certainly felt like the Artist in Hell, *Prometheus Bound,* and "The Little White Cloud That Cried." Unfortunately, I had no concept album to show, no art at all. Tower's *You Turn Me On* album had been stuffed with filler, everything I'd ever recorded, including the poorer stuff, all slapped together regardless. In 1965, I'd been thrilled just to have a twelve-inch album released. But in the present state of the art, I needed something more substantial and significant. Maybe the Denny Cordell London sessions would do the trick? I would hop over to Tower first thing in the morning.

Meanwhile, sleep was the order of the day and so I pulled the Murphy bed down from the wall. But it at once sprang back with alacrity and refused to budge. So I decided to sleep on the carpet and twiddled the radio dial for bedtime music. I was eventually rewarded with a charming reverie that reminded me of Greenwich Village set down in leafy Laurel Canyon: "California Dreamin'" by the Mamas and the Papas. Their music wafted me back to my first days in California, when all was languid, laid-back, and garden lovely. Smooth harmonies, tight light rock beat—no pain, no nothing. I remembered Barry McGuire, the protest singer, raving to me about this group that time we'd been on TV together last fall. He'd said they were Lou Adler's babies and now I had nothing but admiration for the way this pop producer kept in step with the times: from Jan and Dean, through "Eve of Destruction" to West Coast bedrock—an excellent track record and one to take note of and learn from. . . . But how to foresee the next craze?

Capitol Tower, June 10:

Chanced upon some of the Beach Boys at Tower. They'd just been formally presented with three gold albums and they looked healthy, wealthy, and wise. I've been told that vice-presidents at Capitol love to present gold albums but, dreaming of a return to Big Band days, they never listen to every Beach Boys product all the way through unless the record happens to be spinning while they're on the phone or playing office golf.

As we were wishing each other luck, Brian Wilson turned up, trailing his toes and looking like little boy lost. As we'd broken bagels together a few times in the past, I felt safe in asking him, "Can we expect some more surf 'n' turf songs from you, to combat the malaise of protest?" He replied in a curious monotone, "Surfing is a challenging sport. I have never been able to meet that challenge." "What's on the drawing board, then?" "I am fascinated by the mind and hypnosis and things like that." Leaving me to ponder, the entire group disappeared around a bend of the tower.

At Tower Records Corp., all was in turmoil and nobody had time to see me immediately. They were "in meetings," or "tied up," or had "just stepped out." I asked a secretary whether the executive in question had "goose-stepped out," but she didn't get my little joke, so I explained about Hitler and the Nazis. She looked at me oddly and said I must be into that " 'Ballad of the Green Berets' shit."

I took a seat and read the trades, tip sheets, and pop mags. As in doctors' offices, the reading matter was mostly out-of-date and so, in an old copy of the *KRLA Beat,* I learned about "Ballad of the Green Berets" and caught up with much more news too, as people came out of and went into those Tower inner sanctums.

Staff Sergeant Barry Sadler, who reached number one on the U.S. charts in March, is a twenty-five-year-old in the U.S. Army Special Services and recently returned from Vietnam. While in Nam, he fell into a Cong man-trap and had his leg punctured by a poisoned spear made of sharpened bamboo. He operated on himself. While recuperating, he wrote some songs about the war. He's still on active service and is a medical NCO for the Green Berets at Fort Bragg, North Carolina. The Berets carry out special missions beyond the scope of regular troops;

only three out of every one hundred applicants gets to be a Beret. Sergeant Sadler records for RCA.

So does a group from San Francisco and they have an unlikely name —the Jefferson Airplane—but then they come from an unlikely city for pop. They don't care for Barry Sadler, but RCA doesn't mind. The Airplane is RCA's only kookie group and boy are they kookie. *KRLA Beat* discovered that during an interview. It was like talking to six John Lennons at once. How did they get to be the Jefferson Airplane? Marty Balin: "We're not *the*, we're simply Jefferson Airplane. We were working for Jefferson Airlines, so we decided to form a group." Paul Kantner: "A dog led us into a church and there was a bag of JEFFERSON AIRPLANE LOVES YOU buttons, so we figured we'd better make good use of them." They all play their own thing but when they play it's one thing; they play this thing at friendly dog dances to which everyone is invited and hordes of groups play; anybody can play really, just get up and do it; in the middle of their audio equipment sits a three-foot-high yellow-and-brown desert flower. Dig it.

KRLA Beat headlines in May: BRITISH INVASION LOSING ITS POWER . . . WHAT IS A "HAPPENING"? . . . GERRY MARSDEN SPEAKS OUT (*on Dylan: "Rotten"; on the Byrds: "Fair"; on the Beatles: "Fantastic"; on drugs: "Rubbish"; on his favorite music: "Hymns"*).

Love is a new group that lives and practices all together in a hillside "castle." They wouldn't come to the *Beat* office to be interviewed, so the girl reporter had to go to their lair. What a job she had! All kinds of questions were tried, from straight to hip, but all she got at first were monosyllables and giggles. How did they get together? "Walking down a railroad track." "In a gang fight." The poor girl was about to leave when Love leader Arthur Lee said, "It's self-expression, I guess," and shrugged his shoulders. After a while, she learned that Love want their music to "engulf the listener like love engulfs the world. . . . We're not a put-on." Concluded the reporter: "Nothing means much to these young men, but they are determined to get to the top. Lack of manners will stop them."

Sam the Sham has shaved off his beard, let his hair grow long in a pudding-bowl cut, and has traded his turban for a Dylan cap. Following the rock star trend for giving press conferences (Dylan is tops at this, a master of the art of mystically saying nothing), Sam recently threw a conference/breakfast at a Hollywood hotel. He said his ambition is to sing at the Metropolitan Opera House. He will soon be using his real name. A voracious reader, he bought *Manners for Millions* as a boy and can still remember it word for word.

Bill Gavin's Report, a key record tip sheet, has named certain records as propagators of illegal drug use: "Eight Miles High" by the Byrds,

"Rainy Day Women #12 & 35" by Bob Dylan, "Along Comes Mary" by the Association. *Newsweek* has run an article about the epidemic of thinly veiled references to drugs in certain current pop records. I almost fell off my chair when I saw my name and record staring out at me! "Turn On" as a drug phrase! But all I meant was old-fashioned sex! At least they spelled my name right. . . .

Eventually, after what seemed like hours (and, indeed, *was* hours), the A&R office door opened—and out stepped David Mallet. I remarked that a lot had happened in the biz while I'd been away, having in mind all the drug fuss, Sam the Sham minus his turban, and so on. David answered breathlessly that the "camp" craze was the latest and he was riding it like mad. He'd already produced "Supercamp" for Tower and was about to produce Mae West. Hadn't I heard the "hilarious vibrato-run-wild" of Mrs. Miller's "Downtown"? "Camp" apparently embraces twenties' dance-band pastiches, too—so I immediately thought of my recording of "Where Did Robinson Crusoe Go with Friday on Saturday Night?" I must try to get a hit by cashing in on this craze.

Immediately, I dashed into the A&R chief's office, beating several other supplicants by seconds. Locking the door, I started pitching my record to the bewildered and tired executive. "I get your drift," he replied. "But where *did* Crusoe go with Friday on Saturday night? Maybe they went out and smoked a little weed! So maybe we got another marketable controversy disc on the lines of 'Turn On.' In other words, maybe we got a hit!" I was frankly amazed at his suggestion, based on the flimsiest of premises, but I went along with the idea as I desperately need a hit record.

June 16:

On David's advice, I called up Derek Taylor and managed to fix an appointment. I'd like to join his list of clients and so I can—at $250 a month. He occupies a smart office suite in the spanking-new skyscraper at 9000 Sunset Boulevard. Had a demo disc of "Where Did Robinson Crusoe Go with Friday on Saturday Night?" and Derek adored it after hearing only a few bars. Waltzed around with his secretary a while and then called in the Byrds' managers and made them listen to the thing twice. They clearly didn't know where I was at, but they left wishing me well and "trusting everything will work out all right."

Derek and I will get along very well together, having many things in common such as British Old Boy's annuals, Vera Lynn, and almost anything prior to World War II. Many industry people think he's insane but in a nice harmless way. And he does have an absurdist view of life which I would do well to learn from. However, there are certain areas of contemporary life which Derek takes extremely seriously and one of these is the importance of getting involved with the emergent "alternative society" or "counterculture" of just plain *kids on the street*. "There are," he told me soberly over a bottle of extremely smooth Scotch, "insufficient options open to the young and the free in America today. There are those in authority who feel threatened by the maypole offered by the Byrds. In short, these people don't want to dance around such a pole." He's also very concerned with mysterious worldwide conspiracies, such as: Who killed Kennedy? He's worried about incipient violence and assassination. These are questions, I must admit, that have not troubled me in the past, and it was strange to discuss such matters surrounded by copies of *Teen Life, 16,* and *Tiger Beat.*

It was true that there was a growing feeling among those who felt themselves to be in the vanguard of life (and yet outside of the Establishment) that their hearts, minds, and—worst of all—bodies were threatened by great dark forces controlled by the State. Assassination, for example, preoccupied music people from Elvis Presley, Bob Dylan, and the Beatles to lesser-known folk protest singers like Phil Ochs. Certainly they had been shocked by the Kennedy killing. But, the nightmare asked them, would *they* be next? Slightly lower down the scale of priorities was the problem of the authorities and their oppression of youth. The kids against the cops. Of course, it had all started long ago with long hair, but now there was pot involved and in San Francisco word was filtering down that a super new drug discovery was the real key to the meaning of life and must be experienced at all costs. But like all pursuers of holy grails, the seekers would find many obstacles in their path to the Truth and Freedom. The most visible, fat, and blatant being the donut-filled LAPD.

When a cop planted his lardy bulk on the sidewalks of Sunset Strip —fallen arches supported by high, black-leather, kinky boots, belly hanging over gun belt, stubby hands on hips, sneer on lips, and shades hiding laser-beam killer eyes—a member of the New Society was presented with a clear image of the Enemy. It was awful; it was wonderful; it was breathtaking; it was god-given—and it was right here on Sunset Strip. No need to go any farther. No need to go to the Deep South with its dogs, chain gangs, and lynchings. Certainly no need to go to Vietnam. Here was Evil, right here in Lotusland.

Since about January, things had been heating up on the Strip. There were more crazy hangouts, more all-night hamburger joints, delis a gogo, funky little low-lit head shops, swinging motels where no questions were asked—and many more rock clubs. There was, for example, the "total recreation" of the Trip, where in an "infinity space" (once a dance floor) blinking many-hued lights resembled Times Square gone wacko, while way-out movies featuring B-picture horror plasma or the Keystone Kops flickered on the walls; soon, the management promised, trippers could experience New York's latest rage—an automated abstract light painting called "The Translator" which changed colors and patterns in response to the pitch of notes pumped out by the powerful stereo system. At least, that's what the man from *Life* promised. He also told the heads to watch out for the arrival of the chicest of the new "happening" groups—the Velvet Underground from "Andy Warhol's Exploding Plastic Inevitable." If Andy's name was on a product you knew it had to be a true and chic happening. At New York's Cheetah, there were sometimes over a thousand dancers throbbing to the beat, transported by the electric light show (three thousand light bulbs, count 'em); and if they wanted a rest they could always use the well-stocked library or movie theater or TV room. Gray-flannel types who wanted to be only a weekend "happener" could buy or rent such suitable gear as shiny plastic jumpsuits, plastic Dylan caps, wigs, Mod gear à la Carnaby, and other Op Art glad rags from the Cheetah's own boutique. The whole craziness was as well organized, as easy to get into or out of, as a Swedish brothel.

But New York's action was indoors and art-based and cluttered with oldsters recently free of their hula hoops and Chubby Checker Twist instruction booklets. Sunset Strip was where the real action was, twelve throbbing and wailing and sweet-smelling blocks between Hollywood and Beverly Hills, an area that no city council would want to deal with. The rich in the hills, the poor in the flatlands, the parents in the Valley—they all stayed clear of the Strip on weekends, leaving the kids to choke the sidewalks as they ambled or chatted in their bell bottoms, wide-rib cords, luxuriant hair, sandals, and the odd battered top hat painted with the stars and stripes. There were bikers, too, lined up along the gutters in Nazi helmets, greasy leather, Maltese crosses, and war medals. No threat to the kids because they and the bikers share war regalia and dope. In the street, a snail crawl of bumper-to-bumper vehicles—parents' cars, low riders, hot rods, magnesium-wheeled customized works of urban folk art—cruised the area hungry for kicks, despite the pop warning recently released by ex-barber Paul Revere and the Raiders on Columbia ("Kicks"). But maybe the action was just being there with your peers, part of the scene, showing your numbers, showing the Man.

Stalking tall, bullhorn at full volume, clad in tight-fitting leather jacket and cavalry twill jodhpurs—a queen's dream—he rolls into action: "*Attention!* It is now past ten P.M. Curfew law is in effect. Anyone under the age of eighteen years remaining in this area will be arrested!" Then two hundred and fifty patrolmen go to it, rounding up the under-agers, packing them into the paddy wagons, and carting them down to the police department, where they'll await the arrival of their parents who, having signed for their children, will then be obliged to take them home to bed.

Teen Rights Abused. This curfew boiled the blood of some of the more concerned oldsters, the progressive and hip ones. "Boys and girls come out to play/The Moon doth shine as bright as day/Leave your supper and leave your sleep/And come with your playfellows into the street" went the old nursery rhyme. What crimes have these children committed? What harm are they doing—to be shoved, booted, frisked, and arrested by fascistic cops? Teens demand rights—and we can bring them out onto the streets in their thousands to demonstrate. There will be rock- and egg-pelting, you wait. Said Councilman Debs: "The Strip is a dangerous powder keg, ready to explode." AIP Pictures readied a motion picture about this hot topic: *Riot on Sunset Strip*. The Standells, a Tower recording act, would provide some of the music.

Meanwhile, the Byrds' management formed CAFF (Community Action for Fact and Freedom) to counteract the cop harassment. CAFF headquarters turned out to be Derek Taylor's office suite. Derek agreed with Byrd management that it's superimportant to keep in with the new social movements, realizing that his clients would do well to be in the vanguard of the counterculture—but he thought it a bit thick when somebody at a CAFF meeting ripped off his very fine watch. "Never carry any more than you can eat," advised the Byrds.

A little later, I found myself booked at a theater-in-the-round called Melodyland, near Disneyland. Chad and Jeremy were the stars and hosts; I was to do some vaudeville banter with them and they encouraged me to sing "Where Did Robinson Crusoe Go with Friday on Saturday Night?" and anything else in that vein. This stuff went over so-so, but the act that really grabbed the audience was a new outfit with the odd name of Buffalo Springfield (named after a steam-roller, I learned). With two lead guitars (Steve Stills and Neil Young), three lead vocalists (Stills, Young, and Richie Furay), and a beefy, ballsy rhythm section (Bruce Palmer, bass, and Dewey Martin, drums), Buffalo Springfield gave out a unique sound mixing folk, rock, and a touch of Memphis R&B. Sonny and Cher's management company was handling them, Atlantic had signed them, and Derek was working out some lively copy for the mags. They were heavily into the Davy Crockett frontier look and they huffed and puffed onstage to such an extent that one of their members had to be taken off-stage on a stretcher. As time went by and the Strip troubles escalated into full-scale rioting involving thousands of kids, Buffalo Springfield proved themselves to be right on the ball by releasing a number called "For What It's Worth (Stop, Hey, What's That Sound)," which captured the bad vibes and paranoia that were going down. By March 1967, they were at number seven nationally and their song had become a teen anthem. By that time, too, AIP Pictures had released *Riot on Sunset Strip*.

But I am ahead of my story. Based on what I had witnessed at Melodyland, I decided to put on an Attila the Hun fur coat (loaned by Denny Cordell) and play the Strip, hoping to win the approval of the counterculture. Either I was too far ahead or too far behind, but at any rate my new act was met with puzzlement. Still, I did get my first review ever in the show-biz bible *Variety*. The "Niterie" section reviewer, "Dool," wrote: "Ian Whitcomb, an irreverent rock 'n' roll singer as well as piano-thumper, opened Thursday at 'It's Boss' on Sunset Strip, displaying an intensity of energy that seemed more sportsmanlike than showmanly . . . Soberly intense in explaining what he is about to do next, he immediately pounces on his upright piano and in ricky-tick fashion roars furiously over the keyboard while appearing to go into a paroxysm of possession." The critic went on to mention my "interpretations of interpretations" and my "German *oompah* rendering of rock 'n' roll." All very baffling, especially as I had taken so much trouble to be *au courant* with my costume, even to the detail of a plastic cap and plastic two-tone shoes. I consulted a habitué of the Strip, a cadaverous seer with long, matted hair tied in a pigtail. He was a veteran of the beatnik years, a man who had walked with Kerouac and Ginsberg. Locating him at his usual 2 A.M. hangout, Will Wright's Ice Cream Parlor on Santa Monica Boulevard, I bought him a triple cone and in return he told me: "Plastic, man—that's your problem. You wear plastic because you live in Plasticville, U.S.A. I mean Los-fuckin'-Angeles. Forget it and go see what's happening in San Francisco, like right *now!*" I said I'd go to Frisco as soon as possible; in fact, I had a date in Frisco next week at the Teenage Fair. "Look, man, do me a favor and stop calling it Frisco. It's *San Francisco* and don't you forget it!"

In August, the Beatles played Candlestick Park in San Francisco in what was to be their last appearance in America. As you recall, I, too, was there in the audience, having taken time off from selling kisses at the Teenage Fair. After receiving a death threat from an evil-eyed boy who mistook me for a Beatle, I made contact with Gale, the go-go girl now living what I erroneously called at the time "the Beat Life in Frisco." I was determined to find out for myself exactly what was happening in that city and how I could cash in on it. . . .

San Francisco, August 29:

Got away at last from the hysteria at Beatles concert. Had wanted to meet the KYA Radio bigwigs and charm them into spinning *any* of my records, but they were too busy Beatling. Still, Teenage Fair kindly provided me with a long, black limousine and peak-capped driver, so I instructed the man to take me to Gale's address on Haight Street. He threw his head back and chortled. "You really wanna go to Wackoland? Where acid runs in the gutters and fuels the buses; where the weirdos sleep fifty to a room and the result is hundreds more rug rats; where they'd smoke the grass on their lawn if they had lawns? That's what they're escaping from! Having to mow the lawn, wash the car, tie their ties, wipe their asses. You really wanna go to Hashberry? Where the chicks can be sexy but paint everything but their lips; where the guys look like warts sprouting fuzz. Watch out for the ringleaders, those burned-out old fart beatniks who we kicked out of North Beach and who're ornery and horny and urging the nerds to climb out of their skulls and go turn on the world-at-large to dope-fiending. Talk about the Russkies trying to fluoridize our water supply! You really wanna go to that slum?"

He made the denizens sound like bohemians of any place at any time, whether they be existentialists in Paris in the 1950s, smocked painters in Chelsea in the 1890s, or the folkniks of Greenwich Village in the early 1960s. Always the avant-garde carries its trademark of scrofulousness.

The driver is careening around cars on the freeway. Without asking my permission, he's switched on the radio and I'm bombarded with more Beatles music, plus the Yardbirds. Eventually, the chauffeur announced, "Welcome to Haight-Ashbury, eighty-five blocks of decaying Victorian gingerbread with two handy crash-pad parks nearby, where every service is free, from food to love!" The ornate weather-beaten wooden houses I glimpsed were charming, but many of them were covered with messages like DO WHAT THOU WILT, and TODAY IS THE FIRST DAY OF THE REST OF YOUR LIFE. The word "love" was painted on cars, chalked on the pavement, offered at a fast-food stand in the shape of a LOVEBURGER—25¢. We passed a rather unbohemian Bank of America and then a small but neat 1930s store called New Shop 'n' Save. My chauffeur pointed out that his ma and pa used to run that store but had gotten out due to the pilfering and the blaspheming (they are Italian-Americans and apparently were once in the majority here). Another multicolored car passed us, glowing in the dark with a mass of messages that entwined each other like vines. I spied GOD USES LSD before the vehicle was lost from sight. LSD—that only means pounds, shillings, and pence to me. As we roared in, narrowly missing small children and dogs that were roaming the dimly lit streets, I became aware that there were now lots of people around and that they were thronging the pavements dressed as if for a Christmas pantomime show. Some were wrapped in long, black cloaks and some in the Stars and Stripes; I saw witch women in tall, conical hats and youths in redskin half-breed costumes, complete with matted hair, headband, jeans, and cowboy boots. I saw old men with gray beards and floppy hats. Everybody wore some kind of neck jewelry, which flashed and glinted in the hastening gloaming of those dim, dingy, greasy—yet romantic—streets.

Many of the throng were streaming from a ramshackle wooden building whose intermittent flashing sign proclaimed it to be the FILLMORE AUDITORIUM. We were forced to a halt outside this building because the street had become clogged with jigging, flute-tooting, guitar-strumming people. "Crazies" pronounced my chauffeur, giving them his pointed middle finger as a salute. Several of the abandoneers gave him a Churchillian victory sign in return: "Peace, brother!" I asked my knowledgeable chauffeur what these street people worked at by day. "When they're not contemplating their navels, they work at the post office and they deal dope on the side. Everybody's hustling just to have a good time."

While waiting in traffic, I noted a poster on the Fillmore's wall. After a while, I managed to break its twisty-twiney code of illegibility: 13TH FLOOR ELEVATOR, THE GREAT SOCIETY, and SOPWITH CAMEL. Sounded like an uplifting, inspirational evening of hot (possibly full) gospel, followed by a lecture on President Johnson's internal social policy, finishing with a spot of World War I Royal Flying Corps nostalgia. Education mixed with entertainment, a revival of the turn-of-the-century Chautauqua. As I was rolling down the electric window for a better view, a top-hatted and bulbous-nosed face poked in and demanded: "Hey, man. If you ain't a Beatle, then get the fuck outta here. We don't dig tourists from straight society!"

At Gale's Pad:

We pulled up outside Gale's Haight Street address, another tall and skinny Victorian gingerbread house in need of a lick of paint. Loosening my TCD tie and tucking my ukulele case under my arm, I made my way up the broken staircase and prepared to ring—but the door was ajar. Inside was the usual sweet-smelling aroma and, glancing around, I noticed that the pad appeared to be on the lines of Gale's other place in L.A.—except more so. This was the original; this was the real thing—in Technicolor—at last! The original greasy mattresses, bamboo furniture, wine-bottle candelabras, oriental rugs, Op Art puzzle pictures, organic-design posters, blowups of Allen Ginsberg, and dirty dishes, dirty sheets, and possibly dirty work at the crossroads. Throw off your middle-classness! There was much afoot in the front room: hordes and hordes of people of both sexes lounging here and there. Guitars were being studied, flutes and recorders blown; a girl was body-painting a revoltingly obese older man, a cross-legged group was chanting in a foreign language, a circle of cottage-industry types were trinket-making, a caldron of brown rice was bubbling, stirred by a girl who looked like the model for Botticelli's "Primavera," and in the far corner a very solemn bunch, led by a St. Bernard, were staring intensely at something.

And there was Gale, looking like the Goddess of Spring, in the middle of the starers. I went up to kiss her, but she gave me a "Sssh." What were they all staring at? "A plank in the floor," she told me in hushed tones. "Why?" "Because it's a microcosm of the universe." "Who says so?" "Dr. Clark says so."

Dr. Werner Clark, in the days when he wore a suit and tie, used to be a senior lecturer in modern history and political thought at the University of California, Berkeley. He sided with the civil rights marchers in Alabama in '63 (and had a limp to show for it) and with the militant students in the Free Speech Movement of 1964–65. In early '66, the Berkeley dean warned him to desist. Instead, Clark took a large dose of LSD and realized that everything he had been teaching up till now was "bullshit." He also realized that revolution was just around the corner and that, with this new neurological tool of LSD, anything was possible, especially if he were leading the new majority of world students (the under-twenty-fives outnumbered their elders in 1966; half of white American youth was either enrolled in or had attended college). He would be guru, good shepherd, pilot of the new vibes airways. "Call me 'Hadrian the Ninth,'" he said. But the kids preferred to know him as "Dr. Clark."

And what I had taken to be Gale's pad was, in fact, Dr. Clark's new community, "The Magic Powerhouse of Oz," where fifty-odd followers of the doctor lived and loved and did their thing. They had even sprouted a rock group named after the community and led by a stunningly handsome boy named Bobby Beausoleil. "The Magic Powerhouse of Oz" had no time for the "single-family unit" and lawn-mowing, car-washing, and the PTA: "Wash 'n' Wear Society," they called it. The only way was to eradicate the past: the mess of history; the hideous Calvinist work ethic—the idea that you made money for the sake of making money not because of the instrinsic value of your work; the two-car garage and the split-level home; the marriage contract; the "don'ts" of straight society. So here in the Haight and the surrounding mountains and valleys were tribal communities, splintered from a common block.

"In the new youth cosmos on earth," Dr. Clark liked to say, "there is a strong connectability quotient. A friend tells a friend tells a friend—a daisy chain of turning on to the wonders of ancient roots, vines, and plants, and to the cunning of modern chemistry."

"I believe you've contributed to our cause by way of your song 'You Turn Me On.'" Dr. Clark had appeared and was stroking Gale in a lascivious manner, while she gazed at him glassy-eyed. I made small talk while studying him. Early forties, bald on top with thin gray hair reaching down to shoulders. A red Indian headband, tinkling bells around the neck, a bedsheet in the Ghandi style on his tubby body, Chinese clogs on his stubby little feet. A bit of the Wild West, but much more of the Mystic East.

"Won't you join us for a macrobiotic meal? I feel the brown rice is at the crucial stage," the doctor offered. I must confess I was quite hungry. I was also itching to lay my hands on Gale in some dark area, even a greasy mattress. We all sat on the floor to eat, while somebody played a record which ran something like: "If you're tired and a bit run down/Can't seem to get your feet off the ground/Maybe you ought to try a little bit of LSD (only if you want to)." Dr. Clark objected to this ragtimey number, telling one of the guitar bearers nearby that he wanted to hear no more of this "Psychedelic Ranger fun stuff" for the time being. "We will use the mandala and drone as our centering devices," he ordered. Then he toasted me in Kool-Aid and I responded and, for the next half hour, he regaled me with information about his "brave new world."

He showed me the mandala on the wall. "Aids the concentration." Meanwhile, East Indian music was whining away in the background. I've never been too fond of the monotony, but Dr. Clark explained that the drone, like the mandala, is a centering device. "A central tonal stillness in the heart of the whirlwind," he said. The doctor poured me some more Kool-Aid and told me how the three brains of man were always at war with one another. "However, the careful administration of certain new drugs can rectify that mistake. . . ." The room was starting to spin; the ceiling was trying to fly away. The doctor's voice sounded as if he was right inside my ear yet also light-years away from me. "That's right. You're farther than the last frontier. You're taking off and I'm going to navigate you. But first of all, we have to break the locks of your neurotic past, free you from history. . . . Up, up, and *awaaaaay!*"

All around me is a burning, fiery glow, but inside the mandala note I sit on my thick, crispy cornflake revving up my Rolls-Royce engine. "You're not like these cretins here," leers the doctor. "All they have are Ford motors!" But his face is a razorback leper with running sores shooting geysers of pus. When I touch him, I am on a relief map of an infested world, but that globe is bumped by Gale's ballooning breast, just freed from her body. As I negotiate my way across the supper table, which is now the Andes, I see her gobbling Werner's head whole as he unzips his fly to reveal his primeval beast, which frees itself from his fly and proceeds to tell jokes, all of which I've heard before. Suddenly, the house explodes with a great *bang* and I'm in the sky, riding a flaming train which is dressed in pajamas. I look down at myself to see if I still have my ukulele, but Christ! My body is melting away like fried ice cream! And yet over there, a trillion billion miles away, am I, standing stupidly in a blazer and old school tie, the very essence of the professional Englishman. I am as nothing; all my goals and desires and likes and loves are as nothing; not even ashes. Same for Phil Spector, Bill Haley, the Beach Boys, Elvis Presley—they are all nothing. All of us cease to be; we're erased; we aren't even ex-persons. I feel sick. But then gradually, from the Far East, there appears a clear white light that grows brighter and brighter until it sets me free. "You is OK," says the bluesman. "You are Buddha and Christ. You have gone crazy and come back again and now you are descending out of the azure and re-entering the system. So fasten your seatbelts, please, and prepare for landing. We hope you have enjoyed your flight and have a nice day in Los Angeles. . . ."

The mellow, reassuring sounds of Herb Alpert and the Tijuana Brass greeted my return. "How are we feeling, then?" asks Dr. Clark. "I told them you were one of my patients. My, but you've certainly done a lot of babbling over the last eight hours. Was this your first trip?" He told me I had now been initiated into the greater-awareness movement, but please never to refer to it as a cult. He said a million joints of marijuana were being smoked a day at present, but that there is a monthly increase of 5 percent. According to *Time,* a million doses of LSD will be consumed this year. According to Capitol Records, a million copies of their new LSD documentary album will ship. I commented that these figures seemed very round and similar—maybe there was something mystic in this? Dr. Clark winked and said he wasn't in it for the money; he was proseletyzing as a healer and navigator. "And,

God knows, this poor country is direly in need of leaders. Always has been." He offered me a ride into Hollywood in his limousine.

In San Francisco, the food of the gods was acid. Acid had created those gods from regular (and irregular) folks and now, metamorphosed, they were ready to perform missionary work around the country. For acid wasn't just a private pleasure, it was a revolutionary tool for inspiring within common clay a cornucopia of poems, novels, paintings, and music. Acid could end the war between the three brains; it could unite the world and achieve *Nirvana*. Acid was a crash course in the solution of that age-old occidental problem of *alienation*. LSD said, *"We are one."*

But, looking at the new gods—at the inhabitants of Haight-Ashbury—one could be forgiven for thinking that they appeared very much like bohemians through the ages: the Beats, the Dadaists, the long-haired, wild-eyed avant-garde painters, Oscar Wilde rolling down the Strand with a lily behind the left ear. A harmless weirdness confined to a lunatic few—and in certain neighborhoods. But this latest manifestation was different—for San Francisco's life and lore was to spread throughout America and the Western world and was to turn the heads of the Beatles, Stones, and other movers and shakers of rock 'n' roll music. For them, things were never going to be quite the same again. . . .

LSD, hoped the pill pioneers in 1966, would be an elixir that would eventually purify the polluted mainstream. Over the next two years, "Operation LSD" was to find millions of volunteer recruits so that, for a moment, the meandering sidestream of American dissent would actually appear to be flowing into the mainstream itself, flooding shiny, squeaky-clean Main Street, U.S.A. This would constitute a first in American history.

For the Un-Americans, the antijoiners, had never topped any popularity chart before now. They constituted a tiny special-interest group in a land of special-interest groups. The Pilgrim Fathers themselves were one such group. But the antijoiners were true reactionaries because they didn't agree with the nation's dream to become One Big Bloc under the Chief. Though the similarities in language might lead the casual observer to believe that Britain and America were brothers, in fact, the Republic had more in common with the timetable precision and finely structured order of North Germany, in particular the Prussia of the late-nineteenth century. Well-drilled Masses led by the Few. A subtle distinction between Germany and America was that, in the latter, the blocs were treated as if they were sports teams and the whole business was run as if one great game was being played. This made life more fun.

For example, the Constitution was the rule book and pretty rigid in its "do's" and "don'ts." And to be a voter, one had to register. Many colleges, too, had a violent spanking and dehumanizing game as the initiation test. Most aspects of American life were described in terms from organized sport: an original idea was "out of left field," a business venture couldn't even "get to first base," a building contractor's fee was "in the ball park," a lusty bachelor was "playing the field" and might even be a "switch-hitter," for he was known to wear a pink shirt on a Thursday.

The ambition of every red-blooded American was to join the Chief's Brigade, but there was, of course, only room at the top for the tough Few. Anyway, in a game everyone can't be captain. But what was nice in this game was that the captain and his lieutenants were known by their first names and looked just like any Joe. So the head Joe and his shirt-sleeved Jims organized the nation into suckers and con men—the most successful chapter being the crime organization. Early on in the game, the American Fathers had shown a repugnance for democracy—this was a Republic and therefore quite a different matter—and, as late as 1917, U.S. Army manuals described democracy as synonymous with "mobocracy." The Masses were fine, providing they stood in line and paid their admission fee. One of the most shining examples of good business organization was show business: from ragtime to rock 'n' roll, the story had been one of order and conformity, with wild and crazy folk sounds like jazz being soon tamed and packaged by the show business and then—amazingly—sold back to those very suckers who'd created the raw material in the first place!

In contrast, Britain was a loose-knit confederacy of recalcitrant, cantankerous, eccentric curmudgeons. Which was probably why, on the whole, the place simply didn't work very efficiently. Britain was crawling with loonies and loners and so there was no need for current myths starring rugged individualists. Shadowy ancients like Robin Hood and King Arthur would suffice. But in America the rigid two-team conformity demanded a myth opiate and at once. The Wild West provided the heroes. In actuality, the cowboys, trappers, frontiersmen, and bandits had been the bane and bore of the West, the real winners being the solid, hard-working, God-fearing folk who built the towns and stayed in them. But actuality can lead to madness caused by an excess of the mundane and so some of these pesky varmints who had gotten in the way of the real pioneers were called into service as romantic folk heroes, as earnest innocents blazing a lone trail of individuality: Kit Carson, Jesse James, Billy the Kid, etc.

In outlining my theory of Bloc America, I don't mean to put down this ordered neatness. I thoroughly approve, indeed I am envious. To be a member of a group, be it scout troop, football team, or college fraternity, has always been a prime goal for me—but one that has constantly eluded me.

So when I first arrived in the U.S.A. in 1963, I was immediately impressed by the Prussian precision—everything worked and was on time—and by the predilection for uniforms. Everybody seemed to be in glamorous costumes of the musical comedy variety. Even the bagmen at the airports were kitted out like four-star generals. Youth was constantly clicking to attention and barking, "Yes, sir!" to its elders. Even to me. Swimming pools and beaches had guards and posted rules. There were so many "no-no's" in American life. But people seemed to be quite cheerful, brushing their teeth three times a day, driving at the correct speed, eating the same cuisine at chain after chain coffee shop, rooting for the pom-pom girls. I was perfectly content. For the old folkways of black and hillbilly music were not threatened and their existence added a touch of tabasco to the bland consistency of overground America.

However, running parallel with the mainstream was always the sidestream of dissent. It never involved the working classes and it had always been piddling little. The Un-Americans were fired by a fear of machinery and the city. They were usually of an educated-middle-class background, but they liked to disguise this fact by pretending to be "glorious paupers." Herman Melville identified the bohemians of his day as "Painters and sculptors, or indigent students, or teachers of languages, or fugitive French politicians, or German philosophers." But by the 1920s, with post-World War I America swept reasonably clean of aliens, the bohemians were now native Americans and holed up in Greenwich Village, New York, where, amid the usual unmade beds and clogged kitchen sinks, they were free to rail in art against the order surrounding their ghetto. The musically inclined were attracted, at a safe distance, to black jazz because of its furtive and outlaw character.

During the Depression, the bohemians found too much competition from real down-and-outs and the hobby shriveled up and away. But after World War II, when the country made tremendous progress toward a middle-class standard with much upward climbing toward managerial positions and much reading of Emily Post's etiquette book, the bohemian urge took on a new lease of life. Poetry, existentialism, Zen Buddhism, and general slacking were the main features of Greenwich Village life. In music a search was instigated to try and find genuine folk singers, but the more antsy of the New Bohemians went for the stronger meat of modern jazz, of be-bop. They particularly dug Charlie

Parker, not just because of the rap flurry of worry notes that flew out of
his sax but also because he had headed himself toward autodestruction.
The life-style of the cool black hipster was admired and copied by the
white bohemians, particularly the slang and the drug usage. Norman
Mailer dubbed them "White Negroes" and noted that what they admired had many of the characteristics of the psychopath—the instant
satisfaction, the rebellion without cause, the craving to make headlines
—and wrote that though it was liberating to be hip ("an instant understanding through intuition") and crazy, "It is not granted to the hipster
to grow old gracefully."

The "White Negroes," said Mailer, were a new breed of urban ad-
venturers "drifting out at night, looking for action with a black man's
code to fit their facts." Though they had little in common with American intellectuals and arbiters of taste, they did share a *bête noire* of
monstrous proportions: Southern white music, all the way from revivalist "Amazing Grace" sway-singing through hillbilly nose ballads to
rousing rockabilly. They hated such aberrations with a mighty passion
—for they realized that, like respectable black jazz, this music couldn't
be separated from its background, which was White Trash, nigger-in-
the-woodpile of U.S. social history. The dark white heartland, those
full-gospeling, beer-swilling, gun-happy, clog-dancing, guitar-thrashing,
frozen-haired primates—the descendants of the indentured servants of
the Daughters of the American Revolution—scared them to death. Send
Louis Armstrong around the globe as an example of American culture,
but put a Band-Aid on the mouth of those nasal whiners from hicksville!

So when Elvis Presley, King of Rock 'n' Roll and triumph of the
South, burst on the world like a carbuncle, the deep-thinking minority
hoped he was just a passing fancy, another gimmick thrown up by corrupt capitalist show biz, that opiate arm of Big Government. Bop 'n'
Folk, with a smidgen of Charles Ives, was their music and the nastier
the better. Ironically, the young San Franciscans who were to continue
the Un-American tradition would be utilizing rock 'n' roll, Elvis music,
albeit filtered through the merry sound of the British Invaders. For the
little hipsters—the hippies—had learned their credo and lingo from the
local manifestation of Un-Americanism: the beatniks. It was the Beat
way of life that was to be role model for the rock generation that was
to spread from its San Francisco beginnings all around the country and
to certain parts of the world, killing off the old show biz.

For a while, then, we must examine the Beats as hippie-rock mentors.
As a group, they had started in the late forties. The founders were all
writers: William Burroughs, Jack Kerouac, and Allen Ginsberg. Many
of their ideas were based on hipster life, but they were more self-con-

scious about playing outlaw/misfit because they wrote words whose finality stared back at them like monuments.

Their creed was summed up in the command *"Go!"*—which was the favorite expression of their idol, their buddy: Neal Cassady, who boasted the correct Outsider credentials. By the age of twenty-one, he claimed he had stolen 500 cars, screwed 750 chicks, and spent fifteen months in jail. A muscular "rough trade" lug of no fixed address, he wore as his uniform ripped jeans with no underwear and a sausage-skin T-shirt. He was fond of being surprised in the nude. To abolish time was his ambition, but in the meantime he was forever trying to stay ahead of the clock. With mind, body, and desires running at a million m.p.h., he was all *"Go!"* Like any decent psychopath, he believed that the world revolved around his appetites, but he was really at his most characteristic when in transit gloria—stretched out at arm's length behind the wheel of a car roaring bicoastally. He rapped nonstop about how he dug every little deatil of crisscross-country America. He was the archetypal outcast, the drifting mechanized cowboy, and the exact opposite of the 1950s uptight gray-flanneled Mr. "Organization Man" Jones of the manicured suburbs or the poorer, paunchy zombie, Mr. Blue Collar of Levittown.

To his writer pals, Cassady, an unschooled boy-man sprite, was a meaty model of Zen Buddhism in action, penetrating beyond the mundane logical mind into the true core of the human spirit. And that spirit—that all-knowing intuition—dictated the message: the only real goal in life was to be constantly celebrating the ecstasy of the passing moment. To stop and consider was to realize the absurdity of the whole game because the Damocles sword of the H-bomb was saying that "Man is nothing" and the past is a foreign country and the future is nonexistent. So it's all *"Go!"* Experience must be pushed to its utmost limits—even as far as the cliff overlooking the valley of death—in order for one to discover one's real nature and thus attain manhood. You are the center of the universe because all else is nonsense, chaos that can't be trusted. But make friends with chaos and tell society and all its inhibiting institutions to go fuck themselves. Go find the ultimate truth by walking on the wild side of the city late at night—say, in a dingy black bar where the bopper's horn is sending us all heavenward with his jet-propelled blue notes and we get a boost from bennies, bottle, and needle.

Jack Kerouac banged it all down in hot bop prosody. In *On the Road,* a chronicle of the Beat Generation thinly disguised as fiction, he immortalized Cassady as a ramblin' rapper hero. Detailing the picaresque road life in the Other America, the book became a Beat primer and Kerouac became the Hippie Homer. Legend had it that he typed the novel in a trance as one long paragraph on one fat roll of UPI tele-type paper. Truth was, that the book went through many rewrites be-tween the first draft in 1951 and the final version published in 1957. No question, though, that On the Road was a rich read and a tall ad-venture that contained many passages that were to inspire hippie life in the swinging psychedelic years just ahead: "The only people for me are the mad ones—mad to live, mad to talk, desirous of everything at the same time."

In 1957, the book spent a long time on the bestseller lists and, by the end of the fifties, Kerouac was an international name, with Ginsberg and Burroughs not far behind. Mass-circulation magazines like Life helped spread the word and soon a generation of properly accredited Beats assembled and found a suitable resting place on the penultimate frontier of the West Coast. San Francisco, with its long tradition of rad-icalism, embracing anarchists, Wobblies, and an independent commer-cial-free radio network, was most acceptable as an environment: Myste-rious fog, magic mountains, and an ocean view looking toward the East, where the brown rice and the answers came from.

The Beats were thickest in North Beach, a cluster of funky coffee houses, bookshops, and clubs, plus attractive low-rent housing, so that the Outsiders were free to hang loose and do their thing in peace. Soon the press was covering this phenomenon, and the Beats were dubbed "beatniks," spaced-out spinoffs from the recent Sputnik. Ginsberg, happy in his long-sought celebrity status, could be seen by the bus-tour patrons shrieking and gesticulating his famous Howl poem at smoggy poetry readings to a response of "wows" (boos when he said "Moloch" and cheers when he said "love"). Soon he'd be hitting the college cir-cuit and later there'd be Dylan shows and Beatle stardust.

But for Kerouac, the recognition came too late. Maybe he'd once been an Outsider, way back in the early fifties, but that was only be-cause he'd been left out of the team. As a kid, he'd been a hell of a jock with a bright future, but something had cracked during his service hitch. He was really deeply conservative and longed to run with the middle boys, but now the pressure was on the speed-writing champ for more of the same, the crazy On the Road stuff. So he obliged by typing out things like The Dharma Bums—in which lots of the old On the Road cast went through the hoops again, but youth entered as a new el-ement, in a "vision of a great rucksack revolution, young Americans wandering around, going up mountains to pray, making children laugh and old men glad. Zen lunatics—writing poems that happen to appear in their heads for no reason."

As the sixties opened, the vision came true as thousands of kids, for-saking the home attractions of the One Big Blue Eye—the TV—backpacked to Big Sur, Carmel, and San Francisco's North Beach haunts. They were still a select few, but they were too many for Kerouac. Dressed as dharma bums, they trekked even as far as his mother's place in Lowell, Massachusetts, where they bothered the writer for autographs at the door. But he at least managed to keep them outside, which was more than he'd done with Ginsberg, whose beard and garb had scared Mrs. Kerouac. And even worse were Ken Kesey and his Merry Pranksters, who'd made refrigerator raids, put their feet up on the dining room table, and thrown dinner rolls around indiscriminately. Kesey should have known better—he'd been a scholar and a real jock in his time. But these rudenesses, especially the four-letter words, were too much. And the worst thing was the constant desecration of the American flag, which was later aped by Ginsberg and Kesey's kid followers. Can't they keep their fiction within a book? thought Kerouac. Ginsberg was really out to "cash in on the youth racket," he growled. What the hell was all this fuss about the Beats anyway? "All we were out for was to get laid," said Jack. "Look, I may be King of the Beats, but I'm no beatnik!"

By 1964, Kerouac and Ginsberg were among the best-known American writers in the world. Ginsberg, now fond of wearing bedsheets in public, went traveling. In Liverpool, he sensed good vibes, pronouncing the city "the center of the consciousness of the human universe"; at the Cavern, he was struck by the beautiful boys with their "golden archangelic hair." And on and on he journeyed, to be feted by French, Dutch, and German youth. Even the young Turks were lapping up Beat, while back home at his mother's place, Kerouac watched his once-open road jam up with an army of spoiled middle-class brats. Their love of dirt and disorder was hateful and he pinned his hopes on Richard Nixon, so that things might be set to rights. In his twilight years, Kerouac was a guest on a TV show with hippie spokesman Ed Sanders (leader of the Fugs, specialists in obscene songs). When the neophyte Sanders drooled that On the Road had "sparked the hippie movement," Kerouac retorted, "As Buddha said, 'Woe be unto those who spit in the wind—the wind'll blow it back!'"

What really aggravated Kerouac about these hippies was their abuse of hard drugs. A few bennies, a bit of weed, and a slug from the jug were all in a day's work and not out of proportion in a speed-writer's life. But the sixties brats, spoon-fed and Spock-marked, were too lazy to pay their dues, believing that they could get instant Beatitude and become full-fledged artists simply by swallowing tablets of LSD. And this same Ed Sanders had the arrogance to claim: "These drugs are revolutionizing the personalities of individuals, which is the first step in revolutionizing our society and government. I'm for that." Even trendy, youth-trailing Ginsberg admitted that LSD was too strong a potion for him to use as a creative tool.

There was no stopping the rolling stone of Beat gone hippie of the rock movement. Swiss youth, normally placid and sensible, went Beat and Beatle together, for it was thought that they were one and the same, "Yeah! Yeah! Yeah!", "Howl," and *"Go!"* all sounding very similar in a foreign language. What Dr. Albert Hofmann felt about all the hoo-ha is not known. The Swiss chemist, who had invented LSD while working for Sandoz A.G. Laboratories in 1938, had long since dismissed his synthetic concoction as medically useless (he had hoped it might quell migraines) and very harmful if used indiscriminately. Sandoz A.G., learning that many minds were being swiss-cheesed in drug-happy America, stopped distributing LSD in the middle sixties, but by that time their patent had run out.

Dr. Hofmann's first LSD trip back in 1943 had been an unusual experience. As he describes it, he was "seized by a peculiar sensation of vertigo and restlessness. . . . With my eyes closed, fantastic pictures of extraordinary plasticity and intensive color seemed to surge toward me." Although he did further experiments with varying dosages, Dr. Hofmann's research was not recreational. A tall stein of lager and a pipe of tobacco were his usual fare. But there was a demand for the hallucinatory drug in America, where they would try anything once. During the war, LSD was tested as a truth serum on prisoners of war (to no effect). Later, it was tried as a tool for discovering the causes of schizophrenia by producing model psychoses (it was certainly good at slivering up the personality for a few mad hours). Perhaps it would work on alcoholics and homosexuals and all the other deviants? At ivory towers on the East and West Coasts, the experiments went on apace and at Harvard a psychology professor named Timothy Leary turned on to the drug as a panacea. For him, LSD was "Eureka!" and the climax of a mind-boggling search that had started for him in Mexico in 1960 when he'd first experienced visions after eating some toasted magic mushrooms.

Suffering from delusions of grandeur, he declared LSD to be the sacrament of a new religion which he would lead as a sexy messiah. His guinea-pig students and fellow researchers were invited to join the new religion and to embark on a world crusade. Leary and Ginsberg (turned on by the professor) had agreed that LSD, by expanding consciousness, could increase people's intelligence and make them better and more beautiful. They resolved to turn the world on to this instant-answer serum: lysergic acid diethylamide or "mysticism by microwave."

News of Leary's experiments reached the Harvard authorities and, when it was learned that the professor was recommending that the

U.S. water supply be dosed with LSD so as to be one step ahead of the Russians, they fired him. Now the martyred messiah went on the stump, telling all to "Turn On, Tune In, Drop Out." A stunningly simple slogan, as good as any pop-hit lyric. Never mind that the world as a whole wasn't as bright as Leary, as poetic as Ginsberg, as melodic as Lennon and McCartney, and that this majority would come out of their trips the same plodders as when they went in—*if* they came out intact. Many, of course, were swiss-cheesed for life. Others met death. Unknown millions were to carry the drug around in their system for the rest of their lives, like walking sticks of dynamite ready to go off at any moment. Never mind all these side issues; like all drug users, Leary hated to be alone in his dark deeds: he needed company and he also needed a world congregation for his new religion. Supplied with funds by millionaire benefactors, he set up his church on a large estate in Millbrook, New York, and called his outfit the League for Spiritual Discovery. Soon he had a large flock, including children, and all were gobbling up the acid like there was no tomorrow, which there wasn't.

Leary was a fine propagandist as LSD High Priest, rushing from podium to podium and show to show. He was a great media personality and his pop hook phrase of "Turn On, Tune In, Drop Out" was perfect for easy reading. The authorities could do nothing to stop him because LSD was still legal and would be until October of 1966. But he had little success as High Priest in San Francisco—there were already plenty of gurus in residence and their flocks didn't need to be told about LSD, since their local dope dealers had already unloaded supplies of the latest novelty line. There was even a local manufacturer, Augustus Owsley Stanley III, brewing up a top-grade brand in his own psychedelic spaceship lab. By this time, late 1964, a whole new community based on the magic of LSD was thriving in the Haight-Ashbury district, another low-rent neighborhood like North Beach but full of abandoned Victorian mansions and amenable ethnics whose shops and services came in very handy for the running of the acid village. North Beach, anyway, had been cleaned out earlier in an antibeatnik drive spearheaded by the Italian-Americans and Irish-Catholics. The Haight's eighty-five crumbling blocks were to get a new lease on life and coats of many-colored paints.

Leary was too "hot," too high-handed, too mandarin, and too intellectual for this free-wheeling atmosphere, where the Psychedelic Rangers could be found sharing their acid with Hell's Angels. No, the propagandizing of LSD was in more acceptable hands with Ken Kesey. A wrestling champion and Stanford scholar, Kesey had been an LSD guinea pig at Menlo Park Veteran's Hospital back in the days when Hofmann's mixture was still being tried as a medicine. Like Leary, the experience changed his life, but instead of playing the part of the new messiah he decided to stage-manage a psychodrama roadshow with headquarters in his six-acre estate at La Honda, not far from San Francisco (the funds had come from royalties of his best-selling, drug-induced novel *One Flew Over the Cuckoo's Nest*). At La Honda, there was always a party going on. Kesey had several personae but his favorite was "Mr. Stars and Stripes" and he liked to dress up in a flag suit and do a bit of flag burning on the side.

Visitors to Kesey's circus included the Hell's Angels (who were initiated into acid during a party at the estate), Allen Ginsberg (naturally), and Neal Cassady (whose presence placed the Beat stamp of approval on the whole hedonist enterprise). Determined to scatter the good seed, Kesey often took to the road in a riotously colored magic bus—the first psychedelic (or "magic") bus—crammed with his band of Merry Pranksters and chauffeured by Cassady at full rap. With the refrigerator full of acid-laced orange juice, the performers in different costumes every day, and Captain Trips (Kesey) squatting atop the bus with binoculars around neck and grinning like a demented Rommel, the Prankster entourage must have had the desired shock effect on the decent working people they descended upon.

Back at La Honda, Kesey started throwing a series of parties where the object was to blow the mind on acid—but not quite to smithereens. Those who emerged with a few brain cells intact were the winners, having successfully passed the Acid Test, at a time when America's favorite party game was Charades. These tests got more elaborate and more or less loosely organized, with light shows that featured strobes, funny old silent flicks, endless protoplasms, and slides of dead Indians. Music was provided by a loose group of ex-folkies and avant-garde musicians, recently Dylanized into rock, who called themselves the Grateful Dead. They were most useful at the parties, since they liked to play for free and their numbers had a tendency to go on for two or three hours apiece, enabling the trippers to get through their abysses comforted by suitable acid-rock Muzak.

Together with Jefferson Airplane, the Dead became the most well known of the San Francisco acid-rock bands. Like true jazzmen, they played only when the spirit moved them, so that no sets were ever planned and there was no apparent desire to make the Top Forty. Straight society with its timetables was abhorrent and Chance was all-important—for instance, they'd found the name "Grateful Dead" when a dictionary flipped open to a notation on the burial of Egyptian pharaohs. Their musical roots were coffee-house folk—ancient blues, jug band music, bluegrass, and a touch of Edwardian avant-garde (Charles Ives). Their bass player, Phil Lesh, talked about "bringing

Zen consciousness and a polyphonic concept" to their music. Their main spokesman, Jerry Garcia, claimed that "Philosophically, we have nothing to say. We just like to play loud. . . . It's fun to shoot at strangers." The music was very loud, taking its cue from the high-decibeled Yardbirds, and it was mostly blues riffing with tremendous attachment to the drone note, so that the result was a mixture of African and Eastern folk sounds filtered through electronics. The droning, mantralike melody line made Dead music the perfect accompaniment for a trip. Conversely, it could lead to severe headaches if you weren't tripping. One simply had to roll with the flow or get back to Perma-press-ville.

In many ways, the Dead were the children of Beat, living communally and dangerously outside of straight society. The Dead set up their open family in a Haight-Ashbury mansion, where at one time 150 Deadheads could be found living and nearly living. But in other ways, they were different from the Beats, and the main one was in their music: Beats had taken their jazz very seriously and sitting down, with heads bobbing and mouths still except for the occasional "wow" or "outtasight." The Dead and the other acid-rock bands of the Bay Area were into playing music for dancing and partying and this was where they and their fans were to part company with the elder statesmen of Beat. The Acid Tests-turned-dance-parties were attracting thousands of kids who were basically rock fans. Like the local bands, they had come to rock via the Beatles and Stones and now they were proud to have their own local Liverpool with its own sounds, smells, and chemicals.

The Bay, with its burgeoning bands and hungry fans, was ripe for exploitation by entrepreneurs. In the Haight itself, a haphazard start had been made. At one of the rambling old gingerbread mansions-cum-pads—1090 Page Street (twenty-eight rooms and a ballroom)—there had started a series of jam sessions and sometimes actual bands were formed as a result. Big Brother and the Holding Company started here. A fat girl named Janis Joplin would stop by to holler a boozy blues. The Victoriana decor had been hand-painted by members of one of the first Bay bands, the Charlatans. With their hip pizza-parlor straw hats and jug-type music, they weren't about to arouse the rock hungry, but one Chet Helms had been knocked out when he saw them play at a Nevada gig. It gave him the idea for organizing some local dance events, a step beyond the casual jams at Page Street and the arcane frolics in the desert.

Helms was a well-meaning, idealistic soul, very gentle in the true hippie manner. His roommates in another peeling Haight house called themselves the Family Dog and they constituted a kind of village co-op store, with a little dealing in the back room. Helms decided that these jams should become dances at larger local clubs and that the dancers should pay an entrance fee. With this in mind, he went to see local jazz columnist Ralph Gleason—a man over thirty but one who was known to be sympathetic, if not downright excited, by the local band scene.

At home in trenchcoat and tweeds, Gleason was startled by his first sight of Helms and his fellow Family Dogs in their granny glasses, granny dresses, and Sherwood Forest/Wild West gear purchased from the Salvation Army and Goodwill. Helms, shaggy-smiley but firm, announced that L.A. was nothing but a Gomorrah of super-uptight plastic people, then made the proclamation that Family Dog had chosen San Francisco as "the New Liverpool." So would the San Francisco *Chronicle* writer please scour his forty-eight-year-old brain and come up with a cheap-rent locale for their first "dance concert"?

The journalist suggested the Longshoremen's Hall (shades of rip-roaring, radical union days) down at the Fisherman's Wharf. What a crazy idea, bringing the Cuckoo's Nest to San Francisco's very own culinary Disneyland! So in October 1965, the Bay Area rock scene was properly launched at this first Family Dog Dance—entitled "A Tribute To Dr. Strange" (a comic book character). All these dance parties had to seem like spontaneous happenings celebrating something weirdly wonderful and Russ Syracuse, the "All Night Flight" good guy on Top Forty rocker KYA, emceed a bill comprised of Jefferson Airplane, the Great Society, the Marbles, and the Charlatans. Word had been spread by mouth, posters, and radio, and, though these acts were not chartbusters, there was a house fit to bursting. No L.A. act could draw in this manner; it was eerie and exciting. Although the box office did great, the bar business did terribly and, instead of dreary, clinging couple-dancing, there was free-form communal ring-stepping in the Isadora Duncan style with some medieval maypole influence thrown in. The ubiquitous Allen Ginsberg led a Conga line.

Gleason was tickled to death by the colorful turnout and he became an instant convert to Bay Area rock. That same night, at a nearby loft, another older man was experiencing similar feelings as he watched over three thousand people jam into a space that normally might squeeze in six hundred. Bands he'd never heard of blew all night, joined by a stream of players from the Family Dog and other better-known groups. Money was pouring in to swell the coffers of the benefit, which was to aid the San Francisco Mime Troupe. The amazed thirty-six-year-old man was their erstwhile manager, Bill Graham. He saw a percentage in this rocking loft; he saw gleams of a business.

The Mime Troupe were good-time radicals in the Dada vein whose stated goal was to "undermine society" through their street guerrilla theater. Graham had managed as much business as could be mustered—until his patience ran out. He had little sympathy for the griping and pranks of oppressed middle-class kids in a land of plenty. Born Wolfgang Wolodia Grajanka, a Jew, in the Berlin of the 1930s, he'd lost both parents to the gas chambers, but he had managed to escape to the Free World, eventually arriving in New York. Having then toughed his way as a Bronx foster home kid, fought in Korea, gotten a degree in business administration, and finally arrived in 1960s San Francisco as a farm-equipment manufacturer's representative, Bill Graham—filled with all-American business zeal and scarred by European suffering—wasn't about to go wet, woolly, and lovey-dovey with the babes who'd never been bombed—by bombs, that is.

He wanted to stage more benefits and Gleason suggested he rent a bashed-up ballroom in the black ghetto that nudged the Haight. On December 10, 1965, the line to see Jefferson Airplane, the Great Society, and a host of other bands went around the block and beyond. The Fillmore Auditorium made up for its dilapidation with an abundance of space and atmosphere. This could be a groovy—and profitable—environment.

Graham had also booked the Family Dog to perform, so slight was his knowledge of the music game, but Chet Helms soon advised him of his error and the disparate pair were soon in demand as promoters of benefits, dances, and happenings, as heads who could get it all together with no Big Time vibes. When Ken Kesey decided to stage a gargantuan multimedia three-day circus to be called the Trips Festival, Graham was invited to handle the details.

The Trips Festival, in January 1966, marked the culmination of the carefree, hang-loose salad days, the end of psychedelic isolation, and the start of the mass circulation of the news that San Francisco was "where it was all happening." Gleason noted that rock 'n' roll had at last "come of age," implying that the Stone Age of hillbilly beaters and shiny-suited kid crooners was done with. This was the Rock Revolution. Kesey saw his festival as marking a Neon Renaissance and a New Reality, "a new way to look at the world," since the rotten old one was "riddled with radioactive poison." Graham was trying to make sure that the doors of the Longshoremen's Hall were secured, that there were suitable fire escapes, and that the hard drugs were kept hidden.

In effect, the festival was to be an Acid Test without the acid. The multimedia machinery would simulate a trip to *Nirvana* and, if you came a bit stoned, so much the smoother. Over twenty thousand people in a rainbow assortment of fancy dress and arriving in hand-painted, psyched-out cars modeled after the Kesey "magic" bus were to attend, drawn by a bill headed by Kesey and the Merry Pranksters, together with Beatles readings, "the Endless Explosion," "the God Box," Hell's Angels, the vaudeville of Neal Cassady, the music of the Grateful Dead and Big Brother and the Holding Company, and personal appearances by Marshall (*The Media Is the Message*) McLuhan and, of course, Allen Ginsberg. The latter two, surprisingly, were no-shows, but no matter, because the audience had really come to trip on the music and themselves. The Grateful Dead were a huge success, stretching their version of "In the Midnight Hour" until, it seemed, well past breakfast. As for the slide show depicting the plight of the forgotten Indians; "the God Box," in which stoned freaks could bellow over the P.A. about how their heads were expanding on brown rice; and Neal Cassady's vaudeville show of swinging stupidly and dangerously out from the balcony on a rope—it was all the same old stuff to the locals and only the out-of-towners and the press hadn't witnessed such goings on before. Tom Wolfe, outdressed for a change, scribbled away in the men's room.

A silver spaceman kept running around maniacally, stopping to congratulate a fellow freak on his costume, and at one point getting into a nasty row with a tribe of black bongo players who refused to cease and desist: "OK, we've known about all that for three thousand years—but we're now into something *new!*" His tunnel vision did not take in moldy-fig, old-fashioned bongo music. When he later flung open a door to allow a flood of outsiders in for free, the spaceman was in trouble. Graham flew at him in a fury. The silver spaceman pulled off his helmet and grinned idiotically. Of course! It was Kesey himself, in disguise because he was out of jail on probation. Musn't let the fuzz find him at the festival because in court he presents himself as "Mr. Super-Straight Preppy."

There was never any doubt that the whole multimedia simulated drug trip thing was Kesey's creation. He'd pioneered strobes, ectoplasmic slide shows, all the tricks that were to be copied in light shows worldwide. Trouble was, he really didn't understand the power of the music, didn't grow with it—but what was much worse, he was an anarchist. He wasn't organized. The Trips Festival, in Graham's eyes, was an insurance broker's and fire marshal's nightmare. This zoo must be caged and TCB (taking care of business) was the order of the day in the future.

From February on, after the Trips Festival, Graham set the dancehall scene to rights as a business and the first move he made was to take out a lease on the Fillmore Auditorium. The object was to provide a freak's paradise, complete with multimedia trappings and stacks of bands and macrobiotic refreshments, so that the public started their experience the moment they entered the hall and finished it only when they stepped outside back into banality. *But* Graham also took care of business by having an efficient staff to take the money, clean the toilets, post the signs that forbade illegal doings in hang-loose lingo, and bounce the occasional troublemaker. And though the Graham Organization looked to all appearances like part of the tribe, they were nevertheless inheritors of the Barnum & Bailey legacy. Over at the Avalon Ballroom, the altruistic Chet Helms was operating like a clergyman: he was letting them in for free more often than not. He was dispensing the love dream. When it became obvious that Graham was coining in the loot and was well on the way to becoming a millionaire via his dance concert promotions and his management of groups such as Jefferson Airplane, he was accused of being a "rip-off artist." To this he answered: "I don't sell love—I sell talent and environment." Why should he hold back a pop-music development that he could fit into a swell niche in the Grand Order of American Entertainment?

The next obvious step was to spread this new rock around the country—and this could only be done through hit records. There were no labels to speak of in the Bay Area—only Autumn Records (owned by local concert promoter and ex-Top Forty deejay "Big" Tom Donahue), which was in financial trouble. A year back, they'd had great national success with a local group, the Beau Brummels, who'd hit the Top Twenty twice with "Laugh Laugh" and "Just a Little"—but Autumn didn't have the national distribution to sustain the act. Anyway, the Beaus were at the tail end of a curious American craze for British Invader impersonators.

Of the new acid-rock bands, the one that looked most likely to succeed was Jefferson Airplane. Marty Balin, a foxy ex-dancer and sharp-as-a-pin wielder of a large vocabulary, had been running his own club, the Matrix, where he and the Airplane performed a noticeably tidier and more melodic music than the open-ended wanderings of the Grateful Dead. Like the Dave Clark Five, they could be expected to turn up to a benefit or dance concert or Trips Festival *on time*. Graham was impressed and offered them his management; Gleason trumpeted the band in his column. RCA took note, came up to San Francisco, and signed them, making Jefferson Airplane the first Bay Area band to sign with a major label. The L.A.-produced records that resulted were crisp, clean, and rather sterile—a state-of-the-art sound that RCA engineers had spent years perfecting and one perfect for middle-of-the-road music but quite wrong for displaying Jefferson Airplane in flight. How did you capture all the swirling colors and sweet aroma of the acid dream on plain old vinyl? This was to be a continuing problem for the marketeers of the New Sound. Despite this overall blandness of production, the RCA staff and Jefferson Airplane would have two Top Ten singles, "White Rabbit" and "Somebody to Love," and a number-three album, *Surrealistic Pillow*, within the next year.

RCA would certainly have liked to sign up more bands in the fecund Bay Area, but the Colonel refused. No rock 'n' roll outfit was to threaten the throne of his boy Elvis. Sign any more rockers and he would take the boy away—and *bang* goes the company! On the other hand, Warner Bros. Records were hungry indeed. Since their start in the late fifties, they'd been associated with ritzier middle-of-the-road music, light folk music, and comedy. Alan Sherman, Trini Lopez, Dean Martin, and Peter, Paul, and Mary were their stars. Of course, Frank Sinatra (who'd founded Reprise) was a good prestige name, but he was known to detest rock 'n' roll and had even once ordered that there was to be none of that trash on Reprise.

However, Warner Bros./Reprise executives couldn't help but notice that this year's R&R sales figures looked as though they would be 80 percent over 1964 and that, if the trend continued, rock record grosses would be in excess of 25 million units. Early in 1966, a rock record by, of all people, Nancy Sinatra had crashed up to number one ("These Boots Are Made for Walkin'"). A few months later, Warner Bros./Reprise would be surprised by their number seven hit by the Association and even more surprised to learn that the song, "Along Comes Mary," was accused of referring to Mary Jane or marijuana. The company had always been strictly suit and tie. On special occasions, the men would parade in their blue company blazers and it was quite a sight for sore eyes when they marched down the aisle at sales conferences to the music of John Philip Sousa.

But the writing was on the wall—and it was in the form of a psychedelic poster. Joe Smith, general manager of the Warner Bros. half, had already been advising Tom Donahue up at Autumn. The next step was to purchase the ailing but potentially hitbound company. Tom told Joe that he simply must come up and soak in the scene for himself. So Joe made forays, always careful to dress in his usual Ivy League style (he was a Yale man). He witnessed the Grateful Dead in action at Chet Helms's Avalon Ballroom, staunchly standing through the intoxicating smoke and nodding politely when Helms informed him that the under-twenty-fives were now the majority nationwide and not to trust anyone over thirty. Donahue was around as well, urging Smith to sign up the Dead. "This is where the music's going," he said. Smith replied, "I don't think Jack Warner will ever understand this." But he remembered that Warner and his Bros. had had the vision (or the gambler's instinct) to back talking pictures in 1927 when they went with *The Jazz Singer* and he knew that the bottom line for Warner Bros./Reprise was written "R&R." Therefore, bracing himself to his task and keeping in mind—as a onetime disc jockey—that anything goes in the crazy music biz, he ventured into the tribal commune mansion of the Dead. They tried hard, oh so hard, to get Smith to take some acid, but he resisted and lived to return to L.A. to tell his fellow executives that this new rock was worth a shot. He didn't have to work very hard to persuade them: Mo Ostin, head of Reprise and the man who had once had to carry out Sinatra's antirock policy, had already signed a fiery black guitarist who was shaking them up in England—Jimi Hendrix.

And so it was that the Un-Americans, now settled in San Francisco, got the chance to become a moveable feast on vinyl and in concert. Thus the hippies were invited to join the mainstream of American pop. The question was: would they join the tradition and TCB? Or were they revolutionaries who would turn this neat little America of super salesmanship upside down so that the moon would never shine in June again?

* * * *

From KRLA Beat, *October:*

GRANDMA'S VAUDEVILLE SOUND STARTS POP MUSIC TREND

Today's scene has vaudeville music dotting the charts—the New Vaudeville Band's "Winchester Cathedral," Donovan's "Mellow Yellow," Peter and Gordon's "Lady Godiva," and Dr. West's "The Eggplant That Ate Chicago." Ian Whitcomb is well known for his high-pitched falsetto hits, but those who saw him at the Troubadour in L.A. recently saw a whole new side—showing off his ragtime stuff. Many people have wondered why Ian studied history in college and even went on to get his degree while his career was soaring. But when they heard him give a brief history of each ragtime song he sang, when it was written and what was going on in the world at that time, it became obvious. Ian's into the current vaudeville pop scene with "Where Did Robinson Crusoe Go with Friday on Saturday Night?" Record buyer's reaction? Very good—currently, it's at number six on the KRLA request sheet!

October 20:

I'm scribbling this on a couch in the Tower Records reception area, waiting to get an appointment with anybody. George says he'll be right with me, but he said that two hours ago. He's calling across the country to see how our product is doing. I'm pinning my hopes on "Where Did Robinson Crusoe Go with Friday on Saturday Night?" If it clicks big, then I've got a store of ragtime numbers to follow up with and this stuff is wonderful tonic therapy to fill up the holes made in my mind by that dreadful acid trip that I took inadvertently. September flashed by as in a dream. The Troubadour date I remember well, though, as it was such a triumph. The Los Angeles *Times* gave me a good review and among my visitors were painter David Hockney and writer Christopher Isherwood. It's so reassuring to find oneself in real artistic company and, in my own modest way, I feel that I'm bringing a well-timed, healthy Tin Pan Alley sound back to a somewhat jaded pop scene. It is my ambition to make the world into that blue paradise conjured up by such songs as "Halfway to Heaven" (1927). I must say it's been strange to have members of the audience—obviously doped out of their minds—approach me in my dressing room to tell me that my act is a "real crazy trip." Some say they're certain I'm the singer on "Winchester Cathedral" and "The Eggplant That Ate Chicago" and that I must be Napoleon XIV on "They're Coming to Take Me Away, Ha Ha."

I was thrilled that Gary Lewis (of Gary Lewis & the Playboys) dropped in to catch my act. He's had so many sturdy hits over the last year. Productions like "This Diamond Ring" (his producer is Snuff Garrett) show us that America hasn't lost the art of the old slick pop and that the salesmanship that built this country can actually be cooked into the actual final vinyl product. Also, I had a visit from the Swingin' Medallions—all eight of them—resplendent in green paisley trousers, blue shirts, and neatly trimmed hair. Their "Double Shot of My Baby's Love" has become a big fraternity song all over the country after it was pushed by deejays in their home state of Alabama. A nice change to have a baby's love compared to a good old double slug of booze rather than to these sinister drugs. The whole sociology of drink is soaked in history and involves such heart-warming accessories as bottles, cigars, billiard tables, upright pianos, and velvet plush. Not forgetting the old saloon bar rail.

It's odd to be lumped with Donovan in this vaudeville revival trend. "Sunshine Superman," his biggie before "Mellow Yellow," was more good-time blues than vaudeville. I thought it was a terrific number until I was informed it's all about tripping, while "Mellow Yellow" is about the psychedelic potential of smoked banana peel. I must say I find Donovan's press utterances increasingly drippy: *KRLA Beat* reports that he has gone very "magical and mystical" and that his most exciting moment in life is "waking up each morning." He's currently in L.A. and he says he hasn't seen any smog, but he did see "a big, noisy car laying rubber on the road: Twas billowing and blowing, but the pure air sucked ye dirt out." I know I have a tendency to be out of touch with current reality, but this sub-Chaucerian guff really takes the biscuit! Then he goes on to delineate his "rock daydream": a "complete inter-relation of the arts—a concert with Allen Ginsberg recording a Beatles song, John Lennon reading poetry, George Harrison playing the sitar, Paul McCartney making electric tapes, and Bob Dylan taking tickets at the door."

Speaking of real life, I was shocked to read of the death of Bobby Fuller, leader of the Bobby Fuller Four. In August, he was found dead from gasoline consumption in his car. Was it suicide or murder? The Bobby Fuller Four played a transplanted Tex-Mex dance music in clubs and on local TV shows around the L.A. area. They were signed by Bob Keene, who'd earlier scored with Ritchie Valens (of "La Bamba" fame) and, with Bobby's clean-cut good looks, they seemed destined for a decent run in teen-angled movies. Then—tragedy.

Later (Still at Tower Records):

Everybody's still in meetings and George is still tied up on the phone. I wandered around the Capitol Tower, dropping in on a few departments. The sales people are very excited about the number of units sold of their LSD documentary album. Is this exploitation or documentation? The backing music is provided by Fire and Ice, Ltd., who claim to be from San Francisco but I'd guess that San Fernando Valley is nearer the mark. The leader is a flautist who says in his press release that he was born at age zero and is a painter-dancer-singer-poet-and-whatever, famous for spontaneous recitations in Bay Area coffee houses. He also plays reed flute and earth horn. The old reliable *KRLA Beat* is very skeptical and their reporter Carol Deck writes that, "You can't whistle it in the shower." However, she has to admit that this LSD music is where pop is going.

Capitol's own homegrown act, the Beach Boys, are certainly *growing with the music*. They know that if they don't it will grow without them. And they've released an extraordinary masterwork with the topical title of "Good Vibrations." Brian Wilson reportedly says it's the production of his life and sums up his entire philosophy. The record does go through a string of mood changes, which may reflect Brian's mercurial character and his constant search for new philosophies. Derek Taylor tells me that Brian has a huge library of books, none of which is light reading. No Jeeves or Philip Marlowe. He's deeply into astrology and numerology, Derek says, and he wants to absorb everything that's ever been achieved in great art in one big swallow. Currently, he's hobnobbing with a head-spinning avant-garde musician named Van Dyke Parks, reputed to be a genius. Parks's complex weaving of endless fussy rap sentences makes him almost unintelligible and the unfortunate rub-off on Brian has been that it now takes him ages to delineate in words that he would like some cheesecake à la mode. Obfuscation seems to be the order of the day in the once bright, sunny, and simple world of the Beach Boys. "Good Vibrations" has a fine—if erratic—dance beat, with surf echoes and touches of blue-eyed R&B—but it's awfully drawn out and I really prefer my art in more lucid and traditional forms: like a gallery, library, or museum.

"Good Vibrations" was the first commercially successful pop record made on the premise of art for art's sake and never mind the time and expense. The logistics are staggering: fifteen sessions at four different studios over six months, with the use of ninety hours of recording tape, resulting in eleven different versions at an end cost of approximately $60,000. Luckily, the sales justified the means: in December 1966, the record reached number one in the U.S.A. and gave the group their biggest hit ever. Magazines ranging from *The Saturday Evening Post* to little handmade rock sheets like *Crawdaddy* rushed to analyze this work in detail. What was not revealed was the contribution made by hallucinatory drugs to the furious energy and wild imagination of this work. Sand and surf would never look the same again. Nor, hoped the Beach Boys, would the record industry. They were about to give that corpulent bureaucracy some "entirely new concepts" by forming their own label, Brother Records, which was to have "total creative and promotional control over the product." Capitol agreed to connive in this commercialized Boy's Town and everybody concerned looked forward to a bright future in this world turned upside down (where the bottom line was still on the bottom and still black).

While the Beach Boys were revolutionizing their teen image by becoming artists, Bob Dylan had become a complete recluse, locked away in a rented estate in upstate New York while he recuperated from a near-fatal motorcycle accident he'd suffered in July. But in May, he'd released a double album that in its own way was as revolutionary as "Good Vibrations." On *Blonde on Blonde,* Dylan revealed his love affair with Nashville and the country pickers.

Any thinking rock fan could have told you that Nashville was capable of producing only plastic-coated, oily, whine 'n' slide sludge. What did country music have to do with rock? (Indeed, what did Elvis have to do with it?) The South was beyond the pale, as usual. But here was the modern bard relaxing down in Nashville with some good-ole-boy session men, pickers who had picked for (ugh!) Patti Page and her ilk. The result though was mind-boggling: a slew of songs that were the zenith of the poet's life, ranging from the twelve-minute poesy of "Sad Eyed Lady of the Lowlands" to the pizza-parlor dixieland feel of "Rainy Day Women #12 & 35." Here was Dylan turning his back on the problems of the temporal world and looking inward toward his own spiritual salvation. Religious images abounded. There were allusions to rebirth and Zen reflections on the necessity for destroying the alienating ego. However, the accompaniment was as superlative as a lazy afternoon by the ole swimmin' hole and sessioneer Charlie McCoy wrote a folksy article for *Hit Parader* about the good fun and hijinks they'd all enjoyed with the somber-clothed, Beatle-booted poet: "I don't believe I've ever seen anybody that had so much concentration and is so serious. When Dylan is in the studio, everything is strictly business. But it's a lot of fun, too, because he's very open-minded and he takes suggestions from everybody." Dylan turned out to be a lover of moon pies and hominy grits—and also of the records of C&W singer Ray Price. "The night we cut 'Rainy Day Women #12 & 35,' Dylan said he wanted to get a kind of Salvation Army sound, so they asked me if I could find a slide trombone player. I said, 'Yeah, I've got one in my band, Wayne Butler.' So I called him and asked him if he could be over to the studio by midnight. He came over and, seventeen minutes later, we sent him home because we finished the thing. Actually what had happened, we did it in one take and it was so great we let it stay the way it was." A photo of Dylan at the piano accompanied this *Hit Parader* article. The caption read: "See how pensive he is? Actually, he's balancing the budget for Gabby Hayes's fan club!"

I remember that on my first hearing of "Rainy Day Women #12 & 35" I thought, "Great! Here's a superhero joining the vaudeville revival," and I went in and recorded a brass-band dixieland number straight away. But then I heard that the song was all about drugs and then I saw the weird, blurry pictures on the *Blonde on Blonde* album cover and I got a headache and wondered where it was all going and whether I was going with it. . . .

Hollywood, October 21:

George finally got off the phone, but by that time it was late, so I went "home," tried to pull down the Murphy bed, tried to heat up a frozen dinner, finally went to bed on the floor again. We went to Martoni's this evening in order to chat up a few program directors, as George said the deejays have absolutely no power anymore now that Top Forty is boss radio and playlists are tight and safe and chosen by these directors, who are mean, hard men who never smile or pick up a tab. To prove his point about deejays being reduced to automatons reading out the time, temperature, and odd slogan ("This is Boss Angeles Radio!") and often going under air names common to many stations, George got Martoni's host to announce a phone call for a "Johnny Dark"—and five men leaped off their bar stools and headed for the phone booth.

But if a deejay is skilled and pushy enough, he can sneak his own personal slogans into the roaring parade of hits as they rotate twenty-four hours a day and thereby establish a Top Forty personality and maybe even a local TV show. "The Real" Don Steele is such a man and George and I cornered him as he nursed a Jack Daniel's with a twist of lemon in a dark corner of this music-biz gathering spot. I failed to find out why he's called "The Real." But he was very vocal about why his gurgle in the flow of boss hits was different: "I'm a hard-sell announcer with a phonetic hang-up. I dig sound. You don't have to know what I mean with my little spoonerisms, but I like 'em when they have quadruple meanings." "You mean 'aphorisms,' 'Real Don'?" I put in. George kicked me under the table. "Whatever. Here's one I dig: 'It ain't that bad if you fry it right.' I think it sounds *go!*" "I see. Can you think of any more?" "Wait a minute. . . . 'If you got it—flaunt it!' I use these for my IDs. The format requires you to give the time, so I came up with, 'It ain't that bad if you fry it right' at three-thirty and 'If you got it—flaunt it' at four. Then 'Spread your love' at five-thirty and so on." I told "Real Don" that what he was effecting was real art form, but his attention had been distracted by the sudden appearance of a wizened little man with a mass of wild gollyberry hair and large sunglasses. "Spector!" uttered Steele. "The guy's a specter!"

The once-cocky record producer looked very sheepish and surly. George told me that Phil's reign as King of Teen was over and that no longer was there any hush of awe when he entered Martoni's. This was due to the failure of his self-acclaimed masterpiece "River Deep—Mountain High" sung, way in the background, by R&B shouters Ike and Tina Turner. After countless mixes and over $22,000, the Philles record got only as far as number eighty-eight on the *Billboard* chart of June 18. Spector was appalled and dazed and, in this state, he bad-mouthed some radio people. Word spread, tarnishing the Spector name. He just wasn't one of the boys and he wasn't playing by the new rules with this epic-length record in which the same tired old blues licks and shouts were echoed and re-echoed till they almost blew down the Wall of Sound. The Beach Boys are doing fine with "Good Vibrations," but then they're where it's at, as they say, and they don't go around bad-mouthing. At least Brian's spacey gibberish doesn't appear to be sniping at the radio folks. So Spector is no longer King and, George says, he doesn't even show any interest in the business anymore, but just spins out his days playing pool, doing errands for his mother, and roaming the darker and danker byways of Martoni's unrecognized—how sad! I hope I'm right about this upcoming vaudeville trend. I don't want to end up in the trash bin.

Disgusted by the performance of "River Deep—Mountain High," which he believed had been deliberately torpedoed by radio, Phil Spector retired from the business and folded his Philles Records after three more indifferent releases. A great era had been ended by the very medium that Spector had once thrived in. His Little Symphonies were best heard on tinny car radios. On stereo systems, they sounded very Sears, Roebuck and the Top Forty radio that now ruled the AM roost had no place for quirky eccentrics like Spector. He simply didn't fit the format.

The idea for Top Forty—jukebox of the airwaves—had been conceived by T. Storz, a canny media man, while he enjoyed a beer in an Omaha bar, back in 1955. Noticing that in the course of an hour the same jukebox records were picked over and over again, he decided to institutionalize this by establishing a tight playlist on his chain of radio stations. The formula also dictated that deejays must limit their activities to cueing up discs, giving the time, news, and weather, and briefly back-announcing numbers after a music sweep. "Shut up and play the pop" was the order of the day—and the formula was to prove very successful.

On the West Coast, this format was taken over by a quartet of radio programmers headed by Bill Drake. They did careful demographic research to break down their audience by age, area, and income. And to hide the cold business calculation and give the impression of a nonstop swinging party hosted by motor-mouthed zanies, Drake & Company employed screaming "boss jocks" to float segues of phonetic inanities ("Take that piece of meat, put it in your pan, and fry it, baby!") across the stream of pop. These deejays were to have no real power or personality—their sound and fury signifying nothing that might interfere with the flow of established hits. "They just keep on coming!" was one of the required slogans.

Drake's stations kept rigidly to the "Drake clock," which divided up the hour into segments during which business must be conducted (especially the plugging of station IDs) between the playing of only the top thirty-three records of the Top Forty. Drake was trying to cut this number down even further, so that more commercials could be squeezed in, preferably advertising jingles with a current pop sound. On the whole, requests were ignored, the tiny playlist being made up from trade paper charts and record store sales reports. Additions of unproven but promising records were chosen by skilled radio "doormen." Bill Drake himself boasted that he could tell whether a record "had momentum to fly hitbound" by listening to only the first four seconds. "It must come on strong" was his dictum. And, of course, it must "make it in context"—meaning the "Drake clock."

All this was bad news for me, since none of my current work seemed to fit these requirements. I had become very fond of KRLA, the British Invasion station in Pasadena, and George was starting to achieve a rapprochement with the program director there. He was now allowed into the inner office. In 1966, unhappily, KRLA was knocked from its perch as the number-one rocker in L.A. by the flagship of the Drake chain, KHJ of Hollywood. To make matters worse, George had learned that Ian Whitcomb records were blacklisted by the Drake chain because of my backstage bungle in San Diego in 1965, when I had attempted to tweak the beard of a program director who looked like Abraham Lincoln. This man turned out to be one of Bill Drake's partners.

Chemical warfare from San Francisco, coupled with the grim regimentation of Top Forty radio, spelled out a rough ride ahead for yours truly. So it was with some relief that I set forth on a massive series of cross-country tours. Maybe the hinterland would still be open to my charms and to the rebirth of ragtime. . . .

Somewhere in Kansas, November 1:
This isn't a bit like last year, when I was a hot star and *16* magazine held a contest to see who'd win the shirt off my back. A cold wind is blowing across the plains and nobody remembers my hits. They come up and ask, "Didn't you have a record once?" During my crisscross tours so far, I've run into a number of other British Invaders in similarly dire straits. Freddie and the Dreamers have lost some of their bounce, the Hollies are considering moving on to more substantial music, and Dave Clark may be going into the health business. The Liverpool Five were advised to return to Liverpool, which would be silly since they are all Americans.

One of the reasons why we Invaders are finding the gigging hard is that our material is too jolly and nervy for the new mood of the country. The dreaded drugs have taken hold even out here on the lone prairie. Boys in pudding-basin haircuts with pudding faces to match are experimenting with drugs and trying to express the pathetic mangle of Beatles-inspired psychedelic imagery their corn-fed minds dream up ("See the melting cornflake fly across the custard sky") via the technology of the electric guitar. Last year, these country lads enjoyed the simple pleasures of Saturday night auto cruising and making out at the drive-in—and indulging in beer busts and panty raids if they were college students. Now they have been shot pell-mell into the mind-blowing welter of psychedelia. The result is ludicrous.

Mind you, some of the benefits of drug imagery, in which ordinary matter becomes transcendental and surreal, have rubbed off on me. I've been finding that my "Where Did Robinson Crusoe Go with Friday on Saturday Night?" song has audiences deeply puzzled—there are so many hypotheses as to where Crusoe *did* go on that fateful Saturday night. Also, my impersonation of the New Vaudeville Band singing "Winchester Cathedral" has engendered cries of "neosurrealism." The idea of a cathedral being blamed for not tolling its bell when my baby walked out on me has tickled the fancy of these Midwesterners. As for my version of "The Eggplant That Ate Chicago," well, this has them flailing in the aisles in a Holy Roller frenzy, especially when I warn that the monstrous vegetable may eat their own city soon.

Of course, I make it a point *not* to inform my audience that these numbers have in fact been recorded by other people. Why tell the truth when Middle America seems convinced that the tunes are my originals?

I have always admired "one-hit wonders"—those dazzling comets who zoom in with one splendid disc then vanish into oblivion, avoiding the tedious process of going on to become album artists and thus taking themselves seriously. I suppose I fall into this category—unless this rag-time/vaudeville bit gets going. One of the current groups of this sort that I love is ? and the Mysterians, with their masterpiece, "96 Tears." They may well go on to other successes, but for my money they've said it all in this song, relating (to the mesmerizing wail of a surreal fair-ground organ that switches chillingly from major to minor) a tale of sexual revenge whereby the bruised lover—who is right now put down by his laughing lady—will, come the dawn, be on top—with his cried-out girlfriend looking up at him. I learn from teen magazines that ? never takes off his sunglasses, that his real name is Rudy Martinez, and that this Chicano group was recorded in their hometown of Saginaw, Michigan. In photos, the boys scowl furiously, which may be a reflection of decades of white oppression. "96 Tears" sounds like it was recorded in somebody's garage. Could this be a new way of reducing studio costs? In any case, this aggressive music has been labeled "punk."

I keep being switched from package tour to package tour. This must be the work of one of those brown-blazered, stripe-tied agents back in Beverly Hills. I'm currently with the William Morris Agency and last week they sent me to a "Shower of Stars" show in Birmingham, Alabama, with the Hollies and the Dave Clark Five; then I hopped it across the state with the Barbarians to a gig in Montgomery. They are a friendly lot, but Moulty, the drummer, cuts a terrifying figure with his artificial iron claw hand. To play the drums, he unscrews the claw and replaces it with a drumstick. As we drove through one-horse tank towns, the Barbarians had a disconcerting habit of firing off handguns into the less-affluent neighborhoods. I was relieved to say good-bye and hightail it by air to join this current tour of Kansas.

Among the acts here is a group from Tower Records called the Standells. They're Tower's current darlings because of their hits "Dirty Water" and "Sometimes Good Guys Don't Wear White," songs which celebrate surly rebellion without being tied to any specific complaint, either political, social, or economic. Their records snarl and sneer and scorn all parents to a backing of Stones' riffs and fuzz-box guitar. This attitude goes down extremely well in the Midwest, where there's really not much to do after the fields have been tended. The Standells themselves, however, are perfectly gentle boys and very considerate to a seasoned buffer like me. They're very amused by my ukulele songs. I was surprised to learn that their material is written by an older gent named Ed Cobb, who used to be a member of that smooth-sounding close harmony group the Four Preps.

Being from Hollywood, the Standells haven't much time for this hayseed psychedelic/rebellion stage that the Kansas locals are currently effecting. The little teenybopper girls who used to press their noses against the tour bus windows seem to have evaporated. These days, we see so many callow youths, all serious and dazed-looking. They want to talk to us about Frank Zappa, their hero. The main thing that comes to mind about Zappa is that he picks his nose onstage, without shame and obviously as part of his act. The old annoy-the-bourgeoisie game. He seems to have a particular aversion to suburban life-styles and to growing up in the fifties (which I thought a perfect period in which to pass through adolescence—placid, secure, womblike). Back in Hollywood, I met Zappa briefly through a mutual acquaintance and I found him heavily intellectual, rather withdrawn, and curiously ambivalent about his family memories. He showed us some slides of suburban housewives in curlers with their pot-bellied men, which we were all supposed to laugh at. But then, accidentally, he threw some shots of his family taken in the fifties onto the screen and he fell into a loving, nostalgic silence.

Zappa's music is very eclectic, ranging from Stravinsky to doo-wop, and his Mothers of Invention band is first-rate, technically. *Freak Out*, his first album, is trying to shake the Establishment, but I have a suspicion that Zappa is a master of irony—if not sarcasm—and has nothing but contempt for most current rock and for its sheeplike audience. But maybe I'm just getting cynical; maybe *I'm* burned out from too many days of chasing rainbows.

Omaha, Nebraska, November 11 (Armistice Day):
Most refreshing to be touring with Paul Revere and the Raiders: clean bus, dates always on schedule, well-behaved audiences, very little druggery backstage. This is all due to Paul Revere himself, who runs a tight ship but a happy one. I've no clear idea what his age is, but Revere has certainly seen a lot of life, starting out as a barber in his hometown of Portland, Oregon (a very tidy state), and later having to work in a lunatic asylum because his religious convictions prevented him from serving in the military. In the early sixties, he joined the frenetic, largely instrumental Northwest scene when he formed a band called the Downbeats. Stomping, honking numbers like "Night Train" and "Raunchy" were featured and they say that this sound—typical of the area—was a prime influence on the California surf music that followed. Paul's group (now called Paul Revere and the Raiders, with Paul on organ and his pal Mark Lindsay on sax) cut for little local labels and, in April 1961, they managed to reach number thirty-eight nationally with a honky-tonk piano rocker called "Like Long Hair" on Gardena. They also recorded "Louie Louie," which had become something of a high school hop anthem, but Jerry Dennon beat them to the punch with his version by the Kingsmen, also from Portland. In 1965, they were signed by Dick Clark as regular house band on his new series for teens, "Where the Action Is," a show shot on location and all lip-synched. By this time, of course, they were clad in American Revolution jackets and britches. Choreography and comedy were high priorities and their total effect was seen as an antidote to the growing decadence of rock (begun by the second wave of British Invaders led by the Stones).

I remember appearing on a "Where the Action Is," down on the Los Angeles docks sometime in 1965. But I hardly exchanged a word with Paul or the lads because we were all working so hard. On this current tour, I've been able to get to know him much better and I find he's doing a sterling job of steering the kids away from all the temptations of modern life. For example, one of the Raiders' hits is a sort of pop sermon called "Kicks," in which, to a cunning accompaniment of Beatles lead guitar lines and Byrds bass figures, they warn a girl about the dangers of drug use. A highly moral number and I'm pleased to see it was written by Barry Mann and Cynthia Weil, who brought us so many of the Phil Spector-produced compositions.

Many a night as the bus has hummed past the flatlands of Nebraska, Paul Revere and I have discussed the moral turpitude of this once-great land and the insidious spread of the drug culture. I have already had to report to Paul the presence of several pot smokers among our traveling troupe. This is rather like being back at school again—as the house prefect I never was. We keep hearing stories about a very popular new TV series called "The Monkees" that is supposed to be bringing back the cheerful zaniness of the early Beatles; thereby filling a teen void created by the Liverpool boys when they decided to go more serious and more musical. Because we've been scuttling around the country, we've not had time to watch this show in its entirety. So the other night, just before the gig, Paul and I sat down and watched the show.

I have to report that, though there's little to fault in the sheer slick professionalism, I can't really warm to the madcap antics of the Monkees. They're like marionettes and the songs are very vapid. It's all so fast it gives me a headache. The point is, I really should admire this carefully produced package because it has been created by clever New York Brill Building hands who once hobnobbed with Phil Spector. Don Kirshner, who used to run Aldon Music and discovered so many talents like Neil Sedaka, Carole King, Gerry Goffin, and Barry Mann, has packaged the series and got the above writers to contribute songs. They all seem to hit the charts. Yes, I should admire the Monkees. They're bringing back the old show biz, but somehow I'm left cold. Am I going mad?

My sanity on this tour is under severe strain. But I mustn't complain. Here I am where the masses are—and they're all potential buyers of Tower Records. I shall be content if I can spread the optimism of the best of popular music, if I can somehow make the world like the words of the songs: "Smile, Darn Ya, Smile!" and "Happy Days Are Here Again." The world is as it ought to be, somewhere at the end of the rainbow. No sign of "Where Did Robinson Crusoe Go with Friday on Saturday Night?" on the charts.

Meanwhile, the Beatles had released an album in August that marked a departure from the upbeat perky charm of their previous records. While the Monkees kept the merry moptop spirit going (abetted by American magazines, who were celebrating Swinging London a year too late) the Beatles' *Revolver* was a drab-looking record with an odd title. Yet on the record, the four offered a tremendously varied selection of songs, demonstrating that they were not tied to the restrictions of rock 'n' roll. Paul's "Eleanor Rigby," a tear-jerking melodrama about all the lonely people of Liverpool and the world, was sung to a stark and jerking background of a string octet. George attacked the Inland Revenue in "Taxman" and laid on the sitars again in "Love You To," both of which were his own compositions. John got metaphysical in "She Said She Said" and "And Your Bird Can Sing," but he dipped into philosophy of *The Tibetan Book of the Dead* for the imagery in "To-morrow Never Knows." In the background were some very discon-certing sound effects and the tune itself had a drowning smile about it. Combined with the "New Austerity" Lennon look of short hair and wire glasses, the effect was troubling. But Ringo brought us back to the safe past with "Yellow Submarine," a rivival of a World War I number and full of fun.

What the world didn't know at that time was that John, Paul, and George had journeyed into drugs. LSD, of the high-grade and quality-controlled Owsley variety, expanded their imaginations in an airy way that was to result in songs on future albums that would look back cryp-tically in wonder ("Strawberry Fields" and "Penny Lane") and for-ward into a mess of half-baked Eastern fakery. But the boys never let LSD take the throne in the San Francisco manner—their personalities were too strong and obtuse for that—and there was always George Mar-tin, a drug virgin, to tether their yellow balloons. Martin knew that ev-erything in music had been done before and that experiment was the oldest cliché in the business. The secret of the new pop was a fresh mix of old ingredients and, with some scored trumpets and cellos whisked into a basically heavy rock track of "Strawberry Fields," plus a very adroit bit of electronic wizardry (to make the two tracks, which had been recorded at different keys and tempos, sound as one), Martin con-tributed substantially to the "trippy" sound of the final record. A charming slice of nostalgia became a vessel for the pouring in of psy-chedelic dreams.

"Penny Lane" was more straightforward, requiring only the addition of a B flat piccolo trumpet, the closest approximation to the sound that Paul had in his mind after he'd heard Bach's *Brandenburg Concerti*. Both these songs were Liverpudlian memoirs and they were joined by a salute to a great Lancastrian comedian, the ukulele man himself, George Formby: "When I'm Sixty Four" was garnished with three clar-inets to give it the "kind of tooty sound" Paul required. A ululele would have made the record too much of a pastiche. These three Lancastrian numbers, all very much in the British music-hall tradition, were the ten-tative basis for an album that the Beatles were planning during the au-tumn of 1966. Nobody guessed that this was the road to *Sgt. Pepper's Lonely Hearts Club Band*. But there were signs that this was where the trail divided for John, Paul, and Brian Epstein. When Brian popped into the studio one night and offered a small criticism over the inter-com, John snapped back with, "Stick to your percentages, Brian, and we'll take care of the music!" A bitter blow to a man who always saw himself as an artist and who certainly had the artistic temperament. No

consolation to see his fortunes regularly covered in the business section
of the prestigious *Sunday Times.*

In December, I flew home to England and was relieved to find a fantasy island where Tom Jones ruled the charts with a country song concerning the dreams of a condemned prisoner, "Green Green Grass of
Home." Pete Townshend was still furious with Ken Dodd for setting
pop back when his group was trying to take great leaps forward. As I
left California, L.A. radio was effecting a bridge that I had always
feared would lead to madness: setting real-life misery to beautiful
music. The station was heavily plugging Simon and Garfunkel's irony-
laden version of "Silent Night," which had the duo singing like sweet-
voiced choir boys against a background of news reports concerning
Richard Speck, a murderer of many nurses; an investigation into anti-
Vietnam protesters by the House Un-American Activities Committee
(HUAC); the death from narcotics of comedian Lenny Bruce; racial
discrimination in housing; Dr. Martin Luther King's planned march
into the racially tense Chicago suburb of Cicero; and former Vice-
President Nixon's forecast that the Vietnam war would last another five
years. "That's the seven o'clock edition of the news. Good night,"
signed off the firm-voiced newsman—and I was shocked to learn that he
was Charlie O'Donnell, a onetime sunny Southland fun jock at Beatles station KRLA. Reality and pop had met with a great bang that
shook me to my roots. I was so glad to be returning to the land where
Christmas had been invented and I was looking forward to seeing, if
not the Beatles, at least Freddie and the Dreamers and Ken Dodd in
Christmas panto.

The holiday mail flopped onto the floor of my family's flat in London
as the postman stamped off singing "If I Were a Carpenter" (Bobby
Darin's contribution to the new poetic strain in rock). Among the cards,
I found a telegram:

IAN, WE HAVE TRIED EVERYTHING LEGAL TO MAKE "ROBINSON CRUSOE"
HIT THE CHARTS, BUT HE MUST HAVE GONE OUT TO LUNCH PER-
MANENTLY ON THAT FATEFUL SATURDAY NIGHT, SO FORGET REVIVED
VAUDEVILLE AND THINK PSYCHEDELIC. YOURS SPACEFULLY, J.J. WAVE,
VICE-PRESIDENT OF NEW VENTURES, TOWER RECORDS CORP.

6

1967: "THIS IS THE END"

It was the great Serbian psychoanalyst Josef Vilya who concluded that chronic depression is the result of a head-on collision between dream and reality. The patient dreams of becoming King but goes on to become a member of the taxpaying public. Dreams of the night and day, hopes, ambitions, yearnings, goals—all are sighted too high, are too ethereal and mellifluous to blend with the jangling atonality of life on earth. Hence, depression.

This was the case in 1967 when, in the dashing and valiant Summer of Love, the cloud-capped message was spread throughout the rock brotherhood that Flower Power conquers all villainy, that a select band of crusading children—the Beautiful People—by setting an example through *doing their thing* (which was doing whatever you liked, pro-

viding you didn't violate your neighbor's space) would change the
wicked world. Petal against metal, soft words of love, the touch of hand
in hand, and a general demeanor of utter helplessness would wipe the
slate clean of blood and guts. Apart from a little help from some dope
dealer friends, "All You Need Is Love." At last, the music manufacturers were believing the lyrics of their escape reveries, so that now the
sky might actually rain "Pennies from Heaven" because "Love Makes
the World Go Round." (They forgot that these songsmiths of the past
had also warned us that we live under a "Paper Moon" in a honky-tonk
parade where the melody is the cheap jingle-jangle in the amusement
arcade down near the Dodg.'ems.)

Could silly love songs change the world? At the end of the year, San
Francisco's Flower Power wilted and was replaced by the Jeremiah wail
of a grim and daunting band from hard-working, no-nonsense L.A. The
Doors were the pipers at the gates of hell. This is the end of civilization. Redemption comes only through death.

Meanwhile, the straight world got on with the job of making the
world run along the rickety old tracks. They took their Bacharach
lightly, while their babies cried to sleep over the Monkees.

As for me, the sight of the Beautiful People—with their bells, beads,
caftans, frilly shirts, and flower-patterned suits—parading in the monochrome of Britain was simply California Carnaby. I'd seen it all before
in miniature last summer up in the Haight at Gale's pad. I didn't realize that the private club would go public in 1967. Now, as an ex-star, I
had a decision to make: should I join the carnival of progressive rock or
should I have a go at becoming a regular in the duller world of mainstream pop?

Popular music was splitting into the two streams of rock and pop, a
split begun by the Beatles with *Rubber Soul* in 1966. *Rock* meant producing concept albums, holding a life-style in common, subscribing to
certain philosophical views, and breaking down the proscenium arch
that hitherto had separated Pop Art from real life. This could mean
taking your rock stardom seriously, even unto death. *Pop* entailed making hit singles, smiling and being nice to the mums and dads and senior
citizens, and getting a good night's rest and a round of golf on the
weekends.

I looked to leadership, but there was silence. The King was no longer
rocking. He was committed to conveyor-belt movies and their soporific
sound tracks. *New Musical Express* writer Alan Smith complained, "I
think Presley has a fine, wasted singing voice and a tremendous, wasted
potential acting ability." His colleague Chris Hutchins managed to
catch the Colonel in his Hollywood office and to voice the true rocker's
sadness at the present stodgy state of the King of Rock 'n' Roll. Back

barked the Colonel, "People say Elvis's pictures aren't doing so good these days. I tell you we've made twenty-two pictures and nineteen have been big box-office successes. How do you argue with that kind of success? It's like asking Maxwell House to change their coffee formula when the stuff is selling like there's no tomorrow!" But surely, ventured Chris Hutchins, producers could find better scripts for Presley? "I never look at scripts—Elvis does that. I set the deals. . . . If Elvis hasn't found the right script yet, he's earned a lot of money trying to for the last ten years! Isn't it better to get a good price? How could I pay for our Christmas advert in the *New Musical Express* if I didn't get the money?" Then the Colonel checked to make sure the call wasn't collect.

All this money talk was too much for me. Surely the music had gotten beyond mere cash? I decided to investigate the progressive rock scene in London and see what I could learn. New Year's Eve at the Roundhouse sounded promising: GIANT FREAK-OUT ALL-NIGHT RAVE, screamed the pop-paper ads. An intriguing mixture of West Coast "happening" and British "looning," sweet smoke and stale beer, cosmos in the sawdust.

Once a British Railways storage shed, the Roundhouse had become the theater of the local underground movement. In the past, our avant-garde had been a loose band of poets, painters, and happening-makers whose only connection with music had been ill-conceived evenings of poetry read to jazz. Now, with pretentiousness creeping into rock, the avant-garde—as in America—was ready to join forces with eldritch new bands in search of a showcase. Two grubby clubs—the Middle Earth and the UFO Club—gave hearings to such bands amid an atmosphere of incense, health food, and interplanetary news bulletins. The Roundhouse, a North London version of the Fillmore and just as ramshackle, was a theater of sorts and could squeeze in a lot more people than just members of the fringe. In October of the previous year, a party had been held there to launch the *International Times,* nationally distributed newspaper of the new rock-inspired British Underground. The editor knew Peter Asher and the Beatles; Lennon was known to be very interested in offbeat, far-out arts and crafts.

On New Year's Eve, this theater was very cold indeed and I was glad to be wearing my U.S. Army raincoat and Fair-Isle sweater. None of the lavatories were working and the chips were soggy. The promised freak-out wasn't very relaxing, as a savage bunch of geezers somewhere out in the icy gloom were throwing bottles at the happenings onstage. The acts were doing their best to kill contemporary British life by as-

saulting us with the required *son et lumière* show: the Who, Pink
Floyd, and the Move.

I was sorry to see the once-proud Who reduced to performing for
such a bunch of jerks. Due to lawsuits and resulting record label
switches, the Who had yet to break big in America. Back at home, they
were marking time while their management looked hard for a new gimmick to hook on to. The underground would make do for the time
being. Besides, they needed ready cash and this Roundhouse rave-up
could help. Performing to a light show on about the level of a vicarage
slide presentation, the Who did their best to amaze and confound by
sending out smoke bombs while trying to break the sound barrier. At
the height of the happening, the theater's electrical circuit blew and
the ensuing silence was eerie. Just the chattering of teeth and metal
strings on blocks of wood. It was as if pop progress had been stopped
and we were plunged back into the Dark Ages. This would never have
happened in efficient California. Pete Townshend recovered in a few
minutes and, in revenge, smashed up some loudspeakers. He'd rather
have been touring America than looning in this pisspot, but unfortunately the days of British rock rule were long over and the Americans
were once more calling the tune in pop. So it was *all go* on the freaking
out, even in this ice-cold barn.

The Move, a precursor of the Electric Light Orchestra, weren't ready
for America yet. They had their hands full upsetting the locals in Britain. I had a slight connection to the group, since I knew Denny Cordell, their record producer, and I had once brushed up against Tony
Secunda, their manager. When Cordell and Secunda had been working for Seltaeb (the Beatles' spin-off merchandising company that
ended in lawsuits), I had one day sailed into their offices, only to be
savagely attacked by a dog about the same size and with the disposition
of the hound of the Baskervilles. As I complained to Denny about the
damage to my fur coat, I heard an exceedingly coarse and cockney
voice from somewhere deep in Seltaeb shout: "Keep your bleeding Public School gits out of our business!" This, I later learned, was Tony
Secunda. Later, when he was informed that I was breaking out on the
U.S. charts, he became most egregious, sending me out to buy a new
coat of my choice with no expense spared. I had to admire his expansive gestures and, since that incident, I had followed his progress and
marveled at his brazen flash.

Once just another Birmingham beat group, the Move, under the
Secunda thumb, had been decked out first in Chicago gangster suits,
next in East Indian mystic togs ("Brum Raga"), and were now the darlings of the underground set in their new role as neoanarchists. Mind
expansion was not their line, though they had been instructed by their

management to claim that their latest record, "Night of Fear," was about an LSD trip. Spokesman Carl Wayne confided to friends that he hadn't "a bloody clue what it's all about," but the Denny Cordell-produced record (inspired by the *1812 Overture*) was to reach number two on the British charts by February 1967. The Move's tunes were sturdy and catchy and Nancy Sinatra later considered recording their beautiful ballad "Flowers in the Rain." But their live act was built for banner headlines: stages were chopped up, cars were wrecked, TV sets were smashed to smithereens, and effigies of Adolf Hitler were mangled. Chief executioner Carl Wayne claimed to have axed fifteen stages, admitting that "Freak-outs are a bit of a joke, aren't they?" and announcing that the Move's greatest desire was "to cause a riot." Their publicity apogee occurred when they were successfully sued by Prime Minister Harold Wilson, an admitted Beatles fan, for publishing a caricature postcard of him as part of the promotion campaign for "Flowers in the Rain."

At this New Year's Eve bash, I found the Move to be amusing—and most helpful: the warmth given off from the bonfire of TV sets, wrecked cars, and effigies of Hitler was much appreciated by all of us freak-out fans. I did notice a contingent of the Metropolitan Police and London Fire Brigade standing by, stamping their feet and making careful notes. They had little to concern them in the antics of the next ensemble—for Pink Floyd were well within the public safety regulations and the only law they broke was an unwritten one: "Please don't bore." But this group was closest to the psychedelic canon, with their tedious light show, endless numbers crammed with aimless guitar solos supported by organ chords from a submerged cathedral, and lyrics that slid from Fairyland to outer space and back again with no time for a breather.

Like every British group in these chronicles, Pink Floyd had started as an R&B revival band. It is ironic that such an earthy, Afro-American form as the blues—so often concerned with such down-to-earth topics as food and sex—should become a vehicle to convey earthlings on spiritual journeys. It was a light-year's voyage from Dave Bartholemew's "Who Drink My Beer While I Wuz in Der Rear?" to Pink Floyd's "Astronomy Domine" and "Interstellar Overdrive"—but both were knee-deep in the blues. In fact, the very name Pink Floyd was taken from a record by two Georgian bluesmen named Pink Anderson and Floyd Council.

This record was part of a collection owned by Syd Barrett, a student at the Camberwell School of Art (notorious for its encouragement of outré experimentalism). Rescuing Roger Waters, Rick Wright, and Nick Mason (erstwhile architecture students at the Regent Street Poly-

technic, a dim academy) from grim nights pounding out R&B standards
and even "Louie Louie" as the Abdabs, Barrett wrought them into the
Pink Floyd Sound and then—taking a hint from rumors reaching the
grainy Isles that strange things were happening in San Francisco—
simply Pink Floyd. By that time, Barrett had consumed his first batch
of LSD. His mind soared, wind whistling in the holes, and he was
filled with wondrous visions of strange tales from far planets. He was
beoming an interstellar radio receiver.

A local hippie management company, Blackhill Enterprises, was
drawn to Pink Floyd as a homegrown spin-off of a West Coast phenomenon that could catch fire. They signed them and made certain that the
group was always equipped with a mass of aural and visual equipment.
The lighting man, Mick Lowe, became as important as a member of
the group. Freak-out promoters eagerly hired them because they alone
had the correct equipment. In person, as I have noted, they could be tedious or trippy, depending on one's predisposition, but on record they
fit nicely into novelty rock. In Britain at that time, it was still necessary
to make hit singles in order to break into the Big Time. The average
pop fan didn't have the pocket money to fork out for albums as yet,
unlike the affluent American teen, and it so happened that singles were
Syd Barrett's métier: "See Emily Play" and "Arnold Layne" were
charming, whimsical conceits and well within the British tradition of
naughty nonsense. "Arnold Layne," for example, is the story of a man
who steals women's underwear from their clotheslines. Sadly, Barrett's
behavior was to become unpredictable and his speech incomprehensible
due to his LSD diet and he and Pink Floyd were forced to part company (most amicably). He had proved a promising singles writer and
without him the Floyd were to demonstrate that elephants can fly and
to pose the question: "But is it all worth the effort and cost?"

After the Roundhouse rave-up, I thought I'd better make my presence felt, so I pottered around to backstage. Had a bit of strife with the
stage doorkeeper, but eventually I was rescued by Kit Lambert, one of
the Who managers and a passing acqaintance of mine. I was about to
regale him with my firsthand experiences of the Haight when he excused himself to appease members of the London Fire Brigade. Searching for someone to talk to, I glimpsed Roger Daltrey leaning against a
wall, swigging from a lager bottle. He looked so deadly that I avoided
him, though I'd dearly have liked to have spoken with him. He was really living the part of the working-class hero and I, for my part, felt
foolishly out-of-time, even though I was wearing my U.S. Army raincoat.

After a while, Kit Lambert reappeared and I cornered him by the
only radiator that was working. He was extremely well turned out, in

dark blazer and cravat under a camel's hair overcoat. I asked him what was happening and he replied with a shrug, "Nothing, in this pokey little country. We're too damned big, that's the trouble, and we need gigs to match our grandeur. We need someplace like the Fillmore. We need glamour and not the miserable little motheaten audiences of this isle." He went on about the miseries of one-night stands, especially Up North; about the dreariness of the M1 motorway with its despicable cafés selling congealed egg 'n' chips; about louts whose idea of fun was to trip up the roadies as they lugged the equipment up the stairs; about freak-outs in Newcastle, in which one blinking bulb constituted the light show and where the audience lay on the slimy floor, sleeping off the effects of local brews; about the standard greeting of "Get the fuck off!" to any band from London; about Sunday church bells waking them at 8 A.M. with "Pop Goes the Weasel" (a cockney song); and about the endless string of broken-down mill towns and coal towns with their grimy Victorian buildings reminding him of a long-vanished supremacy. "Let's face it—Britain is washed up and we have to break through in America. That's where it's all happening now. They've taken our group sound and made it relevant by applying it to a contemporary social reality. The Mod thing is finished and the Who can be minstrels in this new movement." I took this speech very seriously and I couldn't help asking him whether he thought there was a place for someone like me in the new order. He gave me a quick survey up and down and said: "If you want my advice, you should really milk this upper-class twit thing you exude. Throw away the U.S. Army togs and get with a straw hat and Eton blazer. Be like the New Vaudevilles and *vo-do-de-o-do*. You must realize that, as front-line performers, our class is redundant." And then he exited to his smoked-window Rolls, which was waiting outside.

I'd already ripped off the New Vaudeville Band, of course, when I'd impersonated their "Winchester Cathedral" during my last tour of Middle America. Here at home, they were enjoying another hit called "Peek-A-Boo" and they were soon to romanticize in song a frightful tube stop called "Finchley Central." On investigation, I discovered that, though the group was made up of studio session men on record, in person they included a number of trad-jazz players I'd run across during my time in that field. I realized that the Vaudevilles had this area sewn up and that, while in Britain, I should leave them well alone. But I liked Geoff Stephens, the plump, friendly chap who wrote their material. In an interview with *New Musical Express,* he explained how he tried to write songs that the milkman would whistle on his rounds, adding: "Too many people nowadays are trying to make pop music complicated. I just want to simplify it."

I felt I must change with the trends. Or have a bash at it, anyway. In January, there exploded onto the charts two new acts that, while rooted in the blues, seemed to be paragons of a period charging headlong into the Apocalypse: Cream and the Jimi Hendrix Experience.

Cream were what their name dictated—the cream of the British R&B instrumentalists. They sang as if they had a built-in tremulo lever, and their single "I Feel Free" was racing up the charts. Jack Bruce, bass, and Ginger Baker, drums, had both been in the London R&B band of Graham Bond. Eric Clapton (also known as "God") had recently been with John Mayall's Blues Breakers, a band that stuck religiously to the true blues canon, and before that he'd been a Yardbird. These three top players constituted the first supergroup and when they were good they were very, very good—but when they were bad they were a horrid cacophony. "Super"—this was a word to be bandied about in the late sixties, an age of superlatives with no time for moderation. Superstars were just around the corner.

Cream were best witnessed in concert; records couldn't contain their star bursts of electricity. It was a fireworks display, but a musical one. There were no theatrical antics, no tight trousers fit to bust, no arms windmilling around the guitars, no drum kit destruction. Just great cataleptic hunks cut from prime aged blues and pummeled out, slit up, reshaped, and thoroughly examined with an academic violence.

Whereas the aerial dogfights of Cream sometimes veered into the rarefied realm of free-form jazz, Jimi Hendrix for the most part hugged his guitar close to venerable blues lines. He reeked of a sexuality that had white girls constantly excited—never the case with the likes of Howlin' Wolf, Muddy Waters, or B. B. King. These roly-poly blues greats might get respect but not heavy breathing.

Currently, the Jimi Hendrix Experience (including Noel Redding, bass, and Mitch Mitchell, drums), was in the British Top Ten with a new version of "Hey Joe." The old raver standby was taken at a portentous crawl, as if trying to carry a much heavier weight than the brisk folk tale I recalled from my Seattle coffee house days. During that summer of 1963, Billy Roberts had strummed and sung "Hey Joe" in a gay abandon that had imparted delight but not anguish. Perhaps Hendrix, who hailed from Seattle, had heard a Billy Roberts performance? Anyway, on Hendrix's single, the effect was of a giant in seven-league boots plodding under a storm-filled sky and announcing terrible things to come. It was the first of what was to be a host of snail-paced rock records that would be tagged with the epithet "Heavy!"

Hendrix, before becoming a rock star in the white world, had learned his trade in black R&B. He had been one of James Brown's Famous Flames; he'd backed B. B. King, Sam Cooke, Little Richard, the

Isley Brothers, and Ike and Tina Turner, to name but a few—an impeccable education in genuine R&B. In 1966, he branched out as a performer in a little café in Greenwich Village, and it was there that Chas Chandler, an ex-Animal now involved in management, caught his act. Signing him to a contract, Chandler brought his catch to London and showcased him at chic clubs to an audience of R&R royalty that included Eric Clapton, Pete Townshend, and Paul McCartney. At this point in rock history, the nod of approval from the new Establishment leaders was enough to assure nationwide exposure, if not huge record sales. "Ready, Steady, Go!" followed and, later, after the success of "Hey Joe," a sensational appearance on the early evening mass-appeal show, "Top of the Pops." Here he astounded the pop public (currently buying up the records of such cummerbunded crooners as Tom Jones, Engelbert Humperdinck, and Vince Hill) by playing guitar with his teeth and by materializing the white fantasy image of the flashy black stud. He was a young Satchmo with sharp fangs and a phallic ax.

Off-stage, Hendrix was reclusive and quiet. A *Melody Maker* reporter described him as having a "sad, Dylanish air." Asked about his background and his future plans, he replied: "I don't have no roots—don't matter where I am, so long as I'm living and putting things down." It was noted that his London flat was sparsely furnished, with a layer of soot on the TV set, but that the large and expensive stereo system was "immaculate." In a later interview, he gave some surprising replies to the *New Musical Express:* jazz was described as "a lot of horns and top-speed bass lines—most of those cats are playing nothing but blues, I know that much." Freak-outs were a matter of "getting really high and digging a Mrs. Miller single at thirty-three-and-a-third." On the pressing matter of Vietnam: "After China takes over the whole world, then the whole world will know why America's trying so hard in Vietnam." An odd dude. Maybe I should have warmed to him.

But because I tended to be an admirer of old-time blues by charming old blacks, I found Hendrix too immediate—and therefore too threatening for my tastes. Besides, there was nothing I could steal from him. So, in my continuing search for models to study for my planned comeback, I turned to the twin Beatles hits "Strawberry Fields" and "Penny Lane." If Lennon/McCartney could celebrate the halcyon days of a Northern past, then so perhaps could I. For the moment, from my vantage point in England, I could see no commercial sense in writing songs about my own childhood—of muddied afternoons on the rugby field of my prep school or of amorous walks in the Dorsetshire hills of my Public School, discussing *The Shropshire Lad* with a slim-hipped junior.

Off I went, then, to explore Lancashire, home of the Beatles, Ken Dodd, George Formby, Harold Wilson, the jam buttie, and, of course,

"Penny Lane." Just to be different, I avoided Liverpool and headed for Blackpool, entertainment center of the North and site of George Formby's greatest stage triumphs. After checking in to a first-class hotel and changing into loud checks, plus-fours, and a huge cloth cap, I sauntered forth onto the famous Blackpool Promenade and soon found myself deep within a neon-bright food 'n' fun palace. In my best Beatle accent, I demanded: "Ee bah gum, ah feel right peckish, so slide me over a basin o' black puddin' and a cold spaghetti buttie." The waiter, a burly individual in a red velvet dinner suit and clip-on bow tie, spat back: "Don't come that cheeky London rubbish with me, you chinless drone, or I'll kick yer fuckin' ass to Land's End and beyond!"

It wasn't long before it dawned on me that the North was enjoying a burst of prosperity and subsequent self-confidence and that I'd better tread warily.

Show business was bursting at the seams up here, characterized by a legion of cocky comedians specializing in jokes about Irishmen, Jamaicans, Pakistanis, and idiots like me from the idle classes Down South. Investigation turned up a host of spanking new Workingmen's Clubs the size of aircraft hangars and decorated like Las Vegas casinos. At the Texas Palace, an endless bar disappeared into the tobacco and fry-cook smoke. Mugs were filled with wine to be downed by strapping coal miners and factory workers, while their ladies sipped champagne perries. For one's dining pleasure, there was chicken- or scampi-in-a-basket, accompanied by *pommes frites* (as opposed to the thick, greasy chipped potatoes of the bad old days when the workers were poor). After feeding time came a slap-up cabaret starring one of the latest barrel-chested, Regency-ruffled balladeers like Tom Jones or Engelbert Humperdinck (née Gerry Dorsey). So great was the cash flow in these new clubs that big American acts could be afforded: Roy Orbison and Del Shannon were always popular and Louis Armstrong was scheduled. If a Yank fell through, there was always a supply of once-hot beat groups to fill the gap. With impending summer holidays in Spain along the Costa Packet or on the French Riviera, none of these bold and brass-filled Northerners wanted to be reminded of "Penny Lane." We must not forget that a vast adult public had never had much time for the heavyweights of the rock scene. And "Winchester Cathedral," done in that funny accent, was about all they would tolerate.

Head full of scampi-and-western music and heart full of doubt as to my place in the new order, I returned to London by express train and sought out Mick Jagger for some more career advice. Since I'd last appeared with the Stones, they had proved that the Jagger/Richards writing team was versatile, though not in the Alley tradition of Lennon/McCartney. Stones songs were always rough-edged in performance, but on paper "Ruby Tuesday," "As Tears Go By," and "Lady Jane" looked like decent enough ballads.

However, from late 1966 and well into 1967, the Stones appeared to be set full-speed on a collision course with the mores of straight society. To promote "Have You Seen Your Mother, Baby, Standing in the Shadow?", they were photographed in full drag. Jagger with his lipstick and his ass-cocking was pushing the androgyny bit hard. I was assured he wasn't gay—very few rock stars were of that persuasion—but he was certainly trying very hard to upset our sexual equilibrium. Rumor had it that the group had urinated in unison against a gas station wall. In Germany, on tour, Jagger had enlivened his male striptease by performing a few goose steps. But the greatest shock to the British showbiz fraternity was delivered by the Stones when the band refused to step onto the famous revolving stage (a hallowed tradition) at the end of a broadcast of the popular family TV spectacular "Sunday Night at the London Palladium." Jagger told the press that he hated waving, but there was a terrific reaction, with many famous names vowing never again to tread the same stage as these upstarts. Conduct unbecoming a trouper.

Just as the Beatles were discovering violins and cellos—not to mention the piccolo trumpet—Mick Jagger was flying the black flag and keeping rebel rock afloat. Some of the Establishment were of the opinion he was also flying the red flag because of his statements to the press that his desire was for "society to be overthrown" and that his music was "a protest against the system." The *Daily Mirror,* with the largest circulation of any newspaper in the world, splashed this call to arms in bold print. The adults, the workers, waited to pounce. Where there was this kind of smoke, there must be dope.

One fine February day, I set off into the stockbroker belt of dormitory counties south of London in search of Mick Jagger. I had a rough idea where he lived—I'd gleaned his address from a friend of a friend of a friend—but rock stars had a habit of moving; they seemed most at home behind smoked glass in a racing Rolls. Surrey produced nothing much, except a horde of Beatles fans from all parts of the world, especially Japan. Sussex was explored next and, as I approached the South Downs, I was reminded of the brisk runs and Scout games of my childhood at prep school there. A young German fan in a pub told me that Jagger was living at a manor house called "White Ladies" a mile up the road, so off I went, making sure I had a copy of "Where Did Robinson Crusoe Go with Friday on Saturday Night?" to give him as a reminder of my status.

Imagine my amazement when the door was opened by a chap I'd been to school with! "Farting Jack Smith" was what we used to call him, for obvious reasons, and I was damned if I could remember his real name. "Stuttering Fat Magpie!" he greeted me and, after a few minutes' small talk about the weather, he reluctantly invited me inside. A cocktail party was in progress and most of the guests were as fat and balding as "Farting Jack." The women were twin-set and pearled and in long tweed skirts. Horsey guffaws and lazy drawls filled the air of the richly appointed eighteenth-century drawing room. A silent butler padded about with a sherry decanter. Clearly, this was not Mick Jagger's home.

Eventually, "Farting Jack" asked me what I'd been doing since school. When I told him of my chart successes in America, he looked astounded and, whirling around, announced to all, "We have a rock 'n' roll star among us!" He then insisted that I sing all my hits at once and, when I demurred politely, a loathsome bullfrog of a man launched into a spirited attack on rock 'n' roll and all its practitioners. "And I think it's a disgrace and a betrayal of your background that you should be involved in the Decline of British Civilization. Commoners—poor boys and the like—I can understand, but somebody like you—who was born with a silver spoon in your mouth—should be ashamed of yourself. And I'm going to do my utmost in my limited capacity to prosecute as many drug-swilling, sex-crazed pop fiends as possible—so there!" And he turned on his heel and headed for the sherry. "Farting Jack" informed me that his friend was a prominent lawyer and an expert on Elgar. He had been maddened by the racket coming from the house next door to his—which was being rented by one of the Rolling Stones! "I can't say I blame the poor devil. The whole neighborhood's been inundated with parvenu rock stars. Can you believe one of them bought Lord Ashford's estate and promptly set up a hot dog stand on the 'Capability Brown' lawn! And to cap it all, he changed the name of the house to 'Dunrockin' '!"

Refusing more requests to sing my hits or tap dance or explain how the grooves were molded in the records, I said good-bye and drove up to the house described by the irate lawyer. Perhaps I would catch Mick Jagger in a relaxed preprandial mood, as it was getting to be suppertime.

The address turned out to be a huge estate with high iron gates and a lodge. An old geezer came to the door of the lodge in response to my knocks, looked me up and down, and sniffed. "No autographs. No comprendez foreign lingos. No Stones at home. Scootez off!" I was just about to lose my temper when a smoke-glassed Mercedes pulled up at the gates and honked. It was a pop-producing peer I'd met in 1965, when my publisher Hal Shaper had been showing me the London music scene. He hadn't much time for me, as he was anxious to get inside the gates and remix some tracks, but he did inform me that Mick Jagger was away watching cricket. Cricket? Where was there any cricket at this time of year? "My dear fellow, Mick can afford to follow the sun and I'm sure you realize that cricket is one of the few benefits our Empire bestowed on the far-flung lands that were once our possessions. You must get more sophisticated."

As I headed homeward, I mulled over the astonishing events of the day. My resulting mood was one of severe depression. The fact was, though I might bang and bleat about being an English gentleman upholding fine old values—I was nothing of the sort. All I had was an expensive accent and a vague nostalgia for a land that never was. And I was sure that, if I had lived back in the heyday of the Empire, I'd have hated every minute because there was no Elvis, no blue jeans, and no cheeseburgers and malteds. In this modern whirl of the sixties, I was a charlatan in no-man's-land: I knew nothing of Elgar, didn't care for cricket, and tea made me nauseous.

What to do? Return to Hollywood and make another record!

Seattle, Washington, March 1:

Stopped off here at my professional birthplace to check in with Jerry Dennon. Shocked to find that there's no longer any Jerden Records on the old site but instead there's a brand-new McDonald's. As I'm a hamburger connoisseur, I dropped in for a sample tasting. The manager behind the counter asked me whether I was a student. He said that if I was, they weren't serving me. I replied that I was a rock star. At that, the manager made a clicking sound with his mouth and reluctantly asked me for my order.

I later asked one of the superneat busboys why there was a ban on students. In a whisper, he told me that last week there had been a sit-in under the McDonald arches to protest the firing of a student employee who'd used the word "shit" when he burned his hand while flipping a cheeseburger. I couldn't see much reason for complaint; I've always hated foul language. But apparently, it's the thin end of the wedge: a ban on free speech. Student discontent is endemic across the country and getting worse.

After my burger, I rang the old Jerden Records number. "Jerden Fisheries!" came the sparkling bright greeting. To my astonishment, I learned that Jerry Dennon had gone into the "salmon culture" and was based up on some northern network of lakes. Was I interested in purchasing shares in the operation? I told the female receptionist that I was still bound to the great business of entertainment and was about to have another stab at the charts, bearing in mind the grave changes

being wrought at present. . . . But there was a long buzz and the voice
started its greeting and salmon culture speech all over again. A blasted
recorded message!

I still had Debbie's number—the local girl I had romanced in 1964
and whose father had tried to get us hitched. I hadn't seen her in ages
and I felt a desire to return to the old verities, perhaps go to a drive-in
with her or to cruise suburbia in search of a necking spot.

Her father answered the phone. No, Debbie wasn't there, hadn't
been home for weeks. The police had been notified, but they were
clogged up with hundreds of runaway calls. It was an epidemic and
much of the blame should be placed on rock singers like myself, not to
mention Communist agitators and student leaders. All they'd had was a
card scrawled "LOVE" and postmarked San Francisco. I told her father I
was on his side and that if I found her I'd send her home. He slammed
down the receiver.

Seattle University (Evening):

Before setting off for Hollywood and my next recording session with
Tower, I decided to get some information on the student problem from
Jack Feeny, the Seattle University professor who'd filled me in on the
history of folk music when I'd been playing at the 92 Yesler Club during that hootenanny summer.

He looked much grayer than when I last saw him and his hand
shook as he poured our coffee. No difficulty in getting down to brass
tacks—he was only too pleased to tell me about his student troubles.
"They bombard me with demands, both verbally and from their slogan
buttons. 'Impeach Johnson.' 'Stop the war.' 'Bring the war back home.'
'Introduce courses on rock 'n' roll.' They staged a sit-in right here in my
room because I objected to their use of the word 'fuck' in a class discussion on Irish land movements. I'm as liberal as anybody, but I can't see
what 'fuck' has to do with Irish history!" I agreed with him entirely, ob-
serving that the Irish had always been rather prudish. I spoke from bitter experience, recalling nights trying to get the colleens to unclench
their teeth while kissing.

Professor Feeny pushed a clutter of newspapers toward me and threw
up his hands. The papers were ink-smudged, homemade affairs, with
names such as *Spider, The Third Eye,* and the *Oracle* and splattered
with that twisty-twirly lettering I'd seen before in psychedelic Frisco.
"I'm damned if I can see the connection between the Beatles and revolution," sighed Feeny. An article in a local paper had been circled—
quotes from two Frisco rock seers: Ralph Gleason claiming that "In the
war between the generations, the kids are right and will win. . . . It
may yet come to a battle in the streets. This thing can't be stopped."

And Chet Helms, the rock concert organizer, boasting, "We [the under-twenty-fives] are assuming the role of tastemakers. The next step, as the number of young voters escalates, may be political." I wanted to explain to Feeny that this was only rock rhetoric; I wanted to fill him in on my career in the biz and how I'd tasted the nectar of pop power since our first meeting. But he got to his feet and set about grinding coffee beans violently. "My students are tuned-in to a national network of underground media. I can tell by the jargon they throw at me, half-digested C. Wright Mills, misunderstood New Left ideology. They don't read books—they glance at pamphlets and political buttons. They label me an armchair liberal, a relic of the Old Left. They say my belief in the working classes—the folk—as a revolutionary force is out-dated and that the time has come for the new class of student brother-hood to take political action. They keep talking about the need to put their *bodies on the line,* in order to force revolutionary changes like those made by their fellow students in Turkey, South Korea, Cuba, and Japan. They're darned rude. They made an unholy mess of my room—and they broke many of my precious folk-music records."

Professor Feeny's humiliation was small potatoes compared with the student unrest that was to spread through America over the next few years—until its culmination in the tragedy of Kent State, where peaceful demonstration was no match for murder. "Revolution" had been the watchword—the tyrannical System must be overthrown—but "revolution" in America was *only* a word, and words, threats, curses, and spittle were useless against the mighty metal arsenal that the security forces could use against these cocooned legions of middle-class students.

And much of the militancy was merely theatrical (as in Jerry Rubin's "Filthy Speech Movement" and his dressing up as a Revolutionary War patriot to appear before the HUAC), so that there seemed to be a connection between the student movement and rock. Rock had always been the Theater of the Defiant Gesture—from Elvis's hip-whipping and lip-curling to Pete Townshend's guitar-smashing—but was rock to be the clarion call to arms? Could it marshal the student army? Or was rock locked forever in the capitalist machine that was American show business? For the answer, we have only to look to the fudge-smooth seventies, after rock had triumphed (by steamrolling the spikey but fascinating aspects of pop), to see the surviving rock-stars-cum-bankers filling supershow after supershow with their soporific and brain-numbing wall-to-wall Rockzak.

So, after the sixties' smoke cleared and one could look back from the convalescent quiet of the seventies, rock music was revealed as the opiate of the youth movement: raunchy, moneymaking, electronic escapism. At the time, however, rock appeared to be the exhortative military band leading the show at the sprawling Circus of Causes, an entertainment that also starred Black Power, hippies, Yippies, acidhead dropouts, Women's Liberation, and Students for a Democratic Society.

Since over half the nation's white youth was enrolled in or had attended college and since the majority espoused the social and political complaints rising from the national campus rumpus, it is worth examining the model for student militancy: the University of California at Berkeley, not far from Haight-Ashbury.

A bastion of limply held liberal beliefs situated in an area renowned for radicalism, Berkeley was an easy Establishment to topple and the hollow victory won there set an example for the rest of the nation's college students to follow. It must be remembered that, though the Berkeley administrators might speak in sweetly reasonable tones, they were— like it or not—presiding over a concentration campus whose job was to process an endless supply of finished "products" for the business and governmental institutions of America. To irritate the goings-on at such concentration campuses was to question the whole point of America.

This is precisely what the Berkeley students started doing in the autumn of 1964 when, just returned from civil rights sit-ins and marches in Dixie, they discovered that political activity on campus had been banned. The idealism fanned by President Kennedy was to crash headlong into dollar reality. Civil rights confrontation tactics were now employed by the leaders of the new student army and the resulting dramatic incidents were widely covered by the media and later copied at college after college. The Free Speech Movement, for example, was initiated by speeches from atop a police car stranded in a sea of over four thousand students and others on the Berkeley campus. Student agitators whipped up the crowd with demands for action and references to the police as "Nazis." It wasn't long before there came the demand for the right to say "fuck." From campus complaints, the movement spread to national issues. Soon the students were trying to end the Vietnam war by blocking the trains taking troops to the induction center at nearby Oakland. It was believed that such actions would make the government see the error of its ways. The government knew early on that they couldn't win but couldn't withdraw for fear of losing face—both nationally and internationally—to a mob of ranting kids. On top of this, minorities in America came to realize that the middle-class white demonstrators were only playing a nursery game of taunting their fathers. Come adulthood and the seventies, many of them would in turn don their white collars and direct the blue uniforms of oppression. The blacks, especially, knew from bitter experience that, in a real showdown, the white fathers could bring out the heavy artillery. Violence was as American as cherry pie, but true revolution was as impossible as revoking the right to bear arms.

San Francisco Airport, March 6:

Changing planes en route to Los Angeles, I found the terminal lively with soldiers in transit. They contrasted strongly with the clutches of hippies handing out flowers and handbills. At first glance, the handbills looked like ads for service companies, but soon I figured out that they were evidence of the fast-growing Frisco band scene: Pacific Gas and Electric, Quicksilver Messenger Service, Cleveland Wrecking Company, Emergency Crew, the Loading Zone, and so on. How one yearns for the straight-ahead, tell-it-like-it-is of Hugo Winterhalter! And one suspects that many of these bands are newcomers from out of town— like the airport hippies, who seem to be much younger this year. Memories of my time in Haight-Ashbury last year caused my head to pound and my loins to lust for Gale. I could even put up with her intergalactic small talk during sexual intercourse. And had Dr. Werner Clark returned from his business trips to the material world?

When I phoned Gale's pad, there was an unholy racket in the background—music and laughter and breaking glass. A female voice said, "Uh-uh. No more crashing space." I asked for Gale and, after an eternity, she came to the phone. She too said, "Uh-uh"—but in her case it was because she'd just dropped some acid, as Dr. Clark told me when he took the receiver from the tripping Gale. Bang went my chance for an overnight quickie. The doctor was anxious to fill me in on the mind-blowing progress in the Haight: Beautiful People were pouring in hourly from every state and overflowing onto the very streets. "But we can work it out because there is plenty of free food, free music, free love, and free medical care. We have our shit together, you understand." His voice sounded a bit cracked, like an old record. I asked him about the Berkeley students and whether they too were meshing in. "No—they're dropping out like flies and tuning in to Flower Power instead of horsepower, gun power, or technobureaucratic power. And the New Left politicos are mad as hell!" "Why?" "Can't you dig? The *Ramparts* brigade claim the kids as their property and hate to see potential recruits stolen away from their war!" I told him I was en route to Los Angeles and he growled, "What a rip-off joint! Capitol wouldn't buy my audiosensory album concept. Nor would any of the major labels— and now Plastic City is copying everything we've forged up here." Then he said he had to split. Afterward, I realized that I hadn't asked if he'd run across Debbie from Seattle.

San Francisco was ingesting youth at a phenomenal rate. From all across the nation the tribes were gathering fast, their air transportation facilitated by the cheap youth fares introduced recently by the major airlines. Back on January 14, the siren had been sounded in Golden Gate Park at what handbills and posters had announced as THE WORLD'S FIRST HUMAN BE-IN—A GATHERING OF THE TRIBES, a happening that featured such heavyweights as Timothy Leary, Allen Ginsberg, the Hell's Angels, and the music of the Grateful Dead, Big Brother and the Holding Company, and Quicksilver Messenger Service. Head shop proprietor Ron Thulin, surveying the scene, pronounced the coming ascendancy of the New Community: "Already the minds of hundreds of thousands have been expanded by LSD. After this Be-In, our numbers will mount into the millions and we shall take over the world." Time, demographics, and show-business economy were on his side. For the moment, the good vibrations at Golden Gate Park, expressed in a "cosmic oneness" and a desire to "fuck hate," were carried to future tribespersons by such underground newspapers as the Los Angeles *Free Press,* the *East Village Other* (New York), *The Fifth Estate* (Detroit), and *The Land of Oz* (Chicago). In format, this last paper resembled *Life*—thick, glossy pages and full-color photography—and there was heavy advertising by marital sexual aids companies and soft-core sex theaters.

In March, the message from San Francisco was that the Summer of Love would be proclaimed at a Summer Solstice Festival on June 21. One hundred thousand tribespersons would attend. After all, school was out. By this time, the mainstream media had decided to join in the celebrations: SUMMER HORDE AWAITED—S.F. GIRDS FOR HIPPIE INVASION bannered the Los Angeles *Times.* And at the record companies, plane reservations were made and limousines hired.

But San Francisco had not merely been ingesting youth and announcing festivals. Its bands were sallying forth onto the road to push the message—and their records. Out in the sticks, though, in ill-equipped clubs, it was a real headache trying to simulate the spontaneous swirl-trip excitement of a night at the Fillmore or the Avalon. In fact, it was like a Dick Clark "Caravan of Stars" without Dick's clockwork savvy. For the time being, until the nation could get its act together and be as hang-loose hip as Frisco, the straitjacket of AM radio would have to suffice as the exposure vehicle for the New Culture. At RCA, shrewd executives had issued Jefferson Airplane singles that fit into the Top Forty with just the right amount of titillation. "White Rabbit," with its literary allusions to *Alice in Wonderland,* could be plugged as an accessible art song yet absorbed as the tale of an acid trip. It was number eight on the charts by the end of July.

Unfortunately but inevitably, the material world was adulterating the purity of the cause by reducing a complex and mystic wholeness to a crass and crude psychedelia. This must make a true tribesperson want to puke! How else to react to such ludicrous production/reductions as "I Had Too Much to Dream Last Night" by the Electric Prunes (ugh!) and "It's a Happening Thing" by the Peanut Butter Conspiracy (double ugh!!)? THE PEANUT BUTTER CONSPIRACY IS SPREADING claimed their ads. What a rip-off! Such airhead singles—and especially that insipid, opportunistic travel brochure "San Francisco (Be Sure to Wear Some Flowers in Your Hair)" by Scott McKenzie—would never be allowed on progressive KMPX-FM back home in the Bay Area.

Until recently, no broadcaster of note cared a hoot about FM radio. An FM license could be purchased for a pittance. This odd waveband was left to ethnic, religious, college, or public broadcasters and AM station owners used their FM band—if they had one—to duplicate their car radio programming. But aural tripping demanded higher fidelity, and the heads were buying intricate systems with sophisticated tuners and, from February onward, Bay Area New Music buffs were checking out KMPX-FM. Larry Miller's graveyard shift was brightening the life of this failing foreign-language station. He was spinning a wide spectrum of music from rock to raga to whatever caught his fancy—and he didn't care about the length of a cut. Albums were his thing and he abhorred the Top Forty dictatorship of AM. Then, in early June, Tom Donahue (the ex-Top Forty man) joined the station and, in a flash, was programming "free-form" music night and day. This last-ditch experiment, allowed by a desperate management, proved to be very lucrative: a wide-ranging playlist of up to three hundred records spun by informed and opinionated (yet loose) deejays had, in short order, taken KMPX ad revenues from a measly $3,000 a month to a staggering $25,000 a month. By the end of the year, the station had a major share of the eighteen-to-thirty-five-year-old white males. Madison Avenue paid attention. FM album-orientated rock was on its way. But my hopes that "free form" might expose the charms of ragtime and vaudeville were soon to be dashed. . . .

We are ahead of our story.

Hollywood, April 2:

My career has come to a sickening halt. I can't even get arrested, as they say in the trade. But what is worse, *I can't get a meeting with Tower Records.* But don't misunderstand me: the executives are charming businessmen and frequently I'm invited into their homes for dinner and then asked to read for their children or play my ukulele. When I bring up the subject of my career plans, it is always sidestepped. Timing, they say, is all-important. I'm afraid I am missing the bus as far as today's music is concerned. I must express my Haight experiences via the rock medium. I have decided to take the bull by the horns by staking myself out in Tower's reception hall until I get a meeting—even if it takes days.

At Tower Records, April 6:

My fourth day here and the place is always jammed with traffic coming and going. Freaks are much in evidence, their music-biz connection betrayed by acetates and briefcases. I sip coffee from paper cups, sometimes crushing them violently. Tower has framed some of their best-selling albums and hung them on the wall. Couldn't find mine. But I have examined *Way Out West,* Mae West's album produced by David Mallet. While she was recording for David last year, I was allowed up to her apartment during a break. David kept me firmly in check, telling me to shut up and so on, telling me I was only there because he'd gotten her to record "You Turn Me On" and "N-N-Nervous!" Apparently, she'd expressed interest in meeting the "clever writer." We were screened by maids and flunkies and finally we were left waiting for an eternity in her creamy drawing room. At last, a teenage boy with lacquered hair appeared in the doorway as if making a stage entrance. With a swish of his hand and a high purr, he announced, "Ladies and gentlemen—Miss Mae West!" In came our star, trailing a diaphanous nightgown of unblemished whiteness. "Oh!" She greeted us as if we were an unexpected pleasure.

That afternoon, I learned Miss West's life story from her own lips. She told us of bringing sex 'n' laughs to the screen in the early thirties and becoming such a hot box-office item that she saved Paramount Pictures from bankruptcy. I discovered that she was directly related to Edward the Confessor and that correct eating and regular colonic checkups were two of the secrets of her longevity. But I also learned from what she didn't say or do. Her speech was well prepared and carefully performed and she emitted impeccably timed rays of glamour. She never really loosened up—and this impressed me very much because we were entering a time when public confession was becoming the fashion. Here was a certified star entertaining me in her home and yet still preserving the mystery. Toward the end of the meeting, while David was in the lavatory, Miss West beckoned me to come up and join her on the sofa. When I was close to her—but not too close—she said, "You write such interesting songs. Why don't you write some for me?"

And I did. (More on this later.)

One hour later:

Still having no luck getting into the inner sanctum. I've been given an appointment, but somehow a "crisis" always comes up or some recently arrived person pre-empts me. I *did* catch a glimpse of J. J. Wave, Tower's "freak-out" expert, saying good-bye to a lucky visitor. Wave wears a Nehru shirt (with tails *outside* his trousers), and he said good-bye with a disgusting bear hug. I don't like the look of the man and I sense trouble. . . .

Just had a bright idea: I called up Derek Taylor, my press agent of last year. At first, I couldn't get a word in edgewise because he was so excited about an upcoming music festival he's planning in Monterey. Finally, I managed to tell him about my Tower problem and asked him for help. Specifically, if he'd call the president and drop some Beatles names, perhaps he could get me a meeting. This he agreed to do, provided I dropped by on Wednesday night to baby-sit, as he and the Mrs. were going out to a Monterey Festival "think-in." Of course, I would be delighted.

Later:

The plan worked. I just had almost three-quarters of an hour with the president of Tower Records. We talked about the necessity of changing with the times and about his twenty-five years in the business and about how he, himself, doesn't always empathize with *all* Tower products but he is mindful of Tower's obligation as a leisure service company. At home, he and his family often play my records and derive enormous pleasure from them. Just as I was ready to ask for a budget for a new recording session, who should walk in but Mike Curb.

As always, Mike was nattily dressed, with every hair combed in place. We turned the conversation to his current projects. Mike is a model of keeping up with the times—he is up to his turtleneck in the youth craze in all its manifestations, producing soundtracks for hot exploitation movies like *Riot on Sunset Strip* (which featured the Standells), *Psych-Out,* and *Teenage Rebellion.* He has recorded controversial but relevant songs like "The Gay Teenager" and "Pot Party." In fact, he's come a long way since the days when all he had was the Hondells singing the praises of their Hondas.

He seems to have taken a shine to me. I mentioned my plan to try and bust the charts again and Mike at once turned to the president and said, "Pink Floyd. You have Pink Floyd." Then he recommended that Tower build me into a similarly experimental progressive rock act. When I said I'd seen this act in person, Mike exclaimed with finality, "Well, there you are!" "But what should I record?" "What about reviving your one hit into 'You Turn Me On—'67'? Think about it and

come and see me at my office." He gave me a card that read SIDEWALK
PRODUCTIONS, with an address in the 9000 Sunset Boulevard building,
same place as Derek Taylor. I remembered hearing on the radio news
that a youth had attempted to fly from the top of the building only the
other day. As it's a virtual skyscraper, he became yet another LSD
statistic and made only the morning editions. But this incident gave me
an idea for a song. As both Mike and the president were looking at
each other and their watches, I said good-bye and retreated to my
lonely room at my new apartment tower, the picturesque Tel-El-Pal.

"A GROOVY DAY"

*Written at "home" in the Tel-El-Pal
while waiting for a "Mexican Special" TV dinner to heat.*

I've had such a groovy day,
Everything has been OK,
I've discovered beauty all around me.
Others may see crack-ed cups,
Dishes that need washing up,
I can see a sad eye in that old fried egg.

Beautiful people would not hurt a fly—
Many perch on them, you know.
Beautiful People like Sandy O'Hare,
Who can sail anywhere, yet remain in her chair.
A beautiful day to dissect a flower,
And I could do that for hour after hour.
Or copy the life of a dog friend of mine,
Who watches a plank in the floor all the time.
Beautiful things that keep happ-en-ing
Outside of Mr. Jones's eye.
Beautiful people like Harriet Keble,
Who flew from a steeple and now grooves with God.
An Eastern sultana, she's found her *Nirvana.*

I've had such a groovy day,
Tout le monde has been OK,
Everything has been OK,
OK, OK, OK, OK, OK, OK, OK, OK, OK, OK, OK, OK,
OK!?!

At around 8 P.M., I finished my song and decided to drop into Martoni's
for a drink and some veal parmigiana. George was there at the bar,
tired from a hard day's plugging. Pink Floyd are tough to get added

onto a station's playlist. L.A.'s not quite ready for them yet. George pointed out to me how dismal Martoni's has become lately. Spector is nowhere in sight. Sonny and Cher are always on the road. And the newer hip music business heads find this Italian joint "too Sinatra" for their tastes. Some of the deejays, lined up at the bar, confessed that they've given up trying to grow their hair. Long hair at the sides and bare scalp on top makes them all resemble Benjamin Franklin. No amount of beads, beards, and Roman sandals will hide the fact that these are men from a vanished era. George invited me to ride along with him tomorrow when he goes visiting the radio stations to hype Tower products. I want to go. It's important for me to soak myself in the sights and sounds of what's current.

April 8:
What is reassuring about George is that he hasn't adopted the trappings of the times. To excess, anyway. He has abandoned the shiny suits, but his velour turtleneck sweater and tartan bell bottom trousers make him appear contemporary and yet not out of place on a golf course. He picked me up at 9 A.M. and off we roared in his brand-new Oldsmobile Toronado, a car of the future that threatens to go airborne. After a health breakfast at the Macrobiotic Melange on Melrose, we went to a shoebox shack a few blocks away that George said is a "one-off" publishing house. They put out occasional magazines for the mass market and they always deal with contemporary crazes. Last year they were spotlighting the vaudeville trend, the year before that was probably the British Invasion, and before that surfing. The whole operation was contained in a couple of nondescript rooms and a lavatory. The employees numbered three women of a certain age, plus one pimply younger girl in a mini-skirt. George told me he had to do "a number" with the publisher, something about a psychedelic layout on Tower's more bizarre groups, and I was to make myself comfortable with the ladies while he repaired into an alley behind the shack.

Laura, the younger girl, let me read some of the copy she was writing for a "one-off" in production: *Psycho-Sensational!* She let me have a tear sheet, so here is how Hollywood is reducing the mind-bashing confusion of Frisco and the New Culture to a reassuring norm:

"Once upon a time in the far-off, never-never land of Hollywood, heroes were stamped out of a mold that called for unchallenged manliness. Cropped hair, $200 suits, aquiline noses, and strong chins were required equipment for the sex symbols of Celluloid City.

"Although night baseball failed, *love* has successfully challenged sex as an overriding emotion. We're not talking of love in the physical, boy-girl sense, but rather in an all-the-boys-and-girls-together sense—

love of mankind, brotherhood of man, and that sort of jazz. Take, for example, the inner glow of an exciting new group that radiates out as the fragile but firm essence of Flower Power, a group that strolls barefoot, is well into the bead bag, and in terms of Today and Now has the image that is the absolute end. We're talking about ——" Laura explained that there you fill in the name of whoever is your client. She has variations on this. I marveled and she seemed encouraged, moving her ink-stained hands through piles of dirty tear sheets and proofs and eventually fishing out what she called her "masterpiece":

"Music moods many. Did you ever touch a butterfly? A hurting softness, so soft it pierces through your fingertip and hurls itself through your sense. Touch an orange—it may touch you back with its textury skin vibrating at your finger. Music moods many. Like shreds of red balloons that got caught in the treetops like little tattered flags from some children's army. You breathe all this visual nutriment and there is music. The Sound of Music!"

Laura said she wrote the above on nothing but jelly donuts and Twinkies. "An unnatural high," she laughed as she lit up a Camel.

At KRLA, later:
Yet again, we failed to get into KHJ. Maybe I'm still on their blacklist? George says that pop memories don't last that long. I keep forgetting that 1965 is farther back than the 1920s. George says KHJ will "come across" when Davie Allen and the Arrows make the national Top Ten. They're a Mike Curb production. By comparison, KRLA isn't such a hard nut to crack. Since the coming of psychedelia, the station has been through some changes. Gone are the street parades down Hollywood Boulevard with the "Good Guys" in full costume, displaying the KRLA banner and boasting that they are number one and the Beatle station. Gone are the crowds of teenyboppers on the KRLA front porch and gone are the special promotions like "Scuzzy" ice cream. Even the lobby was quiet, save for grave employees padding to and fro with manila folders and tape cartridges. We poked into a few open offices and George discovered a current playlist, which contained several Tower/Curb records. Finally, we found ourselves in the program director's office and he welcomed us, even offering us a soft drink.

"You should have been here yesterday, George. It was pure pandemonium. Had a visit from the Seeds, pride of L.A. Course, we were the first to go on "Pushin' Too Hard" and we emphasized the fact that Seeds music isn't rock 'n' roll but is real honest-to-goodness flower music. You know, Sky Saxon is so beautiful and real Renaissance. He's just as happy with a flower as he is with an expensive gift. That's what he told me and he says you can quote it." George said that Tower had plenty of Seedy groups, which I thought was an unfortunate choice of words. But the program director didn't seem to mind; he just nodded sagely. George presented him with a shrink-wrapped Chocolate Watch Band album and mentioned that Tower had an option on a sizzling British single about San Francisco by the Flowerpot Men. "Talk about flowers," said the program director, getting to his feet and displaying a very wide belt with a buckle that read LOVE FROM BUSCH and bell bottoms that could have tented a seven-dwarf circus, "We had real rose petals every which way when the Seeds were here. It was crrrazy—strange, too." George remarked that petals were a change from jelly beans. "Don't tell me," said the program director with a shudder. "We gotta shift gears with these freeway fast lane times." He gave me a knowing look. "Now this Lord Tim—he's the Seeds' manager and, I'm telling you, he's hitting 'em high and hard but keeping 'em in the ball park. You should spectate. You might learn something."

George immediately got Lord Tim Hudson's office number and placed the call—outside, in the lobby. "You have to remember him from Invasion days. He was one of the bevy of British deejays we had around. . . . Wait a minute. . . . Hi, Lord Tim. Say hello to an old buddy of yours, Ian Whitcomb of Tower Records Corp."

I don't think Tim knew me from Adam, but he was very charming and effusive. I congratulated him on the Seeds. "Listen, Ian," he said in a very good accent, "Seed music is the original Flower Power music. We coined the expression. It's the first music to truly express teenage emotions. Basically, of course, it's a throwback to pastoral values—the sun, the rain, and the earth—as the bedrock of human experience. Sky's songs are saying that today's youngsters are the seeds of the next adult generation, which will flower into something quite beautiful." I asked Tim whether he'd been back to England lately, how long he had been out in California, and if he had been on a radio station in San Diego when I came down with the Sonny and Cher show. We promised to get together soon.

KRLA has become seriously committed to good works for the teens. Sam the Sham isn't mentioned. They have launched an "Educational Division" headed by Dr. Averell Burman, a historian and broadcasting instructor from Long Beach. I was reading about this development in some free time I had after my talk with Lord Tim—George had suddenly been roped into the studio as a panelist on KRLA's "Teen Topics" forum. Today, they're discussing "Drugs Through the Ages." I volunteered to take part but was turned down on the grounds that my track record showed I wasn't serious enough.

On the way back to Hollywood, I asked George what he'd said on the show. He replied, "Whatever's right," and we left it at that. He later said not to worry because he could probably get me on KRLA's Sunday night show "Radio Free Oz" if I really wanted to hear myself speak. "Radio Free Oz" is free form (it has a nonformat format) with "funky music" and provocative interviews with the likes of Allen Ginsberg and Andy Warhol. I'd certainly like to meet them. "Peter Bergman, the emcee, told me that he's going to have a Los Angeles River 'Fish-In' soon," said George, "and I asked him whether this was a put-on. He said that the brown shoe is on the other foot, whatever that means. It's a crazy world, but we musn't forget that we're entering the Age of Aquarius."

Wearily and with mind bubbling, I gazed at the passing background of velvet hills turning blue in the late afternoon. I imagined the days of yore, when there were buggy rides up to the foothills for picnics while, somewhere over yonder, Western movies were being made. George said the B Westerns were shot farther away, up around Newhall and the far side of the San Fernando Valley. He said one of these days he'd take me up to the Spahn Ranch to see the old owner and spin yarns about horse operas. "Funny thing, isn't it? You dig the Wild West, while I have a craving to rummage around in the ruined castles of Merry Old England!"

At Sidewalk Productions, April 12:

Mike Curb is being very attentive. I know he's a busy lad. Some call him a boy genius. He has a team surrounding him who look even younger than their boss. Everything is as tidy as my old school chapel and smells as sanctified, too. A pleasant drone of air conditioning and the contented clack of distant typewriters. No loud music, thank goodness.

Mike waved me into his office immediately and we got down to business. He said I needed a manager and that the best managers these days are lawyers. He knew one named Bob Fitzpatrick who was two floors below and even better than a regular lawyer. He was a *criminal* lawyer. A call was made and, in no time at all, I was crossing a sea of carpet to shake hands with Mr. Fitzpatrick and then sitting on a leather sofa while he told me of his many famous clients, like Robert Stigwood and Brian Epstein. He told me that Paul McCartney had slept on the very sofa I was sitting on.

A few minutes later, we shook hands again and I was told papers would be drawn up. Back in Mike Curb's office, a conference phone had been switched on so that we could all talk into a plastic box to Tower Records and they, in turn, could all talk into their plastic box. Before dialing Tower, Mike asked me, "Are you committed? Are you in this business for real? You are? Then let's go!" He was soon exchanging pleasantries with G. "Bud" Fraser, the president, and talking "turn-over" turkey. Suddenly, in a pause, he said, "You ought to give Ian Whitcomb another whirl on the carousel." The president called out for me. I answered as loudly as I could from across the room. Then: "What is your concept; what is your sales point?" Quickly, I slung to-gether some of the experiences I'd been having over the last fevered months. I walked over to the plastic box and spoke breathily into it: "*Yellow Underground.*" It sounded good. A mixture of the feelings of the 1890s Yellow Book period—Oscar Wilde and decadence—with the underground rumblings of today. "Sounds Pink Floyd to me. Can you get into production right away? Let me have a budget." We all said good-bye at the same time. I am delighted. What a splendid fellow is this Mike Curb! I called up Derek Taylor to tell him, but he was too busy with his Monterey Festival. I must ask him to arrange for some of Mike's soundtrack groups to be invited to perform at this Monterey songfest.

Palos Verdes, the Barry Haven home, April 13:

Feel guilty that I haven't been in contact with the Barry Havens since the summer of 1963, when they so kindly allowed me to stay in their clifftop ranch-style house and when Frankie initiated me into the world of surfing. When life was simpler.

Anyway, I've tried to make amends by visiting the Haven home—it was such a lovely day and I felt so elated by the Tower breakthrough that I hired a taxi to drive me coastward while I dreamed up songs for my concept album—but I've found that only Mrs. H. remains.

The Union Jack still flies bravely from the front lawn, but that is the only thing to be said in favor of the Haven home. The lawn itself is overgrown with weeds and hideous subtropical plants of mongrel parentage. Parked on the lawn and minus one wheel is the station wagon, all that's left of their fleet of cars. The house itself is leaning westward in an advanced state of dilapidation.

Eventually, I found Mrs. H. pottering about pointlessly in the back garden. She said she was tending vegetables, but I couldn't see any. She was glad to see me, remembering my earlier visit but knowing nothing of my rock 'n' roll success. This was just as well, since her mis-fortunes were brought on by the new rock morality and life-style.

In the kitchen, she sat me down and set about brewing up some tea. In the harsh fluorescent lighting, I noticed that she looked very creased and old. "I know what you're thinking, dear," she said wearily. "That I look like a right old ratbag. In fact, I look like a bleeding hippie!" I was surprised to hear her use the word "bleeding." She had been so refined in 1963. Her tale of woe took several pots of tea and a batch of scones

("I won't touch those English muffins they sell here. Nobody ever ate such a thing in England!") to relate. Frankie, the surf fanatic, had dropped out of college and run away to San Francisco. The last communication she'd had from him was an astrological chart sent months ago. "Not so much as a by your leave," she said, "when he disappeared on Guy Fawkes night." The younger brother, Frederick, was safe in school in Utah (under close guard, as he had become an "incorrigible" after having committed several petty thefts). But the greatest blow of all was that Mr. H. had run off with a local teenage beauty queen and was living near some Aztec ruins in Guatemala. "I ask you!" said Mrs. H. "Is there no rhyme or reason in any of this hoo-ha?"

By the time I was calling Mrs. H. by her first name, Dora, it was dark outside. She very kindly invited me to stay the night and to enjoy some of her famous Lancashire hotpot. While she was preparing the supper, I took a bath. Beforehand, I poked around Frankie's old bedroom to see what literature was available and, with a few underground newspapers in hand, I retired to the tub. The papers made interesting reading and showed me how insidious and slanted reporting can lure impressionable youngsters away from a warm bed, a Union Jack, and a Lancashire hotpot.

The first few copies were of the Los Angeles *Free Press* and they were choking with a fog of paranoia—there were Establishment plots everywhere to deprive youth of their rights and get them into Vietnam; Kennedy was murdered by a conspiracy; the world was coming to an end and L.A. would be the first to go. Next, I picked up a San Francisco paper called *The Fish Rapper*, which was really a publicity sheet for a Bay Area band called Country Joe and the Fish. One of the Fish expressed relief at being back in San Francisco after a promo trip to L.A.: "It's a short-sleeved velour pussycat with a plastic hard-on. It's Disneyland all over." What snobbery!

There was also a rather militant paper from Detroit called *The Fifth Estate*. I suppose they have much to complain about up there. I was surprised to read in the newspaper that Carl Wilson of the Beach Boys has refused Army induction and is being indicted. There was an amusing story about local police disguising themselves in berets and beards in order to infiltrate "beatnik enclaves." The ads in the unclassified section at the back fascinated me because they illustrate so well the strange brew of capitalism and dissent, hedonism and idealism, new street jive and old egghead cant that characterizes our times. This page made me feel, yet again, that the wheel turns yet is forever still:

DRAFT REGISTERS—YOU ARE NOT ALONE.
We have no magic answers to the Draft.
We can't tell you how to dodge it.

We can tell you how to resist it.
Send 10¢ for *Uptight with the Draft* or $1 for a *Draft packet* that includes *Handbook for C.O.s.*

REMEMBER!
The Girl who is waiting for you.
Give her a Square Deal.
Keep Clean.
W.W.I VD Poster 16x20. Send $5.25.

"SEXUAL PARADISE OF LSD"—For copies, write this paper.
Enclose $2.50 for postage and handling.

WANTED: FEMALES! Must be moderately attractive and
extremely friendly—to act as companions to two poor but
ruggedly handsome men. Must have own transportation.

TRAD GENERALIST PHILOSOPHER-THEOLOGIAN (and social
anthropologist, 25). Experienced radical. Needs patron or
imaginative nonservile employment immediately.

SOMEWHERE between Washington, D.C., Antioch, and
Detroit is the best conch shell player in the world. You
know who you are. Please say hi to Cathy.

LOVE NECKLACE MADE FOR YOU. Exotic glass beads. Send
personality sketch, plus $3.75.

I NEED A SOUL TO COMMUNICATE WITH this summer, having lost the one I had to the factories while I am city-
bound. I am a girl-child believing in freedom, peace,
love, stars, music, and tolerance for personal idiosyn-
crasies. No hangers-on, *please!* Write Kate.

FRANKIE HAVEN—where are you, pet? Call your mum collect.

At the weekly Sunday "love-in," Griffith Park, April 20:

I'm writing this while relaxing on the crabgrass in this park, which
was donated to the city at the dawn of the century by a Welshman.
KRLA says the "love-in" will begin at 1 P.M. It seems very well organized, with many familiar franchises here (such as Orange Julius and
Tastee Freeze). I feel it my duty to attend this sort of gathering in the
service of Mrs. Haven. I promised her, as we sat together with dawn
coming up like thunder on the Palos Verdes Peninsula, that I would do
all I can to sleuth out the whereabouts of Frankie. I'd like to locate
Debbie, too.

We're eating a "love-in" brunch, taking a break from the *Yellow Underground* recording sessions. I'm with Ray Pohlman, the onetime
music director of "Shindig" who's helping me produce the tracks, and
his lovely wife Barbara. I must say that Bud Fraser has been very
co-operative on this project, giving us complete *carte blanche*. He explained to me on the phone that he's always had a lot of time for me
and my music. "It's good-time music, the kind of record we used to
market when I first joined Capitol in 1946. Make no mistake: I like it,
my children like it—but we must never forget that we are engaged in
commerce and that therefore all products must be viewed in terms of
the total spending pie."

So far, I've cut a number of vaudeville songs (like "They're Wearing
'Em Higher in Hawaii") which, after a tab or toke, could be taken as
trippy stuff. My Draft evasion offering is called "I've Been Ill" and con-
cerns a youth who'd adore to go to the war, except that his doctor says
no. But he's *with* the soldiers in spirit. Tomorrow, we're cutting my
chef d'oeuvre, a real experimental piece: "Jottings from an Active
Life." These are selected readings from a memoir by Colonel Weston-
Jarvis, whose military career stretched from just after the Crimean War
to the end of World War I. The climax is his conclusion drawn from
experiences in the "School of Life": *Everyone can help.* He also bears
in mind the words of Cecil Rhodes, architect of South Africa and
Rhodesia: "Look here, Weston-Jarvis, never forget that you are an
Englishman and have therefore won first prize in the lottery of life."
Ray Pohlman has found some first-class sound effects to punctuate this
twenty-minute slice of spoken words. We are really going to break new
ground in rock!

May 1:

A red-letter day! I delivered the final mixed-down tapes of *Yellow
Underground* to Tower. Went up to the Capitol art department to confab with the designer about a suitably psychedelic album cover. He

kept referring to it as *Yellow Underpants*, which I didn't find very funny. This afternoon, the Tower executives are going to listen to the tapes and work out a marketing strategy. It's all very exciting and I hope that now I can carve out a niche in the current scene. I shan't be at the listening session—I'm flying back to the Old Country, as I promised the family I'd join them for a holiday in Cornwall, before the crowds flood in and ruin it for everybody.

Later, inside the jet:

We were all strapped into our seats and ready for takeoff when a voice boomed out over the public address system: "Is there an Iron Whittaker in economy?" I'm glad they got my name wrong. I didn't want the world to know I was cutting corners on my air travel. After a while, I strolled up to First Class and, sotto voce, told the chief steward that I was probably this "Whittaker." I produced identification and he handed me a telegram. Felt quite important as I tore open the envelope. Several of the tanned faces in first class regarded me quizzically. This was what I read: "YELLOW UNDERCURRENTS" AUDITIONED. TWENTY-FIVE YEARS IN BIZ, ETC. SPOKEN WORD IS KISS OF DEATH. EVEN YOUR SIR LAWRENCE OLIVER [sic] CANNOT SHIFT UNITS OF SHAKESPEARE. J.J. WAVE AGREES. KEEP KURRENT AND HAVE A NICE DAY. YOURS, G. "BUD" FRASER, PRESIDENT, TOWER RECORDS CORP.

In June of '67, the windows of Hip—as opposed to Swinging—London were wide open to a rare and intoxicating summer heat that wreathed those shuffling peacocks, the silked and satined Beautiful People, in a torpor of sly smiles and silly giggles.

To the average clerk or secretary hastening back to work after a snatched lunch, these exquisite creatures of the British Summer of Love appeared enigmatic if not downright annoying. They gave working-class Londoners the hump. What right had such a shiftless array of fancy-dress partygoers to cavort so brazenly amid slope-shouldered breadwinners? This is how one pinstriped executive expressed the opinion of the real world as he glared from his office window at an inebriated pop star being helped by roadies into his Rolls.

A new kind of spirit on the part of youth was holding the pop aristocracy in thrall. Still selfish, indolent, and throbbing to a pulse it assumed to be the earth's, youth now had high artistic expectations as well—the belief that rock was about to vault into realms where anything was possible, where music had more than charms, and where it might move multitudes into action and even topple governments.

Eric Burdon of the Animals told *Melody Maker*: "Politicians don't count. They are just playing around with people. The Beatles can do a much better job than the Archbishop of Canterbury. They look better and they make better records." In a gentler vein, Donovan related his vision to the press: "I see all the writers together again, and all the film-makers, and of course the musicians. Controlling the whole market with all the art. Like Greece or the Parthenon. All the great minds of the world sitting on top of the world—working it out!"

Perhaps one could forgive some of the excesses of the stars: Keith Richards smashing his Nazi staff-car Mercedes into a Ford Cortina and quickly transferring to a taxi; John Lennon in red cord trousers, yellow socks, and a *sporran*; and the alleged dope orgies held in country estates deep in stockbroker counties where the male participants wore mustaches (normally the prerogative of responsible citizens).

Into this giddy atmosphere of June there appeared the long-awaited Beatles '67 LP: *Sgt. Pepper's Lonely Hearts Club Band.* What a quaint and antiquated name! Or was it a parody of the long and windy names of the San Francisco bands? Quite a stunning package this: a cover, designed by famed pop artist Peter Blake, showing live Beatles decked out in military bandsmen uniforms of the kind one might expect to find at that King's Road boutique "I Was Lord Kitchener's Valet." Around our heroes was an assembly of their own heroes and heroines, including Karl Marx, Diana Dors, Marlon Brando, Laurel & Hardy, Sonny Liston, W. C. Fields, Aleister Crowley, and Mae West. A disparate crew, like a cast of characters from a Dylan epic, but no more bizarre than the cult heroes blown up into posters that were on sale in many a trendy London boutique or youth gear store. The album opened up like a book and inside were the songs' lyrics, together with the kind of cut-out novelties kids used to find on cornflake boxes: a paper mustache, some military stripes, a souvenir Sgt. Pepper picture card, and two badges. Well, not exactly the kind of subject matter for cornflake cut-outs—but this was nostalgia shot with satire, high "camp" fun with a touch of the "con." It was all part of the meaningful frivolity of the times.

The album package was greeted with delight and amusement by the pop press. *Melody Maker* found it a "jolly" record with a "self-mocking undercurrent" and they noted that *Sgt. Pepper's* greatest influences came from George Formby and Lonnie Donegan, rather than Richard Strauss, William Byrd, or Ravi Shankar (the names being bandied about by the serious quality papers). All in all, concluded *Melody Maker,* "The lads have brought forth another saga of entertainment."

Everybody had indeed enjoyed Sgt. Pepper's show and gone away with a gladness of heart and a wistful yearning for those good old days

of childhood joys like circuses, mad flights of fancy in the school painting class, crazy dreams of floating down wonderland rivers, and boys'
adventure stories of daring deeds by steel-jawed officers when Britannia
ruled the world. How clever of the Beatles to romanticize the squalid
practicality of a female traffic warden by offering up an ode to a "meter
maid"! What a good way of softening the bluntness of the present.

But *Sgt. Pepper* was not to be viewed for long as simply a satisfying
entertainment artifact. We must therefore examine its origins. . . .

In late 1966, with American rock refueled by affluent American
youth and now jetting out into the unknown to break the barriers not
only of sound but also of moral (and dress) codes, Paul McCartney realized that the Beatles, in order to stay ahead of the game, must come
up with something earth-shattering. When he had first heard Brian
Wilson's *Pet Sounds* album, he was both impressed and despondent.
He later reported his reaction: "Oh dear me—this is *the* album of all
time, so what the hell are we gonna do?" Wilson's masterwork, a pure
pop flow thick with rococo inventiveness, made obsolete the usual
method of making an LP—sticking a bunch of songs together with a hit
single as the linchpin. The LP had now become a cohesive work and
Paul felt the Beatles could go one step farther by having a *central concept* as the linchpin.

They would take up the American challenge. Instead of copycatting
an idiom, as so many of the British R&B bands had done, they would
concentrate instead on their own vernacular and, indeed, their own
memories of childhood in Liverpool. John and Paul were feeling a mite
retrospective, even nostalgic. During the mad dash through Beatlemania and beyond, they felt they'd lost something and they wanted to
wander back and find it. So "Penny Lane" and "Strawberry Fields"
were written as contributions to this projected snapshot album of childhood scenes. Uncle George had done a fine job spicing up the songs so
that they appeared bang-up-to-the-moment, but basically—as words and
music—they were very old-fashioned numbers (and none the worse for
that!). However, with the premature release of the two tracks as a dou-
ble-A-side single, the original concept was scotched.

EMI and the world were waiting for a new LP in 1967 and all the
Beatles had in the can was the jokey jaunt "When I'm Sixty Four."
Like a school music master, George Martin waited expectantly for the
homework to arrive. By February, there were enough songs—some still
unfinished—to start laying down the miserably few tracks that dear old
outmoded Abbey Road Studios had to offer.

Like all good song weavers, John and Paul had created their own
magical world. The English life they painted was at once well observed
and imaginative, contemporary and timeless. There was also a grim

double meaning lurking behind at least four of the songs—the meretricious cloud of drugs.

But judged on their brilliant surface as melodies, harmonies, and rhymes, the new songs were as clear as a seaside hotel soup and as wholesome as Gilbert and Sullivan. Here they were, pure and unadulterated as Martin received them: "She's Leaving Home," a follow-up to "Eleanor Rigby," about a girl sneaking out of her drab home to elope with a gent from the motor trade. Replete with harmonium harmonies and in waltz time, this song could be taken as a pastiche of Edwardian "heart" songs or as a satire on hopelessly corny tearjerker ballads. Beatles music is full of pastiche and often shot through with a curious ambivalence toward the sentiments in English life—as if John and Paul were scared of being jeered at by their jaundiced British rock and R&B peers for being sentimental. "Good Morning Good Morning" observed with irony the deadening humdrum of workaday married life with its tedious routines. On the domestic front, "Fixing a Hole" dealt with home decorating (a national obsession in Britain, where Black and Decker have their headquarters). "Getting Better" regarded the present day from a bird's-eye view, comparing the horrors of the Dark Age Fifties with the Enlightened Sixties. A disarmingly ingenuous tribute to the idea of Progress.

"Being for the Benefit of Mr. Kite," though still keeping within the theme of the evocation of England, introduced a touch of mind expansion. Based on a Victorian poster hanging in John's room, the "Grand Circus," which starred the Hendersons and Henry the Horse, was aurally visualized by a disturbing spiral swirl of demented steam organs and God knows what else. Then there was John's way-out imagery on "Lucy in the Sky with Diamonds," a simple-enough tune with a title based on a painting by John's young son Julian, depicting his school friend Lucy sitting in the sky surrounded by stars. This chorus was bolstered by a verse asking us to imagine ourselves in a toytown world of tangerine trees, newspaper taxis, plasticine porters (with looking glass ties). Was this charming slice of whimsy inspired by Dali or by Wackyland (as depicted in the famous Warner Bros. cartoon *Tin Pan Alleycats*)? Or was it yet again an echo of the world of Lewis Carroll's Jabberwock? The apocalyptic "A Day in the Life" typified those days when little things pile up to form one big heap of foreboding: sudden death on the radio news as you tumble out of the wrong side of the bed and all you can do is laugh; a trivial item about local affairs in the provinces sets your mind reeling into double meanings and you wish you hadn't indulged so much the night before. At least, that's as far as I could get with an interpretation of this epic ending of *Sgt. Pepper*. Much of it appeared non sequitur, but overall there was a sense of impending doom, as mirrored in seemingly trivial signs. We see THE END in the tea leaves at the bottom of the cup.

Ringo and George were allowed a romp. "With a Little Help from my Friends," an admission by Dopey that he'd really be at sea without his cohorts, was a great vehicle for Ringo's lugubrious drone. And another kind of drone was employed by George on his own composition, "Within You Without You," which preached easy mysticism with a curry flavor. This, then, was the raw material.

Music master George Martin next set to work making these songs into tracks. His musical and engineering expertise enabled him to augment George's friends from the Indian Music Association with a real string orchestra; "Good Morning Good Morning" was pursued by a pack of hounds in full cry and assorted barnyard noises; "Being for the Benefit of Mr. Kite" featured two electronic organs, a bass harmonica played by roadie Mal Evans, and a Dada tape collage of recordings of Victorian steam organs; "A Day in the Life" required a suitably apocalyptic sound, so Martin rented a forty-one-piece orchestra and told them to climb from their lowest note to their highest note. Later, he was asked by the boys to let them record some gibberish on the run-out grooves and also to stick on a note of 20,000 hertz so that any dogs in the audience would have something that only they could enjoy.

Martin found the work demanding, but it was a challenge and it was also darn good fun. Doing things off the top of the head kept him fully stretched and got him out of himself and his straitlaced classical training. Of course, he didn't care for the boys' occasional drug use—he felt it hindered their work—but he tried to turn a blind eye to these youthful excesses. The boys had to lock themselves in the Abbey Road canteen in order to toke up on a joint. John, Paul, and George were dropping LSD by this time, but mostly they kept it secret from Teacher, though one night Martin did observe that John looked very ill. Martin saw the whole exercise as musical and technical, and, oh my, if only EMI would install more modern equipment at Abbey Road.

The Beatles were well into the recording sessions when Paul submitted a light rock song called "Sgt. Pepper's Lonely Hearts Club Band." Martin considered it rather ordinary, but they went ahead and recorded it. Afterward, Paul suggested that they pretend that the four lads weren't Beatles at all, but were the protégés of this Sgt. Pepper who had taught them to play twenty years ago. No putting on of airs, no "heavy" nonsense—Sgt. Pepper's lads would be in spirit what the Beatles had been in practice when they were playing Hamburg or the Cavern. A lark, a laugh, a bit of a *do!* The Sgt. Pepper band could be like some funny old forties' dance band struggling to hold down a gig in a

Working Men's Club up North, tooting out the Tom Jones and Engelbert hits, fighting to be heard above the guzzling of beer, the chomping of scampi-and-chips, and the amplified calls of the Bingo master. "It'll be a nice little time warp and will distance us from being Beatles," suggested Paul.

Martin loved this conceit and from then on the album became not so much a collection of tracks but a *concept*. He and Paul worked out the running order after all the tracks had been completed; after this narrative had been arranged, there followed the applause, the laughter, the crashing of the silence barrier between each track, and the uniforms and all the collage folderol. The album had become a show and the Beatles merely players. They hoped they were home free—but actually they were unwittingly sealing their musical doom.

Thus far, there had been a splendid isolation about Beatles music. When they made their songs, they left the rest of the world trudging behind. They were inside their own creation; they were no longer a sociological phenomenon. In their music, they were timeless. But when they stepped into the summer of '67, they became merely participants in the ever-changing trends of chic rock life. They became champagne hippies, covered in fuzz and silk and plastered with droopy mustaches. Almost hoity-toity, but not as highfalutin' as some of the rare birds around them on the charts. At least they avoided being pseudopoetic and pseudoclassical like Procol Harum who, with "A Whiter Shade of Pale," and their first album, *Procol Harum*, were to enjoy a few hot months at the top before self-destructing.

With a tune borrowed from a Bach organ cantata and a scatter-gun splatter of fake surrealist lyrics, "A Whiter Shade of Pale" was number one in Britain by July, the fastest-selling record in British Decca's history. The trade ads hailed it as a breakthrough for poetry in pop. This was quite a leap for group leader Gary Brooker, who had started out with the Paramounts, a run-of-the-mill R&B band from Southend, where the piercing smell of fried fish and seaweed can turn a sensitive soul a darker shade of green. Understandably, Brooker wanted to get out but, as he wrote only music, he was stranded until he teamed up with Keith Reid, a lyricist with a bulging portfolio. In early 1967, when they had a body of work to show, they found acceptance with my old pal Denny Cordell. He said they'd better rustle up a group and thus (through want ads in *Melody Maker* and on likely bulletin boards) was formed Procol Harum (Latin for "beyond these things"). But "A Whiter Shade of Pale" was a phrase that Reid heard at a party: a guy was telling his chick that he didn't feel too well.

The resulting record, combining baroqueish music with a waffle of poetics, garnered much print praise from critics anxious to help rock grow into a substantial pageant. It was also, in its mystification, a great trip-out.

Procol Harum's achievement was slightly spoiled when it was revealed that a session drummer had been used on the record. Bill Eyden, otherwise known as a solidly swinging jazzman, wanted a cut of the royalties. He felt that, with all this chart action and critical acclaim, he, too, was a contributor to the Procol Harum art. Besides, he had to eat.

Denny Cordell was offering *Melody Maker* some super copy at this time. I remembered when he used to pluck a skiffle bass and revel in the simple boogie-woogie, but some of us change: "Their [Procol Harum's] music is stimulating intellectually as well as emotionally. It's pretty introverted music and definitely not for leaping about. They are mood-makers and should be listened to whilst stoned out of your mind at 3 A.M."

Anyway, the Beatles hadn't gone poetic. Nor were they ever into mind-bending stage visuals. Since their concert at Candlestick Park in '66, they hadn't done a live gig. And even in Beatlemania days, they had never put on much of a show, just twenty-five minutes or so of hit reprising. But now, in this pompous summer, few acts would dare come out merely to sing and strum. The competition was planning big events: Pete Townshend was supposedly at work on a rock opera, while Keith West had released an "Excerpt from a Teenage Opera" (and his single hit number two in November). Pink Floyd announced plans to become a traveling art circus, complete with a big top, a cinema screen 120 feet wide and 40 feet high, and constant "mind surprises." And at the old Flamingo Club, where not so long ago straightforward blues was performed, designers had covered the ceiling in flowers and the walls with psychedelic paintings and had dotted the floor with pedestals topped by stuffed pigeons lit by ultraviolet rays.

Nor were the Beatles on the front line, suffering on behalf of youth rights and the new hedonism. This was left to the Stones. Earlier in the year, the British authorities, having had it with Mick, Brian, and Keith's carryings-on, had busted the infamous three for drug possession. Brian was hit in May and didn't like the attention. Mick and Keith were hit in February and they seemed to enjoy it. The most delicious moment of martyrdom was at Chichester Assizes that summer when Mick and Keith, sentenced to jail terms, were led from the court in handcuffs. Boys in bondage! But next day, they were freed on bail and later Lord Parker, chief justice, set aside their sentences but reminded Mick of the "grave responsibilities" he had as a teen idol. Mick looked suitably solemn in his high-necked double-breasted green blazer. That afternoon, at the press conference, he was in purple velvet trousers, white shoes, and a high-collared white shirt with gaily embroidered collar and cuffs. Soon he was square-bashing again, claiming that the old geezers were on the run and that the time was right for revolution. He suggested burning down the high-rise flats and cruddy factories where kids were forced to rot their lives away.

After the Stones' martyrdom, Paul, John, George, and Brian Epstein admitted to having tried LSD. The *Times* was sympathetic to the new hedonists, pointing out that youth had rights, too. But for those members of the rock entourage who didn't care for drug diets, life could be a nightmare. Cynthia Lennon, John's wife, suffered by virtue of remaining the same as she had been back in their Liverpool courtship days—solid and reliable. The trouble was, that—like a convert to a new religion—John wanted everybody to experience his newfound life and, if they didn't like it, he got paranoid. Cynthia decided she'd better try to join him, in order to save the marriage and to see the hippie life from the inside. From the outside, it was infuriating: "He would return home following a recording session and night-clubbing with a retinue of flotsam and jetsam he had picked up on the way," she writes in her excellent autobiography, *A Twist of Lennon*. "They would all be as high as kites. John didn't know them and neither did I. They all came along for the trip. They would spend the night raving and drinking and listening to loud music, ransacking the larder, dossing down all over the house. The following day the house would be littered with glassy-eyed bodies all waiting to be fed."

So Cynthia took an acid trip with John and she discovered that, from the inside, the hippie life was "hell on earth": the trip made her panic. Through her tears, she hallucinated her husband into a slimy snake and a giant mule with razor-sharp teeth. The biggest bummer was at Brian Epstein's Mad Hatter party when John, tripped out, glared at her as if she were a stranger. She contemplated a leap from an upstairs window. Truth was that Cynthia, traditional homemaker and great scratch cook, much preferred their earlier show-biz life when, with John, she'd been entertained by such straight-ahead couples as the Stanley Bakers and the Mike Nesmiths. You knew where you stood with them; they obeyed the rules of good manners, saying "hello" and "good-bye" and "how are you."

The only Beatle to take an interest in the world-at-large was George, who viewed it as a fortune cookie that might reveal "the secret of the universe" in one cryptic sentence. George (of the bleeding fingers) had actually traveled to India to study under Ravi Shankar and had returned with some Eastern answers. In London, he joined the Spiritual Regeneration Movement and began handing out their pamphlets to anyone he could collar. He was deadly serious and he was weaning himself away from drugs. In August, he visited Haight-Ashbury, in order to understand that life. But he did a bit of proselytizing there, too.

After telling the chauffeur to park the limousine around the corner, George & Company set off. He had arrived with his girlfriend Patti Boyd, Derek Taylor, and Magic Alex, the latter having established himself in the Beatle camp by reason of his conjuring tricks and his electrical games that kept John quiet for hours. Both Cynthia Lennon and George Martin, pragmatists to the bone, were deeply suspicious of Magic Alex. Blond and brimming with innocence, he was to be a harbinger of chaos.

Within minutes, the royal tour had attracted a flock of followers. "You are our leader, George," pronounced a hippie. "It is you who should be leading yourself," George answered. He didn't like what he was seeing; it reminded him of the Bowery—not to mention certain parts of India. He didn't like seeing American kids sitting on blankets begging for money. "It doesn't matter what you are, as long as you work. It doesn't matter if you chop wood, as long as you chop and keep chopping." Someone tried to lay some STP on him, but others got to it first, grabbing and clawing and shrieking. George admitted that, though he had tried LSD in the past, he didn't need it to get high anymore because yoga did the trick. "We're all striving for something which is called God. Everyone is a potential Jesus Christ, really. The whole point of life is to harmonize with every aspect of creation. That means down to not killing the flies or chopping the trees down. . . ." The STP man came back and George told him his purple pill was "bullshit." The hostility that had been in the air right from the start of the tour burst into the open as the STP man confronted George. "I tried to give you a gift that would turn you on and you put me down. I don't like that, man. That was wrong!" George pulled out a picture of an Indian holy man to calm himself down. "This is where it is," he said softly.

The party soon returned, sadder but wiser, to their waiting limousine. They had seen the Haight at its nadir, filled with trippers hungry for instant gratification, poisoned by a few who were at bottom no different than the bums, winos, and murderers of the Other America. The beggars had really disturbed George. Had he ever considered getting rid of his material wealth in order to clear his conscience? "Now that I've got material things in perspective, I feel OK. You see, these material things were given to me as a gift. I didn't ask. All I did was to be me."

George was groping his way toward an inner peace, John was setting course for a new life as a dedicated artist, Paul was getting better and better as an all-around Alley songwriter, and Ringo was always Ringo—as steadfast as the lettering on Brighton rock. Their collective philosophy was summed up in the singalong "All You Need Is Love," beamed to millions all over the world in the hope that the message might be accepted and all strife might cease. It was the first time the Beatles had come out with some direct advice of a universal nature. Were they committed to the Movement?

The boys still felt there was nothing that couldn't be done. But for Brian Epstein, their onetime guru, there seemed very little left for him to do. Ever since the end of the touring and personal appearances—with the need for tight scheduling and attention to minute details—he had felt himself becoming redundant. His creation, once so immaculate and as sunny as a children's comic book, was getting introspective and philosophical. The gay magic bus he had once conducted to a precise timetable was bouncing away down the yellow brick road, leaving him choking in the cloud of a million impossible dreams. Who was this Magic Alex and what were his credentials? Why was he not consulted about the costuming for the *Sgt. Pepper* package? How could the Maharishi Mahesh Yogi guide the careers of the Beatles? Would the boys re-sign with their old manager and mentor when their contract came up in October? Now they were major world artists and had left the trappings of the old show biz behind. But he, Brian Epstein, was no mere spectator; he was an *artist* too—at least in temperament—and it was very taxing trying to be an artist when one's artwork was running away.

He wouldn't bother them musically. He left that to George Martin (but even he, it was rumored, was having his difficulties keeping a rein on the boys' mad extravagances). But if there were travel arrangements, he could take care of them; if there were public statements to be made in support of anything the Beatles did, well then, he would wade in up to the hilt. After joining Paul, John, and George in their LSD admission, he explained to *Melody Maker*: "An awful lot of good has come from hallucinatory drugs. . . . LSD helped me to know myself better and to become less bad tempered." "What is the thing you fear most in life?" "Loneliness—I hope I'll never be lonely." "Ever considered marriage?" "It would be a help, apart from companionship, because I get put out having to run two homes on my own." But back to the subject of drugs: "The pop stars take LSD to find out about their existence, to justify it. Poor people don't take it. Only those who have everything but spiritual peace."

Inner peace and sublime consciousness had been promised to the Beatles by the Maharishi. All you needed was a daily meditation of thirty minutes. On the August Bank Holiday weekend, the boys were going to journey down to Wales with their holy man and embark on a course of spiritual regeneration. Would Brian like to join them? Unfortunately, he had other plans. Yes, he was interested in attaining inner peace, but for the moment unconsciousness could only be induced through sleeping pills.

While I had been holidaying in Cornwall, a New Era had dawned in young America and even the old were dragging themselves into its light. Sgt. Pepper and the Monterey Pop Festival heralded the inauguration; reams of print lent intellectual support; big-time record labels saw black and more black in that crucial bottom line.

First of all, in June, there erupted the pandemic over Sgt. Pepper. Where were you when you first heard the album? Everyone remembers. Langdon Winner, a fan who became a critic, caught the total saturation effect nicely when he recalled: "I happened to be driving across the country on Interstate 80. In each city where I stopped for gas or food—Laramie, Ogallala, Moline, South Bend—the melodies wafted in from some far-off transistor radio or portable hi-fi. It was the most amazing thing I've ever heard. For a brief while, the irreparably fragmented consciousness of the West was unified, at least in the minds of the young." At home—in split-level or crash pad—they sat around transfixed by Sgt. Pepper, playing the masterwork over and over and over, analyzing and rapping it into many shapes, ferreting out a warren of meanings: were the holes in Blackburn, Lancashire, the needle tracks of a junkie or were they a reference to those grisly Yorkshire Moor murders? Why was Paul standing with his back to the camera? Was this a sign of his impending death? At least four of the songs were about turning on, maybe more—"Lucy in the Sky with Diamonds" being obvious and John's public denials a real put-on. As for "A Day in the Life"—*wow!*

The print people, many from the older generation, placed Sgt. Pepper in the realm of High Art. Richard Poirier, chairman of the English department at Rutgers, writing about "A Day in the Life," invoked the names of Wagner, Beckett, and Borges before going on to the vaunted T. S. Eliot. Jack Kroll in Newsweek also brought in Eliot's name and claims to have been raised to an unnatural high by the orchestral climb at the end of the song, describing it as "a growling, bone-grinding crescendo that drones up like a giant crippled turbine struggling to spin new power into a foundered civilization." Was he on some mind-blowing herbaceous plant? To Timothy Leary, the album was clear as Owsley's acid: "The Beatles have taken my place. That latest album is a complete celebration of LSD."

In all this word-spilling, there was no suggestion that Sgt. Pepper might be a summation of much of the past glories of Anglo-American popular music. Why is there so much ignorance of the long and straight road from ragtime to rock (not forgetting the ballad)? Where were the intellectuals when Elvis first appeared?

With grandiloquence and sweep in its very title, The First Annual Monterey International Pop Festival was from its inception predicated on the belief that the New Era must be ushered in with dignity if it were to succeed in its bid for legitimacy. From Friday, June 16, to Sunday, June 18, at the County Fairgrounds of the dainty and circumspect coastal town of Monterey, not too far from San Francisco but far enough from Los Angeles, a bill embracing some of the top talent in contemporary music (not forgetting the new faces, who were given generous stage time) spread happiness to a gathering of at least fifty thousand. But it seemed, to those who were tuned-in, that there were over a million at Monterey, with everyone rejoicing in this new kind of outdoor event, an extension in size and scope of the Human Be-In staged in San Francisco the previous January.

This was the first massive expression of gentle-style "togetherness" and a long way from the crude and nasty behavior to be seen at mass sports events. Flowers were the symbol of Monterey's spirit of altruism, togetherness, and pure, organically grown beauty. You never saw so many goddamn flowers! A mantel of flowers cloaked the festival and its juices affected all present. A nerve gas of good vibes. First off, one hundred thousand orchids, specially flown in from Hawaii, were scattered over the fairgrounds (and the rest were given away). Hell's Angels, biffing in on their snorting dragons to dig some Shankar, were dazed when they were greeted by motorcycle officers decorated from cap to boots with daffodils, poppies, and dandelions; Frank Marinello, chief of these "flower fuzz," was seen accepting a petunia as he dug soul singer Otis Redding who, garlanded in a mixed floral arrangement, praised with amazement the spirit of love among Flower People (for this was a time of great racial strife), but did not allow any loose epicenism to pansy up the stuttering gun of his violent shouts.

Flowers apart, there were twenty-two and a half hours of music for a top admission price of $6.50, resulting in a profit—surplus, rather—of $200,000, every penny of which was to be disbursed among charities. (Eventually, the money went to music lessons for ghetto kids and to the Sam Cooke Memorial Scholarship.) None of the talent got paid, but received only expenses: first-class air tickets, hotels, food, drink, and limousines. The festival was well organized, too: no drug busts, very few arrests, and not one death or birth.

"It was a religious festival. It was a love festival," Eric Burdon told the *KRLA Beat.* "It was a demonstration of what we can do if we put our minds to it and how we can impress the people who think we are incapable of behaving ourselves and acting like human beings instead of savages." An editorial in that same issue praised Monterey as a "real victory for the art of pop music over commercial exploitation." *TeenSet,* a glossier pop mag, went into more detail about the great strides made by rock: "Picture if you will a pop festival in the year 1962. That festival, had it existed, could easily have been held in the town of Elk's Tooth, Nebraska, population 9½. And what a ball it would have been for all those who attended. Both of them." The article maintained that there were few records worth hearing in those days and that too many were penned by Tin Pan Alley moon-in-June formula hacks. "Young music (then known as rock 'n' roll) was at an all-time low. It was simply too pooped to pop and teen interest had turned from singers to television stars, most of whom were about as heavy as egg custard."

But the most colorful reporting on the festival's significance came from Monterey's own house publicists. Derek Taylor, press officer for the event, observed in *The Royal's World Countdown,* a Hollywood-based "underground" paper, that "many of us were able to shed our egos and float downstream on people, music, love, and flowers" with the result that "we are all one and life flows on within us and without us." So transported was Derek by the good-vibe nerve gas that he had a vision of Pigpen of the Grateful Dead (not a lightweight) actually dancing through the air over his electric organ, while all around the press officer were members of the Monterey Public Service Department dissolving from wooden squaredom into real people. Finally, he had the honor of garlanding Police Chief Marinello with a necklace of leather and glass beads; it was further arranged that Derek and Lou Adler, the festival's co-organizer, would personally escort the chief around Haight-Ashbury, showing him all the points of interest.

The full scope of Monterey had been well expressed in one of the first press releases: "It can lift the music from the babbling money arenas of exploitation radio, giving it a chance to flourish or fail in a receptive, free environment. Today's singers have something to say and the manifold ability to say it."

Yesterday's singers, most of whom were still very much around, had had a lot to say, albeit in an *a-wop-bop-a-lu-bop* manner and for money (preferably hard cash). American pop had always been inextricably bound up with money. It sang about what money could buy and its most successful practitioners made a great deal of money by busting the charts. But none of the grand old heroes of rock 'n' roll were at Monterey: no Little Richard, no Jerry Lee Lewis, and (of course) no Elvis Presley. Chuck Berry, a token rocker, rightly declined an invitation because there was no pay. Since there was so much white blues played at Monterey, it would have enriched the festival to have had a few of the grass-roots black bluesfolk perform. But none were represented and certainly the likes of Muddy Waters, Lightnin' Hopkins, Big Mama Thornton, Roy Brown, and T-Bone Walker could have done with the exposure—and the expenses.

So there was no real rock 'n' roll and there was no real down-home blues. Nor was the festival "International," as it claimed to be. Aspects of the British Empire were represented—the Who, Eric Burdon and the Animals, and Beverly, a folk singer, from Great Britain; the Paupers and some members of the Buffalo Springfield from Canada; Hugh Masekela from South Africa—but where was French, German, Italian, or Russian pop? It was certainly flourishing in those nations.

More relevantly, the criticism was made that none of the heavyweights who had labored to forge pop into rock were performing on the Monterey concert stage. Where were the Beach Boys, Bob Dylan, the Rolling Stones, and the Beatles? "Well," said the organizers, "Brian Jones was freely mingling with the fairground crowd and three Beatles were present but disguised as hippies." Which three? Derek Taylor said he didn't know. A brilliant touch, in keeping with the spirit of Monterey. This spirit—that if we wish hard enough, then all things will come to pass—was a crucial factor in the success of the festival.

In the end, Monterey was very much a roundup of West Coast talent and a triumph for the record industry workers of Los Angeles. Bad old money-mad, publicity-crazed, blow-dried, blond-dyed, De Voss-clothed, plastic L.A. had beaten the Friscans to the punch! They were quite simply better at TCBing, they were organizers, they were hustlers.

Music, love, and flowers—it really should have been a San Francisco festival. It sounded like one, on paper anyway. But the Friscans were bogged down in schemes like the two Summer Solstice Festivals planned for June 21. One was to be held at the bottom of the Grand Canyon where no tourists roam, but this Be-In had to be canceled when the Hopi Indians told the Friscans they were a "tribe of strangers" who were "not with each other" and that therefore they should buzz off. So they were left with a gathering to be held on some hills behind the Haight, but this turned out to be a "fog-in" and much too early in the season for most Friscans. Those that struggled up to Twin Peaks were left shivering in the solstice cold and damp, entertained by a few desultory drums and bells and the tooting of a solitary horn. A certain Charlie Brown announced the start of the Summer of Love. But down below, in the streets of the Haight, was an ever-growing slum of runaways, pimps, con men, pickpockets, sex maniacs, and alcoholics. And somewhere in the hustling crowd lurked Charles Manson. Soon the sun would be up and a new brand of circus life would start its working day. By noon, the Haight freak show would be well under way, parading slowly up and down the filthy streets, while on either side of the roadway comfy, air-conditioned Gray Line tour buses delivered their safari spiel: "The only foreign tour within the continental limits of the United States. . . . We are now passing through the beaded curtain, where the favorite occupations, besides taking drugs, are group discussions about what's wrong with the status quo, malingering, and an everpresent preoccupation with the soul, reality, and self-expression, realized by strumming guitars, piping on flutes, and banging on bongos."

It was in working L.A. that Monterey had been dreamed up, planned, and bottom-lined. The original promoters, Alan Pariser and Ben Shapiro, wanted to have a moneymaking festival and they had gone as far as booking the Monterey County Fairgrounds when they were persuaded to change their thinking by the very stars they hoped to hire. John Phillips (of the Mamas and the Papas) and Paul Simon were adamant that such a festival—based on the prestigious jazz festivals of Newport and Monterey—must be nonprofit. Anyway, the two promoters couldn't possibly afford their fee (rock prices now being astronomical) and the occasion should be a celebration of the great strides made by the new art form. Lou Adler, John Phillips's manager, was contacted and he agreed that class and prestige were now of much more import than a mere fee. Lou Adler had made and paid his dues as a record-business operator in the changing trends of sixties pop, from surfing (Jan and Dean) through protest (Barry McGuire and P. F. Sloan) to Laurel Canyon love music (the Mamas and the Papas). He had just sold Dunhill Records (named after a Las Vegas tap-dancing act) and started a company with a more dignified title, Ode Records, on which Scott McKenzie was gently Pied-Pipering the world to come to San Francisco. From such a pinnacle, Lou Adler was not about to fall back into small-time show business. Status was in the offing—and a chance to bring into his circle the aristocracy of rock. Who knows? Even the Beatles might agree to perform.

Adler and Phillips, together with their friends Paul Simon, Johnny Rivers (the go-go record star produced to fame by Adler), and Terry Melcher (producer of hit albums by Paul Revere and the Raiders, the Byrds, and his mother, Doris Day), contributed equal sums of money to buy out the original Monterey promoters. An impressive board of directors was lined up, including Paul McCartney, Mick Jagger, Smokey Robinson (of the Miracles), Donovan, ace music-biz attorney Abe Somer, and Andrew Loog Oldham. Adler and Phillips were to be co-directors of the whole deal. Derek Taylor was to handle the all-important publicity and he did this so effectively that soon the Monterey City Council was fearful, lest their beautiful and artistically inclined town would be despoiled by the hordes of hippies. Adler and Phillips zipped up the coast and placated the city fathers. This festival was not only to be charitable but also educational. The acts invited to play were told that, though there was no actual pay, there would be first-class expenses and staging and sound equipment. And there would be a strict allotment of no more than forty-five minutes for each act. And not to worry about unruly fans because seats would be sat upon and there would be no dancing and thousands of extra police had been hired to quell any disturbance. The press, both working and underground, would be given purple badges enabling them to sit in the press box, but no film or TV cameras would be permitted in the main arena, for ABC-TV had exclusive rights. The paying public would be allowed to go *here* but not *there*—sensible restrictions in keeping with the necessary air of best behavior, necessary to show a certain dignity because the world will be watching and judging the new fraternity. A wide range of pop had been selected, with a special salute to the San Francisco sound, a dash of jazz and folk, and *a whole afternoon* of the mystic music of India, courtesy of Ravi Shankar (George's teacher and guru).

Around the world, the word spread that Monterey was where it was at. By opening night, Friday, all seats had been sold (except for the Shankar concert), but still the folks were arriving, to be greeted by laughing policemen and fascinating concession stands. Even the narcotics squad kept a low profile, disguised as festival judges and turning a blind eye to the open pot smoking. That evening's music leaned nicely toward pop: the Association, suited and precise, opened a bill that included slick L.A. vocalist Lou Rawls and Johnny Rivers with his go-go beat. The audience was appreciative but restless—a hip crowd, mostly from the Bay Area. Then on trooped Eric Burdon with his revamped Animals to bring a whiff of Hashbury via their latest MGM offering, "San Franciscan Nights," in which cops' faces are filled with hate as they stand on a street called "Love." Everybody knew that Eric had recently made San Francisco his home and he uttered the new verities with such conviction, denouncing his old love of guns and booze with such vehemence, that he seemed to out-native the natives. Friday night's show concluded with folk-poets Simon and Garfunkel in an acoustic set.

On Saturday, with the Bay bands scheduled to appear, things really burst loose. Over fifty thousand were present, bobbing and jerking and nodding and smiling at the great shared secret; not bothering emcee Brian Jones and certainly not Monkee Mickey Dolenz (dressed to kill as his Chickasaw ancestor) or Herb Alpert; unconcerned with the cameras and clapper boards, the tangled wires of KRLA's and KHJ's tape recorders; deaf to Jolly Jack the Jock's complaints about being denied a press badge; unaware of the swarms of record moguls on the prowl for future stars and the champagne and strawberries back in the "green room" reception tent.

The smiling ones, in the know, were head-shaking because today was all right, *all right*. Today was blues day and a time for boogie without the woogie. Black blues was fine if you were a historian, but it was a music to induce *sympathy* and what was needed in the here and now of Today was *empathy*. What was wrong with modern, white, urban middle-class blues, born of parent alienation on wall-to-wall carpeting and now dragged out into the street and made to howl? What rocker could truly identify with a Howlin' Wolf black man, as opposed to this afternoon's lineup of white bluesboys who linked music with life? Canned Heat, the Electric Flag, the Steve Miller Band, Al Kooper, and the Paul Butterfield Blues Band were all well versed on black blues history—but they were here to make people have a good time. White blues was *valid*.

Saturday also saw the first knockout scored by unknowns—unknowns, at any rate, as far as the record moguls were concerned. Big Brother and the Holding Company, featuring singer Janis Joplin, were the house band at the Avalon, but so far no major label had gotten a real good taste of them. Warner Bros. and RCA had already made forays into San Francisco and come back with likely specimens. Warner Bros. had the Grateful Dead and that deal looked like being a hard worker; RCA were up and away with their Airplane, who were racking up big sales across the country with their second album, *Surrealistic Pillow*. Columbia had dawdled, but the new president, Clive Davis, was here at Monterey, minus his pinstripe suit but sharp in his turtleneck. The buzz was certainly on in the biz and the question was: will Frisco be the new Liverpool? As *Billboard*, the trade bible, had expressed it a few weeks before: S.F., A CALDRON OF CREATIVE ACTIVITY—CAN THE EXPANDING POP/HIPPIE MOVEMENT TURN THE CITY INTO A MAJOR MUSIC CENTER?

For the Frisco camp, June marked an exciting transition stage, what with *Sgt. Pepper* establishing rock's meaningful significance once and for all and now with the big chance for the Bay Area to make that vinyl art into a visual/aural experience in 3-, 4-, or even 5D. So that Monterey, apart from being a groove and a gas and a sign of the New Togetherness, was also a super showcase. Sure, there might be a few minor compromises in the marriage between art and commerce—but these would originate from the artists themselves and not from the dictates of some corporate fat cat. It was possible to make good bread and still keep your soul—like, for example, Gypsy Boots, one of the first nature boys who had dwelt hippie-style in the Haight as long ago as the thirties. Here he was at Monterey doing his very own thing, wearing that same beard and sandals, spreading his peace and his macrobiotic philosophy, and presently employed as KRLA's special festival horticultural expert!

So we have Big Brother and the Holding Company poised for a knockout. They were going to get out on that stage and play just like they were at the Avalon. No concessions—Janis wasn't even wearing any finery. No concessions—musically. But about signing this release form for the movie people—Big Brother had been warned by the Dead's manager, Danny Rifkin, not to go along with such a rip-off but. . . . Hey, many of the Friscans felt that this festival stank of L.A. efficiency and tight-assed money-grubbing. Not enough natural looseness, too much timetabling. No more than forty-five minutes a spot, what a drag! Hardly time to get in the groove; the Dead sometimes take two hours just to tune up and Country Joe doesn't even bother, ha ha! Screw all this ordering around; it was like school and parents, yakety yak, blah blah blah. Should have been a "freebie" show like the Human Be-In at Golden Gate Park. And if it *was* supposed to be open for the press, then how come *Pool News* were denied accreditation and the Haight-Ashbury *Tribune* only got two badges, while KRLA got seven and *Time* and *Life* swaggered around with whatever they wanted? Who did John Phillips think he was fooling in that long robe and Russian fur hat? Or that Monkee actor dressed up as an Indian?

Ever since the festival idea had first been mentioned in April, there had been rumblings and grumblings from the Friscan camp. And threats that they might set up a rival free festival to be shunted around the commercial affair on flatbed trucks. Derek Taylor, press officer, was dispatched to speak to their leader. Ralph Gleason, keeper of the conscience and defiant in bush hat and knee boots, gave his blessing only after Derek convinced him that Derek and all his festival colleagues were as honest as a summer solstice.

But even this afternoon, as Big Brother was about to go onstage, an impromptu free concert was being held on flatbed trucks at nearby Monterey Peninsula College's football field. And the Diggers of the Haight had promised to perform a feeding of the crowd of 5,000 a little later. During the course of this open-ended concert, there were to be appearances by the Grateful Dead, Quicksilver Messenger Service, and Jefferson Airplane, and they didn't care if they rocked until they dropped. They were signed to major labels; they had clout; they had contracts stating that delivery time for their albums would be exactly as long as their art took to perfect.

Big Brother and the Holding Company, despite their name, had no such clout. Blues energy was one thing, managerial guided-missile energy quite another. They'd gotten tied to a minor label in Chicago, recording a lackluster set that bore no relation to those glamorous nights with the Avalon audience feedback. How do you catch this feeling and shove it in the can? But now they were poised to . . . to . . . to . . . *make it.* Since gelling at a jam in Chet Helms's Haight mansion, they'd scored at Kesey's Trips Festival, gigged regularly at the Avalon, done a load of smaller concerts, and along the way acquired a girl singer even ballsier than Jefferson Airplane's preppy Grace Slick—and this addition made Big Brother a little different from the thousands of other Bay bands. Not that Janis Joplin was in any way a gimmick—far from it, she and the band were clean of any Top Forty crap, stripped down for gut-level action, ready to get an audience off. Like so much of Bay Area music, Big Brother and Janis had to be seen *live.* And then, in essence, it became the Janis Joplin story, a tale reminiscent of Judy Garland, Edith Piaf, Helen Morgan, and all the other battered babies who had become their songs. Ironically, Janis Joplin idolized Mae West and wanted to achieve that consummate sense of style. But Miss West was an ironclad with a built-in Fort Knox and Joplin, for all her battling feminism, was only a stray on the way to the slaughterhouse.

To witness Joplin and Big Brother on a good night at the Avalon, when they were all in the mood and at full tilt and flail, was to be involved in a psychodrama where music was incidental. Maybe the band was sometimes a bit out of tune, maybe Janis's pipes, crudded with the junk food of hell-raising, sometimes gave off too many croaks and wheezes, so that the poor song became lost in a fog made from this abused plumbing—but the spectacle was thrilling, original, sparkling with danger, and the emotions were real. All eyes were fixed on her, entertainer supreme, and the band was left to follow the leader.

Dressed like a fun-fair Queen of Sheba in an ensemble where gaudy ornaments clanged and colors did battle, the leader first clambered into the song, punched it out, gobbled it up, and finally bad-mouthed it into a ragged truth—her own truth, the continuing lurid saga of Janis Joplin. So "Ball and Chain," performed straight ahead by its creator Big Mama Thornton, became a quivering ball of pain flying every which way. And whereas Big Mama (like most blues singers) could always retreat to the church when troubles massed ready to overwhelm, Janis knew no such sanctuary.

But during those stage moments, she was invincible and gorgeous, as if the muse goddesses had painted her, and she radiated a tougher love than flower love. She'd jump down into the Beautiful People and allow them to squeeze her tits if they so desired, but then she'd get back up in search of that bottle of Southern Comfort, uttering "shit" and "fuck" because she couldn't locate it. She was giving booze a good name again and, when she found the bottle, she'd swig deeply and then wave it as a good-bye. Nobody was shocked. In fact, they cheered because this was all part of the show—if you could call it a show, for there'd been no routining, no Vegas faking, no slick soul hamboning. This was real-life rock, with Janis busting to demonstrate that her catharsis could be your catharsis and the whole trip could break on through to pure nemesis. So it wasn't surprising that, if you were backstage, you might look through the gorgeousness and see some specks of blood adding to her costume hues.

And after the psychodrama, with her audience-lovers cooling off, the artist, whom they'd whooped on to higher and higher indulgences, went home alone to curl up with F. Scott Fitzgerald, James Joyce, or her favorite, Wilfred Owen, the poet who had long ago sung of the pity of war.

As a child growing up in Port Arthur, Texas, Janis had been a reader and then, in her teens, a painter of religious themes and more and more a loner. Her world was populated by brassy earth mothers, like Mae West and Ma Rainey, who had built themselves from scratch and could defend their territory. She read books and listened to records and watched movies and never got asked to the prom because no stud wanted to walk a dog. Janis had acne, ran to fat, had frizzy hair, was no beauty. Her clothes started getting bizarre and Port Arthur wasn't ready for a weirdo. She was making the worst of a bad job instead of self-improving and thinking positive like, say, Connie Francis. Only with her father, an oil company executive and a secret reader, could she communicate, in the form of long chats.

Being the only weirdo in Port Arthur became oppressive, so she went to Austin, ostensibly to go to college but actually to realize all her dreams. In an Austin hillbilly bar, she sang country-and-western and sometimes a touch of the barroom blues. Chet Helms, a local, took her with him to San Francisco to see what the North Beach life held in store for them, but by that time, 1962, the beatnik era was at its tail end, leaving only disgruntlement and bad "modern" jazz. At a Palo Alto coffee house, where Jerry Garcia was the main man, Janis got to sing on hoot night and the folkies were impressed by her maturity. Close your eyes and the zit-faced dog with no makeup and with abscesses on her arm sounded like an old race record from the twenties. At this stage, her clothes were ratty, but heavy doses of speed had given her a shortcut to the kind of torn-up, life-battered voice that had taken the likes of Bessie Smith years and years to achieve.

Still, there wasn't much of a living in the deadbeat folk life, so Janis returned to Texas. Besides, she was strung out on bad dope. Two years later, as we have seen, the freaks started massing and establishing a new society centered in Haight-Ashbury. Janis came back and stepped straight into Haight life, no longer feeling such a social outcast. When she jammed with Big Brother, she knew little about rock 'n' roll. She just set Bessie Smith to a rock beat and set her once-scorned body to a workout that often included little jumps. After a while, she was "one of the boys" and the focal point wherever Big Brother and the Holding Company performed.

The whole ensemble was poised to maybe make it in front of the big shots of the industry at Monterey among the flowers. The cameras focused on the singer: Janis seemed to be the very eye of the whirl-wind, the source of all the trouble, the Queen of Complaints. Her Saturday afternoon performance stopped the show and set the wires buzzing. The movie people begged for a release, promising no L.A. rip-offs, so Big Brother finally agreed to a repeat show on Sunday. And Clive Davis, president of Columbia Records, decided he must have this girl on his roster. She had actually reduced him to tears.

Ivy League educated, trained as a corporate lawyer, Davis had no musical background, but he knew what he disliked early on. As a youth, he'd detested Frank Sinatra's "screaming"; he found Bill Haley and Elvis Presley far too gimmicky for his taste; he didn't mind the Kingston Trio. He was fascinated by balance sheets, statistics, and charts. At Columbia, in the deadly, inhuman bunker headquarters called "Black Rock," he started following the ups and downs of the hit charts as, through tact and delicate engineering, he worked his way up the Columbia ladder until he was in a position to call some creative shots, to work with living figures. By the middle sixties, he sensed impending change and concluded, "This was the time for me to step forward and make my creative mark and sign up some of these wonderful new stars" that he was reading about and hearing about. Already Columbia had Dylan, the Byrds, and Simon and Garfunkel, but the only real rockers under contract were Paul Revere and the Raiders. In 1966, Davis stepped forward and signed Donovan ("Very, very ethereal" and a "spokesman for cultural change"). He also struck a deal with Lou Adler and it was at the latter's suggestion that Davis attended the Monterey Pop Festival, casting aside his normal pinstripes and even accepting a necklace and petals for the occasion. The signing of Janis Joplin, though fraught with technical difficulties, was to be the first of his many marriages between corporate clout and heavy—yet sensitive and meaningful—rock artists: by 1969, Columbia would boast a splendid collection of contemporary music stars like the Electric Flag; Blood, Sweat, and Tears; the Chambers Brothers; Spirit; and, of course, Janis Joplin and Big Brother and the Holding Company.

Embracing the ways of the counterculture required all of Davis's tact and patience. Not that his colleagues at other labels were any less taxed or any less successful—all had to become more flexible, less uptight, and to roll with the flow, or else get out of the business. For example, Davis was quietly upset by Janis's habit of suddenly remarking loudly, "Wow, I'd like to ball him!" in the middle of a business discussion; at the very first meeting between Davis and Big Brother and the Holding Company, one of the band boys appeared totally in the nude right there in the office, but Davis shined it on. Later, when Janis wanted to cement her business relationship with CBS by bedding Davis, he politely "deferred the offer." But his conversion to the music was complete and fervent: he insisted that composer Richard Rodgers sit down and listen to Joplin's version of the George Gershwin classic "Summertime" and wasn't fazed at Rodgers' total bewilderment and ensuing depression. The revolution had to come and all else must be swept away in its path.

Saturday night at Monterey saw the largest crowd of the festival, 8,500, but the music verged on the desultory: Moby Grape had a light show, but that was hardly news; Hugh Masekela and Laura Nyro were too jazzy for this audience's taste; the Byrds, already minus key member Gene Clark, displayed more internal dissension when David Crosby tiraded against The Warren Report to Roger McGuinn's obvious annoyance; Jefferson Airplane went through their paces but were clearly exhausted after their free concert on the nearby football field. Otis Redding, the great soul singer and one of Janis Joplin's idols, saved the night with a staggering display of secularized gospel that trailed roots going back to the beginning of pop history and beyond.

Sunday afternoon had religious overtones, too, as Ravi Shankar and his Indian ensemble played their music straight and without any trend concessions for three hours. The audience, sitting in a light rain, obeyed Shankar's request for no smoking or talking and sat devoutly, rewarding the service/concert with the longest standing ovation of the festival. In the evening, the final show, the most thunderous of the new bands appeared. The Grateful Dead, though, were never able to get into a fiery groove, perhaps due to lack of time or perhaps to the old football field exhaustion. The Who came to the rescue, livening things up with the autodestruction show well known to British audiences but still relatively unknown in America. Not a few of the gentler, action-shunning Flower People (and especially the Simon and Garfunkel fans) were shocked by this display of barbarianism, feeling that it set rock back into the mindlessness of the fifties. Ellen Sander, a very sensitive soul, thought "it was a genuine freak-out and that the Who were actually trying to destroy the stage. . . . I broke loose, scampering under the superstructure in full panic, trembling and clinging to a wooden support and praying tearfully." While the smoke was blossoming and the drums were collapsing, Jimi Hendrix was finishing a fried chicken dinner backstage and the Mamas and the Papas were limbering up with honey, tea, and *me-me-me-me-mes*. When the Jimi Hendrix Experience hit the stage, they produced more decibels than the Who and Hendrix bumped and ground out a deal of much-needed sexuality. American girls were astonished to find themselves turned on by a black act. Hendrix humped his guitar; he told the audience in raw whiskey tones that he loved them so much he wanted to just grab them; he giggled sharply (showing that he was flying as high as everybody else at Monterey); and then he announced that he was "gonna sacrifice something I really love, man. There's nothing I could do more for all you Beautiful People out there!" And with that, he proceeded to set his guitar on fire by first setting a small bonfire with the aid of a lighter and a kind of voodoo kneeling and praying and coaxing. Down in the audience, there was a mixed reaction: one of Ravi Shankar's musicians expressed disbelief that any true musician would destroy his instrument (for to even accidentally brush a tabla was considered sacrilege in India); several serious critics voiced disapproval of this distressing tendency toward anarchy and destruction in British-based pop; most people thought it pure magic of the Barnum & Bailey variety.

Of course, what both the Who and Hendrix were depicting was the essence of rock: the narcissistic child entering the apocalypse. The narcissist smashes the things he loves—his face or his limbs or his toys—in order to get sympathy. And the natural conclusion to the devil's music originally whipped up by demon kings like Little Richard and Jerry Lee Lewis is a cosmic cataclysm wrought by God and conducted by His agents, the Who and Hendrix. All will meet the consuming fire. Those who will pass through unscathed will be those who have surrendered themselves to God. Few had thought about such a day of reckoning, but there were to be many burnt offerings in the not-too-distant future.

After Hendrix, on tripped the Mamas and the Papas to quiet everyone down with the balm of their soft rocking lullabies "Monday, Monday" and "California Dreamin'." Then they were joined by Scott McKenzie, another Adler artist, who did his current hit, the clever and immaculate piece that was luring so many to the Far West and irritating the original settlers. Its words and music, so deftly pat in their sug-

gestion that all you need is a flower in your hair in order to join the
New Friscans, re-established that marvelous intimacy between popular
art and commerce: selling back to the masses their very own dreams!
Monterey slept happy that night.

In hindsight, though, reactions were mixed. The British contributors
saw Monterey as just another festival. After all, they'd had the Richmond Jazz Festival (which included rock and blues) for several years
and the atmosphere at this British event was much more relaxed, with
no cops around and plenty of jive dancing. Pete Townshend had enjoyed meeting some of his rock contemporaries but, all in all, he
couldn't raise much sympathy for Flower Power. Basic drive and ambition were lacking in these people, he told the British press. "Dressing up
like a lot of cream cakes only earns young people dislike." As for the
much-touted Grateful Dead, they were, according to Townshend,
"Terrible—ugh! One of the original ropeys!" And the trinket stands
were far too overpriced. Still, the perks were OK: the first-class plane
tickets, hotel accommodations, and so on. Jann Wenner, a young rock
fan preparing to launch an underground newspaper (appearing in November as *Rolling Stone*) filed a report to *Melody Maker* on Monterey
in which he stated that Jimi Hendrix smashed his guitar better than
Pete Townshend, that Paul Simon "will not be remembered as an outstanding lyricist," and that though Monterey was a "gathering of 'New
Americans,' the key makers of new sounds weren't there—Muddy Waters, the Rolling Stones, Chuck Berry, Bob Dylan, and the Beatles."
Finally, on the negative side, the city of Monterey showed no enthusiasm for a second festival the next year. As the city fathers and mothers—
and even the once-flowered police chief—saw it, there had been too
much drugging and cohabitation. Nor had there been a marked increase in local business.

But on the bright side, the future for the new rock looked very rosy
indeed. Entrepreneurs saw pots of money to be made from such festivals and laid their plans accordingly. The rock nation had shown itself
in vast numbers and on good behavior. The only violence had been onstage for art's sake. As for the record industry executives, they were ecstatic: they had seen thousands of fans who were (or could become)
consumers of "units," which would be albums made by artists and
bought for their artistic worth, not just as two-and-a-half minutes' accompaniment to dancing, necking, whatever.

The greening of the record industry had begun, as the executives
grappled with the New Consciousness and tried to hide the old crap-
eroo approach. This greening was not completed until the seventies,
but *Sgt. Pepper* and Monterey had sown the seeds. In the future, the
business bridges would be built by hired hippies, company freaks fresh

from street experience, so that promising artists, who might never make it beyond the threshold of a country club, could be led right up to the desk of the label president himself and not be kept waiting, styrofoam cup in hand, in a reception area. With the chief would be lawyers and managers and creative services experts and, within a year or so, their altered appearance would show that they were all in sympathy with this New Consciousness: beards and, if possible, a full covering of shaggy hair; Nehru jackets and, later, U.S. Army jackets; and jeans, jeans, jeans. Posters on the walls and on the coffee table a copy of *Rolling Stone*, full of groovy ads for the company's latest offerings. Youth had to be persuaded to trust the manufacturers, and the ticket sellers, so the frontal-assault approach was out—like Sam the Sham and Stridex medicated pad commercials. Warner Bros., for example, were to evolve a put-on style with campaigns to make the Grateful Dead and the scatological Fugs seem cartoony lovable: "Enter the giant Pigpen look-alike contest now!" "Win the Fug Dream Date Competition." Warner Bros. could also put themselves down (thus showing real honesty) with an ad campaign admitting that their Van Dyke Parks, acknowledged as a genius by so many of the rock critics, hadn't sold worth a shit: "How we lost $35,509.50 on 'The Album of the Year' (Damn it)." Columbia would not be far behind, with real friendly, real down-to-earth ads. They created: "Know who your friends are. And look and see and touch and be together. Then listen. We do."

Them and Us could work to make beautiful music together for Those Out There. Drinks, smokes, and canapés might now be produced, as boots are removed and contract points hammered out: the artist is assured that cover artwork is of paramount importance and might entail a specially commissioned painting—perhaps even by the artist/musician himself. We live in Renaissance times. Record sleeves are an essential part of the total work concept and we mustn't forget the liner: here could be printed the song lyrics for perusal as poetry and, of course, all the many credits for all the many talents who contribute to the album, even down to the gopher who gets the ice. When the album's ready—however long it might take to create—promotion men dressed exactly like us will present it carefully to radio stations, especially the FM variety because the fast-burgeoning FMs with their free-form playlists of hundreds of records are the best barkers of the new album product. We also have campus representatives and special services men, so we've got every angle covered. The fact is, when you come down to the bottom line, this business is in a raging bull market. Since '67, record sales have grown to a billion a year and, within five years, we should double that figure. Predictions are that records

will soon be the most popular of all American recreations, so watch out
Hollywood! I tell you, the rock machine rules!

And so the executives happily went to bed with the artists. Rock had
come of age and the industry was ready to welcome musicians of intelligence, sophistication, and poetic intentions. Thus this new club seemed
to be a perfect shelter for a misunderstood young genius like myself.
Unfortunately, I couldn't get a membership.

At the beginning of August, a record for a *danse macabre,* dominated
by a sepulchral organ and called by a commanding and sinuous crooner
voice, reached number one in the nation. "Light My Fire," by L.A.'s
own Doors, made a funeral pyre of peaceable canyon rock and re-established the city as a center of black night where even a Murphy bed
could summon up feelings of dread.

The bed in question, my bed at the Tel-El-Pal Apartments in Hollywood, had a nasty habit of springing back to its place in the wall, so
that I had twice found myself literally *up against the wall.* I had never
encountered such vicious beds anywhere before and, on this hot August
night, when my spirits were dim and I couldn't face the dread of the
recalcitrant bed, I tried to sleep on the shag carpet. Its smell brought
back a world I had forgotten during my holiday idyll in Cornwall and
my night was unquiet even in its eventual dreams. I was haunted by a
thousand selves in hopeless search for a lost boyhood, a distant manhood, and a place on the charts. Why had I returned to hell? Was
there a fatal attraction? Certainly not in this waking moment before
dawn when I could hear the shrieks of the police sirens outside and the
groans and squeals from the sex maniacs next door. On my old ex-hotel
TV, long-dead cowboys chased desperadoes down a road whose spikey
dwarf trees looked like those on the way to Camarillo.

So, without even changing out of my pajamas, I got up, grabbed my
book and wallet, and drove out for an early breakfast. I was at the
counter of the Copper Skillet, a twenty-four-hour greasy spoon coffee
shop on Sunset and Gower, dividing my attention between an omelette
and my book, when a croaky voice next to me remarked, "I can quote
the whole of that poem you're readin'."

I'd only been back in America a week, but already I'd heard Jim
Morrison's voice in art-house cinemas, health restaurants, and cars
cruising the boulevard. Radio, which he currently ruled, I'd avoided because I wasn't on the radio. But in magazine photos, he really came
into his own, with his luxuriant mane of dark, curly hair like I could
never grow, his straight Grecian nose, and his sensuous, wavy mouth.
Only the eyes let him down: beyond the broodiness, they were empty.
He was like a hero from *Classics Illustrated.*

At the Copper Skillet counter, he was recognizable but very rumpled and very used. He was all in black leather and it reeked of the same sin as my apartment shag carpet. And yet beyond the boy hustler appearance, I could sense good breeding—he was holding his knife and fork in the British manner and his voice was polite and assured—and I could see that sure sign of civilization: an open book.

I knew better than to get into pop talk, so I said, " 'The Romantic Angst'—it's rather a pompous title, but I've always been fascinated by late-Victorian sexuality." "Me, too." "People used to say that the Victorians kept their feelings too buttoned up, but I think the little they let through was like atomic drops." "You want me to prove I'm not bullshitting you?" "Fire away, old bean."

He quoted Piers Brighton's 1897 poem perfectly:

> "A sturdy lad of seventeen summers hung
> From an old oak and in his death among
> The hollyhocks and leanders his frame
> Though arrow-pierced took on a purple flame
> That fitted him so natural in this scene
> He seemed a life force bloody yet serene."

Two middle-aged homosexuals passing by paused for a short cruise. "They like you," I said. "No, they like *you*," he said. Then he shrugged: "I guess they like us both. You're the Evelyn Waugh lavender type and I'm pure 'rough trade'." I adjusted my pajamas. Nobody else had paid attention to my appearance—Hollywood's forever in costume—and it hadn't struck me yet that Jim Morrison was dressed for a part and that, if he'd been true to his background, he'd be wearing Brooks Brothers' clothes. But his downward journey into rock was the way to go for privileged young in the late sixties. Elvis wanted a Cadillac; Jim Morrison wanted a cold meatloaf sandwich in a greasy spoon. Elvis loved his parents; Jim pretended his were dead.

Jim Morrison was born in Florida in 1943 to a Navy family that was constantly transferred from base to base. His father was marked out for a brilliant career and, in 1967, his diligence was rewarded: he was made an Admiral. Jim always detested his father's mixed-up authority; it didn't tally with the rough justice of service life. For example, after rubbing dog shit in his little brother's face (or farting into it or taping its mouth shut), a boy would expect to be spanked. But all Jim got was a lecture to make him feel guilty; he got sweet reason, while what he felt he needed was a good bashing like any deckhand would have gotten. The words, though, were few and far between. The family was always on the move and his father was going up and up and growing more distant and perplexing. One day, when Jim was a pudgy teenager, his father took him to the current seat of his authority. Accompanied by six Marines, they boarded the aircraft carrier and—lo!—at the wave of his father's hand, two hundred thousand tons began to move, and, in a flash, they were out at sea and ready for target practice with real riot guns. Another wave of the hand and these guns were firing at facsimile U.S. bluejackets bobbing about in the water. Such power! But when they got home, minus the Marines, Jim's mom read the riot act to the Admiral for not having washed the front windows. And the man with the magical hand said he was sorry, very sorry, and he'd get that window washing done soonest.

Jim was uneasy. Life was not fulfilling its promise. It was petty; it lacked grandeur. He retreated, as usual, into his room and his books. Here were Great Men—leaders and philosophers and poets—who could show the way without mercy, without fear of knocking down small persons or animals in the way. He read, marked, and digested Nietzsche on the power of ideas, Plutarch on Alexander the Great, Joyce and his salad of words, obscure medieval writers on demonology. He discovered the *shaman,* a priest who can put himself in contact with the unseen world of demons and ancestral spirits and who can control destiny and cure the sick. Not unlike Little Richard, Jerry Lee Lewis, Elvis Presley, and the other revivalist rockers who had emerged steaming and frothing for a glorious moment when Jim was a lad. But he didn't care for them at the time—they were too tacky redneck and too close for comfort.

His reading told him that the poet had power, much more power than a dad waving his hand on a ship, so he buried himself in poetry, especially that of the lone, misunderstood romantic whose short candle burned at both ends and was snuffed out early. Besides writing verse and dying young, Morrison wanted to be the inspiration of poets, to be the ideal youth. Like Rupert Brooke. He'd have to get into shape and tend to his hair for that. He'd have to lose some weight to get into the kind of tight velvet pantaloons worn by the boy poet Thomas Chatterton in the famous painting of him on his death couch, body posed temptingly, with the lighting just right. Death as the ultimate in ecstasy.

But Jim wasn't entirely locked into nineteenth-century homoerotic necromanticism; he also liked some of the doings of his own age: *Mad* magazine; the "sick" songs of Tom Lehrer; *On the Road* (especially Dean Moriarty—he practiced his insane "hee-hee" laugh); jeering at cripples; sketching huge penises on the rampage for food, and men with Coke bottles instead of penises. He liked the blues and folk music, too.

Like many other kids of the sixties, he was restless at college, experimenting here and there on the East Coast and finally winding up at UCLA in 1964. In theater arts, he could study "film" and avoid traditional academic discipline. Unlike USC, whose cinema department turned out graduates to take their place in Hollywood, UCLA let their students thrash about as true artists, finding their themes, rapping endlessly about film theory, and occasionally making experimental films that made little concession to popular taste.

Jim made his films and they were more than incomprehensible to most of his fellow students: they were revolting. He didn't care because by this time he was well into his role as the wounded artist, misunderstood by a stupid populace, but hellbent on pursuing the greater truth out there in whatever way was appropriate. His art would justify his behavior. In other words: "Whatever feels right is right." Did he realize at that time how close he was to the youth philosophy of the sixties? All he needed was a good song, a good act, and a record contract. He had the lyrics; he was writing them constantly to current pop songs that were floating about in his head, such as "Hello, I Love You" to the tune of "All Day and All of the Night" by the Kinks. He couldn't sing and he couldn't dance and he couldn't play an instrument, but he talked excitedly to his best friend about forming the be-all-and-end-all of rock 'n' roll bands. Even devised a name for this dream band: the Doors, inspired by William Blake's line from "The Marriage of Heaven and Hell" stating that, once our "doors of perception" are cleansed, everything will appear as it truly is—infinite. Of course, most people knew *The Doors of Perception* as the title of a turgid drug book by dullard Aldous Huxley. Most people were as incapable of entering Jim's kingdom as a camel passing through the eye of a needle. But they would suffice as his audience of the future; *actor and spectator*—the world was divided into the two. And when the herd, the rabble, the many-headed monster, got its blood up, the effect was maddening and Jim longed to call up some shamanism to deal with these tormentors of the artist in hell. He now knew what it was like to be Elvis, a great leader destroyed by sycophants (not to mention castrated by a father-figure "Colonel"). Well, this crass outer world must visit Jim on his own terms "in my womb garden," as he wrote in his notebook at the time, "where I peer out; where I can construct a universe within the skull to rival the real."

After UCLA, he went to live in Venice, a hippie colony just south of Santa Monica Bay that had long been a tumbledown haven for the fringe, a folly of pleasant decay, and a home for free spirits in dirty clothes. Several old Beats still lived there, grumbling and gazing into the ocean and constructing dreams of revenge on the straight world.

Such an ambience was perfect for Jim and he found a kind of heaven in a one-room crash pad complete with Bunsen burner and blanket. With countless songs running around his febrile brain, he went beautifully insane and slim on a diet of acid tabs and lids of pot. Soon his hair was long and curly and he was well on his way to breaking down the doors that barred his perception. Venice was full of flakey layabouts buttonholing strangers to tell of their grandiose plans and perhaps some of these strangers might have written Jim off. But Ray Manzarek, a fellow former UCLA student, believed in him, raved about him, saw a million dollars waiting. One day, on a beach littered with hopeless bodies, he'd heard Jim recite some of his songs and he'd exclaimed: "That's it!" These were lyrics like he'd never heard before. "Moonlight Drive," for instance, had Jim suggesting a *swim* to the moon and a *climb* through the tide and a *penetration* of the evening—sort of surrealist but not too cerebral when croak-crooned by this slightly tarnished Greek god. There and then, they decided to form a group. And Manzarek had the experience and expertise as a classically trained keyboarder and just recently a member of Rick and the Ravens, a blues outfit.

Ray, on his electric organ, could provide harmony, melody, and bass. They soon got competent musicians, who'd once played as the Psychedelic Rangers, to provide guitar and drums. Meanwhile, Jim developed his voice by eating more drugs to "open the eyes to the inner self" (a favorite maxim of his) and he tended to his mane by applications of a fabulous organic shampoo he'd learned about from a girlfriend. In return, he gave her some pointers on great themes from Western philosophy.

For a year, the band rehearsed the songs they were putting together and did a few casuals like college parties and weddings. Then they landed a gig at a Sunset Strip club. The London Fog was a pretty sleazy joint patronized by bikers, tough women, and the odd mafioso. But it was *on the Strip,* only a few blocks from the Whiskey A Go Go. On opening night, they papered the house with UCLA film students. The Doors—"A Band from Venice" were hired at $5 apiece on weekdays and $10 on weekends, maybe.

At first, Jim was so insecure about his singing ability that he performed with his back to the audience. But after a while, he got up some courage and was *psychically communicating* with his audience via superb body handling, microphone manipulation, and Alexandrian stances. But business fell off and Jim had some bad communication with the management. A girl booker at the Whiskey took a chance on the Doors, hiring them as the house band. They opened for visiting name acts, but gradually all eyes were on the Doors—or rather on the loony singer who rubbed his bulge on the mike stand, struck sulky poses, and was developing a horror song about a boy who murders his father and has sex with his mother. Of course, it referred to Oedipus and it was symbolic, but "The End" also had a more direct effect on some of the audience. How many times had the yackety-yaks from mom and dad got so nagging that you wanted to blast 'em to damnation? With Jim as conductor, you could cut the bonds, descend into hell, and emerge redeemed to start again as a parentless being! He was also really sexy, whatever your persuasion.

A lot of labels weren't interested, but finally Elektra, a folkie label trying to shake that image, signed the Doors and Paul Rothchild produced their first album, which was released in January 1967. "The End," over eleven minutes long, was there, together with Morrison advice like "Break on Through (to the Other Side)," an old Brecht/Weill song from the thirties, a Willie Dixon blues number, and "Light My Fire," which, in an edited version, was to become a hit single.

Elektra knew that in Jim they had the Face and the Copy. They gave the group a billboard on Sunset Strip, the first of its kind in rock history. They released a bio. sheet on Jim that had him saying: "I am interested in anything about revolt, disorder, chaos, especially activity that seems to have no meaning." His fave groups were the Beach Boys, the Kinks, and Love. He admired Frank Sinatra and Elvis Presley. His parents were dead.

They started touring all over and Jim flung himself into his poetic dramas. But trying to capture the same inner reality night after night was really tough and a real drain. You couldn't simply turn on the demon world like his father waving the carrier into action. And the media weren't about to be allowed to treat the Doors as Top Forty morons, even if Jim did look like jean-creaming pinup material. "We're erotic politicians"—that gave 'em something to think about. The alternative press—now, they were different. They wanted to *understand*. The Doors' message that the end of the world was nigh was *right on* for them. Currently, the underground was bannering stories about assassination conspiracies, police brutality, corrupt government, change and decay all around. God had died in 1966, so there was no "abide with me." Flower Power was giving way to clenched fists, even gun power. Interviews with musicians crackled with angry politics. For instance, Mike Bloomfield of the Electric Flag stated in the Los Angeles *Free Press*: "White people just don't know, they just don't know about anything. They suck entirely. . . . Thank God there are Malcolm Xs and Rap Browns around who are finally, finally getting the people into revolution. . . . You've got a stupid fucking cracker for a President. I mean, there's no doubt when you hear the way he talks with a Southern accent, he's a stinking, lousy, fucking cracker."

In New York, after a gig at Ondine's, the Doors let *Open City* interview them, but the interviewer was bursting with his own observations: "Let's talk about the Doors and alienation. A lot of people look at the group . . . I really don't know, but I think like, at Ondine's, the thing is like the world's a crock of shit and unreasonable and the only thing to do, really, is to protect your cool and look out for your own pleasures and see you don't get too involved in them. They say to themselves, 'This is where the Doors are at, man.' Whatever's right."

OPEN CITY:	Do any of the group play on acid?
DOOR:	No, nobody does.
OPEN CITY:	Jim seems to be stoned. He's a stoned guy, I guess.
DOOR:	That's Jim.
ANOTHER DOOR:	Yeah.
FIRST DOOR:	He's all over the stage. And whether he's stoned or not, he's flopping all over . . . so people think . . .
ANOTHER DOOR:	I suppose a lot of people would have thought Christ was stoned, too. Or Maharishi.

When "Light My Fire" had reached number one, Jim had gone out and bought a skintight black leather outfit. At the Copper Skillet, it wasn't quite so skintight anymore.

"How do you do it?" I asked.

"I never dug Gerry and the Pacemakers. How do I do what?"

I wanted to kick myself for bringing up my obsession with pop success, but I plowed on: "How do you stay intellectual and still be a hit with the kids, the masses?"

"You could have done it. You were into the Theater of the Absurd. I saw you on 'Shindig' and 'Lloyd Thaxton' goofing off and telling the audience that rock 'n' roll was a big joke. That the whole of existence is a big bad joke. You were too comic. Tragedy's the thing. Western civilization is ending and we don't even need an earthquake; we're performing crumble music for the final dance of death and you know what? Truth lies beyond the grave! C'mon, I'll pick up the tab."

Letter to Hal Shaper:

> *August 27, 1967*
> *Mr. Hal Shaper,*
> *Robert Fitzpatrick Management,*
> *9000 Sunset Boulevard,*
> *Hollywood, U.S.A.*

Dear Hal,

I thought I'd write and tell you how I've been faring since I got back here from England. The reason is partly because I need to set my trou-

bles down in type so as to comprehend them better and partly because you've always been such a brick. I mean, you have both feet planted firmly on the ground. Out West, it's impossible to get anybody's full attention unless you're threatening them with violence or love; George Sherlock, my local brick, is out on the road with a new Tower act called the Chocolate Watch Band. I'm sorry I didn't see you in England, but I was determined to spend the holiday with my family and to put pop away for a while. Of course, by doing so I missed the bus over here yet again: I should have been at the Monterey Festival, even if the buggers didn't invite me to play. Apparently, it was a tremendous success and most of those who performed are now stars if they weren't already. Nobody got paid, but I certainly would have gone along with that—had I been asked.

What's bothering me is this conspiracy of silence as far as my career is concerned. Yellow Underground, my latest album, was released but promptly got buried. Can you alert EMI to its existence? Maybe Argo, who have Emlyn Williams and Shakespeare, would consider the spoken-word track? I told you about producer Mike Curb's interest in me. He has his own label called Sidewalk and he's promised to seek out some material for me. He says it must be the right material, Edgar Allan Poe or something. I know he means well, but it's hard to fix a "meeting" with him, as he's so busy with things like his youth market movie scores. He's always very polite on the phone, as charming as an Englishman. Bob Fitzpatrick, my manager, is charming, too. Everybody's charming and delightful, but I do so want a gig—any gig. But Bob says I'm a high-class act and must have my work chosen carefully. He says he worries about me nightly.

He disapproved of my accepting a spot on "The Dating Game," a TV quiz show in which a girl gets to choose one of three hidden celebrities from the answers they give to her questions, such as "Do you kiss on a first date?" I was hidden behind a partition together with an ex-Byrd and an erstwhile Beach Boy. I was chosen, no doubt, because of my accent and Bernice and I won a trip to the Bahamas. One of the other prizes was a trip to London. I coveted this as a free ride home—and I do so want to go home—so afterward, in the green room with all the TV show staff and us celebrities, I asked whether I might trade my Bahaman trip for the London one. The idea horrified "The Dating Game" staff and they uttered comments such as: "Marriages often result from our trips—long-lasting relationships, too—you're pooping the romance aspect of this game." I replied to the effect that we, as showbiz professionals, must know that this show was just another job (I got $500), so couldn't we cut the nonsense and get down to business? A

TV talk show comic called me a "turkey" and I challenged him to fisticuffs; he was starting to remove his turtleneck sweater when the network security intervened. This is a small town and that finishes my career on game shows, let alone talk shows. Am I going mad?

Anyway, I've recently glimpsed a chink of light and a chance to evade this rock world that I don't understand. I have approached Mae West, the great star, with a proposal that she make another album, under my supervision. She has agreed, providing the songs are up-to-date. Maybe this will be a way, albeit an oblique one, of coming to grips with contemporary rock life. One of the songs I have selected for the album is "Light My Fire." All I need now is financial backing and for this I'm going to try Mike Curb.

Bob Fitzpatrick rushed out of his office moments ago (I'm writing this in reception) to tell me the dreadful news of Brian Epstein's death. A drug overdose in his locked bedroom—was it intentional? Either way, it's the end of an era as far as I can see. Like you, Hal, he was an authority figure in the best sense—a guide, a mentor, a guru. Unfortunately, he didn't wear the trendy Indian guru sheets, he was still early sixties. I liked him very much, though I hardly knew him. Bob is most upset—they were close friends and Bob has recently been acting as Epstein's West Coast representative.

What will the Beatles do now? Who will manage them? The right manager is so important. It's up to experienced old hands such as you to keep this ship on an even keel if we are to weather the coming storm. Or am I being unnecessarily dramatic? Perhaps the effect of the air out here.

All the best,
Your pal,
Ian

The Tel-El-Pal Apartments, Sept. 13:
Arrived "home" an hour ago, hot and dusty, from Santa Barbara, where I'd been performing at a local pizza parlor. Not a good gig, but I *must* perform. I kept getting requests for such inappropriate songs as "Ode to Billie Joe." Simply won't work on the ukulele and, quite clearly, I'm not a hominy grits man. Bob Fitzpatrick was dead against me doing a pizza parlor, but as Cream, one of the groups he represents, were doing a concert at the college in Santa Barbara, he let me go up with them in the hope I might catch some of their reflected glory. Eric Clapton and Jack Bruce popped into the parlor after their concert to have a beer. Eric is very sweet and says I'm a "character" and that we need more such characters. Maybe I'll be their opening act someday.

This is the end! Here I am, alone in the Tel-El-Pal with that same tiresome Murphy bed and now an oven that refuses to heat. To make matters worse, those awful sex noises have started again next door. . . .

I thumped the wall and told them to zip up. A voice like an unemployed radio news announcer invited me to "come on over and make it a threesome." What a country!

Should I warn family members of the dangers here? Auntie Iris has written to say that she and Uncle Jeremy are planning a trip over to "sample my adopted country" and could I meet them in San Francisco? She writes: "We hear so much about this city as the jewel of America (and we've seen travelogues showing the little cable cars, the gingerbread mansions, and all sorts of exotic byways and folkways) that we thought we should pay a visit before we 'shed the mortal coil.' Your uncle wants to know what you hear about the golf courses round there?"

On October 6, a modest pageant marked "The Death of Hippie." Organized by the original settlers and filmed by a few TV crews, the occasion featured pallbearers carrying "Hippie" in his cardboard coffin through the Haight streets and burying him after a brief ceremony. The plastic hippies—the foreigners lured by media hype—had destroyed Arcadia. An exodus of true hippies had begun months before, many of them planning to start a new community in New Mexico, where they would not only be free from contamination by outsiders but would also escape the mighty earthquake that they knew was about to destroy California—and good riddance!

"No hope without dope" had become one of the street slogans of the plastics and the dealers readily agreed. Methedrine was the new high: 15,000 milligrams injected intravenously on Monday could float a customer like a hot-air balloon right through to Friday. According to Burton H. Wolfe in his book *The Hippies*: "Young girls turned on to Methedrine were gang-banged in the communes for as long as five days, until their limbs became almost paralyzed and their insides became one with the mystics' basic universal elements of blood and fire." Withdrawal from Methedrine was much more hellish than LSD, STP, and even heroin; serum hepatitis often resulted, which could lead to death; the long-term legacy was paranoia, manifested in a belief that secret police were everywhere and that J. Edgar Hoover was readying enormous concentration camps for the Final Solution to the Hippie Question.

Rough justice for the dealers was left in the hands of their own underworld members. Drug-related murders were cropping up: a biker

murdered a pusher in his pad and then cut off his victim's right hand
and robbed him of $2,600 cash. Something to do with drug impurities.
Superspade, a top LSD connection around the Haight, was found in a
sleeping bag on the rocks below a Marin County cliff. He'd been shot
in the back of the head, stabbed in the chest, and robbed of $40,000
drug money. "No hope without dope."

A week after "The Death of Hippie," I started work in my own
Arcadia, where even the coffee was decaffeinated. Mike Curb had given
me the green light to go ahead and produce an album by Mae West. In
fact, he added, he and Sidewalk Productions would be honored to put
up the money.

And so, in the early afternoon of October 15, snug inside Mae
West's creamy apartment, I sat on a fragrant carpet at my star's feet,
humming song material up at her. She, composed and regal in a wispy
silk gown and towering coiffure, weighed each song carefully.

"Now, Miss West, how about us recording something on the lines of
The Last of the Red Hot Mommas'? You remember, the old song by
Sophie Tucker?"

"Who, dear? No, we ought to be modernistic. Maybe a tune by this
new girl, this Rita Frankel?"

"Ah! Aretha Franklin, the secularized gospel singer."

"If you say so, dear. Must be modern. None of your ragtime."

"Talking about contemporary material, we might try you doing some
of this psychedelic stuff like . . ." At this point, I warbled a lyric concerning a woman wearing a brand new leopard skin pillbox hat. "It's a
song by Dylan, dear," I explained.

"It may well be by Dillinger, but the hat sounds like the kinda outfit
that Stanwyck woman would wear in one of her movies. Try again."

I rummaged and came up with the line from "A Whiter Shade of
Pale" in which the singer is dancing a light fandango and doing cart-
wheels.

"That's useful as maybe an early-morning training exercise, see what
I mean, but, personally, I prefer an indoor bicycle machine customized
to my needs. Try another, dear."

I followed with another Procol Harum song, "Homburg." In this
one, a poor fellow is being castigated for having dirty trouser cuffs, incorrectly laced shoes, and an overcoat which is too long. He is advised
to remove his homburg hat.

She waved her hand, stopping me during the melisma on "long":
"OK, OK! But why does the guy have to remove the headpiece just
'cause the coat's trailing, know what I mean?"

"Well, I. . . ." She had hit at the soft white underbelly of the new
rock poetics.

"Keep thinking, dear."

Eventually, we dredged up some real corkers from the classic days of rock 'n' roll. Only minor carpentry was required to make the songs truly "Westian." For example: "Great Balls of Fire" became graphic anatomical praise for a boxer brute. "Happy Birthday, Sweet Sixteen" became "Happy Birthday, Twenty-one" because Miss West felt that teenagers were too much on the young side for her and I agreed. And in the middle of "Whole Lotta Shakin' Goin' On," we managed to squeeze Westy's celebrated line: "Is that a gun in your pocket or are you just glad to see me?"

Still sitting at her slippered feet, I became inspired and laced together a song in praise of the male and entitled "Men!" The muse stayed, allowing me to contribute to the blues by writing one about how Miss West wins world peace by becoming sex instructor to the United Nations. In the song, we zoom in on our star as she exercises her powers on the makers of war and peace, the fat politicians in their hairpieces. We see her softening them up by hardening them on:

"Just let me meet De Gaulle and get with Mao Tse Tung.
I said, Just let me meet De Gaulle and get with Mao Tse Tung.
I'll *parlez vous* that Frenchman and Mao will hang up his gun."

We discussed at length which other international leaders we might mention in this blues number. I was trying hard to remember who was head man in Russia at the time—Westy suggested "Popoff," but that didn't sound quite right to me—when her flunky announced that a Mr. Gavin Young, foreign correspondent to the London *Observer* (a very stiff Sunday paper) was waiting downstairs for an audience. "Maybe he should get an act," suggested Westy with a guffaw. I said maybe Mr. Young could fill us in on Who's Who in world politics. "Send him up," she ordered. All at once, "Operation Visitor" was put into action—Westy retiring to her inner chambers, the flunky taking charge of the peephole in the front door, and me settling on a sofa to entertain our guest until the grand entrance of Miss West.

Gavin Young eventually entered, looking flustered but clearly impressed. He was wearing a three-piece tropical suit from Stork of the Strand. I beckoned him to a Louis Quatorze chair and offered him carrot cake and Sanka. He was fresh from Vietnam and fairly bubbling with news. After a short half hour, the flunky appeared to announce, "Gentlemen—Miss West!" I stood up at once, thoroughly enjoying this ritual. But Mr. Young, whacked out no doubt after his Vietnam adventures, had dozed off sideways in his chair. The flunky glared and made his announcement again, this time much louder and shriller and punctuated by little stamps of the foot. The poor foreign correspondent, thinking perhaps that the Cong were charging, shot out of his chair, shouting, "What's the drill? What's the drill?"

Miss West glided up to him as if on hidden wheels, rolling to a halt near a male nude statue: "Men and boys first—but he who hesitates is last!" After exchanging pleasantries, we got down to business by demonstrating our United Nations blues song to Mr. Young. He liked it, thought it might do the trick. "The situation is grave," he added.

"Who's the leading man out there?" asked Miss West.

"In Hanoi, it's Ho."

"This Ho is so high?"

I capped with, "He's a high Ho, and off to work we go!" So we continued by singing Mr. Young our revised version of "Rock Around the Clock," which began: "Get your loin cloth on and join me, hon." We finished the song with a flourish, Miss West doing a little shimmy dance from the sofa. Then she said, "Mr. Gavin, I'd like to ask you a personal question: d'you think the boys will be home for Christmas?"

Afternoon after afternoon, we slogged away at our rehearsals. Every nuance—every *oooh* and every *ah-hoh*—had to be timed precisely. Often the phone would ring: an invitation to dinner with Greta Garbo; a woman pretending to be Mae West; Mr. America (1936), who wanted to come up with his ukulele and show off some hot licks.

At last, there came the day when I felt it was time we laid down our backing tracks. Westy said: "Make sure you hire guys who can *pulse,* know what I mean?" Here she wriggled her top parts. "Colored fellows are best. One time I insisted on having the Duke Ellington band for a picture and you can be sure I had 'em all delivered, even though the studio was complaining they didn't want their stages littered with Negroes."

Westy wasn't around for the backing-track sessions. I used my old "Shindig" colleagues, players who passed for white but played colored. The basic tracks for twelve songs were done in only six hours. Those marvelous men had no idea who they were backing, but they played with fire. For all they knew, they could have been sessioneering for a Martin Boorman album.

At last came the day for the vocal overdubs. Miss West was determined to get them all in one afternoon. I was fortunate enough to be allowed ride to the studio in her limousine. For this occasion, she was accompanied by her boon companion Paul, a muscle builder. Downstairs in the basement garage, I waited, watching the flunky (who turned out to be national president of her fan club) climb into his chauffeur gear—a black blazer with gold epaulettes, white riding britches, peaked cap at a jaunty angle. "Say," said the grizzled garage man as he pumped gas into the Cadillac, "Are you goin' yachtin'? If so, give us a hornpipe!" and he pulled out his pump and did a short jig with it.

"Silence, varlet! Our star approaches!" I must say, she did make a splendid entrance from the service elevator. Dressed in an elegant suit and with Paul on her arm, she glided by the line of parked cars and, in no time at all, was safely inside the Caddy, whisked through the air into her seat by Paul's strong arms. The grizzled garage man put away his pump and gave her a round of applause.

Hollywood was glazed and stinking hot, but inside the limousine all was cool and dark. "Did you know I was a direct descendant of King James the First?" she confided in me. She wasn't a bit nervous. Our recording studio was on Hollywood Boulevard, next door to a soft-core porno theater. The studio building was unimpressive, a square crate that had suddenly appeared a few months before and has since vanished. Mike Curb was the present owner, but he couldn't be there at the session. No doubt he was abroad seeking out clean new youth acts, doing his best to hold back the scummy tide. The large recording room was empty; our single engineer sat unseen behind one-way glass in his control booth. He and I had decided in advance to place Miss West behind a tall screen at the rear of the room and on a comfortable, but not too plush, chair. On her right was a large speaker from which were to blast the prerecorded backing tracks; on her left sat our chauffeur (now back in his role as fan club president), on his best behavior; in front of her sat myself, with my lyric sheets and pen and stopwatch. My arms were ready to conduct Miss West, for she needed to be told when to start and when to stop, when to coax out a grunt or a moan or a Westian one-liner. A few feet behind our group sat Paul, bulging all over in his natty suit. As he hitched up his trousers, I caught a glimpse of a bulky service revolver peeping out from his belt.

Rubbing my hands nervously, I called for the track to "The Naked Ape." This was a song I'd written in which I was to play a stuffy professor of history and she was to play his pupil. We are sitting together on a couch and I am reading a passage on the Saxon kings to her from Greene's *History of England.* This private tuition goes haywire because the sexy pupil will keep touching me up, thereby ruining the drift of my dialectic. I shout "Ouch!" and start turning into a naked ape. Westy finished off the number in one take and, with a quick flick of the wrist, threw away her lyric sheet. Next, please! "Light My Fire" was rather trickier. She kept asking me what the words meant and I, in truth, had very little idea. I had to ask her to please concentrate. Paul's hand moved to his revolver. "Who recorded this number?" she de-

manded. I told her about the Doors. "Well, they need shuttin'!" We all
howled with laughter, the tension was broken, and we got it in one
take. I rushed her on to "The Grizzly Bear," a ragtime song from before World War I. Miss West had performed this, with racy hand-to-
body movements, around the time it had first been published. However, we didn't discuss that. She talked instead about her love of all
animals and about, in particular, her first tingling experience: a dream
affair with a passing bear. He had a very swollen prehistoric type of
organ, encrusted with barnacles. "Gosh, it must have hurt," I said.
"Hurt? It was *heaven*." And with another laugh she threw away her
"Grizzly Bear" lyrics. At about four-thirty, we stopped for tea and a delicious meal, served by Paul on a fine muslin tablecloth spread on the
studio floor. He had, I believe, made the watercress sandwiches himself.
After this refreshment, we raced through the rest of the overdubs with
no trouble at all.

At five-thirty, we were ready to wrap. I poked my head around the
screen and, to my horror, saw that the studio was now a sea of musicians. An R&B band had been let in to prepare for a session. We must
have over-run, due to the tea. Paul was polishing up the silver tea
flasks, oblivious to the toots and bangs of the R&B boys; the club secretary was doing his nails. I turned to Miss West and whispered:
"There's a band in the studio. We can exit through the back door."

"What kind of band?"

"A blues band."

"Colored?"

"I should say so."

"Then I'll exit right through them, dear. Make the preparations."

And we eventually made a magnificent departure, emerging from
behind the screen like a medieval Papal procession. True believers,
the R&B boys parted and, as we exited out to face the clamor of the
present day, they raised a fine "Amen!"

Shortly after I'd put the Mae West album to bed, I saw minute signs
that autumn was approaching: some palm fronds fell into the Tel-El-
Pal pool and I had to wear a cardigan at night. The year had flown by,
enormous changes had occurred in pop culture, and I had achieved
very little. I was musing on this as I looked into a cold turkey pie in my
breakfast nook when the phone rang. It was Gale. How had she gotten
my new number? She said that Werner had a third eye and was "intrigued" by me, especially because Gale kept talking about me and
using my "three-dollar words."

There was some spluttering on the line and the man himself came
on: "Greetings, friend! This is Dr. Clark. The Ishi People and myself

would like to extend an invitation for you to visit our flaming vision of reality, our ideal come true. . . . We—" I told him to please cut the crap. "Really, Ian, this is not the gentleman I once knew and saved. . . . Please be so kind as to hear me out. We are organizing a rock festival, a gargantuan one, and we'd like you to be the master of ceremonies and to perform."

I became extremely interested when he went on to tell me that the acts I would be introducing included the Grateful Dead, Jefferson Airplane, Sly and the Family Stone, and the Ishi People's Mantra Orchestra. "This festival will be Big Sur's answer to Monterey—which I hear you missed. You'll love our rancho—it used to belong to 'Whispering Jack' Smith, so you'll feel at home. Maybe you'll summon up his ghost when you strum and croon some twenties numbers. Can I count on you? Per diem expenses, of course."

Without consulting my manager, I agreed. I was determined to get on the map—anyway, anyhow. I had to catch 1967 before it fled forever.

The Ishi rancho was not far from Carmel, the famous beauty spot, and it was at Carmel's world-renowned Highlands Inn that I made reservations for my uncle and aunt. They had cabled to inform me of their arrival date and time in San Francisco, adding that they hoped I'd have time to show them around. Three days would be quite sufficient for them to get the drift of Frisco; after that, they could come to Carmel, enjoy the breathtaking ocean view from the brunch room at the Highlands Inn, and cap off their visit by seeing their nephew perform as an entertainer at the rock festival. An expensive cable, but I was beginning to enjoy the art of cablese.

It was much too cold for an outdoor festival on that fateful November afternoon when my taxi deposited me five miles from the Ishi rancho. Much too cold . . . and where were the posters and underground newspaper ads and FM radio spots for this event? The taxi driver and I were in the heart of the Big Sur country of scribbly dirt tracks, unkempt trees, hirsute fields, menacing birdcalls. "This is as far as I'm taking you, buddy," he said, folding his arms with finality. "I ain't goin' into that nest of crazies. They ain't bathed, shaved, done a day's work in a coon's age." "But. . . ." "See that gas station yonder? You can call those weirdos to come and collect you for whatever witchcraft you're up to." He nodded towards my ukulele. "If that's a machine gun, you'll need it. Sixty-five dollars, please."

I stood in the road under a darkling sky with angry birds screaming at me. I felt a dread engulfing me, but I soon put an end to that by stepping off down the track singing to myself, "I'm Happy When I'm Hiking," a British hit of the 1930s. Several uplifting songs later, I arrived at the askew gate sign announcing: WE ARE tHE ISHI PeOplE —FoRienErs: KEEP OUTTTT!

Still no posters announcing the festival. No power cables, no media vans, and no fans pouring through the gates. Inside was a rubbish dump. Several naked youths of both sexes looked up briefly from a rock pile where they were lounging. But they quickly resumed whatever it was they were doing. Nobody came to greet me. In fact, a snake line of dancers rushing past me hand-in-hand gave me many a scowl. A grossly obese girl in a grass skirt whirled clean into me and, when I protested, she said, "Aw, go fuck yourself." In order to find the H.Q. of Dr. Werner Clark, I had to tip a scraggly middle-aged man who claimed to be Paul Revere (the patriot, not the bandleader). Not a promising start to my new rock career.

Dr. Clark's digs were solid and protected. They were a Tudor-style cabin surrounded by barbed wire, except for the front portico which was English rustic, resembling a vicarage gate. I found it hard to believe that the cheerful crooner "Whispering Jack" Smith had ever lived here. As I trudged up to the portico, a Volkswagen van screeched across my path and came to a halt by a nearby corrugated-iron hut. Out jumped a bunch of dirty boys holding khaki satchels and several ran over to me, spun me around, and shouted: "We got dinner and maybe even a movie!" I asked them what they'd been up to and one said, "Panhandling." Another told him to shut up, then an older man in a blue boiler suit intervened, smiling a false waiter's smile, and told them to go do their thing.

"Can I be of assistance?" he was droning as Dr. Clark came backing out of the front portico with his hands outstretched in the manner of a hot gospeling pastor praising the Lord. The boiler-suit man suddenly blew a whistle and Dr. Clark stepped to the side, revealing a gangly, wild-eyed youth wearing only jockey briefs and wielding a pickax. "Betrayer!" the boy screamed. "You said only God was within me, but instead I find Satan and the CIA! They want my brain for research." "My dear child," said Dr. Clark quite calmly, "I said that the *struggle* is within you. *You* are God and you and He will eventually vanquish all evil. Ah, help has arrived."

As he spoke, four brutish men in blue boiler suits rushed up and overpowered the gangly youth. "Give him some protein," said Dr. Clark as they led away the now-weeping youth, "and get him to wipe his nose. He's worse than the children." The doctor was now facing me, straightening what I recognized as a Navy foul-weather jacket. He was also wearing a silly Indian headband. Nevertheless, I was relieved to run across somebody I knew.

He seemed exultant to see me, gripping me for ages in a bear hug and kissing me disgustingly on both cheeks. "Jesus Christ, but I'm pleased you're here. We've been having trouble all day—the tides, the moon, maybe the food—and some light relief from you is just what the doctor ordered!" He took me by the arm and led me around the corner to where a white Mercedes-Benz was parked. "Only clean place in the camp," he said as he motioned me inside.

The first thing I wanted to learn was the whereabouts of Gale. "Well, that's her love child running about over there," he replied, pointing to a group of babies playing at mud pies in a hole not far from our car. "Gale's is the one with the Pre-Raphaelite hair." "Certainly a beautiful child." "But not toilet-trained yet. None of them are. It's a very real problem. I'm a visionary, not a nurse." "And Gale?" "Oh, she's freaking out in Bilbo Baggins Wood over yonder."

I wasn't that interested in hearing about Ishi People problems—about supermarket bills and gas and electricity and the IRS. But I listened politely and, after twenty minutes or so, Dr. Clark started the car and took me for a tour of the compound. Rancho was hardly an appropriate word. What I saw was vile and depressing, but down where the black people lived, the remains of the old cowpunchers' bunkhouse, I felt at home.

We sat in the car with the engine running and the windows rolled tight. "We've got problems here all right. The blacks have started their own ghetto and won't allow any of us in." Werner drove us back to his H.Q., telling me en route that he admired my "British phlegm," that he would show me to my dressing room, and that the show would start in the old corral as soon as dinner was over.

I should have scouted around more, gotten chummy with some of the campers. I should have been forewarned by the barbed wire and the glazed eyes. I should have called the Highlands Inn and given my uncle and aunt the time of my show and detailed directions. On the other hand, the ensuing donnybrook was most exhilarating and made up for the rough and tumble of rugby that I had missed as a fat child.

I will call it "The Battle of Bilbo Baggins Wood," for the festival stage and environs were hard by that overgrown orange grove. After all, Waterloo didn't actually take place at Waterloo village. And this battle certainly was my Waterloo, as far as my future in rock was concerned.

At 7:30 P.M., I was in my room at the concrete H.Q., fretting with my ukulele and worrying about the absense of the Grateful Dead, *et al.* Why hadn't they invited Allen Ginsberg? He'd be bound to show up, possibly hang around for a week or two of philosophizing. I was moping and staring out of my barred window when I saw Gale stagger by. I dashed out after her, calling her name to no avail. When I finally overtook her, she came to an automatic halt, but still marking a ragged time. I was about to embrace her when I noticed her disheveled appearance. Her hair was a haystack, her jeans ripped and muddy, and one generous breast hung out of her ratty muslin shirt. Only her eyes seemed factory-fresh. They were wide and glinting jet black like a dog's in the dark and, for a moment, they bored clean through me. Then she was on the move again, thrusting me aside with one amazingly strong arm. Pacing her, I told her my conclusions: "You've been Svengalied! You've had a brainwash, I'll swear it!" Without turning from her path, she answered in a monotone, "Yeah, but not by Werner. By the new master, the Snake King. He's made me chef tonight and boy am I gonna give them a dinner they'll never forget. I'm gonna swiss-cheese their brains for eternity, I'm gonna make the camp go faster than the speed of light." And, like a witch of Cawdor planning a devilish caldron, she cackled off into the inky night. Mercifully, I had packed a round of tuna salad sandwiches into my ukulele case, so I was able to avoid Gale's dinner surprise. But what sort of mood would I find my audience in? I had to wait several more hours before finding out.

"When *are* we going to get this show on the road?" I asked Dr. Clark. He made no reply but kept on fingering a string of beads with one hand while nervously stroking his beard with the other. Dr. Clark, a group of his boiler-suit men, a couple of "stagehands," the Ishi People's Mantra Orchestra, and I were all hanging about helpless behind a large flatbed truck. The truck was to serve as our stage, in true free-festival fashion, while in front, out in the corral, were some scattered bales of straw for our audience. But the fans weren't sitting on their seats in hushed expectation. We couldn't get a good view of them from behind the flatbed, but we could hear them moving about restlessly—and hooting, whistling, braying, howling, cursing, occasionally menacing so close to us that we could hear their Bronx cheers. I comprehended their anger: they wanted to know what was keeping the big rock names. Then I heard a distant voice, as deep and ever-rolling as Old Man River himself, demanding Sly and his "whole fuckin' family!"

Dr. Clark was by now trembling. Spastically, he jerked his head around the end of the flatbed truck—and was promptly hit in the face by a large clod of refried beans. I consulted my watch, saw that it was close to midnight, and decided to take action: "I'm going out onto that stage to hold the fort with some amusing songs," I said, starting to unlatch my ukulele case. At that, Werner bounded toward me, raised himself on tiptoe to a ludicrous height, and screamed at me: "*Oh no you don't!* This is *my* camp. Mine, do you hear? I'm going on *first!*" And he scrambled up onto the flatbed and grabbed the mike.

"Brothers and sisters!" The din didn't cease. "My people! What need have we of capitalist entertainers and the gewgaw fetters of a transmogrified Tin Pan Alley when we have *ourselves?* Our very own Ishi Orchestra have a plethora of mantras lined up for you. I myself have collected chants from all over the world. . . . I have . . ." An avocado squelched him square in the face. When he turned toward us with his head shaking in disbelief, we could plainly see green slime sliding down his face to settle in his goatee. Then the accusations began: "Satan!" "Anti-Christ!" "Betrayer!" "Where is the Airplane?" "Where are the Dead?" "Where are the Beach Boys and Sam the Sham?" Where indeed! Werner, still facing us in his perplexity, shouted, "What's gotten into them? What are they talking about?" A boiler-suit man suggested, "Maybe it was something in the Kool-Aid?" "That is *my* job," said Werner, stiffening. But these were his last words, as far as I could tell: For just then a gargantuan cabbage (as only the "salad bowl" of the San Joachin Valley can produce) thudded into his back with such force that he was knocked clean off the truck and down onto a cactus. While the boiler-suit men tended to their leader, I grabbed the situation and clambered onto the "stage." Imagining myself to be at the Hollywood Bowl on a good night, I struck up a lively strum on my ukulele.

At first, there fell a silence, eerie and cosmic. My little song richocheted around the universe telling the bad joke that was the nub of all existence, receiving back in echo the affirmation of its nihilism: "Where Did Robinson Crusoe Go with Friday on Saturday Night?" The silence continued, but it was pregnant now with passion. As I now realize, they couldn't believe what they were seeing and hearing. I had done "I'm Looking Over My Dead Dog Rover" and was just starting in on "I Go So Far with Sophie on Sophie's Sofa" when the first salvos were fired: all manner of rotten, smelly vegetables initially, followed by much harder objects. I stood my ground, tottering to and fro under the attack, trying ragtime, jazztime, swing, strumming, and crooning through the whole story of American music, even attempting "You Turn Me On" as a gesture toward contemporary rock—but there was no stopping this mob. They were out for blood and their ire was focused on me and my uke. I started to wield my instrument like a cricket bat, deflecting as many of the unidentified flying objects as possible.

Then the bombardment stopped. There was a short pause and, at the sound of a whistle, the advance began. The mob had become an army coming at me inexorably from out of that black Big Sur night.

"OK, you guys. Forty-seven, fifty-five, three . . . Hike!" From way out to my right, maybe hundreds of yards distant, came the Old Man River voice, from a tinny bullhorn. The team coach issuing instructions: "Single wing formation! Go! Go! Go! It's a blitz! Run to day-

light! Go! Go! Go!!" Screaming "Yeah! Yeah! Yeah!", the Ishi People's
team marched onward toward me and the flatbed and soon I could see
the first wave of them emerging through the gloom, some thwacking
clubs rhythmically into their palms, others brandishing axes and pitch-
forks, one actually holding aloft a squealing pig. It was the pig that got
to me first, biting and snarling and snorting, and I went down bashing
at its head with my uke. "Pigs! Pigs! *Pigs!*" I heard Old Man River
yelling over a bullhorn and I got ready to meet my porcine fate. But
suddenly I was being abandoned and still the voice was calling: "Pigs!"
Then: "Split, Ishis! Split! It's the pigs!"

In the distance, over another bullhorn, came a sound as mellifluous
as those bagpipes that led the Relief of Lucknow in the Indian Mutiny.
A quavering voice singing a song I hadn't heard in fifteen years, ever
since I'd said farewell at the old gate: a song that brought back at once
the tang of the sea below the chalk cliffs of the South Downs, the call
of the matron—"Chocolate time, boys!"—and the clop of bat on ball and
whack of birch on bottom. Once again, my old prep school song, the
stirring call to Old Roverdonians:

> "The long grey buildings send them out to Afric's sunny shore—
> The boys who know the story, who know what to do and more!
> Their master's words now echo through the corridors of vine:
> 'Heads up, backs down, let's sing the song, Old Roverdonians mine!'"

I lay on my back on the flatbed, rejoicing and thinking that, even
through the distortion of a bullhorn, Uncle Jeremy's voice was unmis-
takable, certain, full of inherited wisdom. And now another voice, less
pleasant and more rasping, took over: "This is the police. You are
unlawfully assembled. You will lay down your weapons and walk
slowly toward the searchlight with your hands on your heads. Now!"

Auntie Iris was in her element. "It's just like the War, dear," she
said as she propped up my head with a rolled foul-weather jacket.
Then she dabbed me here and there with gauze pads drenched in io-
dine that stung and left a yellow stain, so that I seemed much more
wounded than I really was. It was delicious. Uncle Jeremy's face
loomed down at me; he smelled reassuringly of pipe tobacco and
Scotch whisky. "No bones broken then, old boy? Splendid. We arrived
in the nick of time, didn't we? Nice to hear our old school song again! I
don't think you know Captain Steinbrachach of the Los Angeles Police
Force and president of the All-American Peace Officers' Golfing Association." Another face, lantern-jawed and with piercing blue eyes, joined
my uncle. "If you'll excuse me, I must go join my men. They're turning up a veritable arsenal of guns and ammo. Even bazookas—these

people believed the world was against them, especially after a dinner of PCP." "See you on the links tomorrow morn, crack o' dawn?" "Jeremy, *do* remember your heart!" Auntie Iris exclaimed. "Well, nine holes then, Cap'n?" "Yes, sir."

When we were safely ensconced in a snug corner of the Highlands Inn, I learned the details of my rescue. It seems that no sooner had my uncle and aunt arrived at the Inn that afternoon than they ran across the president of the police golfers having a snifter in the bar. With golf and war in common, they soon struck up a lively conversation and, within minutes, my uncle was sharing jokes with other members of the police golf team, plus a few U.S. Marines and Green Berets who were also there. When he happened to mention my concert and ask for directions to the rancho, the police captain grew most interested. Apparently, the police had had tabs on Dr. Clark and his lads for some time but couldn't get any concrete evidence in order to indict. Werner was sought in many states, but obtaining extradition papers in California was proving long and cumbersome. The captain suggested that he and his men give my uncle and aunt a ride to the rancho concert and maybe sneak in and join the audience. "I'm sorry we missed your performance," said my uncle as he poured the other half of my lager and set it down firmly in front of me. "But I've always maintained—and tonight I've been proved correct—that the entertainment trade is *no business for a gentleman.*"

Seacliff, England, December 8:
It is very nice to be convalescing down by the seaside at the home of my uncle and aunt, where they moved from London a few years ago when my uncle retired. They have a simple but tasteful place, a converted fisherman's cottage a quarter-mile south of the sea front. It is very peaceful, and there is no music, as such. But every night around nine o'clock, I am lulled to sleep by the eternal crash of the waves on the pebbles. Altogether my situation—the view, the accommodation, the table fare, *the absence of music*—is most acceptable.

At breakfast, my uncle reads the *Daily Telegraph,* scanning the obituary column first. For the rest of the day, he divides his time between pottering around the garden, walking the dog on the golf course, and eating hearty meals. My aunt takes care of the household chores. And I am left to recuperate in my own time. It is all very convenient.

This morning, I broke a rule of mine. I went out and bought a pop-music paper. Old habits are hard to break. Anyway, they all say I must not make any violent breaks. In the paper, there was a long report about the gala opening of the Beatles' new enterprise, a shop called

Apple at 94 Baker Street, London. John and George were among the throng. The shop will sell clothes and ornaments and lots of electronic gadgets invented by Magic Alex (who also invented John's "nothing box" toy). The decor, designed by some Beautiful People from Holland called The Fool, is highlighted by a "ceiling of snow-white clouds floating across a sky of brilliant blue." Everything is for sale at the Apple shop, even the premises. But, claimed the report, Apple isn't only a shop—it's also a "Corps," with future plans for a record and film company, for the manufacturing of all manner of goods, and for a worldwide network of discothèque clubs.

Elsewhere in the paper, an end-of-year poll gave the "Most Promising Newcomer Award" to the Bee Gees and Engelbert Humperdinck; and the "Biggest Mistake Award" to *Their Satanic Majesties Request* by the Rolling Stones: "A copycatting of *Sgt. Pepper* and a nonstarter saleswise." The current Top Twenty is jammed with love ballads by Tom Jones, Engelbert Humperdinck, comedian Des O'Connor, Cliff Richard, and, surprisingly, the Dave Clark Five and the Troggs. The Beatles have a sort of ballad with "Hello, Goodbye" at number nine. The only time *I* hear pop is when I'm at the local supermarket.

I like to go for walks and bus rides in order to have a think. I've been thinking a lot about the past lately. Not the recent past, but long before. After lunch today, I decided to take the bus to Felpham—a two-hour ride, but I wanted to see the pier and its theater and perhaps recapture that summer of '49 when O. Stoppit's performance sparked off my odyssey.

The afternoon was even grayer than the morning and there was also a drizzle. I like this weather. On the Downs behind the sea front, stodgy clouds were playing ring-around-the-rosie under a patch of clear sky, making Roverdown School shine brightly red. It's been sold for redevelopment.

When I arrived in Felpham, a storm was brewing. There were only a few hardy elderly people hiking the promenade. I tried to gain admission to the pier, but the attendant inside the entrance booth shook his head. He was a pimply youth with a transistor radio clamped to his ear. After a while, I got him to put it down. "May I ask why I can't go on the pier?" Mimicking my accent, he replied, "Hoh yes, you may, squire. This pier's been closed ever since last summer when the fucking theater fell off the end in that fucking storm, didn't it?" I drew myself closer to him with the idea of delivering a punch. Then I noticed a decrepit poster propped up against the back wall. The frame was coming apart and salt spray had frosted the glass, but I could make out the key words:

"FOLLOW THE FUN"
AN UP-TO-THE-MINUTE REVUE FULL OF
ZANINESS, LATEST TUNES, AND BEVIES OF
LOVELIES!!
STARRING THAT CHEERY CHAP HIMSELF,
O. STOPPIT

"Do you need that?" I asked casually. "It's the property of the build-ing contractor, ain't it?" "How much? Five quid?" "Look, mate. You're the second bloke who's wanted to whip that fucking poster. Some old fogey tried it a couple of days ago. Even left his calling card." Eventually, I got the poster and the card for ten pounds. This is what the card said:

CHAS. DANVERS
"SALTASH"
223 CARNABY MEWS
FELPHAM
TEL: 2798.
ENTERTAINERS FOR ALL OCCASIONS:
CONJURERS, VENTRILOQUISTS,
ROCK AND BEAT GROUPS, COMEDIANS.

A chirpy little voice with a Lancashire accent answered the phone. Mr. Danvers was a very busy man. No, *he* wasn't him. Was I in the profession? "In that case, please hold on. . . . Come around at tea time with your present."

The flats were a few miles behind the promenade, so I treated myself to a taxi. By now the storm was raging, the rain lashing down viciously. I stopped the taxi at a department store to get the poster gift-wrapped, then covered tightly in plastic. I wanted to make sure that O. Stoppit got back his memory in as decent a shape as possible.

Carnaby Mews was around the corner from Top Rank Bingo, an enormous ex-picture palace. Although the flats were tower-block mod-ern, they were already showing signs of wear: ashen stains streaked the gravel-faced walls; the entrance was minus one aluminum Doric column.

Inside was no prettier. There was no carpet, only black plastic tiles. Drab battleship-gray corridors stretched away to left and right. The architect (if there had been one) must have been heavily influenced by Kafka. Then the elevator doors slowly ground open and a tiny gnome stepped out:

"I'm the one who left the card. I'm the historian of the family. He hates the past; he thinks it's all a load of rubbish." He was wheezing asthmatically until he stopped to clear his throat in a large polka-dot handkerchief. He pointed to my parcel. "Don't show it him yet. He's in a funny mood." He had another good cough, folded up his hankie carefully and put it in his top pocket, and stuck out his right hand. "I'm Reggie. I used to be his dresser. Come up and have some tea before you catch your death of cold. Eee, thank goodness t'lift's mended—it were right miserable these last three weeks."

"Saltash," the flat, was cheery in a fussy, feminine way, full of knick-knacks and lace and smelling of scented soap. It was also very small and I moved carefully with my present, fearful lest I upset a china doll or a miniature sphinx. "He's in the sitting room, playing around with his cassettes. He's a tape freak, is our Charlie." A toy poodle came yapping at us from a pair of sun doors. I hoped that he was the last obstacle in the way of my meeting O. Stoppit.

He lay, moon-faced and ruddy, in a jazzy modern armchair. It was tilted back but, in response to a jerky movement from him, it sprang to attention. "Hello, young man. Do you have a cassette player?" His accent was cultivated posh. "You should. They're very convenient." He fished up from the floor a handful of black plastic. "Reggie! What about a spot of tea? And while he's seeing to that in his kitchen kingdom, why don't you tell me about the purpose of this unexpected visit?"

Folding his arms, he turned himself and his mechanical chair away from me and faced a TV with a twenty-six-inch screen that was flickering and murmuring in the wall under the cocktail cabinet. Still standing, I took a deep breath and proceeded to describe—minute by minute, movement by movement, joke by joke—the wondrous act I'd seen him perform that summer evening so long ago. I didn't forget the detail of the coat hanger lodged inside his jacket and how, just before exit time, he'd yanked it out hilariously; nor did I forget that, when it had been my turn to perform, he'd given me a wink and a thumbs-up. In conclusion, I told him that he was instrumental in inspiring me to tread the boards. I was in the process of informing him that he was a hunk of the pure British music-hall gold when there was a great rattling and the french doors were pushed open by a tea-laden trolley guided by Reggie.

"Couldn't get Fuller's walnut cake anywhere, so you'll have to make do with Kunzle or lump it," said Reggie as he steadied his trolley and set about organizing tea. O. Stoppit continued to watch the twenty-six-inch screen, saying not a word and hardly moving. Reggie handed me bread and butter and jam, tea with no sugar, and Kunzle cake. He asked me where I had been living and what was my line in show business; he said it was bitter outside, that Americans were a funny lot but that both O. Stoppit and he enjoyed that American TV detective series and that it was on at eight-thirty so supper would be at seven-forty-five and it was a nice bit of fresh cod. "Did you hear that, Charlie?" Charlie said he did and then he turned to me and asked me what I thought about the detective series and what did I think of Cliff Richard's progress and wasn't Lulu a promising little actress as evinced by "To Sir, With Love."

I now knew what Simon and Garfunkel had meant by "The Sounds of Silence." O. Stoppit had gone and now Charles Danvers climbed out of his chair and turned up the sound of the TV. For the next few minutes, we watched youngsters perform magic, tap dance, tell jokes, and sing beat songs and ballads on a show called "Junior Showtime." Danvers chuckled several times and clicked his teeth when tricks went wrong or sour notes were hit. I drank my tea and stole a peek around the room for any signs of show-business life. But I couldn't find any— only prints of dogs and cats and pretty Asiatic girls, a set of encyclopedias, and some condensed novels.

When the TV show ended, Danvers got up again and turned off the set. Reggie packed up the tea things and set off with his trolley. I sat still, listening to the drumming of the rain and feeling melancholy. Danvers moved toward the electric log fire to warm his bottom. Finally, he spoke:

"That was a nice panegyric—or should I say encomium? Actually, it was a eulogy, a funeral oration for a character that deceased years and years and years ago. I mean your little speech about O. Stoppit. Let me give you some advice. We can't live in the past. We must progress. Frankly, I think that my act back then was dull stuff in a rotten time and, if I'd had the money and sense, I'd have emigrated to California, just like my brother and his family did. I think we've made some tremendous improvements lately in the sixties—take "Yesterday" by the Beatles, for instance—and I think this ballad trend is a very healthy sign and will do away with drugs and all that. 'Nuff said?"

In the lobby, I picked up my coat and parcel. Reggie came out of the kitchen, wiping his hands on an apron. "He's in a funny mood today. Must be the weather." I handed Reggie the parcel. "Pleased, I'm sure. I'll find a good position for it. Pop around again when you're next in the district."

I shook hands and thanked him for the tea, but I knew I'd never see Reggie, Danvers, or the poster again—for what need had I for them when I could re-paint an entire world?

Ian Whitcomb,
Altadena, California,
1983

INDEX

374

INDEX

"She's Leaving Home," 314
"She's Not There," 129
"Shindig," 25, 162, 163, 179, 182–85, 186, 187, 202, 210–11
Shirelles, 55, 95
"Shotgun Boogie," 13
"Shout," 94, 129
Shrimpton, Jean, 116
Shuman, Mort, 127
Sidewalk Productions, 302, 306–7, 343
"Silent Night," 280
Sill, Lester, 52, 57, 58–59
Sillitoe, Alan, 86
Silver Beatles, 95, 102–4
Simon, Paul, 219–20, 325, 326, 334. See also Simon and Garfunkel
Simon and Garfunkel, 146, 219–20, 280, 325, 326, 331, 332–33, 334, 361
Simone, Nina, 97
Sinatra, Frank, 16, 66, 121, 185, 189, 208–9, 266, 267
Sinatra, Nancy, 219, 266, 285
"Six Days on the Road," 37
"Six-Five Special," 19
"Sixteen Tons," 68
Skiffle groups and music, 17, 18, 19, 27, 91–94, 100, 109
Slaughter, Tod, 209
Slick, Grace, 329
Sloan, P. F. ("Flip"), 197–98, 200, 325
"Sloop John B.," 72, 232
Sly and the Family Stone, 351, 354
Small Faces (group), 228
Smith, Arthur ("Guitar Boogie"), 101
Smith, Bessie, 52, 331
Smith, Joe, 266–67
"Soho," 138
"So Long, It's Been Good to Know Yuh," 72–73
"Somebody to Love," 266
Somer, Abe, 325
"Sometimes Good Guys Don't Wear White," 276
Sonny and Cher, 60, 62, 166–68, 187, 188–89, 199, 201–2, 232, 244, 303, 305
"Sounds of Silence," 146, 219–20, 361
"Spanish Harlem," 57–58
Spector, Phil, 25, 48, 49–63, 123–24,

127, 135, 136–37, 167, 168, 185, 189, 250, 272–73, 278
Spellman, Benny, 94
Spirit (group), 332
"Sporting Life Is Killing Me, The," 133
Springfield, Dusty, 130
Stamp, Chris, 156, 158–59, 160
Standells, 244, 276, 301
Stanley, Augustus Owsley, III, 259
"Stardust," 53, 55
Starr, Ringo, 83, 95, 110, 125, 171, 216, 279, 315, 320
Statler Brothers, 216
Steele, Don ("The Real"), 272
Steele, Tommy, 91, 92, 109, 113
Stewart, Chad, 129, 244
Stewart, Ian, 29, 116
Stewart, Rod, 29–30
Stigwood, Robert, 158, 306
"Still I'm Sad," 229
Stills, Steve, 244
Stoller, Mike. See Leiber, Jerry
Storz, T., 273
"Stranger on the Shore," 22
"Strawberry Fields," 279, 289, 313
Strong, Barrett, 17, 95
"Stuck on You," 16
"Subterranean Homesick Blues," 174, 179, 181–82
"Sugar Baby," 28
Sullivan, Ed ("The Ed Sullivan Show"), 19, 122, 123, 125, 126
"Summer in the City," 232
Summer Solstice Festivals, 298, 324
"Summer Song," 129
"Summertime," 128
"Sunday Night at the Cavern," 112
"Sunny Afternoon," 233
"Sunshine Superman," 268
Supremes, 135, 153
Surfaris (group), 45, 46
"Surf City," 38, 39, 47, 64
"Surfer Girl," 48
"Surfer Moon," 48
"Surfer Stomp," 45
"Surfin'," 47
"Surfing Songbook, The," 197
"Surfin' Hootenanny," 49
"Surfin' Safari," 47
"Surfin' U.S.A.," 38, 39
Surf music, 38–50, 64, 131, 135, 136, 197, 277